MORAL AGENTS AND THEIR DESERTS

Moral Agents and Their Deserts

The Character of Muʿtazilite Ethics

SOPHIA VASALOU

PRINCETON UNIVERSITY PRESS *Princeton and Oxford*

Published by Princeton University Press, 41 William Street, Princeton, New Jersey 08540
In the United Kingdom: Princeton University Press, 3 Market Place, Woodstock, Oxfordshire OX20 1SY

Library of Congress Cataloging-in-Publication Data

Vasalou, Sophia.
Moral agents and their deserts : the character of Mu'tazilite ethics / Sophia Vasalou.
p. cm.
Includes bibliographical references and index.
ISBN 978-0-691-13145-0 (hardcover : alk. paper)
1. Motazilites. 2. Islamic ethics. I. Title.
BP195.M6V37 2008
297.5—dc22 2007036849

British Library Cataloging-in-Publication Data is available

This book has been composed in Minion.

Printed on acid-free paper. ∞

press.princeton.edu

Printed in the United States of America

10 9 8 7 6 5 4 3 2 1

To my family

CONTENTS

PREFACE ix

ACKNOWLEDGMENTS xiii

1 The Framework: The Muʿtazilites 1

2 Reading Muʿtazilite Ethics 12

Ethics as Theology 12

Approaches to the Study of Muʿtazilite Ethics 26

3 Theology as Law 38

Moral Values between Rational Knowledge and Revealed Law 38

Rights, Claims, and Desert: The Moral Economy of Ḥuqūq 58

4 The Baṣran Muʿtazilite Approach to Desert 67

"To Deserve": Groundwork 67

Justifying Reward and Punishment: The Values of Deserved Treatments 76

Justifying Punishment: The Paradoxical Relations of Desert and Goodness 87

The Causal Efficacy of Moral Values: Between Sabab *and* ʿIlla 95

The Right to Blame, the Fact of Blame: Views of the Person ab Extra 102

5 Moral Continuity and the Justification of Punishment 116

Time and Deserving 116

An Eternity of Punishment: The Baṣran Justification of Dawām al-ʿIqāb 121

Moral Identity and the Resources of Baṣran Muʿtazilite Ontology 132
The Primacy of Revealed Names: Al-Asmāʾ waʾl-Aḥkām 148
Why Not Dhimma? 152

6 The Identity of Beings in Baṣran Muʿtazilite Eschatology 157
Resurrection and the Criterion of Identity 157
Accidents and the Formal Reality of Resurrected Beings 169

APPENDIX
Translation from Mānkdīm Shāshdīw, "The Promise and the Threat," in Sharḥ al-uṣūl al-khamsa 181

NOTES 197

BIBLIOGRAPHY 239

INDEX 247

PREFACE

The study that follows needs to be prefaced by a word of explanation to clarify its aims and orientation, and inoculate it against certain misunderstandings to which it may prove vulnerable. Perhaps the best way to do this is by saying something about the history of shifts that the conception of the task underwent in the process of writing this book, and while by now buried deep within the palimpsest that is the finished product, have played a large enough role in giving it its current shape to hold the key for the intelligibility of some of its most important features.

The original route mapped for this study had been to chart the way in which Muʿtazilite thinkers developed the meaning of merit and desert in their scheme of rationalist ethics. This ethics, so preoccupied with the ontology of moral value, could not but show a similar interest in questions concerning the nature of the connection between the acts a person does and the treatments one deserves on their account. What is this moral force or connection that makes it reasonable to administer pain or pleasure to people because of acts once undertaken, and makes one's conduct a decisive determinant of one's otherworldly destiny—whether heaven or hell?

In response to this kind of query, the Muʿtazilites positioned themselves by intimating a causal connection: one's conduct in this world has as a consequence pain or pleasure in the hereafter; the one leads to the other. As al-Ghazālī might have put it—though not himself a friend of Muʿtazilite ethical rationalism—"The present world is as a sowing field for the next," as "provisions." Such are the values of the acts one has performed over a lifetime: sowed in this world, they germinate in the next. This causal characterization made sense in the context of the overall moral objectivism to which the Muʿtazilites subscribed, according to which values are intrinsic properties of acts—for it is acts that for them constitute the primary bearers of value—and are not, as Ashʿarite theologians maintained, generated by divine command. That desert should be conceived as a feature of the moral economy characterized by the same kind of ontological independence would not be surprising. If it was not God's will that assigned values to acts, it should also not be His will that necessitated that certain "moral consequences" be entailed by one's performance of these acts.

The idea that presented itself—an enticing one—was to explore the approach taken by the Muʿtazilites concerning the nature of desert, and the kind of elucidations offered for the "causal" powers by which reward and punishment arise as moral consequences of our conduct. What made this prospect enticing was of course not simply the desire to understand the Muʿtazilites; it was a desire to think more closely, by working through the conceptual scheme that they presented, about the notion of desert. To say "of course" is to assume one type of motive that might lead a person to engage with a text of this kind. Not: I am interested to know what this thinker has to say on such and such a question. But: I am interested in this question; what does this thinker have to say about it? (Of course the order of priority is hardly ever as simple as this.)

But it was this approach that resulted in the kind of friction that forms the backdrop to this study, for it involved inadvertently casting the Muʿtazilites in Socrates' maieutic role—providing opportunities for personal insight by means of stimulating interventions. And this was a role that these theologians could rightly protest they had never meant to play. As though to prove the point, they set about crowding the view with all manner of unexpected conceptual idioms and peculiarities, which came as distractions from any contemplative ideals underlying the original role in which they had been cast. Clearly they had their own character to play—one that did not coincide with the one I had laid out—and the conversation I had planned had to be reconceived along different lines. For one thing, the conflict between what had been expected and what had been found needed to be placed at the heart of the encounter, and this had to be *about* Muʿtazilite thought in a more conscious way that would pay closer attention to its angularities, using the experience of conflict to throw their ways of thinking into relief. This is the somewhat schematic background of the present study.

The central focus of this study will be on Muʿtazilite conceptions of desert. But it will not be an exhaustive survey of the historical origins of these conceptions. Nor will it aim to order and present the arguments given by each side for their own version of the nexus between acts and consequences—where the two embattled sides, Muʿtazilite and Ashʿarite, divide over the source of moral value—and to give a typology of the rival conceptions; in fact, it will probably even fall short of being an exhaustive survey of Muʿtazilite conceptions of desert. It will be an attempt to present several main aspects of the conceptual edifice built around the notion of desert, but in a way that calls on the prism of our own perspective as well as expectations to throw the Muʿtazilite viewpoint into relief and act as a criterion of selection for the aspects that are to be focused on. This presentation will be prefaced by a number of reflections on the larger moral project of the Muʿtazilites—

reflections that will try to sketch the role, if not Socratic, that Muʿtazilite theologians were cast to play.

After a first chapter introducing the Muʿtazilites—and more particularly the Baṣran Muʿtazilites, who will be my chief interlocutors—the task of fleshing out the subtitle of this book will begin with chapter 2, where taking off from a question about different ways of reading Muʿtazilite ethics, my objective will be to bring into focus the theological aims that frame Muʿtazilite moral inquiry, following this with a discussion of representative approaches taken by previous readers of Muʿtazilite ethics. Departing from a question about the perplexing legal character of several Baṣran Muʿtazilite writings, chapter 3 will take the task forward by training the light on the legal framework informing Muʿtazilite moral thought, and tracing some important aspects of the latticework of relations linking Muʿtazilite ethics and Islamic law. Having introduced the framework and key concepts of Muʿtazilite moral inquiry in these two chapters, chapters 4–6 will be preoccupied with what gives this book its main title—namely, Muʿtazilite conceptions of desert. Chapter 4 will start from broad questions about desert, such as its function as a reason for action and its role in the definition of moral concepts, in order to then look at substantive concerns with the justification of reward and punishment. This discussion opens out to the Baṣran Muʿtazilite understanding of the causal nature of desert and terminates with remarks on the conception of desert as something extrinsic to the person. This will be picked up in chapter 5, which will be concerned with the survival of desert across time, and after an examination of Baṣran Muʿtazilite strategies in arguing the eternal duration of deserved treatments, will give way to a look at the features of Muʿtazilite ontology excluding (or "exhibiting the exclusion of") an account of desert in terms of intrinsic—and durable—features of the person. Chapter 6 will explore this question from a different direction by describing the Muʿtazilite account of the identity of persons within the context of their eschatology and their claims about the resurrection of beings, revealing the stress placed on the material aspects of human beings as a criterion for their identity. Finally, the appendix is a translation of selections from a key Baṣran Muʿtazilite text—the *Sharḥ al-uṣūl al-khamsa* by Mānkdīm Shāshdīw—which aims to open a window on to the Muʿtazilites' discussions of desert and deserved treatments.

Throughout, I have tried not to presuppose a close acquaintance with the works of the Muʿtazilites, and I hope to have minimized—though perhaps not eliminated entirely—the abbreviated ways of reference that such presuppositions lead to and that might have made this work inaccessible to those lacking sufficient background.

ACKNOWLEDGMENTS

The somewhat unusual way in which this book was written means that my gratitude is distributed in equally unusual forms, and many of the people I need to thank played their part less during the writing itself than in the time that followed it. The most usual (in kind) and yet also unusual (in weight) debt of gratitude must be to my former supervisor John Marenbon, who provided the space of communication and the initial impetus to think about the questions that resulted in this book. He has given me unstinting support throughout, not just in scrupulously following the revisions that the book itself has periodically needed to molt through but also in contending with the revisions of my relationship to it, which I have molted off with much greater frequency. His faith has always been greater than my own, and nearly enough to make me doubt him. Most other debts, where these aren't yet more gifts of faith that have already been metabolized but are too old and too many to be named, are due to my family and the good friends who have weathered my uncertainties for part or all of the last four years, especially Dave Robinson, Lila Daskalaki, and Emmanuel Halais.

MORAL AGENTS AND THEIR DESERTS

CHAPTER 1

The Framework: The Muʿtazilites

Questions about the nature of moral values and the conditions that determine one's otherworldly destination—whether to paradise or the Fire—had formed an important part of the Islamic theological curriculum from early on, and generated lively debate. Many of the distinctive features of these debates were molded from the earliest days of the nascent Islamic caliphate when political developments revolving around the succession to Muḥammad placed them at the top of the agenda, and the parameters and membership conditions of the Islamic community came under dispute. At the time from which I will pick up the narrative, two types of responses to the broader questions about moral value and the narrower ones about desert stand out in the Islamic theological milieu, and in particular, in the practice of dialectical theology known as *kalām*: the responses of the Ashʿarites and those of the Muʿtazilites. The latter thinkers shall be my interlocutors in this study, and by way of introducing them, I shall here attempt a brief—and perhaps impressionistic—sketch of their thought and their relation to Ashʿarism.

The name of the Muʿtazilites is usually associated with an approach that gives supremacy to reason at the expense of revealed data, and the master script for the rise of the schools of Islamic theology is usually recounted along the following rough lines: at the time of the caliph al-Maʾmūn (r. 813–33), a famous Inquisition took place at the instigation of a set of Muʿtazilite theologians well versed in and much enamored of disputational inquiries into matters of belief, and wielding great influence over the caliph. The aim of the Inquisition was to compel acquiescence in the doctrine that the Qurʾān was created and not eternal. The Inquisition excited great opposition among prominent traditionalists, who rejected this view and opposed themselves to this type of theological dispute on questions of faith, including the influential Aḥmad b. Ḥanbal (d. 855), who was imprisoned but refused to deliver the required profession of doctrine. The abolition of the

Inquisition with al-Mutawakkil (r. 847–61), the latter's prohibition of such disputes about the Qur'ān, and the release of a triumphant Aḥmad b. Ḥanbal marked the beginning of the fall from grace for Muʿtazilite thinkers. The Muʿtazilites continued to flourish until, some time in the first quarter of the tenth century, a great defection from their ranks occurred that was to alter the course of Islamic theology. After many years of apprenticing in the circle of Abū ʿAlī al-Jubbā'ī (d. 915), one of the most renowned leaders of the Muʿtazilites in the tenth century, Abu'l-Ḥasan al-Ashʿarī (d. 935) dramatically disavowed Muʿtazilite doctrines. He then committed himself to the recovery and stout defense of the traditionalist view of such matters, thereby becoming the founder of the eponymous school of the Ashʿarites, arguably the most prominent theological tradition in medieval Islam. In the writings of al-Ashʿarī and his followers—al-Bāqillānī (d. 1013), al-Juwaynī (d. 1085), al-Ghazālī (d. 1111), al-Shahrastānī (d. 1153), and Fakhr al-Dīn al-Rāzī (d. 1210) are only a few of the glittering names the school boasts—Muʿtazilism was subjected to a devastating critique, and the uncompromising rationalism of Muʿtazilite theology was repudiated in favor of an approach that gave primacy to revelation across the entire spectrum of positions discussed in the Islamic theological curriculum.

This story may verge on the mythological in its stark simplicity and paucity of detail, but for the purposes of the present study it can function as a backdrop for a brief account of the contents of the categories "Muʿtazilite" and "Ashʿarite." The Muʿtazilites identified themselves by a set of five principles that were unanimously affirmed by all, whatever their differences on other, secondary theological questions. Most of these principles are given to us in the account of the Muʿtazilite Abu'l-Qāsim al-Balkhī (also called al-Kaʿbī, d. 931) in the following way:

> The Muʿtazilites unanimously agree that God—may He be exalted—is in no way like any other thing, that He is neither a body nor an accident, but rather the Creator of bodies and accidents, and that the senses cannot perceive Him neither in this life nor the next. . . . And they unanimously maintain that God does not love depravity, and that He does not create the acts of human beings, but it is the latter who do the acts they have been commanded to do and prohibited from doing, by virtue of the capacity for action [*qudra*], which God has created for them and instated within them, that they may obey through it and desist from disobedience.[1] . . . And He willed—great and exalted is He—that they might come to believe out of their own accord and not by compulsion, that they may thus be tried and tested, and that they may deserve the highest form of reward. . . . And they unanimously agree that God—great and exalted is He—does not forgive those who commit grave sin [*murtakibī al-kabā'ir*] unless they repent . . . and that the grave sinner does not deserve to be designated by the noble name of faith

[*īmān*] and submission [*islām*], nor by that of unbelief [*kufr*], but by that of grave sin [*fisq*], as he was called by God, and as the community unanimously affirms.[2]

This passage may appear somewhat opaque without a knowledge of the turns of phrase and concept that characterize Islamic theological discussions, and a full explanation of the principles would take us out of our remit. These principles can be gathered together under two main headings, after a practice initiated by the Muʿtazilite masters themselves: principles of divine unity (*tawḥīd*) and principles of justice (*ʿadl*).[3] All Islamic factions affirmed God's unity, and all subscribed to the Qur'ānic description of God as a being like whom there is none (*laysa kamithlihi shay'*, 42:11), but the Muʿtazilites' approach was distinguished by their austere view of His simplicity and their anxiety over all things anthropomorphic. Things anthropomorphic included the bodily parts (e.g., God's eyes or His hands) and functions (e.g., sitting on the throne) ascribed to God in various Qur'ānic passages, which the Muʿtazilites duly interpreted by the device of *ta'wīl*, or allegorical interpretation, in ways that deflected the possibility of corporeality from God. One of the most contentious extensions of their doctrine was their denial of the beatific vision in the afterlife, since the denial of corporeal aspects entailed that God could not be perceived by sight.

Their adherence to divine unity was expressed in the view they took of the divine attributes, where they affirmed that God's essential attributes were identical with Him, and were not different entities or hypostases. Thus, when one affirms that God is knowing, powerful, eternal, living, one is not thereby affirming any separate "entitative accidents"—a term I will say more about below—or essences. One does not affirm a divine knowledge or life in affirming God as knowing or living. This was not a blanket approach taken toward all the divine attributes, nor was it one that found Muʿtazilites unanimous about the details. Certain other attributes—those that were designated as "attributes of action" (*ṣifāt fiʿliyya*)—were not ascribed to God by virtue of His essence; for example, God's being willing (*murīd*) was theorized in a different way, to deal with certain constraints set down by the Muʿtazilite commitment to freedom of will, and was ascribed to God by virtue of a temporally originated "accident" of willing. Similarly with divine speech (*kalām*)—another unpopular and controversial Muʿtazilite tenet—which was not seen as an attribute predicable of God eternally and by virtue of His essence but one that was predicated of Him by virtue of and at the time of His creating the entitative accident of speech. This view grounded the doctrine of the createdness of the Qur'ān, which some scholars have suggested may have been adopted partly as a solution to certain questions relating to human freedom of will.[4] It is worth stressing the degree of diversity characterizing Muʿtazilite theological professions as well as the inevitable revisions of doctrine that came with the passage of time, among the most significant of which was Abū Hāshim's (d. 933) theory of modes or states (*aḥwāl*) as a means of understanding the divine attributes, developed in the first part of the tenth century.

In this ontological economy the Muʿtazilites were at odds with the wider Islamic view, which was represented by traditionalists such as Aḥmad b. Ḥanbal, who recoiled from the rationalism characterizing the Muʿtazilite approach and the way it seemed to undermine Qur'ānic authority. If the Qur'ān affirms knowledge of God, who are the Muʿtazilites to so boldly interpret it away? If the Qur'ān speaks of God's hands or God's eyes, then what hermeneutic device can legitimize the denial of them? Which is not to say that God has hands and eyes in the way in which we normally understand these features; we must simply accept such aspects of God without asking how (*bi-lā kayfa*) and resign our claims to knowledge of their modality. When al-Ashʿarī opted out of Muʿtazilism and took up the Ḥanbalite banner, it is this sort of return to a primitive acceptance of scriptural authority that he advocated, and the denuded, achromatic, and unQur'ānic God of the Muʿtazilites that he was rejecting.

Yet al-Ashʿarī did not wholly repudiate the methods of *kalām* that had served as means for the exposition of Muʿtazilite ideas, and this meant that the door to the temptations of rationalism remained open; so while on certain matters the rich Ashʿarite tradition that sprouted after him continued to challenge Muʿtazilite views on the nature of the divine attributes—for example, in denying the identity of God's attributes with His essence and affirming His knowledge, power, and so on—soon the Ashʿarites began to inch closer to their opponents in several respects, such as their discontent with a no-questions-asked, uninterpreted acceptance of the anthropomorphic features of God. In this, they provided grounds for an abiding hostility on the part of the traditionalist camp, which had been distrustful of al-Ashʿarī's self-appointment as defender of their cause from early on.

It is the second principle or general heading, however, that gives this study its subject matter. It would make little sense to issue unrestricted judgments about the relative importance of these two principles. Both were the subject of acute controversy that continued to engage the energies of theologians from both sides for centuries after their initial launch. Moreover, the topics grouped under one principle are never entirely insulated from those discussed in another (it is, after all, the demand for a perfect consistency, and thus for a communication between all constituent parts of the doctrine affirmed, that made of *kalām* such a *technē*). Nevertheless, what may be said is that the topics discussed under the principle of justice percolated into seminal streams of Islamic thought and practice to a greater extent than did the theological discussions of divine unity. This was in great part a function of the relations these topics bore to legal thought, in which the values of acts were theorized, making works on legal theory (*uṣūl al-fiqh*) and often also substantive law (*fiqh*) vehicles for the expression of theological commitments. This, in turn, was a reflection of the multiple roles Muslim thinkers frequently bore, for they were never just jurists or theologians but quite often served in both capacities.

The positions gathered under the Muʿtazilite principle of justice converged on the affirmation that God is just and good, and will not commit acts that are wrong or evil. If the principle of unity in many respects emphasized the unlikeness of God to human beings, the principle of justice laid greater stress on the likeness. The standards of good and evil, justice and injustice, are those that we human beings know by our own reason, and are univocally applied to God and human beings. God and human beings are bound alike by a single code of moral values, though God is unlike human beings in that He will not commit evil due to His lack of need (that is, self-sufficiency) and knowledge of moral values. Moral values are intrinsic qualities that attach to acts by virtue of their satisfying certain descriptions that are accessible to reason: if an act is a lie, it is evil; similarly if an act is injustice; gratitude is always obligatory, and so is the repayment of debts. The Muʿtazilite thesis that human acts are not determined by God was linked to the defense of divine justice, for the evil acts of human beings would otherwise be fixed on God. God does not prejudice anyone's ability to become a believer, lead anyone astray, or close anyone's heart against belief—as some Qurʾānic passages and prophetic traditions seemed to suggest.

The Zaydite Muʿtazilite Mānkdīm Shāshdīw (d. 1034) provides us with a pithy portrait of the God of the Muʿtazilites when he describes Him in these words:

> His acts are all good, He does not do evil, He does not fail to perform what is obligatory on Him, He does not lie in His message nor is He unjust in His rule; He does not torment the children of pagans for the sins of their fathers, He does not grant miracles to liars, and He does not impose on people obligations that they can neither bear nor have knowledge of. Far from it, He enables them to accomplish the duties He has imposed on them, and acquaints them with the qualities of these duties . . . so that he who perishes, perishes in the face of clear signs, and he who is saved, is saved in the face of clear signs. If obligation is imposed on a person and he fulfills it as he is bidden to, then He will necessarily reward him. And when He—glory to Him—afflicts people with pain and sickness, He does so in their interests and for their benefit, for otherwise He would be failing to perform what is obligatory.[5]

The Muʿtazilite defense of the belief that God is bound by the same code of value as human beings was often conducted via a defense of the view that moral values are independent from revelation, since the contrary perspective, taken up by the Ashʿarites, consisted of the belief that acts acquire their values when divine command or prohibition attaches to them, and that it was revelation that promulgated the values of certain acts. The universal human knowledge of such moral truths—even on the part of those who adhere to no religion—was cited by the Muʿtazilites as proof of their independence from revelation. The claim that moral truths are apprehensible by reason was linked with the claim that the moral obligation to reflect on the existence of God is a rational one that precedes revelation; indeed, were there no such prerevelational moral imperative, it is hard to see how human beings could be held accountable for their failure to believe.

The Muʿtazilite claims about moral value tied in with their views on desert and posthumous destinies, which formed the subject matter of the principle of "the promise and the threat" (*al-waʿd waʾl-waʿīd*). Since the moral values of acts are independent of God's will and command, so is the desert one acquires through such acts. Reward and punishment in the afterlife—what I shall call posthumous treatments—were inexorably determined by one's deeds, though here two separate principles collaborated to guarantee this determination: not simply the moral value of one's acts but the word God had sent forth once and for all by promising and threatening certain treatments in scriptural passages. God would not retract, for lying is intrinsically evil.

Closely related to these concerns was the rubric titled "the intermediate position" (*al-manzila bayna al-manzilatayn*), in which the Muʿtazilites argued their answers to the following questions: What is the status of grave sinners? And what destinies are reserved for them in the afterlife—in particular, are they to be consigned to eternal punishment? The first was a question about the definition of faith: the status in question was whether the grave sinner remained a believer, whether his sin rendered him an unbeliever, or whether he should be designated as a tertium quid. The Muʿtazilites were distinguished by taking the third view, saying that the grave sinner was in an intermediate position, and defined faith with a strong bias toward acts of obedience at the expense of internal belief. In answer to the second question, they affirmed that the grave sinner would receive eternal punishment unless he repented of his sin before dying. The intermediate position in this life resolved itself into the status of unbeliever in the next (and everyone agreed that unbelievers would receive eternal punishment).[6]

The Ashʿarites countered such views with their vocal and challenging brand of voluntarism, which construed good and evil as qualities generated through divine command and prohibition. What was it that piqued Ashʿarite theologians about the creeds of their colleagues and excited their zealous indignation? The creation of an order of causality that was not subject to God's sovereign power and seemed to operate autonomously from the divine Will. God himself, Ashʿarites affirmed, cannot be subject to a *Law,* nor can moral concepts be applied univocally to His acts and those of human beings. Desert and moral value do not operate in this quasi-autonomous manner, nor indeed do human beings behave in an autonomous manner such as would set them up as little "creators"—creators of their acts—side by side with God. The doctrine propounded by al-Ashʿarī attempted to preserve divine omnipotence by claiming that God created human acts, and human beings "acquired" them. In addition, whereas for the Muʿtazilites it is external acts that are the primary bearers of value and the ingredients of faith, possessing decisive significance for one's posthumous treatment, the Ashʿarites gave primacy to the internal, cognitive act of belief in God's unity as a criterion for faith, and thus included grave sinners in the community of believers. And while both schools shared a scriptural legacy that tended to depict deeds as a form of moral currency that could be stored up and put one in credit or debit, the Ashʿarites backed off from this model when its independence from God's will became too conspicuous.[7] The Muʿtazilites immortalized this model in the structure of their theodicy.

If one was to schematize the conflict, one might try juxtaposing the competing theological perspectives in the following way. The Muʿtazilites said of God: "It is obligatory for Him to . . . it is not permissible that He . . ."; the Ashʿarites replied: "God—may He be exalted and may His names be sanctified—is not under a Law [*taḥta sharīʿa*] . . . nor is there anyone above Him who permits and forbids Him, who commands and proscribes."[8] "He is the sovereign ruler [*mālik*] who is subject to none and above whom there is none to permit or command or rebuke or forbid . . . and as such, nothing He does can be evil."[9] The Muʿtazilites said: God does not do wrong, for one who does wrong is a wrongdoer deserving of blame, and thus God does not create wrongful human acts; the Ashʿarites countered: "We do not say that the liar and wrongdoer is the one who *creates* lying and wrongdoing; rather that the wrongdoer is the one in whom wrongdoing *inheres* and the liar is the one in whom lying *inheres*."[10] The Muʿtazilites said: Good and evil are intrinsic attributes of acts; the Ashʿarites objected: "The meaning of 'good' (*ḥasan*) is an act whose agent is commended in the Law, while the meaning of 'evil' (*qabīḥ*) is an act whose agent is reproached in the Law; when the Law speaks of acts as being good or evil, this does not involve the ascription of such attributes to the acts."[11] The Muʿtazilites said: It is obligatory to reward good deeds and evil to reward the undeserving; the Ashʿarites responded, "Nothing is obligatory on [God]"; "reward is not an inalienable right (*ḥaqq*) . . . but it is a voluntarily rendered beneficence (*faḍl*) from God Almighty"; "if it were impossible that God not reward, the Creator would be a necessitating cause of that reward (*ʿilla mūjiba*) and not a voluntary agent."[12]

This was a conversation only in part, and it is open to question to what extent Muʿtazilite or Ashʿarite *kalām* can be wholly reduced to the reactive character of a dispute (a question that gives the impetus for the issues forming the subject of the next chapter). Extroverted conversations aside, the Muʿtazilites themselves were not without their internal divisions. The distinction between the Baṣran and Baghdadi schools of the Muʿtazilites was only at first a reflection of actual differences in location, and soon came to designate differences in theological positions, albeit ones secondary to the fundamental principles by which the Muʿtazilites identified themselves. By the end of the tenth century, the Baghdadi school seems to have been eclipsed by its Baṣran counterpart in number of adherents and importance.

Perhaps the last prominent member of the Baghdadi school in its later years was Abu'l-Qāsim al-Balkhī, who was a contemporary of two seminal thinkers of the Baṣran school, Abū ʿAlī al-Jubbāʾī and his son Abū Hāshim, who succeeded his father as head of the school on his death (d. 915 and 933, respectively).

And if debates between the two schools of the Muʿtazilites abounded, so did debates within the schools themselves. With Abū ʿAlī and Abū Hāshim, the Baṣran school splintered anew over disputes concerning such questions as repentance, desert of blame, and Abū Hāshim's theory of modes or states (*aḥwāl*).[13] History favored the son's school, and by the eleventh century its members had outnumbered those of all other Muʿtazilite schools and produced some of the most important thinkers through which we have come to know Muʿtazilism. ʿAbd al-Jabbār (d. 1025), the Zaydite sharīf Mānkdīm Shashdīw (d. 1034), Ibn Mattawayh (d. 1076), and Abū Rashīd al-Nīsābūrī (d. before 1076?) are among the names that have put their signature on our understanding of Muʿtazilite ideas. It is perhaps ʿAbd al-Jabbār who must take pride of place among them all, not simply because he stands at the head of this sequence of thinkers, but also on account of his astonishing output and in particular for his work *al-Mughnī fī abwāb al-tawḥīd wa'l-ʿadl*, which runs to over twenty volumes, and whose length is only matched by its formidable complexity and capacity to perplex.[14]

It is on this branch—the Baṣran branch—of Muʿtazilism that the focus will be placed in this study, as the strongest and also the best-documented school. In talking about this school, I will often be referring rather cumbersomely to the "Baṣran Muʿtazilites," as opposed to the abbreviated "Baṣrans," out of a sense that it is crucial to keep in view the broader intellectual platform with which the school was associated and not to allow the internal divisions, generating eponymous subschools—a tendency stoked by hostile heresiographers eager to portray the Muʿtazilites in their factiousness—to obscure the sources of unity. The more parochial appellation "Baṣran" should not obscure that these thinkers were first of all Muʿtazilites in their loyalties. The central theme with which much of this study will be concerned—namely, the conception of desert—is itself a development of the fundamental ethical vision of Muʿtazilite theology.[15]

To prepare for our discussion of this theme, several comments are in order concerning the nature of the sources to be used and especially the complexity referred to above in connection with ʿAbd al-Jabbār's *Mughnī*. The complexity in question is partly a result of the fact that many of the works that have reached us—the *Mughnī* being a prime example—were the products of a process of oral dictation, which has left its mark on their organization in the form of frequent repetitions, discontinuities, and interpolations. The mode of composition is connected to and serves to heighten the effects of the disputational character of Muʿtazilite theology. While Muʿtazilite works do contain expository sections, these are often outweighed by the dialectical sections that consist of arguments responding to objections that previously had been or might in the future be brought against the positions canvased. The proportion of the expository to the dialectical varies from one work to another: ʿAbd al-Jabbār's *Mughnī* and al-Nīsābūrī's *al-Masā'il fi'l-khilāf bayna al-Baṣriyyīn wa'l-Baghdādiyyīn* outstrip a work such as Ibn Mattawayh's *al-Majmūʿ fi'l-muḥīṭ bi'l-taklīf* in the space given to this "if someone says, we will reply" sort of argumentation. (And it is for this reason that likening ʿAbd al-Jabbār's *Mughnī* to Saint Thomas Aquinas's *Summa Theologica* is not helpful: beyond parity of length, the analogy must fail when it comes to the quality of systematic exposition.)[16]

It is the dialectical sections of Muʿtazilite works that usually need to be winnowed if one wishes to get the Muʿtazilite view on a question in any detail. But the challenges such a style poses for the student cannot be overestimated. It is not only that it makes it difficult to pronounce with confidence that one has surveyed the entire body of texts where one might expect to find statements relevant to the question under investigation (given the interconnection between theological theses, texts relevant to a given question may exist in wide geographic dispersion). Nor is it just that one must scavenge for relevant statements and strands of argument from widely scattered places within the Muʿtazilite corpus and weave them together on one's own looms to produce what one will then describe, somewhat sheepishly and self-consciously, as "the Muʿtazilite view" of a matter. It is also that often, the locations in which such statements are met will be arguments in which the angle of interest does not coincide with the angle of interest that one carries to the investigation. These angles—which dictate the focus, choice of topics, and organization of means and ends in the argumentation—are frequently determined by the history of the debates, and that is not something that can be read off their sleeve. The origins of the debates will need to be reconstructed by crisscrossing through the body of arguments, so as to finally permit one to dispel the unfamiliarity and oddity of a particular view in light of the interconnecting whole.

A good example of this deep embeddedness of Muʿtazilite discussions can be mentioned by way of introducing some of the sources I will be using, and concerns a topic included in the Baṣran Muʿtazilite corpus whose title would have readily recommended it as a first port of call for gaining an understanding of the Baṣrans' view of desert. Attractively and suggestively titled "Desert of Blame," this topic is discussed by ʿAbd al-Jabbār in one of three books that comprise volume 11 of the *Mughnī,* and by his successor Ibn Mattawayh in a similar thematic neighborhood in his *Majmūʿ*. The subject of debate was one internal to the school of the Baṣrans, dividing Abū ʿAlī (whose side was taken by the Baghdadi Abu'l-Qāsim al-Balkhī), on the one hand, and Abū Hāshim and his followers, including ʿAbd al-Jabbār, Mānkdīm, and Abū Rashīd al-Nīsābūrī, on the other. The delicate question around which the debate revolved was parsed in the following form: in the case in which an agent failed to do what was obligatory, was the true relatum—or simply, "the ground": *mutaʿallaq*—of blame *the fact that the agent had not done the obligatory* (the "not-doing") or was it *the act one had done instead*?[17]

The origin of the debate, as Muʿtazilite writings suggest and the Ashʿarite heresiographer al-Baghdādī also testifies—not without a measure of pride—went back to a certain reductio directed by Ashʿarite opponents against a central Muʿtazilite claim—namely, that human beings determine their own acts.[18] This claim had been spelled out in the position that the agent's power of autonomous action (*qudra*) precedes in time the action which it empowers one to do, and is not simultaneous with it, as opponents of a libertarian position held. The reductio consisted of saying that if this power precedes the act by a certain amount of time, then there is nothing to specify the length of time by which it should precede, and it may precede by "one time" or "many times" (*waqt/awqāt*). It is then conceivable that an agent endowed with this power may go through life without undertaking a single act—whether of commission (*akhdh*) or omission (*tark;* and this, it must be noted, is conceived as the *positive* act done instead of commission)—and thus complete life without coming to deserve anything on account of works done. Yet it is accepted by all parties that human beings must ultimately be *either* punished *or* rewarded, so it is impossible that they should deserve nothing at all.

Abū ʿAlī and Abū Hāshim responded to this objection in different ways; while Abū ʿAlī rejected the possibility that a capable agent could ever be free from acts, Abū Hāshim lent his weight to the position that it was indeed possible for an agent to be *qādir* but not *fāʿil* ("capable" but not "acting"), to be endowed with the power of action but not to use it to produce any acts and thus to be altogether free from them. He complemented this with the view that blame may accrue on account of not-acting; in this and other ways, he eschewed the final entailment that it was possible that no desert should arise. This complementary position crystallized in the statement that the "relatum" (*mutaʿallaq*) of blame may be that "one has not done the obligatory," and that blame need not attach to a positive act, such as the act of omission done instead of the obligatory act.

While the origin of the question may have been an external challenge, the intramural debate between the two masters holds the field in the book of *Istiḥqāq al-dhamm*, and gives rise to intricate discussions of the concept of omission, the definition of obligation, and the counterfactual possibility of God's not rewarding those who obey His commands, and all these discussions—long and arduous—are conducted with primary reference to the debate about the relatum of blame. One would have had to admit that one's expectations had been confounded by the agenda of this book, if one had expected a treatment of the central issues relating to desert as a principle connecting acts to consequences. Why must punishment be perpetual? What kind of causality is involved in the relation between an act and what one deserves by it? And what is the relation between God's agency and efficient powers and the type of causality that engenders deserts and necessitates deserved treatments? Such questions are among the ones that we might have expected to find answered in a book thus titled. And it is important to have expectations, for the perplexity they generate whets the need to understand.

Indeed, this need is one that continues to press on one even after one's grasp of the situating dispute has modified one's sense of its relevance for the above questions; for even obliquely, there is much to be gleaned from this book concerning the Baṣran Muʿtazilites' approach to desert. The need to utilize these resources is rendered more pressing by the vagaries of manuscript transmission, which have deprived us of texts of central relevance to our interest, such as the sections of ʿAbd al-Jabbār's *Mughnī* concerning *al-waʿd wa'l-waʿīd,* in which matters of desert would have received their most concerted treatment, compelling us to fall back on other, more indirect means of garnering some of his views.

These, then, are some of the challenges and puzzles one needs to face in educing Muʿtazilite views out of their dialectical warrens and situating disputes. So it is not surprising that at the end of one's task and detective work, one should be left with the confident belief that one knows the minds of the Muʿtazilites better than they knew them themselves, nor to notice a somewhat imperious or triumphant tone creep into one's exposition of "the Muʿtazilite view." These challenges also give the reason why it often proves difficult to adduce sizable and continuous textual quotations in the course of mapping their positions, for the textual grounds are frequently both too dispersed and too deeply embedded in contexts of argument and angles of interest to lend themselves to such a presentation. Hence, it is critical to bear in mind these qualities of Muʿtazilite writing, for the way in which their views have to be studied affects the ways in which these views can be presented.

CHAPTER 2

Reading Muʿtazilite Ethics

Ethics as Theology

Whatever the origins of a particular dispute, however, and whether the opponent was a fellow Muʿtazilite or an Ashʿarite, these disputes and conversations clearly contribute to the distinctive character of Muʿtazilite theology. Thus, when one seeks to understand Muʿtazilite views on moral value, it is necessary that due attention be paid to these situating disputes, for many features of these views can only be grasped through their contrary. But now, if Muʿtazilite ethics can only be understood by being brought into relation with its gainsayers, what consequences does this hold for the student of their texts, and how does it determine one's understanding of one's task? Is the only coherent and legitimate task one could set oneself that of playing the role of a belated middleperson between two parties in conflict, mapping convergences and divergences, and tracing the complex course of arguments and counterarguments, mutual misunderstandings, exchanges sometimes actual and sometimes imaginary, often triumphal and even more often at cross-purposes? The Muʿtazilites said, and the Ashʿarites answered.

There are several reasons why this notion of the task may seem hard to accept. The most intuitive source of resistance would be the difficulty of believing the reductive view it seems to demand that we take concerning the motivations driving the Muʿtazilite theologian to his work. Is this all one is to make of the outpourings—copious despite the ravages of time—that stand before us? Are the twenty volumes of the *Mughnī* painstakingly dictated over some two decades by the aging judge of Rayy driven by nothing more than the wish to argue back? Certainly medieval critics of *kalām* such as al-Ghazālī might have dismissed it as a purely reactive and defensive intellectual practice, but is this all we have to say of it and the motivations of its proponents? Here one finds oneself wanting to insist, "Surely this cannot be all it means!" This intuitive reaction might find support in the observation that Mu'tazilite works do not uniformly seem to be engaging with a recognizably Ash'arite—or indeed even fellow Mu'tazilite—disputant.

Much would have to be done to give an adequate reply to this intuitive unease, and above all what would be needed here would be a deeper understanding of the nature of the dialectical practice constitutive of *kalām*, which would give a fairer account of the motivations sustaining this type of theology, revealing the thick social meanings realized in the practice of disputation—a practice that represented a widespread tool for the demonstration and development of knowledge, and the determination of intellectual hierarchies—and thus challenging the well-meaning but shortsighted dismissiveness of this "*all* it means."[1] This would at the same time illuminate the notion of the adversary or the interlocutor—Ash'arite and Mu'tazilite, historical and preemptively imaginary—that organized it. Some of the adversaries were certainly imaginative anticipations, while others were part of a reliquary of early Mu'tazilite voices that later members of the school considered as contestants to truth whom, centuries later, they still felt obliged to convince. And it was this skein of internal dialogue, as much as the central positions of unity and justice that it interpreted, that contributed to the warp and woof of the Mu'tazilite "body of knowledge" that, so some affirmed, was transmitted from generation to generation from the time of the Prophet.[2] But it would take a separate study of each area of debate, and each response and objection appearing within it, to determine the identity of the historical interlocutors it engaged.

While this is not a task that can be attempted here, it seems certain that such an intuitive resistance to considering the sustaining motivations of *kalām* mainly in terms of a reactively dialectical reflex must be presupposed by many of those who have rejected this conception of the scholarly task—as one exhausted in the study of a stichomythia—and been attracted to a different model.[3] Rejecting the seemingly reductive view of the meaning of the Mu'tazilite corpus in terms of a mere reaction, this model looks for the possibility of meaning in the engagement of this corpus on its own terms, and detached from the disputes and conversations, actual and imaginary, that situate it. It is a model that has had several adherents among students of Mu'tazilite thought, and it is the task of this chapter to bring into view the character of the Mu'tazilite moral project that engenders difficulties for it and prejudices its chances of success.

It will help set us on our way to pick up the theme of "conversation" that occurs in the contrast between the two approaches one may take toward Mu'tazilite theology, where to see it as a conversation between two theological schools is to see it in its dependencies. This theme echoes, though it does not correspond to, a similar theme that occurs in the contrast that has been drawn in the broader debate over how to approach past conceptual schemes. In the debate conducted by historians of philosophy, the two main rivals that have emerged are an approach that makes "conversational partners" of past thinkers through radical translation, and an approach that considers such conversation illegitimate on the grounds that it rides roughshod over the historical specificities and context of philosophical discourse, and insists that while an antiquarian approach can be avoided, the meaning of texts must be properly contextualized.[4]

The outcome of this debate could not take the form of the sharp choice of one alternative against the other, and could never make an understanding of the background conditions entirely dispensable. But the degree of temptation to dispense with the latter, and the difficulties of legitimacy in doing so, would depend squarely on the identity of the conversational partner who is (inevitably) initiating and the type of conversation one is interested in carrying out. One point particularly deserves to be emphasized here. And this is that the urge to raise questions of this sort concerning how a text ought and can be read is often a reflectiveness that is forced on the reader by the disruption of a preexisting meaningful engagement with the text. Not all texts need to be broken by efforts to reflectively relate to them. (And of course what counts as reflectiveness will depend on the particular habits or "norms" of scholarship through which one has learned to do this reading in the first place.) The attempt to resolve this question in terms of a conversational partnership may in turn often represent a bid for meaning that an unreflective and unself-conscious—again, on the scholarly norms—reading for some reason or other was unable to yield.

What are the factors that might disrupt such an unreflective relationship or make it difficult to establish in the first place? Several types of discontinuity between the thought-world of the reader and that of the text could be mentioned here: the reader of religious texts who is not a member of the religious tradition one is interested in has a more self-conscious task than one who is; similarly with the reader who is not heir to the larger cultural community one studies. The last point, made in the context of Western scholarship, strikes the larger and familiar note sounded with increasing frequency since the publication of Edward Said's *Orientalism.* The study of medieval Islamic thought is beset by a different set of problems from those that affect the study of its medieval Christian counterpart. "All historians intrude upon the past as outsiders, but medieval Islamicists who are not personally from a Muslim background are outsiders in both time and culture," as Richard Bulliet has more recently put it.[5] And the development of this type of discourse brings out once again the fact that it is norms of scholarship—norms that shift and evolve—that determine what counts as a self-conscious or reflective reading.

But not every type of meaningful engagement with a thinker would be disrupted by these discontinuities, and whether this occurs would depend on the type of engagement one is seeking. I want to focus, then, on the particular conversation that is of interest here, in which Muʿtazilite ethics is detached from the dialectics situating it to be treated "on its own merits." In practice, this has meant treating it as a species of philosophical ethics, which involves seeing the Muʿtazilites as contributing to a particular intellectual tradition defined at least in part by its ends—namely, a primary concern with the nature of moral values. The next section will be placing under scrutiny some leading examples of this approach. Here, my aim is to explore on a more general level the reasons why such approaches cannot work by sketching the character of the Muʿtazilites' moral interest, starting with a remark about why they might have been thought to work in the first place—namely, the formative effect on one's expectations exercised by a narrative of Islamic theology characterizing the Muʿtazilites in terms of a thoroughgoing commitment to the role of reason in human knowledge.

This so-called rationalism, which earned the Muʿtazilites their notoriety in the Islamic tradition, was evidenced in their assertions about the capacity of the human intellect to apprehend moral truths (truths that were seen as a precondition for one's acceptance of revelation) and attain to a certain knowledge of the Creator. It was also highlighted in their hermeneutical approach to the Qur'ān, as revealed by the pejorative tone that came to attach to their mode of interpretation ("*ta'wīl*" came closer to signifying a "reading into" rather than a "reading"). Developments within modern Islam, in which Muʿtazilism has often been appropriated as emblematic of a spirit of reason that betokens Islam's internal resources for facing the challenges of modernity, have contributed to the tendency to magnify the meaning of the Muʿtazilites' rationalism.[6] This understanding of their approach makes them the most likely cynosure for those who look to find continuity of spirit with the thinkers they study. Those students of Islam who are not members of the Islamic tradition or heirs of its cultural history could do worse than apply themselves to the study of Muʿtazilite thought.

Recent accounts of Muʿtazilite thought have striven to adjust our vision to a more temperate conception of their rationalism, stressing that it cannot be understood in the exacting sense discouraged by Daniel Gimaret—"to formulate a system solely by the exercise of reason, independent of all revelation." Apart from emphasizing their hermeneutical (rather than system-building) aims, it is important to point out that their use of reason had much in common with that of other schools of *kalām*, especially as concerns their view of the role of reason in the knowledge of God, and all the more as Ashʿarism moved into the later periods of its history, which were marked by a heightened absorption of Greek philosophical influence. Yet if there is one area in which the Muʿtazilites' rationalism was distinctive, Gimaret tells us, this would be in their approach to matters of ethics.[7] The hallmark of this approach was the claim that moral values are generated by objective features of acts that are accessible to human reason; revealed commands and prohibitions constituted neither the epistemological access to nor the ontological cause of moral values. This was a claim that the Muʿtazilites supported by a variety of arguments drawing single-handedly on the resources of reason.

Their rationalism thus limned, their ethics would seem to be the best candidate for a philosophical kind of attention. The difficulty that such an attention would have to face can be educed in two stages, both of which may be partly organized as attempts at tracking the all-important notion of "necessary knowledge" (*ʿilm ḍarūrī*) that cements the Muʿtazilites' moral epistemology. Necessary (or as we might say in an idiom more accessibly modern, "self-evident") knowledge represents the explanatory limit—the limit of reason—by which the firmament of the Muʿtazilite moral world is bounded. The distinction between two types of knowledge, necessary (*ḍarūrī*) and acquired (*muktasab*), was one that was widely shared across schools of *kalām*, whether Ashʿarite or Muʿtazilite. Necessary knowledge, in the Muʿtazilite Mānkdīm's definition, is knowledge that we do not bring into existence ourselves, and it is not in our power to do so, and that we cannot "repel" from ourselves at will. "Necessary" is a term that derives from the notion of coercion: this is a knowledge to which one is coerced. It is self-evident and brooks no doubt, thereby imparting to any epistemic course its foundations.[8] Acquired knowledge, by contrast, is that which is acquired by proof. Differences in theological convictions appeared in the contents ascribed to these epistemological categories, and the distinctiveness of the Muʿtazilite position lay in the claim that among all other things we know necessarily—such as our internal states, objects of perception, and certain basic logical principles—we also possess a knowledge of fundamental moral principles. At this crossroad, of course, Ashʿarite and Muʿtazilite epistemology parted company.

These fundamental moral principles were understood to take the form of universal moral propositions—"injustice is evil," "thanking the benefactor is obligatory," "it is obligatory to repay debts"—while it fell to one's own reflective efforts to judge (that is, to seek for proofs and thus acquire the knowledge of) whether a particular act was an instance of a given class of acts. Not all universal moral propositions are known necessarily, with one significant example of acquired moral knowledge being the proposition that all lies are evil. One does not necessarily know that all lies are evil—including those that are beneficial—but one has to arrive at this truth by proof; what one knows by necessity is the evilness of lies when these do not avert harm or produce benefit (in the latter case, the lie is a "vain act," *ʿabath*).[9] Our moral judgments therefore depend on a combination of necessary and acquired knowledge, of which it is the latter that might be vulnerable to error. Once one has identified the (act) description or ground that an act instantiates (*wajh*, as in *wajh al-wujūb, wajh al-qubḥ*), one necessarily knows its moral value (*ṣifa* or, less frequently, *ḥukm*: attribute, property, quality).[10]

It is against this unyielding epistemic limit of the Muʿtazilite moral firmament that one keeps knocking when looking for the stars. It's hardly a place to feel lonely, as it is precisely this limit to which medieval critics of the Muʿtazilites congregated in order to concentrate their flak, essentially contesting their opponents' right to pontificate concerning the truths inscribed in our minds. These critics were provoked by the Muʿtazilites' lavish refusal to address them by fortifying themselves behind epistemological claims and turning a deaf ear to the gainsayers. To one who denies the evilness of certain acts—meaning the acts' possession of *intrinsic* moral qualities—"there is nothing left to say, save to indicate to him his denial of necessarily known truths." Yet (the critic retorts) don't the Muʿtazilites assert that the surest path to truth is by "turning inward" (*al-rujūʿ ila'l-nafs*) and looking into the data one's own inner reality presents to one?[11] But we turn inward and find no necessary knowledge of moral principles, the critics contend. If such a contest cannot help descending into strident counterassertions, at least it will have been shown that there is nothing to favor either side in its claims about necessary knowledge. One Muʿtazilite response was to suggest that the majority did not deny their claims; another was simply to repeat that those who were denying their claims about necessary knowledge were in error and had been led astray by false beliefs, or in the words of Sherman Jackson, that "they were guilty of feigning moral agnosia."[12] But there was little one could say to such deniers of the obvious. A more nuanced response was to say that the dispute was one that concerned not *whether* we know certain moral truths or certain truths hold but *why* these truths hold—and on this necessary knowledge could not adjudicate.[13]

Whatever the success such ripostes might have had with their medieval targets, for the modern reader this lavish provocation represents a stopping place for explanation that is acutely felt when one's expectations have rallied around a certain conception of the rationalist foundations of Muʿtazilite ethics. Bold claims that excite one into the anticipation of bold argumentation often send one away in a state of flaccid chagrin, having discovered that the task went no further than claiming, and that the Muʿtazilites frequently seem to beg all the questions to be asked.

An example of this is the bold and exciting position that the Baṣran Muʿtazilites took on the moral value of lies, where they claimed that all lies are unconditionally evil regardless of the consequences, and proposed to use this claim as a proof of the existence of universal moral knowledge. The proof in question, to run through it briefly, goes something like this: we know that if a person has the option of lying or telling the truth and knows that the consequences of both acts will be equal in terms of benefit or harm, they will tell the truth. Thus, if a person knew that they "could obtain a needed dirham either through lying or telling the truth, they would not choose lying over truthfulness, but would inevitably choose the latter."[14] This is meant to apply to all human beings, but for the purposes of the proof, the Muʿtazilites focus on unbelievers and those who do not adhere to any revealed religion. The claim is intended as a factual one that refers us to our common knowledge, not merely of others' motivations, but in the first instance of our own motives as they present themselves immediately to our own consciousness. It shows, the Muʿtazilites assert, that one knows that it is evil to lie—for why else, when all other features of the acts are the same, would one choose to tell the truth? The fact that such choices issue even from those who have not been instructed by revelation demonstrates that moral propositions are known by reason.

Ashʿarite critics had several lines of criticism. Some denied the claim itself. Others accepted the claim, but argued that had the person been enculturated with different social norms, they may not have chosen, as they did, to tell the truth. To deny this counterfactual possibility would be begging the question. In responding to such criticism, however, the Muʿtazilites did not go much further than simply reiterating their claims with inconsequential amendments, referring us to our own psychological data, accessible by introspection, for corroboration of the claim.[15]

This case is one of many in which one's expectations would be disappointed by coming up short against the stopping place of explanation fixed by the necessary knowledge of moral principles. The "given" of Muʿtazilite ethics that this knowledge presents us thus modifies in a crucial way the picture of the rationalism that characterizes it. It is a feature to which I will return at several junctures in the chapters that follow as well as using it—and in particular, using the observations about just *where* the stopping place is pitched—to illustrate the further qualification I must now make to the picture of Muʿtazilite rationalism. And it is worth stressing that what is at issue is not the application of a particular term—what counts as "philosophical" and what counts as "rationalist" (these are terms lacking the fixed and transhistorical references that are often heard as honorifics)—as long as one is clear about the combination of methods and ends involved.[16]

Whatever categorial names one chooses to apply to it, the Muʿtazilite exercise of reason must be seen in its subordination to a set of clear *theological* concerns, which stimulate it and set its boundaries. To be sure, this view of the order of means and ends would not encompass all sectors of the Muʿtazilite intellectual syllabus equally well, and it has been argued that questions belonging to the "subtler" subjects designated as *daqīq al-kalām* that relate to the physical world and its ontological structure are not as readily described in terms of primary theological concerns. There, to focus on the theological and apologetic orientation of the *mutakallimūn,* including the Muʿtazilites, is a mistake, in Dhanani's view, in that it "disregards the perspective of the *mutakallimūn* themselves and ignores the non-theological aspect of their writings."[17] In this sector, it might be more appropriate to consider the speculations on ontological or physical issues themselves as constituting the primary concern, with theological positions functioning as a secondary means of argumentation for or against a primary question of this sort. Clearly what we make of this claim will depend on where we set the boundaries of this particular subject matter, as many of the ontological speculations of the *mutakallimūn* were originally closely linked to controversial questions concerning divine nature.

It is in any case with far greater confidence that one can assert this order of means and ends when turning to that sector of the Muʿtazilite syllabus that is concerned with matters of value. Muʿtazilite moral speculations are bounded by a clear set of theological ends that make their presence acutely and ubiquitously felt in imparting to Muʿtazilite moral theory—if one may isolate it as a distinct subject matter without this constituting an ideologically charged move—its very reason for being. To treat Muʿtazilite ethics as a philosophical discourse, to the extent that it depends on a resolve to abstract from these ends and present it as an independent body enclosing its ends within itself, is a venture that cannot go far.

These theological concerns are announced in no uncertain terms from the first pages of ʿAbd al-Jabbār's chief volume on matters of ethics, *al-Taʿdīl wa'l-tajwīr* (volume 6/1 of the *Mughnī*), which he introduces with the following statement of purpose:

> Know that the *purpose* of this section is to show that God only does what is good, and will do what is obligatory without fail. . . . This cannot be shown without first explaining the nature of acts, the characteristics [*aḥkām*] of acts, the nature of evil and good . . . and without explaining the grounds on account of which an act is entitled to these characteristics, for it is *only after* these principles have been explained that what ought to be denied of God or ascribed to Him can be made clear.

"What ought to be denied" (*tanzīh*) signifies the denial of evil.[18] He goes on to enumerate several theses that are guided by the same purpose—namely, that of denying evil of God. A few lines down, another set of remarks broadens the sweep, indicating that the volumes of the *Mughnī* dealing with the principles of divine assistance (*luṭf*), compensation (*ʿiwaḍ*), the optimum or "most beneficial" (*al-aṣlaḥ*), and prophecy all form part of the same theological project. This is a project that ranges itself under one of the two main principles mentioned in the previous chapter—that of justice (*ʿadl*)—in which the distinctive Muʿtazilite position concerning God's justice was developed: moral concepts such as justice and goodness apply to God's action in the same way as they do to those of human beings, God is not above all moral standards because of His status as Sovereign and Proprietor, nor are moral truths generated by His command.

Thus, it is this strategic theological concern that Muʿtazilite moral positions are marshaled to support. These positions belong to a variety of areas of inquiry: one of these concerns the choice of substantive values; another, the principles of moral psychology and epistemology; and yet a third, the ontology of moral value. Carving them up in this way is calculated to indicate correspondences with familiar categories of philosophical inquiry, so as to make it clear that the teleology of theological concerns spares none, but it shouldn't be permitted to obscure the thick mesh of interrelations in which each area coexists with the others. Hence, and most notably, positions on the second level serve to establish theses on the third: the claim that moral values can be apprehended by reason is seen to be instrumental to the claim that they are independent from revelation, and thus—a Muʿtazilite "thus"—independent from divine will or command (an independence on which in turn rests the possibility of evaluating God's willing, acting, and commanding). The former thesis is sometimes supported by attempts to demonstrate the fact—taken to be an empirical one—that human beings are motivated by their knowledge of the moral values of acts even when no revealed evidence is available to them that could have informed them. These empirical claims are supplemented by arguments of what one might call a "transcendental" sort, following (rather crookedly) a certain mode of philosophical parlance, in which the objectivity of moral truths is argued to be a condition for the acceptance and fruition of divine revelation. Therefore, the objective truth of the proposition that lies are evil is seen as a precondition for according our trust to the divine message, the rational accessibility (thus objectivity) of the obligation to avert harm from oneself is seen as a precondition for undertaking the obligation to inquire into religious matters (*wujūb al-naẓar*), which one does because of the fear of harm that might befall one on account of neglecting to do so, and it is this inquiry that leads on to revelation. A more diffuse suggestion is that a God whom one believes to act in despotic injustice is one whom one would have no reason to trust in.

Several examples could be given to illustrate the circumscription of Muʿtazilite ethics by theological concerns, and more particularly how one's encounter with these concerns will be marked by the experience of a contrast between their moral thought and what one's broader cultural tradition—but even more so, a familiarity with philosophical tradition—would have led one to expect. The best place to turn for this is the Muʿtazilite discussion of substantive moral values, in which what is in question is not what it is for an act to be evil, obligatory, and so on but which types of acts are evil, obligatory, and so on; here we may finally return to the "given" of Muʿtazilite moral epistemology, this time to scrutinize some of its particular contents more closely for the light they cast on the purposes of Muʿtazilite ethics. Approaching this area naively and with a philosophically informed spirit, one would no doubt land oneself in no small perplexity. One's perplexity would partly derive from the peculiar fashion in which substantive values are introduced, as they are in ʿAbd al-Jabbār's *al-Taʿdīl wa'l-tajwīr,* where he takes us through the grounds or descriptions (*wujūh*) that render an act evil, good, or obligatory.[19] The discussion of these grounds is ranged around the question, "What is it that distinguishes an evil act from an act that is not evil?" and on the face of it, the purpose of the exercise is an explanatory one. This purpose seems to be clearly signposted by the following statement, where ʿAbd al-Jabbār writes:

> If it has been established that a rational [i.e., rationally *known: ʿaqlī*] evil act, such as injustice and lying, must be distinguished from other types of acts by a feature exclusive to it, there must be something that necessitates its being thus, were it not for which, there would be no reason why it should be evil rather than good nor why *this* act should be qualified as "evil" as against *another* act.[20]

The kind of methodology employed here is one that is familiar from many other spheres of Baṣran Muʿtazilite thought, and one might designate it as a kind of "modal heuristics" or a method of modal distinction. A marvelous display of the Muʿtazilites' keen appreciation of contingency, it runs thus:

we *see, know, observe,* a certain entity before us of which we apprehend that it is qualified by a certain property or attribute. Having observed this, we proceed to ask a modal question: "*Why* should it be qualified by *this* attribute rather than any number of others that were equally possible?" (And of course, since this question can only be an *expression* of one's sense of contingency, the ability to ask it is here presupposed and not questioned.) One of the most important areas of Muʿtazilite metaphysics in which this method is deployed is in establishing the existence of entitative accidents (*maʿānī*), which are the ontological grounds to which created entities owe their possession of most of their attributes—attributes as disparate as location and motion or will and belief (there the modal question would be, Why is this body *here* rather than *there?* Because it has an accident that determines that it should be so).[21] The notion here is of a passage from our *necessary* perception of a thing's quality—without which it would make no sense to wonder at its being so and ask whether it could have been otherwise—to the *acquired* or *proof-based* understanding of its ontological cause.

Likewise, in this context, a reason for an evident fact is being sought: Why is an act evil when it could have been otherwise? This piece of methodology presupposes *our* perception of moral attributes. It is because we necessarily perceive them that we can ask about their ontological ground; one's back is turned to gainsayers of the claim that moral qualities are known by reason. These grounds, then, are intended to be explanations for the ascription of a moral attribute to an entity (namely, an act). What are these grounds? In ʿAbd al-Jabbār's words: "A lie is evil because it is a lie, ingratitude because it is ingratitude, enjoining obligations which a person cannot fulfil because it is enjoining obligations that a person cannot fulfill, and willing evil, ignorance, commanding evil, vain action likewise for possessing these attributes."[22] The ensuing paragraphs in this passage undertake to explain why certain acts—speech, willing, beliefs—may be evil, in the same cataloging spirit: speech may be evil because it is lying, vain action, a command for evil, a prohibition of what is good, an enjoining of what is not obligatory, a promise of reward for that which does not deserve reward, a command that enjoins obligations that a person cannot fulfill, and so on. Willing may be evil because it is willing evil, because it is willing an action that a person cannot fulfill, because it is willing an action from a person who has not fulfilled the conditions for the imposition of the Law, because it is vain action, and so on.

A first reaction to this listlike cataloging of these categories of acts would be bafflement. For what order of account is this, signposted as it is by an explanatory intention? Yet in itself, this should probably be no more baffling than any other variety of act-description ethics, as one might classify this approach. It comes complete with the intuitionist epistemology traditionally associated with this type of ethics, in which there is no further question to be asked concerning how one knows one's moral truths after it has been stated that one does—one simply does, and if *that's* contingent, well, all explanations have to come to an end somewhere. The Baṣran Mu'tazilites nowhere speak of conscience, but if that is understood merely as a reification of one's moral knowledge, then one might say that for the Mu'tazilites, "our conscience simply says so."

More to the point, however, would be a second type of perplexity addressed less to the listlike character of the exposition than to the list's specific contents. A reader approaching the Mu'tazilites with an appetite philosophically whetted would have expected an inventory of value-bearing acts to reflect the variety of ways through which we realize our capacities to harm and benefit each other, keep and breach trust, and create and exact claims over one another. And it is not so much that the inventory of moral act-descriptions fails to contain such moral precepts of a more general sort and with recognizable relevance to human ethical concerns (the evilness of lies and the obligatoriness of gratitude are just two examples) but that it contains too many act-descriptions of a more particular sort. These compel us to ask a modal question in turn, one similar to the question asked by readers of G. E. Moore's *Principia Ethica* who saw aesthetic enjoyment included in his catalog of goods and readers of Aristotle's *Nicomachean Ethics* who saw magnanimity included in his catalog of the virtues: Why *this* act-description in particular and not others? Why "vain action"? Why "enjoining what cannot be fulfilled"? And why, later on, "rewarding one who does not deserve reward"?[23]

And this last act-description makes plain what must have already been suggesting itself—namely, that the contents of the inventory are sharply oriented not to the actions constituting one's relations with one's fellow human beings but toward the range of actions peculiar to God. All three of these descriptions—like those enjoining what is not obligatory and promising reward for that which does not deserve reward—are ones that the Mu'tazilites have made it their business to prove God will never instantiate in His acts: for these kinds of act are always evil, whether the agent is human or divine. "Vain action is evil"; *read*: God always acts with a purpose, and purposefully created humankind to benefit them, giving them the opportunity to attain reward through their just deserts, and so no action of His is vain. "Rewarding the undeserving is evil"; *read*: God rewards and punishes according to one's deserts, and so the grave sinner who does not deserve reward will not enter paradise, for *such* an act—an act of giving an undeserved reward—is evil. "Commanding what cannot be fulfilled is evil"; *read*: God does not command human beings to do what exceeds their capacity, and so ought (here: a command) implies can, for it would be unjust to punish someone for failing to obey commands when they could not have done so.

These references—the result of a reading that could hardly be called subtle—contextualize the choice of descriptions for us and thereby explain away the contingency that adhered to them, revealing the theocentric nature of Mu'tazilite moral inquiry and its preoccupation above all with the values of divine acts. The descriptions are theologically functional, and bespeak the curriculum of moral questions that had been discussed in early Islamic debates and impressed themselves on all subsequent theology—about the status of the grave sinner (and hence the constituents of belief), the ascription of the evil acts of human beings, and God's justice. And all of this, in the final analysis, is as it should be in a project whose charter is spelled out by ʿAbd al-Jabbār succinctly in these words: "If such an act is not found among those that [God] performs, then there is no point in taking pains over its characterization."[24] If there is anything at all worthy of perplexity, it is that it should take so little subtlety to notice the derivation—*not* because of any Muʿtazilite interest in concealing the nature of their project (it is only we, deceived by our expectations as well as a division between ethical and theological that did not obtain for our authors, who can experience it as a concealment after we suddenly discover its real character). It is rather that the Muʿtazilite project of demonstrating the equivocity of moral values between the domain of the worldly or perceptible domain (*al-shāhid*) and that of the otherworldly or unseen (*al-ghā'ib*) had rested on establishing a correspondence of valuing categories between the two realms. What seems peculiar then is the absence of a greater effort to assimilate the categories relevant to the two domains more successfully into a type of action that could be predicated of human agents as well as God, producing a set of descriptions that would be neutral and uninformative as to the identity of the agent, in a way that talk of "rewarding" or "enjoining what cannot be fulfilled" is not.

My intention in the above has been to reinforce an awareness of the theological aims that bound Muʿtazilite moral discourse, and the task would not be complete without including a salient example attesting to these aims that is drawn from the Baṣran Muʿtazilites' conception of desert. This example can be described in terms of the annihilation of a necessary contrast between what ought to be and what in fact is the case, and it consists in a principle that states that "it is not possible to deserve something whose realization [or effectuation] would be impossible."[25] This was included by the Baṣrans on the list of conditions on whose prior satisfaction the realization of desert was made contingent.

A full explanation of this principle could not be given without anticipating the investigations of later chapters, but plenty can be done even at this stage by sketching the background theology from which this idea derives its meaning. This background was roughly as follows: in order to guard the claim about the univocal application of moral concepts to humans and God, it was absolutely imperative that one should be able to utter counterfactual statements about the possibility of God's deserving blame. Moral laws needed to be supported by counterfactual statements: *if* God were to do evil, He *would* deserve blame. For such is the nature of evil, whatever the identity of the agent. At the same time, the Muʿtazilites did not wish to permit analogous counterfactual statements about punishment ("if God did evil, He would deserve punishment"). But how could a distinction be drawn between the two types of claims, so that one would be admissible but not the other?

The *Baṣran* Muʿtazilites in particular could not justify making this distinction on the basis of a claim that "God would never do an act of such *magnitude* as would deserve punishment." That is, it would seem that nothing in the *moral nature* of the *act* could be employed for this purpose, given their commitment to the position they maintained in the face of opposition from their Baghdadi colleagues—namely, that God is *capable* (*qādir*) of committing evil, even if He *will* not do it for reasons explained by the model of moral motivation. According to this model, knowledge of the moral value of the act and lack of need to perform it (both of which would be true of God) are sufficient conditions for choosing the good, and if one satisfies them one will choose the good *unfailingly,* though not *necessarily,* in the sense of necessity that a lack of *qudra* ("metaphysical" possibility) would involve.[26] (This was in contrast to the Baghdadis, who held that God was not capable of committing evil.) Thus, a distinction was made in terms of the possibility of receiving the treatment: since God is not susceptible to benefit and harm, it would not be possible to punish Him.[27]

But now, considered as an independent moral precept, this principle would seem to countenance an unwarranted intrusion of what is in fact possible—whether it is *possible* that something that is deserved be received—into the realm of what ought to be, including what is deserved. "If you cannot punish someone then he cannot deserve to be punished"? Surely such considerations ought not to affect what is or can be deserved, and this order of moral truths should not be contingent on anything that happens to be true about the nature of the world—which would include what happens to be the case about the nature of the moral agents. Of course the question is not a simple one, and there are many contentious questions that might be raised here concerning the broader issue of how "can" relates to "ought." Clearly the nature of the moral agent is highly relevant where the possibility in question has to do with one's ability to *do* an act: where I cannot do something, I cannot be under an obligation to do it. The Muʿtazilites recognize this sort of constraint when they speak of the ability to guard against evil (*al-taḥarruz min al-qabīḥ*) as a restriction on the generation of desert.[28] But the sort of possibility to which the Muʿtazilites make morality hostage here is of a different order: it is not about whether an agent can do something but whether something can be done to an agent—whether one can experience something (sc. *after* the act); "whether someone can do something" versus "whether something can happen to someone." One solution, of course, would have been to accord a certain kind of privileged status to the agent in question that would differentiate between them and other existents, and justify a differential application of ethical norms. This is a solution that the Muʿtazilite views on the univocity of moral standards between *shāhid* and *ghā'ib*—between the worldly (more particularly the human) domain and the otherworldly (more particularly the divine) domain—would seem to foreclose. In ʿAbd al-Jabbār's discussion, the above principle is embedded precisely in such a context, in which the argument is directed against the view that the identity of the agent has any bearing on moral value.

It is interesting to note that the difficulties involved in the attempt to prevent such counterfactual predication are confined to punishment (about which, after all, the embarrassment would be greater). This principle is not needed when it comes to reward, because here it is indeed something about the *nature of this type of desert* that makes it impossible for God not just to be in practice rewarded, but to *deserve* reward. As we will see in greater detail in chapter 4, a condition for coming to deserve reward is that one suffer hardship, and this God cannot do, as a being insusceptible to benefit and harm. In this case, it is a reason at the order of the *ethical* that accounts for the impossibility of His deserving, and not a reason of the order of practicality. (Yet at the same time, this asymmetry connects to a troublesome difference between the justification of reward and that of punishment in the Baṣran Muʿtazilite scheme, about which there will be more to say at a later point.)

The theological aims of the Muʿtazilites and the boundaries to moral thought that they provide will have been amply attested by all the above.[29] In sum, it may be stated that the specific contents of their moral categories; the thesis that these are known by reason; the strident insistence on certain deontological principles, such as the evilness of lies regardless of the consequences; their analysis of moral motivation; down to the details (as we have seen) of their conceptualization of desert—all these facets are instrumental to the theologoumenon of divine justice. In all these areas, the theological concern of the Muʿtazilites bounds their thinking in ways that even a temperate philosophical interest should quickly discover.

But now it is important to return to the track from which I began, in which it was suggested that a reading practice (a conversation) that sought to ignore these aims would not "go far" or "work." The particular type of conversation I had in mind was one that sought to address Muʿtazilite moral thought in terms that construe it as a philosophical ethical discourse, where the latter is taken in a minimal (though admittedly still contestable) sense: that its focus is anthropocentric, and its ultimate concern lies with questions about how human beings should act or live. Placing a philosophical construal on the Muʿtazilites' efforts thus involves leaving out of one's ken the theological ends that guide their moral formulations. In what ways could a conversation like that work or fail to work?

One way would be in the opposite sense of the utilitarian or consequentialist tone that such words carry. For the conversation one tries to hold is not a private one, and so to conduct it in a way that does not give a faithful representation of the thinker is problematic to the extent that it conflicts with a responsibility to do so in one's capacity as a student and a scholar, whose task is partly determined by the expectations of others and their understanding of what the conversation is about. Such a conflict will need to be taken into special consideration when the account one is taken to be presenting is a historical one.

Yet what if it proved profitable to do so (to sound the utilitarian note more clearly), and what if the conversation was understood in such terms by all parties involved? Here, the doubt to be voiced is rather whether one could expect to garner a gain of this sort in this case, should one choose to approach Muʿtazilite ethics with the aim of "appropriating" their ideas in order to enrich existing philosophical concerns. As I hope the foregoing discussion will have suggested, so different are the angles of concern, and so great the effort it would command to translate them into our own, that contemporary ethics would hardly seem to stand to profit from the exercise and the result would not requite the effort.

Holding down the utilitarian note, one can say that to accost texts such as these with expectations and questions rolled into shape by current philosophical custom—a custom defined not merely or primarily through its terms as much as its aims—may be to let oneself in for frustration and disappointment when the shape of one's curiosity fails to be met by the reflective categories of the thinkers' discourse. The importation of alien prisms and standards of justification may fail to work simply in the sense that it forecloses the possibility of meaningful engagement with the thinkers one seeks to render conversible.

My principal aims in the foregoing have been to bring into focus the theological character of Muʿtazilite ethics and point toward some of the difficulties that will arise when one seeks to wring out of their talk the theological timbre that grounds it in order to retreat to the tranquillity of a direct (philosophical) conversation. Several of these difficulties, here pursued on a more general level, will become clearer when we turn to a brief examination of the previous scholarship on Muʿtazilite ethics and consider particular examples of attempts to engage with it detached from its theological ends. To this task I now turn.

Approaches to the Study of Muʿtazilite Ethics

The inappropriateness of initiating a philosophical conversation of this sort with our Muʿtazilite authors may have been taken to be a matter of course by many students of their ethics for whom its theological timbre was not a background distraction that could be eliminated but rather the only pitch at which their talk was at all audible. But this has been far from an exceptionless rule. In this section, I will take a look at two opposed types of approaches to Muʿtazilite ethics through a pair works that best exemplify them.

The name inextricably associated with the study of Muʿtazilite ethics is that of George F. Hourani, who pursued his interest through several works—most important, his monograph on ʿAbd al-Jabbār's ethics, *Islamic Rationalism*, which was published only a few years after the edition and publication of the latter's multivolume *al-Mughnī*. This was followed up with several studies elaborating aspects of ʿAbd al-Jabbār's thought and plotting the features of Muʿtazilite ethics more widely against broader characterizations of Islamic moral discourse. His works provide a portal of access and a reference point for all those interested in the subject, and have rendered our understanding of the Muʿtazilites an invaluable service.

Hourani's hope in this monograph is to establish ʿAbd al-Jabbār's philosophical credentials, and the audience he is interested in addressing is clearly the wider philosophical community. To such an audience he directs his thesis that ʿAbd al-Jabbār's and, more broadly, the Muʿtazilites' concerns were such as made them share the same philosophical curriculum as well as grapple with "the same kind of questions with which their Greek predecessors and modern successors have struggled"; and by the latter he has the British intuitionists in mind. In the *Mughnī*, "we have at last an extensive theory of 'modern' ethics from medieval Islam."[30] His aim is to recommend to our attention a work that might change the way the history of moral philosophy is written, and bring into question the common model that has "almost skipped over two thousand years and, to put it crudely, expected to find Hobbes taking up where Epicurus had left off."[31]

In several places throughout the work, Hourani draws our attention to the parallels and similarities between ʿAbd al-Jabbār's moral positions and those of British intuitionists such as G. E. Moore and W. D. Ross. On the one hand, these parallels might be seen as straightforward comparisons between the ideas of the respective thinkers. And certainly Hourani was not unaware of the theological ends motivating the Muʿtazilites' moral speculations, remarking in the introduction that "it may even be said that his [ʿAbd al-Jabbār's] ultimate interest is theodicy, the justification of God."[32] In his subsequent writing, indeed, these theological dimensions receive greater attention. But these ends are consigned to the margins of the work, and their presence is rather too discreet to serve as a counterweight to the explicit analogy between not merely particular moral positions but the aims motivating their development. This analogy between the aims of the modern moral philosophers and those of the Muʿtazilites is expressed in the statement that "in both groups we perceive the same attitude to ethics, a desire above all things to 'preserve the phenomena,' if necessary at the sacrifice of theoretical elegance." "Phenomena" refers, in part, to the "judgements of common morality" with which moral theory must be made to accord. The Muʿtazilite thinker is a "partisan of truth" who is anxious to "present the truth as it is" and "takes care to adhere to the phenomena of ethics."[33] Elsewhere, Hourani couches the point in somewhat more earnest terms and speaks of the "sincerity" of the Muʿtazilites' moral purpose.[34]

Put in these terms, this view would be hard to deny without seeming to presume the right to judge the hearts of men, but thankfully one does not need to do so in order to remark (or repeat) that the Muʿtazilite concern for truth is not to be doubted but rather to be understood as one oriented toward theological truth as against the self-contained ethical one that Hourani is considering. While this is not to deny the Muʿtazilites' need to remain sensitive to the phenomena, the implications of "preserving the phenomena" are rather too strong a description of their attitude toward moral inquiry. And to suggest a kinship of purpose between their ethics and that of Greek or British philosophers misidentifies the type of practice they were each engaged in.

More instructively, it will help to track some of the difficulties with which such a conception of Muʿtazilite practice hamstrings the attempt to give an account of it. A leading example to consider is Hourani's proposed explanation of the principles utilized by ʿAbd al-Jabbār in selecting which attributes of acts are to be made absolute grounds for their moral value and which are only prima facie grounds. A prominent instance of the category of absolute grounds is lying, which unconditionally attracts the moral value "evil."[35] Hourani writes:

> The line of division between attributes of acts that are absolute grounds and those that are only [prima facie] aspects . . . is untidily drawn, if drawn at all, by ʿAbd al-Jabbār. It is not clear, for instance, why lying should be a ground while inflicting pain is only an aspect. He seems to have worked by rule of thumb.

In his subsequent section on lying, he suggests that the emphasis laid by ʿAbd al-Jabbār on the evilness of lies may be a result of his Persian origin and environment, and reflect the deep-seated Zoroastrian repugnance to lies.[36]

But it would here underestimate ʿAbd al-Jabbār's systematicity to present him as taking recourse to a rule of thumb in laying down what constitute, after all, the very foundations of his moral system. As for the Zoroastrian milieu, I will be returning to it from a different direction in a moment. In any case, there is no need to go so far afield in search of an explanation. The mystery—and any worries about untidiness—clears up once we recall the theological end points and, in particular, the position of paramount importance that the Muʿtazilite view of lies occupies in their defense of the principle of justice. The absolute prohibition of lying was a centerpiece in that defense as well as the argument for the epistemological and ontological independence of moral values from revelation. To rehearse the basic argument: if one is to put one's trust in revealed truth, one must be certain that God would not lie under any circumstances, and hence lying must be evil prior to the advent of revealed commands and prohibitions.[37]

The treatment of lying is a case in point; an example of a different sort occurs in the discussion of the grounds of obligation, where Hourani adverts to the competing definitions of obligation proposed by the "*aṣḥāb al-aṣlaḥ*" and their opponents, which (latter) included ʿAbd al-Jabbār. The question of *al-aṣlaḥ*—"the optimal" or "most beneficial"—was a theological question par excellence—one that was debated between Baghdadi and Baṣran Muʿtazilites, and concerned the obligations God could be said to have toward

His creatures. In contrast to the Baghdadis, who claimed that God was obliged to do what is most beneficial for human beings in what pertains both to their worldly welfare and welfare in the afterlife, the Baṣrans limited God's obligations to the latter, and held that God is only obliged to do His utmost in assisting human beings to fulfill the obligations of the Law imposed on them and attain posthumous felicity.

Debating the issue of course involved intricate discussions about the grounds of obligation; but to what extent can these be severed from the theological interests that frame them and discussed directly as rival concepts of obligation? Hourani proceeds to do so, and one of the questions he raises in this connection is whether ʿAbd al-Jabbār's view of obligation is "unduly egoistic," to which he attempts an answer by comparing it with modern utilitarian or intuitionist counterparts. He concludes that his theory "leaves plenty of room for heroism and altruism in the class of gracious acts," if not in that of the obligatory.[38] But what a peculiar question to raise—that of its egoism—to a concept of obligation chiefly understood with reference to God. And who here is to be taken as the implied subject of heroism or altruism? Surely not the reader of the Muʿtazilite treatises, whose principles of action and ideals would rather have been set down by the concrete teachings of Islamic law. Questions such as these impress an anthropocentric focus that naturally leads one to hear statements such as the one ascribed to the Baghdadis—"it is obligatory to bring benefit to others . . . so long as this does not result in harm to the agent"—as those concerned with human morality and its practical application, rather than statements that are part of a theocentric debate about divine obligations, to be placed in the context of an interest in theodicy.[39] This difference in focus—between a theocentric and anthropocentric concern with value—is part of what is captured by remarks such as those of A. K. Reinhart and George Makdisi, both of whom go on record with the view that the inquiries into value of the *mutakallimūn* do not constitute ethics in the proper sense of the word. For Makdisi, the "Rationalists"—those engaging in *kalām*—fall foul of the description of the science of ethics because "ethics is a science that seeks to know which actions should be done and which avoided. It is a practical science; it seeks knowledge not for the sake of knowledge, it seeks it in order to apply it." While in itself this is an excessively narrow definition of ethics, we may here sidestep unrewarding taxonomic arguments about what is or is not (to be called) ethics and still recognize the merit of this view in calling attention to the focus of Muʿtazilite moral thought, whose aim is neither to discover the nature of value "for its own sake" as it were or out of an anthropocentric concern with the practice of value.[40]

The overall tendency is to abstract from the theological contexts that give ʿAbd al-Jabbār's positions their meaning and purpose. And on the one hand, Hourani gave due notice of his intention to exclude from his scope the "divine side" of ethics and confine himself to the level of ethics on "the human side," "as in modern ethics." But it is perhaps his belief that "the dangers of distortion are less than might be expected" that may have to be questioned.[41]

Something more also needs to be said about the transformation of notions of genre and, as a corollary, of authorship through which such a distorted picture of the "continuity of concerns" is brought about. Hourani's elegant, economical, and limpidly distilled presentation of ʿAbd al-Jabbār's ethical thought is problematic precisely in its virtues, in imposing on the latter's thought a discursive order that shields us from the very features of style and genre—above all, the refractory flow of argument and counterargument—that would have challenged claims about intellectual continuity, but that now assimilates ʿAbd al-Jabbār's theory more nearly to a familiar type of philosophical treatise. To an extent, of course, such shielding is inevitable in talking about the Muʿtazilites, short of giving direct translations or descriptions, or composing our own scholarly works in the form of captious stichomythias. But in this use and context, it proves misleading, especially when combined with a notion of authorship that, had the original dialectical genre been kept in view, would have been immediately called into question.

This notion is once again rendered problematic by its virtues: anyone acquainted with the character of ʿAbd al-Jabbār's writing—its stiff and dry style, the indefatigable monotone of argument and counterargument, so typical of the doggedly dialectical spirit with which *kalām* is often synonymous—will be impressed with Hourani's generously personal treatment of ʿAbd al-Jabbār. In several places in the work, he speaks of the latter in terms of his "cool sagacity," "cool patience," or the "tranquillity" with which he meets the challenges of his opponents.[42] On the one hand, this can serve as a corrective to the lack of imagination with which one is prone to encounter dialecticians like ʿAbd al-Jabbār. Yet is it after all an accident that one should do so? To what extent is the dialectician writing his work as an individual of whom such qualities of character can properly be predicated? To consider him in this light of course helps assimilate him even more successfully to the notion of the philosophical thinker Hourani has in mind, in which a notion of individual creativity and independent reflection plays a big role, but here this would disregard the scholastic context in which "ʿAbd al-Jabbār's views" were articulated. This context was in great part constituted by school traditions of problems and solutions, arguments and counterarguments, handed down from one generation to the next, to be criticized, extended, and amended or accepted, and then passed down for the next round. Thus, the dialectical style of writing evokes the institutional framework—"institutions" taken in a loose sense—in which such activities took place, in which it seems more correct to conceive of the activity as (the public, interactive) one of speaking, rather than (the private, isolated) one of thinking or writing.[43] One's capacity to ascribe thoughts or views to the individual *mutakallim* is one that must be qualified by placing it in such a context.

Here it is worth returning for a final remark on the question of the unconditional prohibition of lying, whose discussion by Hourani was referred to above. The difficulty involved in ranging this discussion around a question concerning "'Abd al-Jabbār's reasons" for taking this view of lies is revealed by the explanation it provokes. One of Hourani's suggestions here had been that this view might have arisen through the influences of Zoroastrianism pervasive in the Persian culture that surrounded him (the composition of the *Mughnī*, we will recall, dates to the time of his judgeship in Rayy.) This emphasis on responsiveness to the needs and influences of historical and social environment is consonant with the picture of 'Abd al-Jabbār's authorship that has been cultivated by Hourani. Yet to place such an emphasis is to greatly downplay the importance of school traditions that diminish this responsiveness to the present, and make each member's views the reflection of a more diachronic and participative exercise entailing that the individual lives at least as much in the past concerns and experiences of the school as in those generated by their own present. The unconditional prohibition of lying is a case in point: judging from the time when one of the dominant arguments for it entered into circulation, this position may be estimated to date at least to Abū Hāshim's time more than two generations back.[44]

All of the foregoing could be taken simply as a reminder of the significance of conveying an accurate picture of what the inquiry was about for the thinker under study. As suggested in the previous section, one can have other aims than producing an accurate picture—for example, cultivating a certain philosophical attention in which the value of a thinker's ideas is set by purposes of one's own—but in such cases it is crucial to call attention to the change of use, and the self-description of *Islamic Rationalism* as a "historical exposition of the thought of its subject" leaves much to be desired in the way of signposting.[45]

The importance of making one's intentions explicit is evoked by considering another and much briefer treatment of Mu'tazilite ethical views, which Oliver Leaman wrote in response to a certain claim made by Hourani concerning 'Abd al-Jabbār's view about the evilness of vain or useless actions (*'abath*). This is a category generally taken to encompass acts that involve unnecessary exertion and harm. Mānkdīm's definition runs: "useless is every act which the acting subject does without a proportional recompense." An example of this kind of action, cited by Hourani, involves the person who is hired to pour water from one part of the sea to the other. "No harm is done to anyone, but it is evil as useless."[46] No harm is done, that is, in the sense of unjust harm—the laborer receives his wages.

Leaman's response in many ways acts as a magnifying glass to the problematic features of Hourani's approach. Hourani had remarked on 'Abd al-Jabbār's exposition of the evilness of vain action that it was "not very satisfactory," the examples with which it was illustrated not appearing sufficient to warrant the moral judgment that these actions are evil. Leaman's aim was to question this view and show that "the Muʿtazilite does succeed in providing a firm foundation for his doctrine *and* that in doing so he throws light on a class of actions not much addressed by moral philosophers."[47]

It is the double intent contained in this statement that makes the piece problematic. For on the one hand, Leaman speaks of grasping "*what is behind* ʿAbd al-Jabbār's objections to uselessness" (itself a rather ambiguous way of putting the matter) and *ʿAbd al-Jabbār's* success in providing foundations. While he promisingly begins with an outline of what he calls the "essential doctrines of the Muʿtazilah," his interest does not lie in connecting this particular moral position to the larger Muʿtazilite thought-world. His concern is rather to engage with this moral conception on its own merits and for the value it might have for us rather than to engage in an exercise in understanding the writer's intent, and this is signaled by Leaman's designation of ʿAbd al-Jabbār as a "philosopher," in an embrace of Hourani's invitation.

While Leaman is not unaware of the link between this view and the Muʿtazilite belief that "there is a moral purpose in the whole of creation," his attention to it is only a glancing one, so that neither Hourani nor Leaman discuss the theologoumena underlying the Muʿtazilite inclusion of this type of action in the class of evil acts. But as it is the theological applications and implications of this substantive evaluative principle that account for its presence in Muʿtazilite ethics, of course an examination of features of the actions themselves will fall short of providing an explanation.

What are these applications? As Leaman rightly observes (without, however, adequately stressing), the immediate connection of this view is with the broader Muʿtazilite position on the purposefulness of creation—that is, with their belief that God always acts with a reason or purpose (*ḥikma, gharaḍ*), and that God created humankind to benefit them.[48] In ʿAbd al-Jabbār's words, "All of God's acts must be beneficial . . . otherwise it would be vain."[49] This fundamental conviction acts as a reference point for the Muʿtazilites' articulation of their positions with regard to several questions of a more specific kind, and the belief in the purposiveness of divine action acquires a number of contexts of relevance. One seminal context is set up by the Muʿtazilites' belief that God imposed obligations (*taklīf*) on human beings with the purpose of benefiting them—or giving them the opportunity to be benefited—by attaining reward, and this view of the imposition of obligations supports the Muʿtazilite perspective on freedom of will, for its absence would make *taklīf* vain.[50] In another context, it acts as a pivot for the Muʿtazilites'—and more specifically the Baṣrans'—theological narrative on the place of pain in the economy of creation, and thus for their views on theodicy. There must always be good reason for the infliction of pain and harm, and no pain is justifiable unless it is a necessary condition for attaining a benefit; where there are alternative means of arriving at the same benefit, one of which involves pain while another does not, it is a pointless or vain action to use pain as a means.

One important topic subsumed under this principle is that of compensation, in which the majority Baṣran view was that the fact that a person will be compensated by God for the pain they have suffered is insufficient justification for inflicting pain on them. There must necessarily be a further reason or purpose in the infliction of pain: it must also serve for instruction and therefore act as an assistance (*luṭf*) in fulfilling the Law; otherwise, it would be useless.[51] With this background, it is easier to grasp the logic of one of the examples cited by Leaman from Hourani: "A permits himself to be beaten by B if B rewards A with a benefit greater than that available to him were he not beaten. Although no wrong is then involved, such an act would still be evil, since it is useless."[52] This is the position on compensation transposed from its primary domain of application—divine action—to the domain of human acts and cast in the form of a general principle, whose substance is that the equilibrium or mutual cancellation between benefits and harms is not sufficient to make undergoing the harm good.

Explanations that omit to mention these facets will miss the mark, as long as the mark has been set up as to "grasp what is behind ʿAbd al-Jabbār's objections" (Leaman) and what "ʿAbd al-Jabbār had . . . in mind" (Hourani).[53] And insofar as their respective treatments are presented as explanatory accounts of his thought, then the omission of such facets in favor of explanatory suggestions such as that "our occupation with useless activities may be condemned for crowding out valuable ones" or recommendations for the improvement of the system (ʿAbd al-Jabbār "should have fastened on pain, sorrow, unhappiness as an independent ground") results in a misrepresentation of the moral theory in question and its aims.[54]

This trouble arises because of the attempt both writers make to engage with Muʿtazilite ethics on a level that goes beyond mere textual interpretation, and in which it is possible to issue judgments such as that "this view is not satisfactory" and strive to discover ways in which "*we* can make sense of this concept" (Leaman's phrase). While this harbors the danger of blurring the lines between the perspective of the thinker and their commentator, it might be said that this is an eradicable problem whose solution lies in adapting the self-description appropriate to the commentary. On the other hand, little in this type of writing suggests that modern moral reflection stands to profit from the exercise, and that the Muʿtazilite approach to moral questions can significantly enrich our own angles of engagement.

This approach contrasts with another, more prevalent form taken by commentaries on Muʿtazilite thought, in which the role of the commentator is characterized by a desire to let the theologians speak for themselves. The aim here is to present their views in a way that, while imparting order and cohesiveness to the thought of the writer(s), stresses the importance of truthful and accurate description above all, and effaces the commentator behind the personae one gives voice to. Given the nature of this genre of writing and the high value it sets on faithful presentation, confusion about the aims of the Muʿtazilites is unlikely to arise.

One may take as an example of this approach Margaretha Heemskerk's recently published *Suffering in the Muʿtazilite Theology,* a study of ʿAbd al-Jabbār's (and his disciples') views on pain—its ontology and the moral judgments producing it attracts—and on divine justice. Unlike Hourani, who to a great extent had imposed the order of his exposition *ab extra,* and had addressed himself to questions and problems that were not "given" by the texts themselves (Is ʿAbd al-Jabbār's view of obligation egoistic? Does the distinction made between neutral and plain good acts really work? Is the view on vain actions satisfactory?), Heemskerk's presentation is governed throughout by the questions and problems internal to the texts. While the opening sentence of the book ("Many questions may arise for a person who reflects on the phenomenon of pain") might suggest that it is *our* preoccupation with this phenomenon that is being invoked and that will provide part of the vantage point of interest from which the texts are examined, the perspective turns out to belong entirely to the Muʿtazilite theologians whose views are being presented.[55] The curriculum of topics is determined by the subject matter discussed in the original texts, and the role of the commentator is to raise questions that will elicit the relevant subject matter: "ʿAbd al-Jabbar asserts that . . . but how does he think about . . . ?" followed by an exposition of ʿAbd al-Jabbār's thoughts on the question raised.[56] Something similar holds with regard to what is identified as a "difficulty" and a "problem" for the views under examination, which is determined by reference to the original texts. A difficulty usually consists of an aspect that was considered problematic and debated among the Muʿtazilites themselves, and is thus one internal to their conceptual paradigm.

The text strikes one as being very much an apostrophized narrative by virtue of the frequency of phrases referring to the vantage point of the thinker ("in ʿAbd al-Jabbār's theory," "according to ʿAbd al-Jabbār's doctrine"); even when absent, they are implicit. The verbs that form the joints of the narrative and carry it forward—the verbs of "intellectual action"—all have the Muʿtazilites as their subject: ʿAbd al-Jabbār explains, asserts, discusses, argues, considers. The author herself is effaced behind the persons she brings to life. Her efforts are focused on the task of understanding the intent of the writers she is studying: "What did his master Abū Isḥāq b. ʿAyyāsh *mean* when he denied that pain is a *maʿnā*?" "How does he *think* about the actual perception of pain?"[57]

The project embodied in this work is to render a faithful description of another's conceptual universe. Given the care taken to understand the viewpoint of the thinkers, and the emphatically disinterested effort to convey their perspective and examine the contexts in which this is embedded, the theological ends toward which the latter is oriented are not obscured. Thus, the matter-of-fact observation that "[ʿAbd al-Jabbār's] object is not to set up an ethical system to be applied to human acts but rather to show that all God's acts are good," leaves nothing to be desired in terms of a presentation of the ends of Muʿtazilite moral theory.[58] Indeed, remarkably lucid in this formulation is not just the presence of an explicit statement about the aim of Muʿtazilite ethics but also the negative remark about what this aim is *not*. Such fidelity to the perspective of the thinker is accomplished at the price of an uncritical engagement, as Leaman was the first to remark. His mild reproach to the author concerned the absence of any attempt to assess the arguments of the thinkers and explore their wider implications, with the result that the topic "seems only to exist in a hermetically sealed historical discussion between a number of Muslim theologians."[59]

These two different ways of engaging with Muʿtazilite ethics exemplified by Hourani and Leaman, on the one hand, and Heemskerk, on the other, are situated at opposite ends of a continuum that is populated by a variety of other approaches. Here I will not attempt to discuss these, given both my limits and aim, which was to indicate representative trajectories in the study of Muʿtazilite ethics, and to highlight the way these relate to different perceptions of the finality of their moral discourse.[60]

In light of all the above criticisms and remarks, it seems necessary to say something more concerning the orientation of the present study and the place it occupies on this continuum of possible styles of conversation with the Muʿtazilites. The starting point of this study, already adumbrated in the preface, was in many respects closer to Hourani's spirit than to Heemskerk's. On the one hand, the syllabus had not been explicitly intended or expected to be an invasive one that depended on importing questions alien to the body of the Muʿtazilite syllabus of interests. Clearly the Muʿtazilites exhibited a keen interest in professing an objective ethical reality, and clearly desert was one of the founding stones—if not *the* cornerstone—of this reality (in what ways, I hope the next chapters will help show). And their texts offered at least one bait that gave promise of a captivating textual expedition, in the form of a passage in ʿAbd al-Jabbār's *al-Aṣlaḥ* that tantalizingly spoke of desert (*istiḥqāq*) as one of the ways in which a cause can bring about an effect side by side with natural causality, in the context of a discussion of the nature of harm (*ḍarar*) and grief (*ghamm*). Harm, ʿAbd al-Jabbār writes there, consists of pain and grief that are not followed by benefits that would requite them. He continues:

> This is why acts of disobedience are described as "harm," insofar as they lead to punishment; and if one were to describe in this way [i.e., as harm] one's giving a person to eat delicious but poisoned food, it would be insofar as this leads to perdition. Now what leads to [harm] can do so by way of desert, or because it occasions [harm] by custom [*bi'l-ʿāda*].[61]

ʿĀda is shorthand for *ʿādat Allāh*: the custom in question is God's custom, which represents natural causality.

Such remarks stimulate the imagination to raise a thick rush of questions. Formally, these would be parsed in the mode of Heemskerk's framing question: "What does the thinker mean when he says . . . ?" What kind of causal powers attach to this principle and how far do the Baṣran Muʿtazilites take its explanation? In what detail do they work out the contrast between the two types of causality? Concerning the ways in which the spirit of these questions was a more demanding one than their formal framing might suggest—redolent of expectations closer to those of a philosophical dialogue—I have already given an indication in the preface. More to the point here is to ask how the product of this exercise could receive justification in light of the remarks I have made in both sections of this chapter. For it was suggested above that approaches formed by such expectations will be frustrating, fruitless, or simply unacceptable as attempts at a faithful representation of the thinker's intellectual universe. How, then, could the present exercise be spared such afflictions?

Certainly they can be frustrating, and certainly unacceptable as attempts at representation—if at least they are implicitly understood as such (and if one can allow oneself to take the notion of "faithful representation" as one that we can intuitively grasp). On the other hand, reading one text or intellectual vantage point in light of another can produce representations that may be explicitly signposted as ones generated through a process of textual or intellectual neighboring, and these very frustrations can be a way of discovering things that would not have been visible from any other perspective except one that expected to find something different. The mesh of theological and—as I will be stressing in the next chapter—legal variables that determine the shape of thinking in this area would not have emerged as sharply had it not been for such expectations. The juxtaposition of different approaches can be a critical source of mutual illumination. Thus, the account of Muʿtazilite conceptions of desert to be presented here can in part be understood as a comparative one, anchored in expectations that are in turn moored in a broader philosophical concern.

One of the results of this approach is that the features evoked are as often negative as they are positive, emphasizing how the Muʿtazilites *don't* think, rather than how they do. It is through this context that the discussion of moral qualities—or rather, of their absence—for example, comes to take its place. This approach may strike some readers as an exercise in counterfactuals that is not only tiresome but also, and more important, incomplete. An explanation of this type might have been redeemed by its completeness, but to provide a complete account of why something was considered in one way rather than another, far more of the intellectual context and antecedents of the Muʿtazilites would have had to be brought into view. Granted this relative shortness of sight, my hope is that it is compensated by other benefits arising from closer analytic attention to the conceptual structure of the texts, and that, as the well-known Arabic adage instructs, "a thing is known by its contrary" (*al-ashyāʾ tatabayyanu bi-aḍdādihā*), so that knowing what a thing is *not* is integral to knowing what it *is* (a belief from which, after all, the study of *kalām* in terms of school divergences derives its value).

The final criticism I want to anticipate is closely connected to the above. Some of the conclusions reached in this study may seem problematic not because they are negations as such but rather because they are jejune ones: the conclusions may seem expected and unsurprising by those whose expectations would have been more congruent with the Muʿtazilites' context and antecedents. Whatever made one expect in the first place that one would find a solid concept of the person or moral character in the metaphysics of these atomists who were—as their very metaphysics betrays—as impressed by a sense of God's omnipotence as any other *mutakallim*, despite what their libertarian impulses might suggest? Yet the mere predictive certainty that something will happen in a particular way doesn't make it dispensable to explore how and why that happens, and to gain a clearer view of the operative mechanisms, no more than the certainty that the sun will be coming up in the east tomorrow makes it dispensable to find out why and how that is the case. And if an eccentric visitor from another planet whose suns sometimes combust overnight was to investigate the matter—unacquainted with the labors of us earthlings—with the eccentric expectation that the sun would fail to do so, that would not diminish the interest of their results, if turning out a prodigy, the visitor should discover several new laws—however local—involved in determining that it should inevitably rise, and describe the operating mechanisms in a way that deepens our existing understanding.

The Baṣran Muʿtazilites no doubt would have been highly gratified by such complimentary comparisons with the solar system, which evoke flattering allusions to the lawlike consistency to which they aspired in their dialectical system. At the same time, there is another feature of their scheme that would find itself accommodated by the terms of this comparison, if only the term "law" was read in a somewhat different sense. And this consists of the special relations in which theology and the traditional Islamic science of law—both in its methods and conceptual resources—were brought within their moral thought. It will be the task of the next chapter to address the various presences of Islamic law in Baṣran sources, and the questions they raise for us.

CHAPTER 3

Theology as Law

Moral Values between Rational Knowledge and Revealed Law

The presence of legal material in the writings of the Baṣran Muʿtazilites and the heavy seasoning that it gives to their conceptual system offers a riddle to which any student of their theology would have had to apply himself, but this is even more so with the type of student and the type of task we are concerned with here. For while the theological ends that govern their moral formulations are a critical factor to include in any account of the latter, they would not be the only ground of perplexity to be met by one seeking to engage the Muʿtazilites in a philosophical conversation. An additional cipher arresting the fluency of such a conversation would have been presented by the use of legal resources as a staple currency within their ethics. This is a use that provides fresh markers of the historical particularities contextualizing and conditioning the texts, from which it would be hard to disengage them and that furnish the bounds of the rationality peculiar to them. At the same time, this very use may serve to call into question one of the ways in which the aims of Muʿtazilite ethics were parsed in the previous chapter—namely, that it is unconcerned with the practical application of moral principles by human agents—when adumbrating the difficulties that this type of conversation would stumble against.

This legal currency can be traced on many levels within the Baṣran Muʿtazilites' moral perspective. The most fundamental level concerns their moral terminology, where terms such as *ḥukm* (ruling, judgment, status, and thus quality) to refer to the moral qualities of acts, or *ʿilla* (necessitating cause) to refer to the grounds of their qualities, reverberate with the connotations these terms have in the domain of law, and more particularly—or self-consciously—that of the theory of law (*uṣūl al-fiqh*). A further level concerns the substantive acts chosen as the bearers of value, where act-descriptions such as returning a deposit (*radd al-wadīʿa*) or paying back a debt (*qaḍā' al-dayn*)—grounds of obligation, both—give strong pointers to the contents of substantive Islamic law (*fiqh*).

These ports of entry of Islamic law into Muʿtazilite *kalām* are already deep enough in the territory of the latter to merit comment. But even deeper, and rendering even more necessary an attempt to focus on the relations between law and theology, is the role that legal resources play within the fabric of the conceptual structures with which this study is primarily concerned—that is, the Baṣran Muʿtazilite understanding of desert (*istiḥqāq*). Given the function of the concept of desert as a cornerstone of the Muʿtazilite moral system, there could be no deeper infiltration than this one, and it is a precondition for understanding this system that one should devote some attention to the relations it bears to law.

In this chapter, I will try to bring into view the presence of Islamic law in Baṣran Muʿtazilite *kalām* along with the questions this generates by focusing on a particular aspect of the *kalām* syllabus that piques one's interest by the heavily legal cadence that sets its pace and style, and that is the treatment of repentance (*tawba*)—with particular focus on ʿAbd al-Jabbār's *Mughnī* (volume 14). Listened to carefully, this cadence may be traced to the larger horizon of the Baṣrans' view of the relation between reason and revelation, and especially the relation between the normative truths known through the former and those known exclusively by the latter. This larger horizon, which determines the approach taken by the Baṣrans in legal theory, seems to underlie the assimilation of legal material in the discussion of repentance. As I hope to show, it is an assimilation with crucial consequences for the conceptual tissue of their ethics—including, specifically, their thinking concerning desert.

The broader interest of this volume of ʿAbd al-Jabbār's *Mughnī* lies in its status as a testimonial to the multiple internal divisions with which the Muʿtazilite movement was riven. Each of the three books that comprise it recounts a different aspect of this story of fragmentation. The first book—titled *al-Aṣlaḥ* ("The Optimal" or "The Most Beneficial")—tells the story of a dispute polarizing the Baghdadi and Baṣran factions, already alluded to above. The dispute concerned the limits of God's obligations toward His creatures, and whether these were exhausted in the obligation to maximize religious or otherworldly welfare (as the Baṣrans claimed), or whether it included an obligation to maximize worldly welfare (as the Baghdadis insisted). The second volume—titled *Istiḥqāq al-dhamm* ("Desert of Blame"), about which something has already been said in chapter 1—registers a dispute internal to the Jubbā'ite school, in which Abū ʿAlī (joined by the Baghdadi Abu'l-Qāsim al-Balkhī) was pitted against Abū Hāshim in a controversy over the proper relatum or object (*mutaʿallaq*) of blame in the case where one failed to do the obligatory, and whether this was the not-doing (Abū Hāshim) or the act-done-instead (Abū ʿAlī).

But it is the third book—the book of *Tawba* ("Repentance")—that commands the greatest interest at this point and confronts us with the most ticklish puzzles. Here again, the discussion holding the field is one that received its motivating fillip from an internal dispute, often mentioned by later chroniclers of the Muʿtazilite school along with the dispute over the relatum of blame as one of the major points of conflict between Abū ʿAlī and Abū Hāshim and their respective (and often impassioned) partisans.[1] The principal node of the dispute concerned the conditions for the validity of repentance, and represented a tension between two different tendencies—a particularist and a universalist one. Abū Hāshim's distinctively universalist claim was that repentance from a single evil act could only be valid if accompanied by repentance from all other evil acts, and invalid if one persisted in any other form of evil-doing, however light or grave it might seem. One could not isolate or compartmentalize evil acts in the way suggested by Abū ʿAlī's partisans, who upheld the validity of repentance over a single evil act even while the agent persisted in another. One cannot be said to have truly repented of shortchanging a given customer without repenting of shortchanging any single one of one's other customers; one cannot repent of shortchanging someone without repenting of beating them up without just cause; these harms are all species of the genus of wrongful treatment. Or to avail ourselves of one of ʿAbd al-Jabbār's grislier examples: one cannot display contrition to a person for killing one of his sons "while persisting in killing another son . . . or wounding a third, or while usurping his possessions or violating his women . . . and it makes no difference whether [the evil] is small or great."[2]

Abū Hāshim's universalism was tied to a definite view of what constituted repentance. Repentance is defined as a conjunction of regret (*nadm*) and resolution (*ʿazm*)—the first a backward-looking regret over the evil act committed or the obligatory act omitted, and the latter a forward-looking resolve not to repeat it. His claim was that the "relatum" or object to which one's internal attitude must be directed is the *description of the act as evil.* For there are many aspects of the act to which one's regret may be directed:

> One may regret [an act] because it constitutes harm, one may regret it because of inadequate benefit gained from it, or because of the blame it draws, or because of its reprehensible outcome, or because it is evil, or because it constitutes disobedience of a given person, or because it constitutes obedience of a given person, among other things.

The regret that is specific to repentance "must attach to an evil act because of its evilness," and this means that true repentance must embrace all evil acts that the person has committed.[3]

Unlike many other Muʿtazilite views, the aspect of Abū Hāshim's position that concerned the description of the act that ought to form the object of one's motivation did not prove an insular one within the Islamic milieu. And later Muslim theologians and jurists who share it cast an interesting and suggestive light on it in remarking that from the perspective of a legal classification of acts, repentance constitutes an act of worship (*ʿibāda*)—that is to say, an act specifically directed toward God as His due. The defining feature of such acts is the intention (*niyya*) with which they are undertaken, which consecrates them to God and would be defeated if any worldly considerations were present as part of one's motive. Yet at the same time, many of the same writers—especially those of an Ash'arite persuasion—refused to join Abū Hāshim in the claim concerning the nonfragmentable scope of repentance that he derived as an ineluctable implication of this view of the penitent's motivation, and maintained that repentance from one act is valid even while one is persisting in another, though *not*—it was conceded—one that belongs to the same type. (And all of these writers interpreted the scope of consequentialist motives that would invalidate one's *niyya* as one confined to this world: for one of the chief motives to repent, after all, was the fear of otherworldly consequences should one fail to do so.)[4]

It is in this book of the *Mughnī*—in which ʿAbd al-Jabbār takes up the cudgel for Abū Hāshim's side of the disputed question—that there appears a series of sections designed to make one stop short and wonder quite where, within the map of the Islamic sciences, one had found oneself in, and whether one had strayed into the wrong neighborhood. The source of one's bafflement is the pronounced and concerted legal character of these sections. While Josef van Ess did not have this aspect of Muʿtazilite theology in mind when he described it as "juridical in its outlook rather than metaphysical," nowhere else would the description be felt to be more apt.[5] What is a discussion of the nature of ownership and property (*milk*) and the causes that may engender it doing in a treatise on repentance? What, similarly, the exposition of rulings consequent on delicts (*jināyāt*), such as retaliation (*qiṣāṣ, qawad*) or blood money (*diya*) for homicide? How are we to understand the detailed account ʿAbd al-Jabbār delivers of the rulings consequent on the usurpation (*ghaṣb*) of objects—what is required in case the object was destroyed; in case the rightful owner is dead, in a distant country, or cannot be found; in case the usurper has no means of restitution; and so on? And how are we to make sense of the frequent references to the jurists (*fuqahā'*) and their disputes?

The ostensible link can be spelled out succinctly. It was an integral part of the exacting view of repentance taken by Abū Hāshim's partisans that just as one was obliged to bring all evil acts committed into the scope of regret *in foro interno*, one was under the obligation to right things *in foro externo* in an equally comprehensive way. The blame one deserves on account of one's past acts will not be annulled merely by the internal response; one must also strive to efface the marks that these acts have left on the external world. One's aim, in Mānkdīm's suggestive words, is "to make one's status such that it were as if one had not done the evil one in fact did," or in ʿAbd al-Jabbār's, to make one's act "as though it had never been" (*ka-annahā lam takun*), within the bounds set by the counterfactual impossibility of "not having done what one did" (*lā yumkinuhu allā yafʿala mā qad faʿalahu*). Such a task cannot be accomplished without reversing the consequences of one's acts to the degree possible.[6] Talk of the "external world" should not mislead, however: what is in question is the restoration of the *normative* order of the world, and in particular, the order dictated by the crucial normative currency of *ḥuqūq* (sing. *ḥaqq*).

Detailed remarks about the normative currency in question will have to wait until a later point in this chapter, but here I will briefly introduce the term *ḥaqq* by a simple translation as "right" or "claim." The same term can express an obligation as well as a right/claim, depending on the prepositional structure it is embedded in—*ḥaqq ʿalayhi* versus *ḥaqq lahu*—so that to say of a person that there is a *ḥaqq lahu* is to say that one has a right or claim over someone or something, whereas to say that there is a *ḥaqq ʿalayhi* is to say that one is under a claim or obligation toward someone else. The definition given by the Muʿtazilites' own, al-Sharīf al-Murtaḍā (d. 1044), bespeaks this duality: "*ḥaqq*" denotes "every exclusive assignment to a person as a result of which something *for* or *from* the person who possesses it becomes good."[7]

The obligation to set things right in the world derives from the way in which one's acts have disrupted the rights and claims of other human beings. This obligation therefore only attaches to the class of "transitive" acts (*mutaʿaddiya,* which affect others). Thus, homicide represents a violation of a person's right over their body; usurpation, the refusal to return a deposit, or the refusal to repay a debt represent a violation of a person's rights over their property. These violations will respectively engender a *ḥaqq ʿala'l-nafs*—a claim over the wrongdoer's person and more particularly their body—and a *ḥaqq fi'l-māl*—a claim over the wrongdoer's property.[8] A third broad category of rights and claims concerns a person's honor (*ʿirḍ*), though this is one that receives less attention in the sections I am considering. Together these categories represent the type of right or claim termed *ḥaqq ādamī* or *ḥaqq li'l-ʿibād* in Islamic law, and it is crucial to note here—what will receive greater stress at a later point—that it is this division that ʿAbd al-Jabbār faithfully follows.[9]

The stiffly legal sections that one finds in the book of *Tawba* might then be interpreted simply as a natural expression of the universalist scope of Abū Hāshim's definition of repentance. In repenting of any act, one must repent of all evil acts, and in doing the latter one must in turn reverse the consequences of all evil acts. Hence the expansiveness of these long sections: its aim is to provide detail to the reversal or restitution that must accompany a person's repentance. The need for an exposition of the conditions of ownership, for example, is summarily explained by the following laconic remark given by ʿAbd al-Jabbār:

> The penitent is obliged to examine what is in his possession. If it is legitimate for him to maintain it and dispose over it, then his repentance is valid. But if any of it must be removed or be given in reparation, then he is obliged to do so. This is why we mention it [i.e., the nature of ownership] in this section as part of the discussion of repentance, due to the strong connection it bears to the topic.[10]

This, then, is the explanation with which ʿAbd al-Jabbār himself would satisfy our curiosity.

Yet from our own perspective, how much would it really explain? Above all, how well could it help us understand the target of ʿAbd al-Jabbār's addresses? Were we to submit to the suggestiveness of this brief self-description, it might seem that the envisaged reader was the prospective penitent, interested to know what their obligations consist in: What should one give back? What could one keep? If that is the case, should we be compelled to revise our initial idea of Muʿtazilite ethics as fundamentally theological in orientation, indifferent to an anthropocentric concern with the practical application of morality?

The questions raised by the legal timbre of these writings multiply once one casts one's glance toward related writings in the field of Islamic law. For a brief comparison between the discussion of repentance undertaken by our Muʿtazilite theologian and that of the same question encountered in legal writings reveals a captivating degree of correspondence. The correspondence goes beyond the basic ingredients included in the definition of repentance by most writers—whatever their theological faction or particular discipline—in terms of regret, resolution, and desistance from the act. It encompasses the fundamental idea, repeatedly rehearsed in legal works, that where the person has aggressed against the right/claim of a human being (*ḥaqq ādamī*), repentance must involve a reparation of violated rights (*radd al-maẓālim* or *radd al-ḥuqūq*)—rights that are understood in terms of the threefold scheme of goods: body, property, and honor.[11]

Further, within that basic frame, one can recognize a host of details appearing in ʿAbd al-Jabbār's exposition, especially when one turns to writings stemming from the Shāfiʿite school of law to which the author belonged. Take ʿAbd al-Jabbār's views concerning one's obligation to surrender oneself to rightful punishment if one has committed a crime of physical aggression, including crimes of homicide, where the owner of the right (*ṣāḥib al-ḥaqq*) may choose to forgive or exact punishment, whether retaliation or blood money. Take the contrast he draws between the obligation to surrender in this case and the absence of a similar obligation where it is a matter of what is termed "God's right or claim" (*ḥaqq Allāh*—to be discussed below), where the punishment of *ḥadd* is applicable, as in the case of adultery or theft.[12] Or finally, take his discussion of the obligations attaching to the return of wrongfully held property where the owner is dead or cannot be found. All these seem to be nothing more than studious rehearsals of the contents of substantive law (*fiqh*). And as for the latter—to add to the thread of questioning initiated above—we do not need to settle the precise understanding that Muslim jurists had of the status of the principles they articulated as *ideals* in order to say that these ideals were ones that they intended to see *practiced*. Hence the description, by modern scholars, of the late Shāfiʿite Ibn Ḥajar al-Haytamī's (d. 1567) *al-Zawājir ʿan iqtirāf al-kabāʾir*—in which one finds a discussion of repentance rich in reminiscences of ʿAbd al-Jabbār's—as a work on "the practical morality of Islam."[13]

Such, then, being the correspondence between the two domains—that of *kalām* and *fiqh*—under what description, with what end in view, has this transmigration of material been carried out by this theologian and those, such as his disciple Mānkdīm, who follow in his footsteps, even if less expansively?[14] Is there a particular relation between the two domains that we can understand this use to be arguing?

One response that might be made to these questions would be to query the assumptions that underlie them, and especially the expectation they reflect that Muslim thinkers in ʿAbd al-Jabbār's time and milieu would have considered the subjects and disciplines of law and theology to be bound by firm lines of demarcation. These lines are known to have been crossed with special regularity in the theory of law (*uṣūl al-fiqh*). Further, the difficulty of separating the two subjects reflects the difficulty of separating the two roles as jurist and theologian, which the same person would often fulfill. ʿAbd al-Jabbār is the best-known but not the only example: his teacher Abū ʿAbd Allāh al-Baṣrī (d. 979) before him and his disciple Abu'l-Ḥusayn al-Baṣrī (d. 1044) after him—Ḥanafite and Muʿtazilite both, the latter the author of two important works on *uṣūl al-fiqh* (*al-Muʿtamad fī uṣūl al-fiqh*, and a commentary on ʿAbd al-Jabbār's *ʿUmad*)—similarly exemplify the cross-disciplinary interests of Muʿtazilite theologians. ʿAbd al-Jabbār's principal distinction in this connection was the rite of law—Shāfiʿite—that he followed, for it was to the Ḥanafite school that most Muʿtazilites tended to belong, as was the case with ʿAbd al-Jabbār's disciple Abu'l-Ḥusayn as well as his teacher Abū ʿAbd Allāh, who was one of many Muʿtazilites to be associated with the well-known Ḥanafite scholar Abu'l-Ḥasan al-Karkhī (d. 951).[15]

And while these Muʿtazilites might have been responsible for forging a stronger connection between the domains of theology and law, it is clear that earlier members of the school had shown a keen interest in legal questions and especially legal methodology. Indeed, the works produced by these later Baṣrans serve as a museum of early Muʿtazilite voices on questions of *uṣūl al-fiqh* such as the status of consensus (*ijmāʿ*), independent reasoning (*ijtihād*), or analogy (*qiyās*).[16] Other preoccupations proper to the subject of *uṣūl*—such as the concern with the methods of interpretation of revealed evidence—betray even more clearly the untenability of a firm separation between the two domains, legal and theological. Finally, as concerns *substantive* law, leafing through the biographical and bibliographic dictionaries we will discover numerous references to early Muʿtazilites with an interest in *fiqh* expressed in their qualification by the compiler as *faqīh* (jurist, knowledgeable in the law) or their composition of specific works on the subject. Given ʿAbd al-Jabbār's strong juridical profile, should it give us ground to wonder that material deriving from his knowledge of substantive law should be grafted to a work on *kalām* where the identity of the subject matter—the question of repentance—makes cross-pollination particularly inviting?

The above reflections would provide a sound corrective to the temptation to create artificial divisions between the two subjects, yet at the same time, a theory of inadvertent cross-pollination seems too unreasoned to function as anything but a final explanatory resort. This is especially so, as lines of demarcation between the two subjects do exist, and reflect no less than the distinction between two bodies—and two means—of knowledge: the knowledge attained by unaided reason, and that made available by revelation. The crucial feature about the discourses that the *Mughnī* comprises, as a work of *kalām,* is that they are understood to represent the fruit of reflection peculiar to the domain of reason. The demarcation of this domain is clearly indicated within ʿAbd al-Jabbār's work, in his declaration that the scope of his discussion concerns that of rationally known obligations (*takālīf ʿaqliyya*), a declaration born out of his practice of drawing the limit to a discussion when judging that a particular precept falls outside the range of what is rationally known.[17] A second indication of this demarcation consists of frequent references, in discussing the various obligations, to the source by which a certain principle is known, whether by reason (*ʿaql*), revelation, or the revealed Law (*samʿ, sharʿ*)—and the latter would here include the substantive rulings of *fiqh.* The contrast is one we may handle in terms of a contrast between moral and legal norms, as long we do not charge the former term with anything more than an indication of the source of normative knowledge. So what is the latter doing in a work such as this?

In trying to answer this question, the presence of seams between these two bodies of knowledge within the text cannot but seem a strongly suggestive one. These seams are marked out explicitly by ʿAbd al-Jabbār through numerous references within his text that relate and distinguish what is known by reason and what is known by revelation. Here reason conforms to the law, here the law came to promulgate something more; here the obligation is rational, and there the obligation revealed. The suggestion such seams would appear to urge most particularly is that the inclusion of legal—that is to say, revelation-based—material in the horizon of the work is intended in some fashion to promote a specific account of the relation between the two domains. It is by scrutinizing these seams that we are clearly in the best position to assess this suggestion.

But before turning to this task, one point that was passed over without comment in the foregoing remarks has to be explicitly discussed, and this concerns the Baṣran Muʿtazilite use of the language of *ḥuqūq* (rights, claims). For it could rightly be remarked that in the previous chapter, where the Muʿtazilites' catalogs of substantive values were discussed, hardly a vestige of this language had been encountered. Indeed, what I had stressed there about the Muʿtazilites' substantive acts was their theocentric nature; by contrast, these rights and claims possess a clear focus on human action. Without explaining this contrast, it would be hard to see how an ambiguity between domains—between the rational and the revelational, or if we wish, between the moral and the legal—could arise in the first place. In the catalogs of substantive acts examined in the previous chapter, the legal presence was seemingly exhausted by the two common act-descriptions of returning deposits and paying back debts.

The sense of a contrast or discrepancy here is not out of place, and it has to do with the existence of two different ways of structuring the account of substantive values, the relation between which does not seem to be explicitly remarked and explained by our theologians. The first account, instanced in ʿAbd al-Jabbār's *al-Taʿdīl wa'l-tajwīr* (but also elsewhere—for example in *al-Aṣlaḥ*), is the one we are already familiar with. Here, act-descriptions are tabulated under the headings "obligatory," "evil," "good," and "supererogatory." Act-descriptions such as returning deposits and repaying debts appear under the heading of obligatory acts.[18] Yet this account of the values coexists with another, which is produced in connection with *obligations* in particular, and in which the relation between different grounds of obligation is brought out by structuring them in terms of the fundamental currency provided precisely by the language of *ḥuqūq* introduced above. The two isolated acts of returning a deposit and repaying a debt are here subsumed into a wide-ranging and systematic normative framework.

This second account is produced in *al-Aṣlaḥ* in a context that, like the one we are considering, is redolent of a heavily legal spirit. Here, ʿAbd al-Jabbār divides obligations into the self-regarding and the other-regarding; the latter is said to be determined in terms of the rights or claims of others (by what is *ḥaqq li-ghayrihi*). Within the latter category, a further subdivision follows: "What constitutes another's right/claim divides into two kinds: one is God's claim, which He deserves on account of His bounties—such as His claim to thanksgiving and worship—and the other is the claim of human beings, which must be set up by antecedent grounds." And these will vary according as the antecedent grounds (*asbāb mutaqaddima*) that set up a *ḥaqq* vary. For example, the obligation to return a deposit is set up by the prior "ground" of another person's entrusting it to one's care, and "the return of the deposit is a right (*ḥaqq*) of the depositor if he has previously deposited it."[19] Similarly with the obligation to both repay a debt and thank the benefactor, which is now described as a right of the one to whom it is due.[20] Thus, values included in the first catalog are spelled out in terms of *ḥuqūq* in the second. Crucially, just as the act-descriptions comprising the first catalog are made the objects of necessary or self-evident knowledge (*ʿilm ḍarūrī*), so ʿAbd al-Jabbār speaks of a necessary knowledge of *ḥuqūq*, and in volume 17 of the *Mughnī* on matters of the law (*Sharʿiyyāt*) refers to "*ḥuqūq ʿaqliyya*" (where the term *ʿaqlī* means not "rational" but "rationally known").[21]

While it was said above that the language of *ḥuqūq* appears to be an anthropocentric one, this cannot be asserted without qualification. For rights and claims are distinguished into two broad categories, one of which—already mentioned—is private or "human," while the other belongs to God (*ḥaqq Allāh*). The difference between the two broad categories relates to the possibility of their being repealed: God's rights or claims cannot be repealed or annulled by human beings, whereas one may waive one's own rights.[22] Examples of the latter are the penalties (*ḥudūd*) that must be administered for drinking wine, unlawful intercourse, the accusation of chaste women of unlawful intercourse, brigandage, and theft, which cannot be dropped at the will of human beings, for this punishment is classed as a divine claim and must be exacted—even if, in practice, it infrequently was, because of the numerous conditions that had to be satisfied in full before this could be done. By contrast, with ordinary homicides, the claims they generate are categorized as private, and thus a person can choose to waive their claim to the various types of compensation to which they are entitled on account of the murder of a relative. Yet in contrasting the scheme of values discussed in the previous chapter with this one, it would be clearly right to describe the orientation of the latter as an anthropocentric one, even though, as we will see in a later point in this chapter and the next, there are certain key values that act as joints between the two schemes and unite them under a theocentric concern with divine justice.[23]

I have said enough now to be able to return to my main trajectory, in which I had been pursuing the puzzle carried by the curious juxtaposition of the theological—the domain of rational moral truths—and the legal—the domain of truths known by means of revelation. It is this tissue of *ḥuqūq* that lends ʿAbd al-Jabbār's theological exposition a legal timbre that renders the boundary between the two a mysterious one. We have already seen how these *ḥuqūq* are made the objects of rational moral knowledge and thus accorded the status of rational moral truths. Yet decked out in this language, our moral reason has come to sound singularly similar to the special dialect that marks the subject of Islamic law, in which *ḥuqūq* form the conceptual stock-in-trade. The centrality of the language of *ḥuqūq* in the latter would have been betokened by the single fact that it gives the terms in which the founding concept of legal responsibility or competence (*dhimma*) is parsed: *dhimma* denotes the capacity to be the subject of relations of *ḥuqūq*—of acquiring claims over others and being the subject of claims in turn, of having rights and obligations.[24] But one may read it off any discussion unfolding in the various branches of substantive law with equal facility; for whether dealing with family law, contracts and commutative transactions, or penal law, *ḥuqūq* are the currency of the discourse: one will speak of the right of a wife to receive maintenance (*nafaqa*), the right of someone to have their deposit returned to them, or the right of the next of kin (*walī al-dam*) in cases of homicide to retaliate or receive blood money.

It is to the seams between rational and revealed normative truths that ʿAbd al-Jabbār traces out for us that I then turn in order to interpret this assimilation of the special dialect of law into the universality of moral language. At first sight these seams generate fresh bafflement, with the mysterious display of legerdemain by which they seem to be drawn. There is a breeziness in the ease with which ʿAbd al-Jabbār appears to sift through his bag of propositions and identifies the body of knowledge to which each belongs. In connection with the obligation to return a usurped object, we hear that reason does not tell us the specific kind (*jins makhṣūṣ*) of objects that must be given, whereas revelation does. In connection with a usurped object that is destroyed and must be replaced with its equivalent, reason enjoins us to replace it as soon as one possesses a relevant equivalent, without regard for one's circumstances—even if one is in need of the object, one is under the obligation to hand it over because the other's right has priority over one's own need; revelation, by contrast, makes allowance for dire need. In connection with objects that chance throws one's way—such as a garment blown by the wind into one's house—reason does not demand that one declare or acknowledge the discovery, whereas revelation does.[25] Whence this confident separation of the truths of revelation and those of reason? By what feat of self-examination are these Muʿtazilite believers, thoroughly imbued with revealed norms, interrogating their individual consciences and succeeding in this task of peeling away the topmost layers of the palimpsest to discover engraved the original moral script (the *takālīf ʿaqliyya*) that God had implanted there?

Help in answering the above questions could be expected from two areas of the Muʿtazilite corpus: one is the Muʿtazilites' discussion of prophethood (*nubuwwa*), which is located precisely at the crossroads between the domain of rational and that of revealed truths, and concerned with the passage from one to the other. The other is their discussion of the theory of law (*uṣūl al-fiqh*).

I need to begin with the former by rehearsing the basic perspective articulated by the Baṣrans on the question of revelation. While the subject of prophecy—the proofs that supported it and the reasons that necessitated it—was a lodestone of religious reflection for Muslims of all theological stripes, what made the Muʿtazilite relationship to the topic a distinctive one was their claim about the rational apprehensibility (and hence objectivity) of moral values. This claim gave rise to a difficulty that their account of prophethood was obliged to negotiate: for if the Muʿtazilites averred that the Law (the *Taklīf*) was already given in reason, which yielded immediate knowledge of the values of acts, and concomitantly that the performance or nonperformance of these acts resulted in deserts—whether for reward or punishment—by which one fulfilled or failed to fulfill the purpose of the Lawgiver in promoting it—namely, in the Baṣran Muʿtazilite view, to give one the opportunity for reward—then what could possibly be the function of revealed prescriptions and prohibitions? Either revelation could tell us the same things we know by reason—in which case it would redundant—or it would ineluctably conflict with it.[26]

The Baṣran answer to this question made the concept of *luṭf*—"assistance"—its centerpiece. In itself a concept neutral between agents, the Muʿtazilite usage of *luṭf* promoted its application predominantly to acts of God, where it signified the acts by which God provided human beings with the assistance necessary for them to fulfill the obligations imposed on them.[27] Crucially, the obligations here are understood as rational ones: the word used is *ʿaqliyyāt,* or again *wājibāt wa-qabāʾiḥ ʿaqliyya.* Revelation then was considered to be good (and indeed obligatory on God to provide) by way of conferring assistance to and serving the welfare (*maṣlaḥa*) of human beings in their fulfillment of the rationally known truths. "It is as if one had been told, 'Follow this law [*sharīʿa*], so as to fulfill what is known by the intellect.' "[28] What is crucial is that it is these rationally known moral acts that generate the consequences of reward and punishment—consequences that give the meaning of the *maṣlaḥa* in question ("*al-thawāb . . . huwa nihāyat maṣāliḥihi*")—by way of desert. Rationally known normative truths (*ʿaqliyyāt*) are such that "their performance makes one deserve reward and preserves one from punishment because of the qualities [*awṣāf*] they possess, and it is . . . because of these attributes that desert is realized."[29] By contrast to the intrinsic value of *ʿaqliyyāt*, the value of revealed injunctions is an instrumental one. They are obligatory insofar as they are the means for one's performing acts that are intrinsically obligatory, and eschewing acts intrinsically evil, and thus do not themselves constitute independent grounds for reward and punishment. One of the verses of the Qur'ān cited most often in this regard is 29:45: "prayer restrains from shameful and unjust deeds" (*inna al-ṣalāt tanhākum ʿan al-faḥshāʾ waʾl-munkar*), which is seen as a clear indication of this instrumental logic for the prescription of prayer.[30]

In talking about an instrumental role, the facts that the Baṣrans had in mind were ones belonging to the order of empirical psychology: *luṭf* encompasses those circumstances that will (in fact, empirically) strengthen my motives to choose what is good and make it (empirically) more probable that I will avoid what is evil. It is for this very reason that according to the followers of Abū Hāshim—who insisted, against Abū ʿAlī, that revelation had to convey information that reason could not come by—the maxims of revelation could *only* be given from above and could not be attained by single-handed reason.[31] For God alone, *ʿallām al-ghuyūb,* was capable of such psychological prediction. The insight needed here was "akin to a knowledge of the unseen [*al-ʿilm biʾl-ghayb*], of what acts will or will not issue from the subject of the Law, and what will strengthen his motives or fail to strengthen them."[32] And these are things that hardly came into the range of human intellectual capacities.

The same idea was inextricably bound up with a second essential aspect of the Baṣran account of revelation: the particularism and relativity of revealed norms. For what strengthens one's motives at one time may not do so at another, or what does for one person may not do so for another. The norms of revelation possess a fine-tuned sensitivity to circumstances that enables them to be responsive to the plethora of conditions that affect a person's capacity to fulfill the rational Law. Hence the revealed norms are sensitive to particular times, places, conditions, and the circumstances (states, situations: *aḥwāl*) of the subjects of the Law (*al-mukallafīn*). ʿAbd al-Jabbār encapsulates the point in the following statement:

> The special character of revealed laws [*sharāʾiʿ*] is founded on variations in the situations of the subjects of the Law, and variations in time, place, and the conditions of acts. For it is possible that what is obligatory for Zayd is evil for ʿAmr; what is permitted to one, forbidden to the other; and what is obligatory may be obligatory on a particular condition, and evil on another. So how could it be proved through reason [alone] that prayer without purification does not lead a person to perform what is obligatory but rather leads him to do what is evil, whereas when it occurs in a state of purification, it leads one to do what is obligatory and leads one to refrain from shameful and unjust deeds?

In their conditional nature, revealed norms contrast sharply with rationally known norms, in respect to which "once their ground [*sabab*] is present, the situation of the subjects of the Law is one and the same."[33]

Where does all this leave us with regard to our questions? We will be better equipped to take stock of our position once a final facet of the Baṣran account of revelation, connected to the above, has been brought into view more sharply. And this is the claim that the role of revelation is to give the particulars for something that is known by reason in a general form. In Mānkdīm's words, "What the prophets convey . . . can only constitute the particularization [*tafṣīl*] of a general knowledge [*jumla*] already established by reason."[34] It is on the interpretation of this idea that our ability to interpret the baffling treatment of legal resources by ʿAbd al-Jabbār and his disciples turns.

Now there is one obvious sense in which these words are meant, given in Mānkdīm's prompt continuation: the general ground we already know by reason is the consequentialist principle that what leads to harm is evil and what promotes one's welfare is obligatory (*qubḥ al-mafsada, wujūb al-maṣlaḥa*)—a statement that basically rehearses the value assigned to *luṭf*. This is connected with—and indeed dependent on—the rationally known obligation to deflect harm from ourselves and seek after benefits.[35] Legal causes (*ʿilal sharʿiyya*) accounting for the status (*ḥukm*) of a revealed norm are defined by the Baṣrans precisely in terms of the capacity of the act prescribed by revealed Law to serve as a divine assistance and promote one's welfare by making it more likely that one will be motivated to choose the acts whose values are independent of revelation.[36] Thus, let's take a classic case: the prohibition of wine; the cause of its prohibition is its intoxicating effect, and it is *all* intoxicating substances that are encompassed by the prohibition. And this proximate, as it were, cause is determined by a broader consideration of *maṣāliḥ*: the social consequences of intoxication, resulting as it does in the spread of enmity and animosity (which, one must assume if the loop of teleological reasoning is to close, in turn prejudices the moral choices of individual agents).[37] Similarly, fasting is a practice that by training one to brace oneself against physical appetite, may place one in a better position to resist the appetites that incite one toward things prohibited by reason (*muḥarramāt ʿaqliyya*).[38]

Elements of this brief sketch will turn up in later points of the discussion, but now the important question is whether the particularizing function of revelation we have seen—namely, its prescription of specific acts on account of their consequences—exhausts the sense in which revealed norms particularize rationally known moral norms. For what must be observed about the acts that consume the pages of the *Mughnī* at its legal, is that they are not of a consequentialist kind. The normative relationships constituted by *ḥuqūq* are such that, in ʿAbd al-Jabbār's crucial formulation, they "must be set up by antecedent grounds" (*lā budda min taqaddum asbābihi*). Thus the return of the deposit is a right of the depositor set up by the antecedent act of depositing. A similar, though slightly more complex story applies to the obligation to repay debts, which depends on the existence of a variety of antecedent causes.[39] The difference between the two types of acts can be distinguished more clearly by recalling what was said above about the circumstance sensitivity of revealed norms. This, as has already been briefly alluded to, contrasts sharply with rationally known norms. Hence the seminal distinction spelled out by Abu'l-Ḥusayn al-Baṣrī in his commentary on ʿAbd al-Jabbār's *ʿUmad*: revealed law may change according to the interest it serves (*maṣlaḥa*), whereas rationally known norms may not.[40] This, in turn, seems to give us the major division marked between rational and legal causes (*ʿilal ʿaqliyya* versus *ʿilal sharʿiyya*). Rational causes "*necessitate* a state or quality for an entity"; "their necessitating action cannot depend on any other concomitant or condition"; and "their necessitating action cannot be confined to one particular individual but not another, or to one particular moment in time but not another." By contrast, a legal cause does not necessitate, and its effect is highly conditional, as Abu'l-Ḥusayn al-Baṣrī explains:

> Inasmuch as its influence on the quality [or status: *ḥukm*] [of an act] is not by way of necessitation, but rather . . . lies in its constituting an assistance for the subject of the Law and motivating him to choose another act [i.e., rationally known acts], its influence is dependent on choices. In matters that concern choice, we consider it possible that qualities may differ as between different individuals or different times.[41]

And it is in terms of rational causes that the moral treatises of the Baṣran Muʿtazilites have taught us to understand grounds of value such as evilness or obligation (*wujūh al-qubḥ, wujūh al-wujūb*), and correlatively of *ḥuqūq*.[42]

The difference between the two types of acts is likewise tracked by an explicit distinction between grounds of value with which ʿAbd al-Jabbār furnished us in a few rare passages occurring in the context of a discussion of the purpose of revelation. There, the grounds of value constituted by consequentialist considerations—whether an act yields benefit or repulses harm (referred to as the act's purposes or *aghrāḍ*)—are contrasted with the grounds of value that concern an act's form (*ṣūra*), class (*jins*), attribute (*ṣifa*), or name (*ism*)—or what may be termed act-descriptions, whose orientation would contrast with the first in being deontological. For "the fact that an act serves one's welfare does not derive from its class or form or any other of its characteristics [*aḥwāl*]."[43]

While the distinction is clearly marked, one's efforts to trace out the relation between the two types of acts are hampered by the programmatic focus on the second type—consequentialist acts—in both types of Muʿtazilite writings from which one seeks illumination—namely, discussions of prophethood and discussions of legal theory. For the first, this bias is due to the fact that it is acts of worship (*ʿibādāt*) such as prayer or pilgrimage (whose value is understood on a consequentialist logic by the Baṣrans) that occupy center stage in justifying the need for revelation, and not the *ḥuqūq* figuring in human transactions (*muʿāmalāt*). For the latter, it would seem to be because it is the discovery of the value ascribed by the Law to acts whose value is still unknown (and thus not already known through reason, such as the fundamental *ḥuqūq* of paying back debts or returning deposits) that dictates the interest of legal theory.

Nevertheless, the passages we have been considering—in which appears the peculiar imbrication of moral and legal whose puzzlements I have been striving to dispel—enable us to put these difficulties aside and make a strong case for interpreting the use of the law in such places in terms of the Baṣran view of the particularizing function of revelation, as the theory that illuminates their practice, by reading this claim as one intended to cover both types of acts whether consequentialist or deontological—only with different applications to each. For having set out this piece of theory, we may return to the instances cited above as examples of the curious legerdemain with which the data of reason and those of revelation were sifted apart to examine them anew. If an object has been usurped, reason does not tell us the specific kind (*jins makhṣūṣ*) of object that must be given, whereas revelation does. If an object has been usurped and one possesses its value, one must deliver it to the right holder as soon as one can, without regard for one's need. The first case can now be seen as a straightforward one in which revelation comes to specify something that reason has left vague, only bidding us the general principle that something must be given in replacement of the object. The latter, again, may be read as a case in which revelation has come to limit the universal application of a precept known in general form by reason by telling us how the application of this principle should go in the particular circumstance of one's personal pressing need. (And in this case, the more particular revealed or legal maxim that ʿAbd al-Jabbār perhaps had in mind was the priority given to necessity (*ḍarūra*) in Islamic law, which often produces mitigations of rulings and is capable of modifying the scope of one's obligations.)[44] In the Baṣran account of revelation given above, we may recall that the particularizing function of the latter was spelled out in terms of its sensitivity to different times, places, conditions, and situations or states of the subjects of the Law. The last principle can now be interpreted precisely as a particularization deriving from the special situation of the subject under an obligation to act.[45]

The reading can be given a broader sweep to encompass many of ʿAbd al-Jabbār's lengthy disquisitions on the details of the obligations arising from violations of *ḥuqūq*. Thus, for example, in considering the return of usurped objects, one must take into account the state (*ḥāl*) of the person to whom they are returned, the state of the penitent who is to return it, and the state of the object to be returned. A proliferation of conditions ensues, once again conveying an impression of the strongly legalistic spirit at work:

> If the [original usurped] object still exists but the penitent is prevented from access to it, its return is not obligatory. If it is destroyed even though it would have been accessible to him it were it still existing, he is not obliged to return it. If the person from whom it has been usurped cannot be reached for various reasons, its return is not obligatory.[46]

Next ʿAbd al-Jabbār turns to the penitent's obligation to deliver a like or equivalent (*mithl*) object to the right holder if the original is lost—in which connection, as I have already mentioned, the discussion of the nature of ownership is launched. The latter discussion arrives as an interpretation of the condition "if claims already attach to one's property," which necessitates an understanding of the rightful grounds of property—for *if* claims already attach to it, one cannot use it to satisfy the claims of the right holder from which one has usurped something. Other conditions are scattered throughout the ensuing passages: if the right holder dies, if the right holder does not show great insistence in demanding their right, if the penitent has nothing to give as a replacement, if the person under claim is not fully in command of their reason.[47] All of these conditions can thus be seen as particularizations of general principles known by reason—above all and in this context, the moral principle that one is obliged to right one's wrongs and restore the world to its normative order as a condition for the validity of one's repentance.

This, then, is the reading one may give to these passages in light of the Baṣrans' view of revelation. Among the facts that would embarrass its application, the most germane is the following: within the passages engrossed by the detailing of conditions, it is not always unequivocally clear which side of the divide between reason and revelation these conditions are intended to fall on. Certainly it must be admitted that the mere presence of a condition in itself does not automatically constitute a signifier for the revealed domain.[48] And certainly it would also seem a simple task to analyze most act-descriptions that the Baṣrans entertain into conditional statements, thereby trivializing any distinction—for instance, "if one accepts a deposit into one's trust and another comes to demand it, then it is obligatory to return it." Indeed, given the view that it is essential to *ḥuqūq*-based obligations that they arise through antecedent grounds (*asbāb*), the obligations they give rise to can be said to be essentially conditional (the obligation to return a deposit is conditional on the ground that someone has deposited an object with another and comes to demand it). This suggestion is made more compelling by Ibn Mattawayh's slippage between the term *asbāb* (grounds) and *shurūṭ* (conditions) in referring to such obligations.[49] In fact, one of the most important things to notice is that overall the "divide" between the two domains—rational and revealed—is hardly a well-tended one, in spite of the seams that trace it out for us in many places. The generous and casual sprinkling of references to *fuqahā'* and discussions of *fiqh* attests to the permeability of the boundary separating the two domains. With this connects the following impression: that while indeed the practice as we see it in these writings may be explained by, or seen as an expression of, the theory relating reason and revelation discussed above, it would be stretching things to say that the *aim* in these writings is to raise an explicit argument for a particular view of the relation between rational and revealed truths.[50]

Yet here we need a more global look at the Muʿtazilites' moral position in order to appreciate that it may be precisely this blurring of the divide between the two domains that constitutes the distinctive and most important feature of ʿAbd al-Jabbār's approach. The significance of this ambiguity can be located in both directions toward which its effect flowed: in the infiltration of the domain of Islamic law by moral reason; and conversely, in the infiltration of the domain of moral reason—or more accurately, the theological practice through which moral reason was defended—by the law.

As far as the latter direction is concerned, I may put the suggestion briefly by invoking George Makdisi's well-known thesis concerning the primacy of legal studies in the Islamic mainstream. In his essays on the relations between *kalām* and the schools of law (the "guilds," as he called them: *madhāhib*), Makdisi argued this thesis with great verve and—in his uniquely colorful way—spoke of the cunning infiltration of the schools by practitioners of *kalām* of all stripes, who perceived that there was no better way to legitimate their activities than by appending themselves to the vehicles of legitimacy—to schools of law.[51] "Islam," in his words, "is, first and foremost, a nomocracy. The highest expression of its genius is to be found in its law; and its law is the source of legitimacy for other expressions of its genius." The thesis may be expressed too strongly in such words; but even if not as a total description of the spirit of Islam, surely as a characterization of a key component of it, it would not be contested.

The Muʿtazilites' sensitivity to this point is suggested by an incident that we find recounted in their biographical literature.[52] The story goes that someone approached ʿAbd al-Jabbār inviting him to compose a book in "*fatāwā al-kalām*"—that is to say, theological pronouncements delivered after the model of legal works and legal opinions. This was a task in which ʿAbd al-Jabbār, as a Shāfiʿite jurist and onetime chief judge in Rayy, could certainly acquit himself with success. The story continues that ʿAbd al-Jabbār being otherwise engaged at the time, he delegated the task to Abū Rashīd al-Nīsābūrī, who composed his *Dīwān al-uṣūl* (which has not reached us).

The loss of Nīsābūrī's work is one to be lamented, as it would have made for a particularly illuminating document, on the assumption at least that the request had been carried out as prescribed—for what, after all, would it mean to compose a work of *kalām* in the manner of *fatāwā*? Not that it could not be done; quite to the contrary, it would seem that it was a description to which the practice of *kalām* already answered. For the questions and challenges (*su'āl* and *shubha*) recorded within works of *kalām* are essentially requests for clarification of theological doctrine not so different from requests for clarification of legal doctrine—however much the often polemical intention of the former might have differed from the pious intention and practical orientation of an ordinary *mustaftī* (a seeker of legal opinion)—differing little from *fatwa*s except in minor aspects of stylistics, such as the formality of beginning "What would you say to a man who . . . ?" Yet *kalām* works were essentially a record of responses to what was said to "men who . . ."—here, to men who asked or objected on different occasions, often included in the works shorn of identifying or historical reference.

The gap is closed even more in those areas of the Baṣran corpus that are taken over by a spirit of law. Thus, a reader of the following opening of a passage in ʿAbd al-Jabbār's *al-Luṭf* may well wonder whether there was much of a gap to be sealed.

> If someone were to ask concerning property left by a man who died and was survived by a brother and grandfather, and to say: tell us about the case where a person unjustly usurps it; the compensation for the amount that exceeds the grandfather's claim has been a matter of disagreement among jurists—is it to be given to the grandfather or to the brother or to both?[53]

But even without the information with which Nīsābūrī's work would have supplied us, we are still in a position to consider the story on a general level and ask, What is the significance of such a commissioning? The simplest conjecture is this: it expresses an awareness of the centrality of legal studies in the Islamic milieu, and as the vehicle and seat of religious status, the desirability of emulating its features.[54] And while Nīsābūrī's *Dīwān* did not survive, a work of his that did may yet provide for interesting reflections—namely, the work titled *al-Masā'il fi'l-khilāf bayna al-Baṣriyyīn wa'l-Baghdādiyyīn*—in that the terms it employs (*masā'il, khilāf*) were identical to those used to designate the genre of legal literature dealing with the differences of opinion between doctors of law, whether within or between different schools. One may interpret this as yet another instance of the appropriation and reenactment of the legal framework and legal culture, and the enjoyment of its powers of legitimation.

The blurring of the bounds between the discourse peculiar to *kalām* and that peculiar to *fiqh* could then be taken as a response to this same awareness of the latter's ascendancy, and the same drift toward where the current pulled strongest. Yet at the same time, this was no one-way or undogmatic appropriation, nor should we be misled by the apparent facility—one may say docility—with which material redolent of its jurisprudential provenance is lifted bodily from one domain into another to be presented in jurisprudential diction and tones. For in effecting this migration of legal conceptual tools and frames, and incorporating them into works whose subject was signposted as that of moral knowledge accessible to reason, the accomplishment of these Muʿtazilites may have been nothing less than the audacity by which it lay hold of Islamic law as an annex of moral reason. It is in this light that the easy passage from *ʿaql* to *sharʿ* that we see should be interpreted, and we should not allow to pass unobserved the scatter of occasions in which an exposition of rational truths is followed up by the—unobtrusive, yet for all that pregnant—remark, "This is why it is the case in the Law that . . ."[55] What such a statement implicitly represents is a claim about the basis of the revealed Law in rationally known truths, and the continuity between *ʿaqliyyāt,* on the one hand, and *sharʿiyyāt,* on the other.

It is the brazen "this is why" in this statement that constitutes the hallmark of the Muʿtazilite perspective on the objectivity of moral truths, permeating through and through the Muʿtazilite approach to the revealed Law by a rationalizing spirit that surpassed the bounds set by many of their contemporaries in the domain of legal theory. The bounds in question were negotiated by legal theorists with particular urgency in relation to analogy (*qiyās*), where it was a matter of deciding on the limits on its legitimate use in seeking new applications for the law, and in relation to the nature of the legal cause or *ratio legis* (*ʿilla*), the reason underlying a legal ruling. In trying to ascertain the legal value of an act or other object of evaluation that was not catered for by an explicit textual prescription, the temptation for jurists was to move in the direction of rule formation. If wine was prohibited because it was intoxicating, then perhaps all intoxicating drinks were prohibited. If it was permissible to use water at which a dog had lapped for ritual purification, then perhaps the permission of use could be extended to cases where other types of animals had come to drink. "One naturally sought categories," Bernard Weiss observes, and "through such generalizing activity the law became more systematic." Yet the trend toward ever more extensive categorization was curtailed by the caution of those jurists who espoused a more "textualist" or particularist approach. While the use of analogy came to enjoy near-universal acceptance among legal schools, limits to its use were set down, and it was understood that the general principles that they tended to suggest were to serve as guides to the formulation of rules, but were not to constitute rules in their own right.[56]

Although the Baṣran view of revelation strongly stressed the need for revealed norms just as it stressed the jurist's dependence on the sources of revelation in the process of discovering these norms, in many respects the rationalist attitude to the law expressed in the Muʿtazilite writings we have been considering constituted a bold rejection of such circumspect particularism. Its proposals for a rationalization of the Law can thus be seen to run on two levels, already adumbrated by the above. On one level was the rationalization that we have already remarked as the kernel of their account of revelation, whereby the very reason for the existence of the revealed Law was claimed to be its contribution to human welfare. Carried over to the practice of legal reasoning, this general claim encouraged an analysis of legal norms (*aḥkām sharʿiyya*) in terms of a cause (*ʿilla*) that revealed the interests a norm served. The strong tendency to generalizations ("every intoxicating substance is prohibited") was complemented by a willingness to sanction certain types of theological statements that partly motivated other jurists in shunning generalizations insofar as they feared that such statements would be their natural corollaries—namely, the ascription of such generalizations to God as the reasons motivating Him to institute these prescriptions. The legal cause, in ʿAbd al-Jabbār's words, is as good as God's announcement "I made this act obligatory for such-and-such a reason [*ʿilla*], or in order that such-and-such a thing might come about, or in order for such a thing not to come about."[57] And here we may imagine the shudder of the Ashʿarite listening in; for who—reverberate Ashʿarites from Bāqillānī to Shahrastānī and beyond—should dare to ascribe to God the indignity of motives with a determining power over His will? And this formulation, in connecting God's action of obligating to talk of causes and grounds, certainly seems to come dangerously close to such audacity.

As for the second level of rationalization, it consisted precisely of the identification of many of the revealed prescriptions as objective moral truths, among them the truths defined in terms of the rights and claims signified by *ḥuqūq*. The relationship between the two levels reflects the contrast between rational and legal causes, and that between the grounds of value that consist of (deontological) act-descriptions and those determined by consequential considerations. The spirit of rationalization adopted toward legal and revealed norms that is expressed in these two levels is one pervasively leavening the writings of ʿAbd al-Jabbār, as the discussion of repentance has most strongly suggested. And while such writings, as we may readily observe, may not have been produced with the explicit design of urging an argument about the relation between reason and revelation, or between legal and rational norms, they can be seen as the fruit of an explicit account, which indeed they could be said to promote all the better insofar as the latter is put into use unmarked and unobtrusive.[58]

Rights, Claims, and Desert: The Moral Economy of Ḥuqūq

In all the above, I have been pursuing a trail whose origin lay in the bafflement aroused by the legal spirit found in some of ʿAbd al-Jabbār's writings on matters of value—a scintilla of which, as I have remarked, is carried by his disciple Mānkdīm's briefer work, though without breaching too far the familiar boundary between the domains of *fiqh* and *kalām*. And while the discussion of repentance marks a particularly strong legal note, it should be said that it is not the only part of the Muʿtazilite syllabus in which a legal accent infiltrates, though in those parts where it does more concertedly—for example, in the discussion of compensation (*ʿiwaḍ*)—it may be said to contain itself within the bounds of a subordinate role.

My objective in all the above has been composite. On the one hand, I have aimed to highlight yet another intellectual condition bounding the Muʿtazilite approach to ethics and limiting one's capacity to interact with their ethical thought by detaching it from the features that environ it—whether its theological ends or its legal fibre—and bestowing on it an attention referred to in the previous chapter as a philosophical one. Of course—to resume a thread of reflection left unresolved—some of the remarks made in the previous chapter concerning the aims of Muʿtazilite ethics may now be qualified in light of the present exploration. For to the extent that the enterprise of moral inquiry comes to approximate to the enterprise of Islamic law in such writings, and thus to the teleology inherent in the latter, one has no reason to demur against one who wished to say that the aims of the former partake of a practical (and anthropocentric) orientation. In the section on repentance that we have been focusing on, the statement "*it is obligatory*" could appropriately be heard as a statement prescriptive of practical action, as in the admonitory force of the remark, referring to the penitent incapable of independent reasoning (*ijtihād*) who faces uncertainty, "It is obligatory on him to seek a legal opinion [*yastaftī*] from someone whose knowledge and religious probity he trusts in."[59] In actual fact, the reader of these sections of the *Mughnī* may not have been the penitent seeking moral direction, but it is not impossible that had one happened to look for direction there, one would have found some.

The focus on the relations between theology and law—or between reason and revelation—therefore contributes a further brushstroke to the characterization of the Muʿtazilite moral project. At the same time, it gives us the material we need for understanding several aspects of the conceptual latticework peculiar to the Baṣrans' thinking about desert. Some of these aspects will have to await a later stage of the discussion. The features that we need to focus on here, and for which the foregoing has equipped us, concern the central role of the concept of *ḥuqūq* in the Baṣran Muʿtazilite understanding of two key concepts within their system: desert and injustice.

The concept of *ḥuqūq*, as we have seen, is one that forms the normative currency foundational to the economy of Islamic law, and I tracked the assimilation of this currency in one of two competing structural schemes of value deployed within Baṣran Muʿtazilite works—one that tabulates substantive acts under the value they share (evil, obligatory, and so on), and another that tables them under obligations divided into self-regarding and other-regarding, then analyzing the other-regarding in terms of the claims or rights that others possess (whether human beings or God). Now which of the two structural schemes of value is to be considered as the master order? A big step toward answering this question can be made by considering those sectors of the Muʿtazilite moral system in which the role of *ḥuqūq* proves foundational: their constitutive role in the act-description of injustice (*ẓulm*); their definitive role in the concept of desert (*istiḥqāq*); and hence their role in the definition of moral qualities such as evilness or obligation.

There are several reasons why the act-description of injustice might be identified as the master category of Muʿtazilite ethics. Heading the list is the fact that from the earliest days of Muʿtazilite theology, it had been the magnet notion around which the concern with divine justice had ranged itself. Another reason has to do with the unusually composite nature that the concept possesses: an act is unjust if it brings harm that neither leads to greater benefit or averts harm, nor is deserved. Either of the two grounds—the absence of beneficial or harm-averting consequences, and the absence of desert—could make an act unjust. In the next chapter I'll be coming back from a different direction to the disquiets harbored by this conjunction of grounds and the troublesome "either/or" that relates them. For the present purposes, however, the accent must fall on an aspect of injustice related to its composite character, but not equally evident, and this concerns the founding role played in it by the currency of *ḥuqūq*.

A first step toward identifying this role is to focus on the concept of desert internally deployed in the definition of injustice, which gives us one reason why an instance of harm may be unjust: it may be undeserved. "Desert" is the translation for *istiḥqāq*. What is the relation of this term to *ḥaqq*? From a lexicographical point of view: derivation. Legal writings make this derivation clear, as in the following words by the Ḥanafite jurist Ibn Nujaym (d. 1563): "*al-ḥaqq mā yastaḥiqquhu al-rajul*" ("a right is that which a person deserves/is entitled to").[60] This, in itself, would not be sufficient to establish the relation between the two concepts in Baṣran Muʿtazilite usage in the absence of clearer indications.

Indications to this effect are furnished by ʿAbd al-Jabbār in a number of places. Explaining the concept of *ḥaqq* (specifically in its meaning as right: *ḥaqq lahu*), he makes *istiḥqāq* a term in its definition: "When we use the expression '*ḥaqq lahu*,' it signifies that a person deserves [or 'is entitled to': *istiḥqāq*] another's performance of an act."[61] Yet these indications in turn carry us only part of the way, and need to be clarified by examining more closely the notion of an "undeserved harm" that the definition of injustice contains. Now what form of harm would be *undeserved*? And what form *deserved*?

The intriguing answer to the first question is suggested by the remark made by ʿAbd al-Jabbār in the context of a concern with the relation between obligatory acts and injustice. ʿAbd al-Jabbār comments that if an obligation "concerns another's claim [*ḥaqq*], then the failure to fulfill it must constitute an injustice [*ẓulm*]."[62] The implication is obvious: one of the chief reasons why harm inflicted on another will be unjust is that it constitutes a violation of the other's rights (*ḥuqūq*). The reach of these *ḥuqūq* is a broad one, as some of the above discussion will already have suggested. These rights and claims mark out the sphere of a person's legitimate enjoyments and benefits, and most saliently the enjoyments arising from the possessing of property, which is defined precisely in terms of the benefits it confers on its possessor (thus "what matters is not particular objects per se [*aʿyān*] but rather benefits and harms").[63] Not only the refusal to return a deposit, pay back a debt, or refrain from physical aggression but according to the Baṣran masters—who in this instance seem to have lost their sense for the facetious and thus given us an opportunity to laugh—even "if Zayd was to sit on ʿAmr's chest, he would be obliged to compensate him, and he would be obliged to remove himself from that position." More sedately, even such a simple thing (though perhaps less simple at a time when books were expensive and knowledge a precious religious duty) as your preventing me from reading a book that I own and benefiting from its study would violate my rights. As such, this violation would constitute an injustice.[64]

I have already noted that the category of injustice is a composite one, made up of two different elements: consequentialist calculations, on the one hand, and considerations of desert, on the other. It is the latter that the violation of *ḥuqūq* interprets for us: the harm that is not deserved—that is not *mustaḥaqq*—is a harm that violates a person's *ḥaqq*. And by this I may now capture with sharper strokes what constitutes the singularity of the composite character of this moral category. It is the Noah's ark of Baṣran Muʿtazilite ethics in that it instantiates in microform the two cardinal sources of value that the ethics is founded on: consequentialist grounds (the calculus of benefits and harms that offset the harm under judgment), and nonconsequentialist grounds (namely, *ḥuqūq*, mediated by the concept of desert). I've already brushed against this double allegiance above in discussing the distinction between acts whose value arises from their form (*ṣūra*), kind (*jins*), or attribute (*ṣifa*)—again, what we may call act-descriptions—such as thanking the benefactor, returning deposits, or lying, whose value is stable, and acts whose value depends on their beneficial or harmful consequences, whose value shifts with the circumstances. The category of injustice straddles both types of ground.

Yet the conceptual latticework we have begun to trace can only be complete once we have answered the reverse of the question we raised—this time: What form of harm would be *deserved*? One harm that would clearly be a deserved one, and that it would be just to inflict, is the harm of punishment. And now why might a person deserve to be punished? Clearly because that person has done something wrong and violated some moral principle.[65] Yet as we have seen, in the structural scheme described above, moral principles are spelled out unequivocally in terms of rights and claims, in the language of *ḥuqūq*. And as the scheme also makes clear, not all claims will be those of human beings; some claims are peculiar to God.

The complex pattern of relations, then, can be unpacked as follows: one commits an act that fails to respond to the normative order spelled out in terms of individual *ḥuqūq*, and inflicts a harm that is not deserved (*mustaḥaqq*). The result of this failure to respond to the normative order of *ḥuqūq*—a failure described as an act of injustice—is that one in turn comes to deserve (*yastaḥiqqu*) the harm of punishment. The relation between the two concepts of *ḥaqq* and *istiḥqāq* is therefore far from being merely lexicographical; it is these *ḥuqūq* that give rise to deserts.

Crucial in this scheme is that the same term—*istiḥqāq*—is applied to actions that respond to the normativity of claims by adjusting a person's relation to valued goods (paradigmatically: property, honor, and physical integrity) according to the order dictated by existing claims, but is *also* applied to actions that constitute a requital for one's success or failure in responding to this normative order (where the term "requital" is intended to be neutral between positive and negative deserts). The foundational fact that it primarily applies to *actions* is evident in 'Abd al-Jabbār's formulation: "*mattā qulnā innahu 'ḥaqq lahu,' afāda istiḥqāqa fi'lin 'ala'l-ghayr*" ("when we say 'it is one's right,' this signifies an entitlement to [or 'desert of'] an act from another"). And here we may also recall al-Murtaḍā's definition, cited above, in which *ḥaqq* was defined "as exclusive assignment to a person as a result of which something *for* or *from* the person who possesses it becomes good"; this "something" is the action that is *mustaḥaqq*.

The first direction of the usage is indicated in a phrase such as this one: "if we take over the deposit or the debt from a person from whom this is deserved/claimable . . . (*min al-mustaḥaqq 'alayhi dhālika*)"—where the demonstrative "this" refers to the act of taking. Similarly in the phrase "one from whom performance is not deserved," or better, "over whose performance there is no claim" (*man lā yustaḥaqqu 'alayhi al-adā'*).[66] In both examples, it is the action responsive to *ḥuqūq*—taking a deposit or making a performance—that is referred to as what is deserved. This direction of the usage concerns the worldly domain, in which alone can good and evil be committed by human beings. But the converse is the use of the term to refer to punishment and indeed reward, preeminently such as God will mete out in the hereafter by way of desert—that is, in response to actions bearing moral value performed in this life.[67] Thus, the moral proposition "I have a right to take the deposit" (it is a *ḥaqq lī*, and hence your giving it to me is something that I have a claim to: *mustaḥaqq*) in this life translates into the moral propositions "I deserve (*astaḥiqqu*) compensation" and "You deserve (*tastaḥiqqu*) punishment" in the next (positions that I will explore in the following chapter). Both actions adjusted to the order, and actions adjusting violations of the order, are covered by the same word. Further, the deserts that one acquires are themselves spoken of as *ḥuqūq*—with reward conceived as a *ḥaqq lahu* (a right one holds) and punishment as a *ḥaqq ʿalayhi* (a claim held against one)—so that the latter form one's point of both departure and arrival.[68]

This twofold usage is lubricated by the following interesting fact: ultimately, for both mainstream jurists and Baṣran *mutakallimūn*, the normative order of *ḥuqūq* is analyzed into a currency of benefits and goods, and it is the apparent univocity of these benefits between the here and the hereafter that supports the possibility of adjustments of the moral order between this world and the next—the same kind of thing that was taken away in this life can be given back in the next. This is made plain in ʿAbd al-Jabbār's characterization of *ḥuqūq* as consisting of "either benefit or the repulsion of harm."[69] In this, ʿAbd al-Jabbār would be falling in line with a dominant trend in Islamic legal thought, in which *ḥuqūq*—specifically human—are defined by reference to the benefits accruing to their owners. Thus the Mālikite jurist al-Qarāfī (d. 1285) in his *Kitāb al-Furūq*: "*ḥaqq al-ʿabd maṣāliḥuhu*"—the right/claim of a human being is their welfare, benefit, interests.[70] Reward and compensation, referred to as *ḥuqūq*, are defined precisely in terms of benefits (*nafʿ*, *manāfiʿ*).

Of course one must remark, in connection with the use of *istiḥqāq* just described, that as much in our own moral language so in the Muʿtazilites', there are two ways of talking about desert, highlighting different aspects of the normative relations involved. We say that a person deserves goods or evils (benefits or harms), and that a person deserves *to be given* goods or evils. Now the primary order of talking might well seem to us to be the first: when one speaks of a person deserving reward and punishment, what one expresses is a normative relation between a moral person and a set of goods or evils—namely, that a person who acted in certain ways ought or ought not to enjoy or suffer—and not primarily whether another party is obliged or not obliged to establish the relation. The other's *action* of requiting—of rewarding or punishing a person—would seem to attract a value of an instrumental order: its value derives from its serving as a means to achieve the end value of a person's enjoying or suffering. At the same time, there is a justificatory wedge dividing the two propositions; the fact that another person deserves something is not itself automatically a justification for another person to give it to them.[71] By contrast, the distinguishing feature of the above conceptual matrix is that it forces open a space of questioning concerning the *agent* who is responsible for making the adjustments of the order when violated or respected—that is, of giving deserts. Framed as the normative proposition is around actions, this conceptual matrix demands the naming of the agent. And in the worldly order, the placeholder of the agent is filled clearly (it is clear who must pay a debt, and to whom the debt must be paid). But who is the placeholder—who the right holder—in the case of deserved punishment, reward, or compensation, and who is the one obliged to make payment?

These questions will need to be shelved until the next chapter, where they will be brought out for an answer once several other aspects of the Muʿtazilite approach to desert have been set in place and some of the above structures have been fleshed out in greater detail. Here, my chief concern has been to lay the groundwork by revealing the extensive reach that the normative matrix of *ḥuqūq* possesses within the Baṣran moral system. The task would not be complete without mentioning that the concept of desert, which has here been shown to be deeply embedded in this matrix, is to be identified as the capstone of the Muʿtazilite moral system in imparting to it the chief definiens deployed for the basic moral qualities of acts such as good (*ḥasan*), evil (*qabīḥ*), and obligatory (*wājib*). It will be the next chapter's venture to set out the relationship between these terms in detail, thereby launching us on the first of several stops from which to examine the Muʿtazilite understanding of desert, in all its peculiar plumage.

But as we are fresh from a discussion of the legal baggage of Baṣran moral thought, and even more particularly of the legal baggage carried by the concept of desert, this is the place to explore a scruple that has recently been raised in this connection, in which it is argued that the legal environment of the concept defeats our very capacity to identify it. Such a scruple, if sound, would evidently threaten the possibility of engaging the subject in the way I outlined at the end of the previous chapter, which was signposted as having emerged from an approach marked by a certain degree of philosophical expectation. For the possibility of such an approach squarely depends on the minimal achievement of identifying that the same thing is being talked about by the Muʿtazilites and ourselves—both laypersons and philosophers—when we use the term "desert." Without this reliance on "our" notions of desert in this study, its task would have been impossible to accomplish. One might now worry that this represents an illegitimate act of imposition on the character of the ethics to be examined. But it is altogether doubtful whether any study can be free from such supposed imposition even when its ideal is that of the good listener rather than the conversational partner. While a study of the Muʿtazilite understanding of desert conducted in Arabic might evade certain problems, any other language of research could not, for in the very translation of *istiḥqāq* as "desert" one is utilizing one's own notions and concepts. How do we know the Muʿtazilites *are* talking about desert? Clearly, one's identification of the subject matter is guided by noting the similarity of conceptual structures, by seeing "how the concept works," by observing its functions and the relations into which it enters with other concepts—mainly, the moral qualities of good and evil. This is how one succeeds in *recognizing* the concept. Without this foundational sort of reliance on our own understanding, we would have to succumb to incurable skepticism about the possibility of understanding another scheme of thought. This, apart from suggesting that a complete purification of our lens from the refractions of our own time is an unattainable as well as undesirable ideal, is a good occasion to stress that were such similarities not there, the study of the differences would have been impossible. And this should act as a foil to all that is said below, where the tone will often be set by the differences.

Nevertheless, it is this basic capacity to recognize the concept at issue that A. Kevin Reinhart seems to question in his *Before Revelation,* where he denies that the term *istiḥqāq* is rightly rendered as "desert" or "deserving." "We must not be misled by the English term 'deserves,' which has implications of valuation," Reinhart writes. "The Arabic terms *ḥaqq* and *istiḥqāq* are not valuative but are expressions of ownership and correctness. *Istiḥqāq* means 'having a claim on,' 'owning,' 'belonging to.'"[72] This position, let it be said, and while indeed it may hold special interest for the present study, would require a revision of understanding on the part of most scholars of Muʿtazilite thought.[73]

Now if there is anything from which Reinhart's position derives its persuasive appeal, this is the intimate nexus between the domain of law and the domain of rationally articulated norms that I have been considering. More particularly, it may be seen as a reflection of the twofold usage of the term *istiḥqāq* that I remarked above, where it was proposed that this is applied both to those actions demanded by the order of *ḥuqūq* in this world, but also to actions that requite one in the next world for one's failure or success in meeting this demand. In the discussion of this point, it may have been noticed that the translation of the term was allowed to skid between different possibilities when applied to this-worldly actions (such as exacting a deposit or debt): to deserve, to have a claim over, to be entitled to. It is in this light that one must understand the passage cited by Reinhart to buttress his case. In that text, ʿAbd al-Jabbār responds to—and counters—a suggestion that the primary referent in our necessary knowledge of the fact that pain can be good because of *istiḥqāq* should be considered to be the *istiḥqāq* of the return of a deposit or the payment of a debt (*radd al-wadīʿa wa-qaḍāʾ al-dayn*).[74] Reinhart correctly points out that the term cannot be rendered as deserving (*deserving* the return of the deposit). "Having a right" or "having a claim" on the deposit or the debt would be more suitable as renditions. And in their context, these translations are correct; in the domain of worldly actions demanded by the normative order of *ḥuqūq,* desert may often be an inappropriate translation for the term in question. But this should not lead one to neglect the existence of another domain of usage—*intimately* related to the first, as we have seen, so much so that one hesitates to call them "different" domains—in which the term *istiḥqāq* accepts desert as the only appropriate rendition.

So on the one hand, Reinhart's position can be seen simply as stemming from a one-sided and partial attention to the conceptual reach of the term. At the same time, it is worth noting that it is in both cases constraints encountered in our own language that we rely on in adjudicating between different translations, and that compel us to give up the term "desert" and look for a more appropriate idiom—for it is in *our* language that we feel there is something awry in talk of a person "deserving to take a deposit" or "deserving a performance." Once again, it seems to be our own familiar sense of the relationships into which particular concepts enter that acts as a criterion for the translation we choose.

But now what about the other part of the claim, concerning the term's nonevaluative character? Here the claim would appear to be simply wrong, *whichever* domain of usage one might choose to focus on. It would be hard to see how "having a claim on" or "a right to" (as one would translate expressions with *ḥaqq* as their term) could escape categorization as evaluative concepts, unless the application one grants to the term "evaluative" itself is drastically restricted. Under normal conditions of application—and without engaging ourselves too deeply in the scrutiny of the concept—the justificatory meaning of "rights" and "claims" would entitle them to be included in the class of evaluative terms. The case with "ownership" might not seem so obvious. With respect to the above-quoted passage, Reinhart writes that "the thing owned, and the deposit, are the property of the creditor, and the debtor, respectively. They belong to them"—suggesting that "belonging to" differs from desert (or deserving and being deserved) in failing to constitute an evaluative concept. But the terms "property" and "belong" (and similarly with the term "to own") are not reports of fact, in the sense that statements about actual *possession* are such reports (e.g., "I have this money in my pocket"), but express the presence of justifications for possession; belong would mean "it is rightfully mine" in such a context. This is sometimes explicitly brought out in renditions of the terms, as in Makdisi's translation of "*mustaḥiqq al-milk*" as "rightful owner of the property."[75]

To gain support for his view, Reinhart abandons the domain of legal and ethical applications, and appeals to the usage of the term *istiḥqāq* in Muʿtazilite ontology, adducing the expression "The atom has as its property (*istaḥaqqa*) this attribute" (*inna al-jawhar yastaḥiqqu hādhihi al-ṣifa*). He comments, "It is not that this attribute is entitled to, or deserves, the atom but that this attribute belongs to the atom." Of course, the relationship has been described the wrong way around here: it is not the *attribute* that is entitled to the atom but the *atom* that is entitled to the attribute. But putting this to one side, here again "belongs" is an expression that conveys the sense of rightful ascription, which is used in the context of an ontology whose prime preoccupation is with establishing the grounds that explain and entail the possession of attributes. If the ground of possession and actual possession appear not to be distinguished in certain contexts (as in Richard Frank's quotation, adduced by Reinhart above), this should perhaps be seen as a consequence of the close relation drawn between the ground and the attributes it entails; the ground works its effect—the bestowal of the property—in a manner of inerrant necessitation.[76]

I will have occasion to return to the Baṣran Muʿtazilite ontological scheme in what follows, and this picture can only be painted in broad strokes here. For the present purposes, the above should suffice to show that *istiḥqāq* is indeed an evaluative term that expresses a general concern with justifying grounds, adapting its meaning to the context in which it is employed. Once these misgivings have been removed, and once it is seen that *istiḥqāq* is used to convey the idea of a claim, ground, or right, it is merely a matter of deciding which translation is best suited to convey the meaning of the term depending on the semantic domain in which the instance of use is situated, and on the class of things to which the claim is made or the entitlement is grounded. It is not too difficult to locate the particular semantic domain of the concept that relates to the moral assessment and consequences of acts in which no translation serves us better than that of desert. And all of this is not intended to deny—that which this study is meant to underscore—the multiple differences in terms of functions and relations that distinguish our conception of desert from that of the Muʿtazilites.

CHAPTER 4

The Baṣran Mu'tazilite Approach to Desert

"To Deserve": Groundwork

The last two chapters have supplied many of the ingredients necessary for situating what constitutes the main subject of this study, the Mu'tazilites'—and more narrowly the Baṣrans'—conception of desert, marking out in bold two frames that bound their intellectual vantage point: their theological purpose and theocentric attention; and the osmosis effected between their ethics and the resources of Islamic law. Enough has already been said to suggest the importance of the concept of desert in the Mu'tazilite scheme, but not quite enough to elicit the full picture. This picture can be drawn more sharply in this chapter, which will be one of several stops in the attempt to map the Mu'tazilite view of desert and related issues concerning the justifiability of deserved treatments such as reward and punishment. As I've already indicated in the preface, the map will not be an exhaustive one: the angle from which it will be drawn is partly made up of questions anchored in a broader—philosophical—perspective, and thus partly defined by an interest in the differences that are picked out when one retains such an anchor and does not wholly throw oneself into the texts.

The first task, then, will be to outline this perspective with broad strokes, starting with a general question about the concept of desert: What does it mean for someone to deserve something? The centrality of the concept in our moral thinking makes it elusive to define, but attempts at definition capture the fact that desert is a "relation" of some sort, and that to deserve is to be "suitably related" to a certain type of treatment (on certain conditions).[1] The grounds that set up this relation consist of certain facts about the person that carry moral weight, whether actions performed or characteristics possessed by a person, and these constitute reasons why the person deserves to get, have, or keep a certain thing, or enjoy or suffer certain experiences. Deserts can be termed as the "moral consequences" of these facts.

Which actions and characteristics give rise to desert is a question of substantive ethics, on which the concept of desert—itself a formal one—depends for its content.

What kind of justificatory force desert carries is then a further question, and it is again a matter for substantive moral debate to determine whether the claim that a person deserves to suffer, enjoy, gain, or lose something, is a claim that one *ought* to suffer or enjoy, or rather that it would be *good* for one to suffer or enjoy. The outcome of the debate will crucially depend on the particular deserts and grounds of desert at issue. Thus one analysis practiced on the concept is to reduce and discuss it in core normative terms such as obligation, permissibility, or goodness, and say that "X deserves *y*" means "X ought to receive *y*" or "it is good that X receive *y*," or that it is just or unjust, right or wrong, for someone to receive a given treatment.[2] This approach has been charged as vacuous or rendering vacuous the concept of desert, yet it is a vacuity one cannot afford to indulge.[3] For example, whether to analyze "X deserves to be punished" into the claim "it is *obligatory* to punish" or rather that "it is *permissible* to punish" is one of the central questions in the justification of punishment. In this debate, desert will appear as a possible *reason* for the moral value assigned to the suffering inflicted in punishment, and hence cannot be collapsed by analysis into other terms. Why ought one to punish the murderer? "Because he killed with malicious intent" is no explanation in itself; it is still merely to line up one act next to another without explaining the connection that joins them. On one account, one ought to punish him because, having killed, he deserves it. The position that desert is a necessary and sufficient reason for punishment is what is usually termed "retributivism," and desert is thus to be distinguished from other reasons that may be canvased as justifications of punishment, most notably utilitarian or forward-looking ones, such as the value of punishment as a deterrent (of the agent in the future, or of other agents) or a means of reforming the agent. Desert, then, lies at the heart of questions to do with the justification of punishment.

A further clarification to the notion of desert can be introduced from a different direction, by considering the things or experiences ("treatments" to mark the fact that they are usually provided by another) that desert puts one into relation with. These will always be things that are considered goods or evils, things desired or feared: removing the liberty of a wrongdoer or consigning them to hard labor, slapping the child who talked back to its parent, giving a gift in token of thanks to the friend who stood by in a time of trouble, or simply praising or blaming, forming a moral judgment on a person and expressing the judgment to them—all of these are treatments that a person desires or fears. Although I have referred to deserts as moral consequences, one might have described them as the "values" of acts were it not that the term "moral value" is usually used to refer to the qualities of acts such as "good," "evil," or "obligatory." The statement that one deserves *x* for an act can also be put by saying that the act is *worth x* or that it is valued at *x* (a replacement that some languages make more evident than others: in modern Greek the term that means "to be worth"—αξίζει—also means "to deserve"). This possibility is revealed in the words "blameworthy" and "praiseworthy," which can substitute the expression "deserves blame or praise." But the commutation of the value of the act into the value of the consequence involves a shift in the kind of value at issue. Whereas the former concerns what is morally good, the latter concerns what is good for a person; deserved consequences must be desirable or desired. Thus one desires praise and honor, and shuns blame and dishonor, and—to move closer to the axial terms of Muʿtazilite ethics—one desires reward and not punishment. The distinction between something being desirable and its being desired raises a host of separate questions (could one not desire to be praised or not wish to receive eternal life?), but one assumes certain psychological—and in many cases physiological—facts about human beings and certain facts about the deserved objects in assuming that human desire attaches to them.[4]

This use of the word "value" to cover both what is morally good of a person to do or be, and what is good for a person to enjoy or suffer because of what one has done or who one is, strikes a strong cord with the outlook of the Baṣran Muʿtazilites. This will become plainer when I examine the definitions of moral terms, and the groundwork for doing so will be complete once a last question concerning our concepts of value—directly related to the above point—has been asked: What would "evil" really mean if it did not involve any reference to moral consequences? Could the concepts of good and evil be conceived in isolation from desert?

The affirmative answer could be called "the terminal conception of moral value," in which the "career" of value is seen as terminating with the instantiation of that which is valued. On the terminal conception, when a person is honest or kind, gives to the poor and tells the truth at a difficult moment, the quality of goodness characterizes these features; when the person ceases to instantiate these features, the career of moral value comes to an end—that is all there is to value. Similarly, when a person is coldhearted and invidious, when one cruelly hurts another, lies, or goes back on obligations, these features are bad, and disvalue attaches to them as long as they are instantiated; but the career of moral disvalue terminates with the extinction of the feature.

The affirmative answer can best be understood by contrasting it with the negative one, which could be termed the "demand conception of moral value." On this conception, the instantiation of moral value creates a demand for something further; when the person instantiates the above features, something remains even after they have ceased to exist. After a hurtful remark has issued from me, after participation in another's misfortune through vicarious grief, or after a lie or an act of injustice, moral value generates a demand for something further. Theories of moral value in which desert is made integral involve this type of demand conception of value—and which theory seems more compelling may depend on the particular features or acts one is considering: it may be that the notion of a demand attaches most insistently to acts that adversely affect others against their will, as a response to the experience of violation. In the demand conception, that which is deserved is a normative consequence—a consequence of the feature that ought to follow. Those who adhere to such a conception may feel that nothing but a mere ghost of the concepts of good and evil would remain on abstraction from the relation between these and the moral consequences connected to them. It would be a ghost cloaked in deontological garb, for to speak of desert and deserved moral consequences is also to give a *reason for action*—and it is of course the status of deserts as things valued or disvalued, as goods or evils, that bestows on them this motivating power.

This point had been well understood by everyone working within the Islamic tradition, and had been articulated by both theologians and jurists interested in the theory of law (*uṣūl al-fiqh*), who exercised themselves in finding definitions for the legal categories of acts such as "obligatory" or "forbidden" (*wājib, maḥẓūr*). And as *uṣūl al-fiqh* was an extension of the grounds on which theological disputes were fought, for those theoreticians who were hostile to the positions of their Muʿtazilite adversaries it became imperative to define these concepts in such a way that they did not lend support to such positions. In defining the legal values of acts, Ashʿarite theoreticians from Ghazālī to Āmidī and beyond made reference to the notion of preponderance (*tarjīḥ*); for example, obligatory acts are those in which performance is preponderant over nonperformance. But *why* would performance be preponderant, and what did this mean? To say that an act is preponderant is to make a statement about the agent's reasons for preferring it. Clearly, the reason for its preponderance was the prospect of punishment for the failure to perform and the prospect of reward for performing, and this could not but be stipulated in the definitions. As Āmidī put it, "Obligation must necessarily involve the preponderance of performing over abstaining on account of the blame or reward that attaches to [the act], for obligation is not realized if both performance and abstinence are equal as to their result [or end: *gharaḍ*]." In itself, the recognition of the motivating function of the consequences of acts was neutral between different views of the nature of the connection holding between acts and consequences. The Muʿtazilites had averred not just that God *will* punish wrongdoers for their evil acts but that wrongdoers *deserve* punishment. The Ashʿarites disavowed this interpretation as a blasphemous exaltation of desert to the status of a necessitating cause (*ʿilla*) limiting divine liberty, insisting, with Bāqillānī, that "God's—may He be exalted—infliction of pain on those He afflicts with pain does not occur from Him on account of a cause were it not for which it would not have occurred; rather God made the acts of human beings indications of the destiny He pre-ordained for them." Yet the denial of the *necessary* or *normative* occurrence of these future events was compatible with a properly hedged incorporation of these consequences into the definition of legal values.[5]

That the Muʿtazilites likewise ascribed enormous significance to the function of blame and praise, and reward and punishment, resulting from one's actions as motives for doing them is evident in a pithy statement such as ʿAbd al-Jabbār's: "One may say regarding evil acts that one should not perform them *insofar as* the agent will be exposed to an [adverse] consequence [*tabiʿa*] if he does so."[6] This view of deserts was reinforced by the strategic claim to which it was conjoined, according to which deserts were constitutive and definitive of the moral values of acts—a claim that represented the precise point of dispute between the Muʿtazilites and their opponents in grounding a normative description for the way in which such consequences "resulted" from one's acts (and about which I will have more to say in a moment).

The role played by the deserved consequences of acts in motivating one's moral choices was exhibited plainly in the contents of the knowledge that the Baṣrans diagnosed as indispensable to human subjects for fulfilling the Law: the knowledge that one deserves reward and punishment as a result of one's actions was designated as an "assistance" (*luṭf*) in the fulfillment of the Law, and it is the capacity of these projected deserts as motivating or deterring factors (*dawāʿī, ṣawārif*) that gives them this function.[7] Indeed there is no stage of the drama of salvation, as the Muʿtazilites conceive it, that is not shadowed by a consideration of deserved consequences; it is this that gives content to the motives of both the promulgator of the Law—who promulgates it in order to bestow the opportunity for deserved reward to its subjects—as well as the subjects of the Law—whom the concern for their own welfare and the fear of being exposed to harm carries from door to door—from the motive it gives them to inquire into religious truth in the first place ("what if I did not do so and thereby exposed myself to punishment?"), to the repentance from evil deeds that it motivates in the last.

If there is any question to be raised concerning the account of human motivation proposed by these Muʿtazilites, it would not be whether desert should be one's reason for action but whether there is anything *else* that could serve in this capacity. The tension here is one familiar from other forms of religious ethics in which the possibility of reward and punishment stalk the affirmation that one must be motivated by the values of acts (taken in the first sense of "*good*," not "*good for*")—that one should do the good for its own sake, and not for the way it affects one's own interests. This tension undermines the capacity to draw a tenable distinction between deontological and utilitarian (consequentialist) grounds of value. How well can such a distinction hold within Muʿtazilite ethics, when even with those norms expressed as act-descriptions—such as the normative claims of *ḥuqūq*, which I looked at in the previous chapter—the agent's fulfillment of them is ultimately pursued in terms of the contribution they make to his desert of praise and reward, and therefore to his welfare in the next world?

Yet it is clear, on the one hand, that there were several areas of the Muʿtazilite scheme that meant that the Muʿtazilites *needed* such a distinction to hold. One of the most crucial consisted of the project of proving the independence of moral values from revelation by means of empirical claims about the *moral* content of human motivation, as exemplified by the proof of the evilness of lying discussed in chapter 2. That they *intended* it to hold is manifest in several places throughout Baṣran writings. Thus Mānkdīm, discussing the return of a deposit, remarks that "the ground for this obligation is not the eternity of reward [which one will thereby deserve]; rather a deposit must be returned *because* it constitutes a return of the deposit, and the same applies to the repayment of debts."[8] The strongly deontological note sounded here takes programmatic form in the conditions set down by the Baṣrans for the realization of desert (to be discussed below), where positive deserts were made conditional on an agent's having chosen to do what was obligatory—or avoided what was evil—*because* it was obligatory or *because* it was evil.

ʿAbd al-Jabbār irenic solution to the problem was to suggest—no doubt aptly—that motives need not be exclusive and may be composite: one may choose an act for *both* its moral value *and* the value it holds for one's self-interest. "If [an obligatory act] is performed for the sake of the ground that makes it obligatory but also for another reason, this does not impugn the fact that it was performed because it is obligatory."[9] A further solution would seem to be implicit in the strategic difference in causality—in how one action *led* to another—that was reflected in the difference in scope—between benefits and harms accruing in this world, and ones accruing in the next. To return a deposit in order to win the heart of the depositor's daughter would not leave one deserving of reward for one's action, whereas to return it because one hopes to gain greater things in the hereafter might do so if this hope was founded on the knowledge, not that reward is an event that simply "happens to come after" the particular act, but that it *is entailed* by the act *as deserved*, as a consequence of the intrinsic value of the act. By contrast, in this world, this action merely *happens* to win the heart of the one wooed.

If the distinction between reasons for action was not easy to make on this level, this had a lot to do with the close relations into which the Baṣran Muʿtazilite account of values drew moral qualities and the moral consequences of desert—and it is to this crucial component of their account that I now turn. The relationship between deserts—designated as the *aḥkām* of an act (rulings, characteristics, or effects)—and moral qualities—usually designated as *ṣifāt*—was understood by the Baṣran Muʿtazilites as one between definiens and definiendum. The Muʿtazilite moral palette was made up of four main qualities: obligatory (*wājib*), recommended or supererogatory acts (*nadb* and *tafaḍḍul*), "plain good" or permissible (*mubāḥ*), and evil (*qabīḥ*).

The first three qualities were in fact grouped into an overarching category termed "good" (*ḥasan*), so that, in effect, acts divide broadly into good and evil. These three qualities were all conceived as sharing the rulings of "goodness" as their base, and as being differentiated by the desert-related characteristics or rulings (*aḥkām*) that supervened on that base. All of these acts have in common that the agent does not deserve blame for doing them. But the distinctive *aḥkām* of obligatory acts are that one deserves blame for omission and praise for commission; those of supererogatory acts are that one deserves praise for commission but no blame for omission; and those of plain good acts are that one neither deserves blame for omission nor praise for commission. Thus, unlike the categories of *wājib* and *nadb* or *tafaḍḍul*, which engender deserts, the last category, plain good or permissible, is constituted solely by the base quality of goodness, and its special ruling or *ḥukm* is that inasmuch as one does not deserve blame or praise for doing nor for not doing, valuewise it is a sterile act. Common examples that might illustrate this kind of act include eating—under ordinary circumstances (not, however, if one is in danger of death by starvation)—or breathing. By contrast, evil acts are those that make the agent deserve blame for commission and praise for omission.[10] Relying on the concise picture of the moral epistemology at work as this was set out in chapter 2, what should be rehearsed here is that the knowledge of the value of an act follows and is conditional on the knowledge of the act-description or ground (the *wajh*) of value. The desert-based value of an act is *generated* by these grounds.

The status of the deserts referred to as an act's *aḥkām* can only be appreciated fully by taking stock of what the Baṣrans have in mind when speaking of definitions. A couple of suggestive statements by ʿAbd al-Jabbār will set us on our way. Describing the *aḥkām* attaching to obligatory acts, he says:

> Good acts include acts which one knows their agent deserves praise for doing and does not deserve blame for not doing under any conditions, as well as acts that one deserves blame for not doing under certain conditions, and this [i.e., the latter] division is *described* as obligatory, in order to distinguish it from other types of act. The *meaning* of this *word* is thus that the act has a bearing on the desert of blame if it is not done, and so every act in which this obtains is *described* as being obligatory.

The implication of the highlighted words is made plainer in the statement that follows up the enumeration of the deserts attaching to evil acts, where ʿAbd al-Jabbār states, "Acts that are such [lit. that have such a state: *ḥāl*], we *refer* to as evil, and with this *expression* [*ʿibāra*] we refer to this *meaning* [*maʿnā*] that obtains in it."[11]

The implications of these passages are pulled together by two linchpin considerations. The first is that in talking of definitions, the Baṣrans here have in mind lexical definitions—that is, they consider themselves as giving an account of ordinary linguistic usage (*mā yūṣafu fī'l-lugha*, and more precisely the *primary* meaning they have in language: *ḥaqīqat al-alfāẓ*).[12] The second is that the Muʿtazilite view of language took as its capstone a belief in the epistemological priority of meaning over words: we have immediate intellectual access to meanings unmediated by and independent of language, and language is then instituted in order to set up correspondences between linguistic expressions and meanings, the latter forming criteria of application for the former. This is a view that is intimated most concisely in Ibn Mattawayh's formulation that "a thing does not become intelligible (*maʿqūl*) through its name but rather it must be intelligible first and then the name follows it . . . so if something has not been grasped by reason, it is impossible to apply a name to it."[13]

The stark implication seems to be this: the *real* moral facts—those of which we have immediate intellectual apprehension—are constituted by the rulings of desert, and the qualities obligatory or evil are simply—*merely*—words. We call obligatory that type of act to which we know that such-and-such deserts attach, and so on with other qualities; the deserts form the criteria of application for the word. And although some stray phrasing here or there may seem to suggest that when we know what the deserts of an act are, *then* we know its quality—suggesting, that is, that the former knowledge is a *ground* for the latter, and that the latter constitutes a separate cognitive achievement—it would rather seem to be the case that to know the deserts of an act *is* to know its quality, in the sense that the quality is merely a linguistic expression that describes the intellectually perceived reality given by the *aḥkām* of deserts.

It is in this light that we must understand ʿAbd al-Jabbār's distinction between the two types of disagreements that might be generated by the claim that a particular act (e.g., lying) deserves blame, and that this act is evil: a disagreement "over meaning" (*fi'l-maʿnā*), and one over words (*fi'l-ʿibāra*). The first would be to challenge the substantive or synthetic judgment—namely, that this act deserves blame—and is summarily dismissed as a denial of necessary knowledge. The other would be to deny that an act with such *aḥkām* is called evil. And ʿAbd al-Jabbār was not alone in the Islamic tradition in waving away this challenge as a mere quibble over words, nor in the confident assertion that the real "discussion is not over words but over meanings; once the latter have been arranged in the soul, let the speaker express them with whatever words he pleases."[14]

This interpretation of the relation between moral qualities and moral consequences reveals deserts as occupying the position of the prime moral data in the Baṣran Muʿtazilite scheme. In light of it, it is not difficult to see why the distinction between an act being good and one being good for—discussed above in connection with the reasons for action—should be an elusive one. One more piece must now be moved on this particular chessboard before I can continue, though it will be moved only partially in anticipation of the more prominent role it will play at a later point. It is a remark that comes to qualify the nature of the "primary moral data" that arises upon the knowledge that a given person has committed a value-bearing act, and that I have said consists of the deserts an act engenders. But this is not yet entirely precise. First of all, it must be noted that the term used to describe these data—

ḥukm—is equivocal between the meaning of "status, quality," which is predicated of an *act*, and "judgment, the *act* of ascribing a quality," which is predicated of the *judging subject*. It is through the latter evaluative response that one has access to the former. This mentioned, the preponderant form in which the primary moral data is given by the Baṣrans is in fact constituted *not* by the knowledge of the deserts an act entails (objective moral data predicated of the act) but rather of the value of an evaluative response that constitutes a deserved treatment: the primary moral datum—that which one knows when one knows a person has done evil, for example—is *not* that "the person deserves blame" but that "it is good to blame that person."

This rather densely put observation, the slant toward subjective judgments and evaluative responses that is encoded in it, and the substantive evaluation of blame that it involves ("good"), will have to wait until a later point to be unpacked. Here, having plotted the role that deserts play in the definitions of moral terms, an important qualification has to be introduced to this account, thereby bringing into view more clearly the workings of moral value in the Baṣran Muʿtazilite scheme. For to say that "evil" and "obligatory" are words whose criteria of application are the blame and praise a person deserves for omitting or committing them, is not to say that any person who performs an act instantiating a ground of value such as justice or injustice, gratitude or ingratitude, will *in fact deserve* praise and blame on performing the act, and it is certainly not to say that they will in fact *receive* these treatments.

There were two main sorts of conditions that the Baṣrans recognized as limiting the realization of desert and affecting the causal efficacy of act-descriptions, considered in the capacity of primary causes. The first set of conditions was one antecedent to or contemporaneous with the act, and concerned features that its agent had to possess. A principal feature was that one should not be acting under compulsion (*iljāʾ*), defined as an overwhelming strength of motives. A second feature registered a distinction between bad and good deserts. In order to incur bad deserts—blame or punishment—the condition that was stressed was that the agent should know, or be in a position to have known, the value of the act. In good deserts—praise and reward—this condition was implicit but given a stronger form in the demand that the agent should have performed the act *because* of its moral value—that one should have done what was obligatory *because* it was obligatory, or refrained from an evil act *because* it was evil.[15] As motives are given an intellectual definition ("the motive to perform an act is the state of the agent in terms of knowing, supposing, or believing"), these conditions reduce to entirely cognitive features.[16] The acts of minors, the insane, or those acting while asleep or inadvertently failed to generate desert because they did not satisfy these conditions.

A second set of conditions was rather subsequent to the act, and here there were two main factors to be taken into account: whether a person would defeat their past act by regretting it or repenting of it, or whether they would produce acts whose value would counter the value of the previous ones. I will say more about these issues later in this chapter, in "The Causal Efficacy of Moral Values," when setting out more fully the understanding of the causal operation of desert that is carried by these elements. But here I may note in anticipation an important difference between the two sets of conditions: the first were conditions determining whether a person would *acquire* deserts at all through a particular action; the latter, by contrast, were conditions for the *effectuation* of deserts that are thus presupposed as already existing. It is the *deserts* of one's past acts that are defeated by regretting them, just as it is the deserts of one's past good acts that are defeated by the outweighing deserts of one's subsequent evil acts, as this was envisaged by the dominant theory of how this happened—the so-called theory of *takfīr* and *iḥbāṭ*, or the "expiation" of punishment and "frustration" of reward—that held the field in later Baṣran Muʿtazilism.[17]

The dependence of deserts on this complex gamut of factors is reflected in the conditional formulas employed in the definitions of moral qualities, as in the one given by ʿAbd al-Jabbār for evil acts. An evil act is one that "if it occurs under a certain description [*wajh*], is such that one who performs it while knowing that it is occurring from him thus, and who is at liberty to choose it, deserves blame unless a preventive factor arises."[18] It is captured also in the frequent inclusion, in most definitions formulated by the Baṣrans, of the clause that the acts attracting a given value "have a bearing" (*madkhal*) or "effect" (*ta'thīr*) on the desert of blame. That is to say, morally valued acts are acts that are *such that* one may deserve blame or praise for them *if* certain conditions hold.[19] Thus—according to the view that prevailed among the later Baṣrans such as Abū ʿAbd Allāh al-Baṣrī, Abū Isḥāq b. ʿAyyāsh, and ʿAbd al-Jabbār and his disciples—even though acts performed without satisfying the relevant conditions might not give rise to desert of praise or blame, they would still generally be qualified as evil or obligatory, as befits the particular ground they instantiate.[20]

Before turning to our next set of questions, one last thing should be pointed out, which perhaps by now volunteers itself as a natural corollary of what has already been said: the Baṣrans do not seem to have attempted to define the concept of desert. This should be no surprise in light of the status they assigned to it as the ultimate and unanalyzable definiens of all moral language, and hence as the primary moral data available to human reason. The repository of necessary knowledge to which such data are allocated is one that as we have seen, delivers postulates whose hallmark is that they should admit no further explanation.

Justifying Reward and Punishment: The Values of Deserved Treatments

Many of the above elements will need to be drawn together at a later point in this chapter once a few more bolts are in place, enabling us to assemble an account of the causal nature of desert as the Baṣran Muʿtazilites understood it. Now, having limned the founding role that desert plays in both the account of moral motivation and the definitions of moral qualities, and having left several loose ends to be woven into the story later, we can move on to more substantive questions concerning the normative force of desert. The most important point to discuss here will be the difference between the force assigned by Muʿtazilites to good and ill deserts, which is expressed in the asymmetry between the moral values assigned to the treatments of blame and praise, and concomitantly, reward and punishment, and thus between the types of analysis sketched out in the opening groundwork of this chapter. In the Baṣran account of these justificatory forces, it will be the value assigned to bad deserts—to blame and punishment—that will have to worry us the most, and to which the next section will be devoted.

A few words of introduction, however, are needed for the goods and evils—the benefits and harms—that form these Muʿtazilites' currency of deserved treatments, and fill the slot of "what is good *for* a person to *receive*" that requites them for having succeeded or failed in "what is good *of* a person to *do*." We have already seen that blame (*dhamm*) and praise (*madḥ*) function as the building blocks of the definitions of moral qualities. Reward (*thawāb*) and punishment (*ʿiqāb*) were considered to constitute the counterparts of these responses, in the sense that the person who deserves blame is such as also deserves punishment. Blame is the moral prototype of punishment: it is the paradigm accessible to us in this world (*al-shāhid*) by which we may grasp the principles that apply to its counterpart in the other world (*al-ghāʾib*), and thus the justification for the one is the justification for the other.[21] Likewise with the paradigms of praise and reward. Blame is defined by Mānkdīm as "a type of utterance (*qawl*) that expresses the low status of a person." Conversely, praise is "a type of utterance that expresses the elevated status of a person." The status that forms the subject of these predications is clearly a moral one. Ibn Mattawayh adds a further touch that will prove significant for my purposes at a later point: this utterance is a predicative statement (*khabar*).[22] Blame and praise as conceived here are both acts; it is the utterance of the statement that is blame or praise, and not, for example, the internal judgment.

In discussing these responses, Mānkdīm is careful to draw a distinction between what has been called in our day "praise and dispraise" as against "praise and blame," the former signifying an evaluation of natural features of the agent, and the latter of moral ones. One may praise people for their beauty or physical build, and dispraise them for being ugly or lame, but this is not a moral type of evaluation associated with reward.[23] The distinction is significant because of the homonyms that convey aesthetic *and* moral standards. *Ḥusn* is a term that can refer to both beauty and goodness, and *qubḥ* can refer to both ugliness and evilness. Critics of Muʿtazilism had been inspired by this linguistic connection in arguing that the ascription of both qualities was alike in reflecting merely subjective preferences and tastes.

But now, we will gain a better insight into the Muʿtazilite—and indeed the Islamic—order of goods by going on to ask: Why would the description of someone's moral status be so injurious to them that it is included in the consequences deserved on account of evil? The cluster of terms the Muʿtazilites associate with blame cast a suggestive light: *to insult, to belittle,* and *to derogate* are among the treatments blame bears kinship to.[24] The harm involved, one may venture to suggest, is the harm involved in the loss of honor and good repute. The conception of honor as a good in its own right is plainly indicated by its presence in the trinity of valuables spoken of in various prophetic traditions and made central in legal thought: *ʿirḍ, māl,* and *badan;* honor, property, and physical integrity (literally, "body")—goods to which the rights and claims discussed in the previous chapter are reduced. One may point out in this connection that one of the major sins that make a person liable to the *ḥadd* penalties is the false accusation of adultery (*qadhf*), in which the good exposed to harm is a person's honor (though in fact the Baṣrans considered even lesser forms of injury on a person's honor as harms for which the victim would have to be compensated).[25]

Indeed the intimate connection between the concept of *ʿirḍ* and that of praise and blame is codified in the way Arabic lexicographers define the former. Among a variety of more or less related meanings, *ʿirḍ* is said to signify those aspects of the person that are affected by praise and blame (*mawḍiʿ al-madḥ wa'l-dhamm min al-insān*).[26] While *ʿirḍ* had formerly attached to the special cluster of values characterizing pre-Islamic society—whether these pertained to one's tribal group, one's family, or oneself as an individual (the latter including such qualities as courage, generosity, chastity of the wife, and faithfulness to one's word)—the concept survived the transition into the Islamic era, but with concomitant changes in the criteria constitutive of honor, whose content was now advised by religious morality. *Madḥ* and *dhamm* are formal evaluative concepts that await a substantive morality to give them content.[27]

The high value attached to honor is carried over to the definitions given by the Baṣran Muʿtazilites to the notions of reward and punishment. They are, respectively, defined as great benefits that are deserved and constitute a form of honoring or exalting (*taʿẓīm, ijlāl*) a person, and great harms that are deserved and constitute a form of derogation and visiting retribution on a person (*istikhfāf, nikāl*)—and like praise and blame, rewarding and punishing are acts. It is the honor involved in reward that distinguishes it qualitatively (because there is also a *quantitative* distinction) from the notion of compensation (*ʿiwaḍ*), which likewise consists of benefits. This difference derives from a difference in the grounds that give rise to each type of desert: it is one's action—one's effort, inevitably painful, to do what is good—that generates the desert of reward, whereas it is one's passion—one's suffering pain through another's action—that makes one deserve compensation.[28] As to the precise nature of the benefits and harms deserved, the Baṣrans held that the motivating function they had to fulfill entailed that they had to be familiar to us from the experience of our present life. In this vein, Ibn Mattawayh writes that "promises and threats"—revealed admonitions concerning the consequences of good or evil actions—"must involve familiar benefits and harms, for the purpose of promises and threats lies in the desire and the fear that they excite, and this they could not do save through the kinds of benefits and harms we already understand."[29]

These, then, were the goods and evils that were seen to flow as deserved consequences from the morally valued acts one performed. Good acts made a person deserve reward; evil acts made one deserve punishment. But now what—in the terms laid out in the prefatory groundwork—did the Baṣrans mean in saying that such things were deserved, and what justificatory force did they intend to charge this with? It is here that Baṣran and Baghdadi Muʿtazilites divided on one of the most important controversies over posthumous treatments. The controversy was derivative to a position that commanded unanimous Muʿtazilite assent—and this was that God would necessarily punish the grave sinner and the unbeliever, unless of course they were to repent of their deeds. But what kind of necessity was this? Here the road bifurcated, and each party took a different view of the value of deserved treatments, which involved in each case a different type of asymmetry.

The Baghdadis, according to the account given by Mānkdīm, held punishment to be obligatory on the grounds of its being deserved. By contrast, their view of reward was that it was obligatory only in the sense that an act of beneficence (*tafaḍḍul*) can be considered obligatory—which the Baṣrans believed to be no sense at all, being a *contradictio in adjecto*.[30] The Baghdadi stance on reward—that it was not obligatory due to desert—was the corollary of a belief that the grounds of our earthly obligations were of a "backward-looking" type. It is the abundance of past benefits that God has already bestowed on us that gives rise to obligations, and by performing our obligations we are merely paying back what we owe to God on account of the benefits received. The moral value of our acts is exhausted in discharging a debt and cannot give rise to deserts—that is, a fresh debt on the part of God.[31]

The Baṣrans inverted this asymmetry by considering the normative force of reward to be stronger than that of punishment. As concerns negative deserved treatments—blame and punishment—they claimed that such treatments were good (that is, "*merely*" good: *ḥasan*) to give, adopting a position of weak retributivism; positive treatments—praise and reward—were by contrast judged to be obligatory (*wājib*). God was thus obliged to reward but not punish.

The reasons for this differential strength were interesting, and can be tracked on several different levels. First, it seems to have been because of the Baṣrans' inability to discover a ground justifying the necessity of punishment with a force comparable to that which held in reward, where a certain commutative precept struck them as obvious. The performance of good acts was seen to necessarily involve hardship (*mashaqqa*), insofar as it demands "doing something that one's nature is averse to, and abstaining from something that one covets."[32] The central role of such hardship in the moral economy is enshrined in the very term *taklīf* ("the imposition of the Law" or simply "the Law") used to refer to the normative order human beings are subject to, which includes a reference to hardship (*kulfa*). It seemed obvious then that the hardship suffered in fulfilling the Law had to be given its equivalent (*muqābil*) in reward: harm must commute into benefit. "One deserves reward for [good acts] *insofar as* one does them in a way that involves one in exertion."[33]

The difficulty was that this logic does not seem to reverse with respect to evil actions, making it impossible to justify punishment as a commutation of benefits—benefits gained as a result of transgressing the Law—into the pains of punishment. One principal reason for this is that not all evil acts redound to the benefit of their agent, and some even involve them in considerable hardships, as ʿAbd al-Jabbār explains:

> The subject of obligations [*mukallaf*] may deserve punishment for acts of disobedience that involve neither pleasure nor any benefits—on the contrary, he may deserve it in the face of great hardship, if this was sustained through acts that it is evil of him to do, as is the case, for example, with the worship of idols or the actions of monks.

The point is made with equal clarity in the statement that "it is not a condition for deserving punishment because of evil acts that the act be beneficial."[34] The asymmetry between the justification of reward and that of punishment is reflected in the great frequency of statements about reward in terms of equivalence or correspondence (*muqābala*), and the shortage of analogues about punishment.

Here one might have proposed a different commutative principle, according to which harm suffered by a person as a result of another's evil action is converted into harm suffered by the agent of the action in the hereafter. But even where evil acts inflict harm on a certain recipient (and as we will see in a moment, not all evil acts are acts of harming), elements involved in another sector of the Baṣran scheme militated against such a commutation across persons. This was the theory that concerned the compensation (*ʿiwaḍ*) that had to be provided in the hereafter to a person who had suffered harm without due cause—and this included the effects of injustice perpetrated by human beings as well as the various illnesses and afflictions that God metes out to human beings during their lives. Victims of such harm had to be compensated by supplying them with a quantity of pleasure that would be the equivalent of the pain they had suffered. Now who was the subject of the obligation to compensate the victim? Naturally, this had to be the wrongdoer. Yet in what sense, and by what means, could the wrongdoer do so in the hereafter? The answer, in a nutshell, consisted of an operation that one cannot find a better word to describe than as a grandiose transfer of funds, in which God plays a role that one cannot find a better word to describe than, following Heemskerk, that of a master "bookkeeper" responsible for settling accounts and executing transfers.[35]

For our purposes, what is important about these funds is that the target account and the account of origin had to be of the same *moral kind* and the same *currency*. One could only transfer from an account of compensation to another (and not from an account of reward, supposing that it existed), and as a corollary of this, one could only employ a currency of benefits to pay debts demanded in a currency of benefits. Thus, even though the very demand for compensation rested on the possibility of converting harms (those unjustly suffered) to benefits (those that had to be given in compensation), the harm one had inflicted was not in turn converted into an experience of pain suffered in punishment but to the loss of pleasure owed to oneself as compensation.

We may well note the obvious perplexity that this account raises: What if the wrongdoer is short of funds and can't make the payment of pleasure that is morally required? What if there is not sufficient compensation due to be received by the wrongdoer? It took the Muʿtazilite genius for bookkeeping to devise as a possible expedient a free divine gift of sufficient funds to the wrongdoer that would enable them to make the payment. This was the solution proposed by certain Muʿtazilite masters. ʿAbd al-Jabbār, for his part, rejected this solution as a nonsensical conflation of the concepts of free gift (*tafaḍḍul*) and obligation (for the obligation to compensate entailed that God would be *obliged* to deliver the means to provide it), and instead affirmed his faith that the wrongdoer would in fact have the required funds in their possession, as God in His justice would not permit a person to commit injustice save with the knowledge that the latter had the means to make recompense for it.[36] What means of "permitting" or "forbidding" ʿAbd al-Jabbār had in mind we cannot speculate on here. Nor can we pause too long to wonder what afflictions this proposal would sanction as a means of raising the necessary funds, or indeed what burden it placed on the denial of the existence of happy villains in whom happiness and vice are combined. But the following remark by ʿAbd al-Jabbār gives pause enough: "It is a well-known fact about those who commit injustices, that God afflicts their hearts with sorrow, grief, disquiet, and fear, such as He does not cast on the heart of the upright believer."[37] The denial of such a possibility is not only made explicit but coupled with a claim that one has every right to find startling: that it is distress deriving from a person's vice and wrongdoing that gives rise to the obligation to compensate them.

In any event, what is certainly made clear is that compensation and punishment were judged by these Muʿtazilites as two separate treatments that were justified by entirely different processes, thereby precluding the reversal of the commutative principle that justified reward and its use for the justification of punishment.[38] Therefore, if someone were to defraud me of my life savings, the harm I have suffered would be converted into benefits that the perpetrator must provide to me by having them subtracted from compensatory benefits that they may have come to deserve because a fellow human being likewise made them suffer unjustly, or because God afflicted them with illnesses and pains. This being so, only the transgression of the moral principle—here, the prohibition of theft—would remain as grounds for punishment, and these grounds do not afford a logic comparable in cogency to that of reward.

One of the main arguments brought out by the Baṣran Muʿtazilites in justification of punishment gave plain evidence of such a lack of cogency. Briefly put, the contention was that were it not the case that punishment would be deserved on account of evil acts, this would be tantamount to a temptation or inveiglement (*ighrāʾ*) to evildoing, and far be it from God to tempt His creatures to evil. In Ibn Mattawayh's words, "If the performance of evil acts did not give rise to deserved punishment that would deter one from doing them, God—May He be exalted—having created the . . . subjects of the Law with a desire for evil, would be as one tempting them to perform them."[39]

But if the main concern was with motivation, the only necessity that one could deduce from this argument, as the later Ashʿarite al-Jurjānī (d. 1413) for one was quick to notice, was that human beings should *believe* in the occurrence of punishment.[40] Once motives are past being affected—once the utilitarian value of deterrence has lapsed—what reason remained for the actual event of punishment to take place?

What reason indeed? The difficulty of accounting for the necessity of this event was stepped up by the analysis to which both deserved treatments—that of reward and punishment—were subjected and through which they were translated to the (by now familiar) language of *ḥuqūq*. The normative force that was assigned to each of the two treatments derived from the differential analysis they received, for they were contrasted as two different kinds of private claims: the right to reward constituted the *private claim of human beings* (*ḥaqq liʾl-ʿibād*); the right to punish was a *private claim of God's* (*ḥaqq Allāh ʿalaʾl-khuṣūṣ*). This analysis in fact contains two distinct elements that it is important to distinguish and discuss as separate issues: one concerns the *subject* to whom each claim is identified as attaching; the other concerns the *normative force* that redounds to each deserved treatment by construing them as claims belonging to particular subjects.

So let us start with the first, and immediately grant that the ascription of reward to the person who has performed good deeds as their right seems intuitively reasonable (recall here that the question still concerns merely the *identity* of the claimant and not the *force* of the claim). But what about the analysis of ill desert into a divine claim? In a world conceived in terms of owners of rights—that is to say, a world in which particular persons stand in exclusive relations to particular goods, in which goods are *assigned*—why should it be God that stands in a special relationship to the breach of moral principles? The question I am resuming here is the one wedged open in

"Rights, Claims, and Desert" in the previous chapter, where I remarked that the formulation of desert created the space for the mention of an agent answerable for things deserved. The question is rendered sharper by what we saw above: harms suffered by human beings through wrongdoing are expunged through transactions between human beings, and compensation consists of the settlement of interhuman *ḥuqūq* in which God has no "personal" stake as it were save His obligation to carry out justice on behalf of human beings. He is merely the executive power, as it were, of a judicial order realized in terms of *ḥuqūq*. Thus, the only claim that is left over once these claims—which essentially revolve around benefits and harms—have been liquidated is merely the bare "deontological" fact that a moral principle was violated, shorn of any implications or consequences to any being (God Himself is essentially insusceptible to being affected by the consequences of anything, to being benefited or harmed). So why should *God* in particular be "concerned" with these bare violations? The answer to this perhaps startling-sounding question is implicit in its initial formulation: it is the very fact that the normative world is reduced to the currency of *ḥuqūq* that makes it necessary to carve up this world in terms of relationships to particular persons. For as we have already gleaned, the reduction of norms to *ḥuqūq* involves codifying the necessity of a person to whom these will be exclusively assigned. The breach of moral principles must be *somebody's* right; it must be someone's *ikhtiṣāṣ*. It *cannot* belong to no one. Perhaps the only question that could have led outside the system would have been to ask, Why is it a *ḥaqq* at all?

Among the arguments that Ibn Mattawayh gives for the claim that it is God who must punish, the one that carries the brunt of the defense is essentially a method of elimination that reflects this fundamental assumption about the essential relatedness or belongingness of *ḥuqūq*. "Why couldn't human beings be those responsible for meting out deserved punishment?" Ibn Mattawayh queries. The answer is as follows: "Were a human being to deserve punishment from another human being, there would be nothing to choose between its being deserved from any one [any *particular*] person as against any other. For the reason for which punishment is deserved for an act . . . is its evilness and nothing else."[41] That is to say, it is a matter of an exclusive disjunction: either one could deserve punishment from God or human beings; that the claim has no assignment was inconceivable.

One clarification needs to be added here to impart complete transparency to Ibn Mattawayh's reasoning. We saw above that blame is considered to be the counterpart of punishment; but this statement was not quite a complete account. For the Baṣran Muʿtazilites distinguished between two different types of blame (and similarly of praise), which corresponded to an act under the different descriptions it might satisfy: the description as evil (*qabīḥ*), and the description as an offense (*isāʾa*). The latter was a major yet nonetheless not exhaustive subcategory of the former: all offenses are evil, but not all evil acts are offenses. The distinction between the two rested on the criterion of transitivity or other-regardingness (*taʿaddī*); offenses—as revealed by the verb from which the word derives (*asāʾa*)—are "transitive" acts, meaning that they affect others.[42] Under the category of *isāʾāt* would fall the breaches of rights and claims that we are already familiar with, such as not returning a deposit, usurping someone's property, harming a person physically, not paying back debts, and so on.[43] If an evil act does not affect another person, it is just evil, not an offense. The category of acts that are intransitively evil is filled mainly by internal acts: false beliefs—including unbelief in God—or willing evil. Lying would probably be included, though this is not explicitly mentioned; the category of evil acts that are not offenses is not a populous one.[44]

The crucial fact about offenses is that they give rise to a special claim of the offended party to blaming the agent of the deed: the offended party, says ʿAbd al-Jabbār, *ikhtaṣṣa bi-ḥaqq lā yusāwīhi ghayruhu fīhi*.[45] This right to special blame (*dhamm makhṣūṣ*) is *additional* to the blame deserved for the act under its description as evil, and the two types of right or claim are differentiated by the different moral responses they demand for their elimination (to be discussed in greater detail in "The Right to Blame, the Fact of Blame"). As to the latter blame, it is said that *all* rational beings have a right to give it: everyone has the right to blame a person under the description of their act as evil.[46] It is the blame for the act qua evil that is more precisely considered as the counterpart of punishment. But now the right to special blame—for the act qua offense—is the exclusive property of the offended. To whom, then, belongs the right to blame for the act qua evil, and thus the right to punish? To no human being in particular, and thus by method of elimination to God. Hence the logic of Ibn Mattawayh's argument. If it is God who possesses the *ḥaqq* to punish for the breach of moral principles, this is primarily because the need to punish is parsed as a *ḥaqq*, and derivatively because the *ḥaqq* could belong to none other.

In settling the identity of the terms of the *ḥaqq* relations, the case of reward once again presented an easier target than that of punishment. For on the one hand, as was granted above, the position that reward is a claim of the person who performed good deeds seems intuitive, as far as the direction of *ḥaqq lahu* is concerned. Yet the specification of God as the one answerable for making the claim good in the direction of *ḥaqq ʿalayhi* is a separate move. Nonetheless, a far more compelling case could here be made to support it. For as we have seen, the ground—a cogent one—given for the desert of reward stemmed from a commutation of the hardship suffered in obeying the Law. This was a ground that contained two elements: one was that the Law—the set of moral obligations—had to be obeyed; the other was that it was difficult to do so; and between the two there was no intrinsic connection. Now God could not be held responsible for the fact that an act was obligatory and another evil, for these values were, as the Muʿtazilites emphatically maintained, features of acts that neither God nor any other subject determined by their choices or preferences. Yet He *could* be held responsible for the fact that He had created the beings made subject to this Law in such a way that moral choices do not come effortlessly. "It is God—may He be exalted—who made these [good] acts strenuous for us, revealing to us the obligation that attaches to them, whether by way of performing or abstaining, and making our nature averse to performing them or abstaining from them." Ibn Mattawayh continues: "If God—may He be exalted—was capable of revealing to us what was obligatory and making us desire it so that no hardship be suffered in performing it, but instead made us averse to it, there must needs be some sort of benefit that corresponds to it as its equivalent [*muqābil*]."[47]

The above remarks, which pertain to the question about *who* should punish and reward, are intrinsically related to questions about *whether* and *why* one should do so, which concern the differential normative force ascribed to each type of deserved treatment on account of their reduction into the currency of *ḥuqūq*. As concerns the human right to reward, the above gives a sufficient indication of the sources of its normative force. (And this of course is not to say that its force was beyond question: Ashʿarites rejected in stentorian tones the idea that "anyone might have a claim over God through his works" or "because of any antecedent ground," and not unlike the Baghdadis, spoke of reward as an initiated act of beneficence.)[48]

But what about the divine claim to punishment? It may be recalled from the previous chapter that one of the principal properties of God's rights or claims—such as the *ḥadd* penalties administered for the major sins of theft, adultery, and so on—is that they cannot be repealed or annulled by human beings, whereas one may waive one's own rights. Yet the point is even broader: for every claim, the holder of the claim has the license and liberty to waive it. This was a principle familiar from the legal domain, and it was its logic that buttressed the position that reward was a matter of *obligation*: for God could not rightly deny human beings the reward they deserve—not being the right holder, He could not choose to annul the right. It is the converse that accounts for the position that punishment is merely good and not obligatory. For since punishment is conceived as a divine right or claim, it follows that this claim could also be dropped by God should He so choose: "He can [choose to] waive it or He can exact it" (*lahu an yusqiṭahu kamā anna lahu an yastawfiyahu*).[49]

The Baṣran Muʿtazilites followed this logic with great scrupulosity, and readily acknowledged that it was permissible that punishment be foregone, even admitting that we know by reason that it is good to forgive and pardon wrongdoing—a choice for which revelation itself gave ample encouragement (see, for example, the Qurʾānic exhortations to forgiveness in 3:134, 2:237, and 64:14). Thus Mānkdīm: "It is our belief that it is good [*yaḥsunu*] for God to pardon."[50] What, then, of the necessity of punishment on which I have already said that all Muʿtazilites concurred? The force of this necessity, it transpires, derives from a moral ground entirely unrelated to considerations of desert—and that, in the view of the Baṣrans, is the word God sent forth in His revealed message, by which He committed Himself to the punishment of wrongdoers (unbelievers and grave sinners). And none of God's subsequent actions could be such as to render His word a lie. Therefore it was the prohibition against lying, and *not* the force of negative deserts, that emerges in the Baṣran Muʿtazilite scheme as by far the stronger deontological principle.[51] The difference between these two grounds was made by marking a distinction between two types of necessity. The *moral* necessity represented by the notion of *wujūb* was withheld from the act of punishment (it could not properly be said to be *obligatory*), and it was instead described as an act that "could not but happen" (*lā budda min wuqūʿihi*). But one may see why perhaps it did not require an excessively bad faith on the part of later Ashʿarites such as al-Jurjānī to confuse the two types of necessity and still make their opponents answerable to the former.[52]

The foregoing remarks serve to reinforce the account developed in the last chapter arguing the centrality of the language of *ḥuqūq* in the moral fabric of the Baṣran Muʿtazilite scheme. It is one of the more interesting aspects of this scheme that by ascribing the response to moral violations to God as a private claim, it reveals a readiness on the part of the Muʿtazilites to attenuate the austere objectivist view of values that they are customarily associated with. For to countenance the waiving of deserved punishment—and thus the annulment of what was the scheme's fundamental moral currency: desert—implied that whatever the strongly nomological account given of moral ontology, moral values were not granted absolute independence or promoted to the status of natural laws—or at least no more than natural laws were granted such independence in the Muʿtazilite atomistic metaphysics—but were rather circumscribed by the will of moral subjects who could decide what force to give to their own rights. This revealed a tendency toward mitigating the bare deontological component of the system—a component that was after all so ill at ease in the larger moral economy with which both Muʿtazilite theology and more broadly Islamic thought identified, and in which considerations of welfare—*maqāṣid* and *maṣāliḥ*—formed the rallying concern. The prohibition against lying itself, with which the pardon of negative deserts collided, was in fact one that while postulated as a deontological demand, was a deontology in the service of the larger welfarist project that the imposition of the Law represented. For without this deontological principle, the Baṣrans insisted, reliable communication between God and human beings, and hence the communication of salvific precepts indispensable to the fulfillment of the Law, would be impossible.[53] Only the terrible deontological demand to punish thus remained outside the pale of the concern with welfare and the pursuit of otherworldly good, and it was the price that was considered necessary to pay in exchange for the possibility of setting up this salvific pale in the first place and extending its offer for welfare.

Justifying Punishment: The Paradoxical Relations of Desert and Goodness

There will be several opportunities in what follows to return to the above points, and in particular to the question concerning the ontological status of moral values and deserts that the Baṣran Muʿtazilites envisaged (A "nomological" one? If so, what species of law, and with what kind of efficacy?) But now my task is a different one, though one that will be furnishing several of the additional provisions that will be needed for discussing the former question. From this point onward, the focus will be trained most intently on the question of punishment and the resources deployed for its justification, and in this section the resources I'll be considering are those involved in the qualification given to the act of punishment as "good" (*ḥasan*). This qualification, as we will see, comes with an entourage of paradoxes and challenges; and it is the Baṣran analysis of the concept of goodness that forms the chief breeding ground for these paradoxes.

As we saw in the beginning of this chapter, goodness forms the base of three different qualities: obligatory (*wājib*), supererogatory or recommended (*nadb* and *tafaḍḍul*), and plain good or permissible (*mubāḥ* or simply *ḥasan*). All of these share the quality of being good as their base, which corresponds to the desert-related ruling or characteristic (*ḥukm*) that no blame is deserved for commission, and are then differentiated by their particular rulings (e.g., obligatory acts attract the desert of blame for omission, praise for commission, and so on). The third quality *only* exemplifies the base ruling. And in describing punishment as good, it is this quality that the Baṣrans have in mind: punishment is plain good or permissible.

This category of moral value seems to have puzzled the Jubbāʾīs, father and son, as it did the members of the school that succeeded them, continuing to be debated for over two centuries after them. While the *ḥukm* of plain good acts (or good acts, as I shall henceforth refer to them to avoid cumbersomeness) was not a question of dispute—their sterility in terms of desert was affirmed by all—what caused perplexity was the nature of the descriptions or grounds (the *wujūh*) that made an act good. For on the one hand, it was perceived that the grounds of goodness did not have the independence and finality of other moral qualities. Whereas grounds such as lying or ingratitude were sufficient for the moral qualification of an act as evil, and grounds such as thanking the benefactor sufficient to qualify an act as obligatory, the grounds of goodness were not, and the quality of goodness could be defeated if the grounds of other moral qualities were present in the act. If an act was simultaneously an act of truth telling (*ṣidq*)—normally valued at *ḥusn*—but also led to harm, the moral value of good carried by the first description was defeated by the value of evil carried by the latter, and the act became evil. Yet on the other hand, and for a variety of reasons, Abū ʿAlī and Abū Hāshim were uncomfortable with the idea of defining goodness as, or by principal reference to, a kind of privation—the privation of grounds of evil.

Their approach to the problem was to say this: there are grounds that make an act good in the same way that there are grounds that make it evil, obligatory, or supererogatory—these grounds, too, *necessarily entail* (*taqtaḍī*) the moral qualification; however, they differ from the latter in that if a ground of goodness and one of evil are simultaneously instantiated by an act, the ground of evil preponderates and the *ḥukm* of the act is as evil. But even though the efficacy of the grounds of goodness is in a sense conditional on the negation of evil grounds, this negation itself cannot be said to be a determinant of the moral value. The grounds of goodness they named included: that the act redounds to one's own or another's benefit, or averts harm; that it is deserved; that it is an instance of truth telling; and that it constitutes the remission of a right/claim (*ḥaqq*). Note that the category thus filled includes *both* the exaction of a claim (which is what giving someone their deserts constitutes) *and* its remission, thus recalling what was said above concerning the liberty of the holder of a claim to waive or exact it as he chooses, which was transferred to the divine claim of punishment.[54]

This approach was judged to be problematic by most of their successors, and the source of the problem was the threat it posed to the consistency of the theory enunciated concerning the nature of moral grounds and the qualities they entailed. The *wujūh* or grounds of moral qualities were meant to operate in the manner of necessitating causes:

> That which necessarily entails [*yaqtaḍī*] the evilness of an evil act—such as the fact that a statement is a lie or a pain is unjust—functions in the manner of necessitating causes [*yajrī . . . majrā al-ʿilal al-mūjiba*] in respect of the fact that it entails this [effect or qualification]. Just as it is impossible that the cause be present without necessitating its effect, thus it is impossible that the ground of evil be present without necessitating [*yūjibu*] that the act be evil.[55]

In the view of these Muʿtazilites, it was inconsistent with the nature of these causes that their action should be made conditional on the presence or absence of other factors or causes. Since the grounds proposed for goodness did not unconditionally work their effect—that of bestowing the quality of goodness—and their operation was dependent on the privation of evil ones, there could be no such thing as *wujūh al-ḥusn*, grounds of goodness. Either *wujūh* as we know them or none at all.

The alternative proposed seems to have been first articulated by Abū ʿAbd Allāh al-Baṣrī (d. 979) and achieved perhaps its clearest expression at the hands of Ibn Mattawayh. Rejecting the claim that there were grounds of goodness, it was argued that the quality of goodness is established once two conditions have been met: the act serves some kind of end (*gharaḍ*), and the grounds of evil are absent. The distinction lay in the fact that the "ends" are not themselves grounds of goodness but only one of the two conditions—and one could not, properly speaking, consider these conditions as *wujūh*, whether the individual conjuncts or their conjunction. These ends would include all the things listed by the Jubbā'īs as distinct grounds of goodness, and they would be required to lend the act a quality over and above that of mere existence—there had to be something to be said for the value of these acts apart from the negative fact that they are not evil. Thus, against the Jubbā'īs, it was said that it makes no sense to raise such a question as, "If a ground of goodness coexists with a ground of evil in the act, what is the act's quality?" for a ground is not affirmed good independently. The older masters' discomfort notwithstanding, subsequent generations of Baṣrans essentially adopted a definition of goodness that made the privation of grounds of evilness the criterion, thereby making this the only moral category that was not filled by conclusive *wujūh*.[56]

'Abd al-Jabbār seems to have wavered between the option of postulating grounds of goodness whose conferral of moral value would be conditional on the privation of evil ones, and that of holding the conjunction of the two elements mentioned above as the joint determinants of value. Thus we find him saying that an act "is rendered good through the presence of a rational [i.e., rationally known] ground, once the grounds of evil have been negated" (Jubbā'īs' conception), and yet we also hear (following the revised conception) that

> it is not possible that grounds of goodness and grounds of evil be combined [in a single act], for we have shown that goodness does not have a ground to which the quality [or ruling: *ḥukm*] of the act attaches—and in this respect it is unlike evil, which indeed has a ground to which the quality of evil attaches.

Yet it is the latter alternative for which he eventually appears to have settled.[57]

The Mu'tazilites who subscribed to this view of *ḥusn* did not purge the old terminology from their writings, and continued to use the term *wujūh* when referring to the first of the two elements required for goodness. In most cases, the term must be understood as bearing a nontechnical sense (a sense in which it does not designate a necessitating cause).[58] In some cases, as in that of 'Abd al-Jabbār, it reflects some ambivalence about the conception of goodness. But this may also be a reflection of the Mu'tazilites' awareness of certain of the problems concomitant with the denial of *wujūh*—problems that have a direct bearing on their conception of desert.

A first port of call in pursuing these problems involves briefly considering a twofold ambiguity that enters the Baṣrans' qualification of the divine act of punishment. Taking my cue from our theologians, I may describe it as one that concerns the level of words and another that concerns the level of meanings. As concerns words: while in referring to plain good acts above, both the terms *mubāḥ* and *ḥasan* were used, a distinction was in fact drawn by the Baṣran Mu'tazilites between the two terms, which was then used to argue for the Baṣrans' resistance to applying the former to divine acts. The distinction was not always perspicuous, but the term *mubāḥ* was said to carry the implication that one had been *informed* about the value of the act by another. And it was also sometimes added—as by Ibn Mattawayh—that the term was confined to acts that are performed by their agents for their own benefit. These semantic charges suggested that the category of *ḥasan* was wider than that of *mubāḥ,* though the two would thereby appear to remain identical with respect to their basic desert-related entailments. What is important is that both charges of the term *mubāḥ* obviated its application to God; thus the act of punishment, predicated of God, could be called *ḥasan* but not *mubāḥ*.[59] The same would hold true of blame, though the Baṣrans hardly predicate the latter of God, since in the otherworldly realm where deserts are exacted, it is their counterparts of reward and punishment that are given.

A more important ambiguity concerned whether God's act of punishing *was* indeed *fī ḥukm al-mubāḥ*—that is, whether not only can the term "*mubāḥ*" not be predicated of divine punishment for the reasons given above but whether even its desert characteristics are those of the category of good acts, *whichever* particular term one might use to refer to them. While the point seemed to command general consensus, the trouble arose from the definition of good acts as ones in which it is all the same whether one does or does not do them in terms of the desert this would engender (*fiʿluhu lahu wa-an lā yafʿalahu sawāʾ fī annahu lā yastaḥiqqu dhamman wa-lā madḥan*).[60] But this, quite clearly, was not the case with punishment: God *would* deserve praise *if* He did not exact it, for that would be an act of beneficence, so it is *not* indifferent whether He does or does not perform it. And this thought led ʿAbd al-Jabbār to deny that punishment falls in this category, at the risk of both inconsistency and creating a lacuna in the structure of Muʿtazilite categories of value.[61] A deft solution to the problem was provided by Ibn Mattawayh, who rejected ʿAbd al-Jabbār's formula and chiseled the definition to greater precision, specifying that the value is predicated of the *actual* act (*innamā yurāʿā hādhā ʿinda al-wuqūʿ*), thus deliberately excluding the consideration of counterfactual possibilities.[62] Through such a strategy, then, the act of divine punishment could be formally subsumed into the *aḥkām* of good acts.

But whether we are speaking of the punishment undertaken by God or the blame practiced by human beings—both of them acts experienced as harm, though to radically different degrees—the qualification is the same: they are both good. The problematic nature of this evaluation can begin to emerge by pointing out that it is to the definition of goodness as set out above that one must refer when considering the evaluation. On the definition given, it is simply inadmissible to ask the question, "What makes blame good?" or on a broader level that brings out the reason why such a question needs to be asked in the first place, "What makes the infliction of suffering good?" and answer, "That it is deserved." And that is because the latter is not a ground of goodness. For the distinction between two conceptions of *wujūh* mentioned above, that which recognizes *wujūh* operating conditionally, and that which does not, makes all the difference in one's ability to make such statements. To put it in a way that may be dry but nonetheless revealing: in the first conception, one would be able to say, "(An act is good if it is deserved) unless it has grounds of evil." In the second conception, one would have to say, "An act is good (if it is deserved and does not have grounds of evil)." The difference in scope makes all the difference in our ability to say that desert itself constitutes a moral justification of the act. The theoretical impediments erected by the later Baṣran Muʿtazilites to such talk become acute when they attempt to discuss the question of pain and the reasons that may make it good. Here the theory comes under its greatest strain and the conception of goodness finds itself exposed to its greatest threat of inconsistency. For clearly it is important to be able to say "pain may be good because it is deserved" and give desert as a reason. And this indeed the Baṣran Muʿtazilites proceed to do—their discussion of pain would be stultified were one to delete the statements asserting that pain may be good *because* of desert (*li-ajl al-istiḥqāq*).[63] On their own terms, however, it is far from clear that they are justified in doing so.

Close on the heels of this problem follows another, which is a feature not so much problematic as greatly counterintuitive. On the conceptual terms offered by these Muʿtazilites, the goodness of an act of blame depends on the privation of any grounds of evilness. That is, blaming the agent is good only if it has no other grounds making it evil. This conceptualization seems strangely surprising; for it will strike us as a singular way of thinking about what an agent deserves, to ask ourselves what blaming them would *not* be and thus to arrive at its goodness by a method of elimination. The paradoxical nature of this exercise is evoked when one of those ubiquitous interlocutors entrusted with the task of objecting in works of *kalām* asks a question that directly comes to bear on this. In your view, the objector reminds the writer, "there is no *wajh* on account of which an act is good," for goodness consists in privation; yet here, in the goodness of blame, we have a *wajh*.[64] How so?

The pull toward speaking of deserts as reasons is sharply felt once again, and while ʿAbd al-Jabbār reiterates the familiar position on the grounds of goodness, he yields to the pull to the extent of suggesting that desert may be "as a *wajh*" or "have the status of a *wajh*" (*fī ḥukm al-wajh*). But more important for the present purpose is the part of the response that concerns the necessity of establishing that all grounds of evil are absent before the act of blame is shown to be good. For this means that one must ensure that blaming the wrongdoer "is not lying, nor injustice, nor vain action, nor any of the other grounds that make an act evil," which would include ingratitude, commanding someone to do what exceeds their capacity or forbidding someone to do what is good, failing to return a deposit, usurping a person's property, and so on.[65] Once we have ensured this, "we come to know that this blame is good."

Yet what a comparison class—what a field of possibility we must scan, and what conceptual leaps we are invited to make, in inquiring whether blaming the wrongdoer might be an act of ingratitude or a withholding of a debt. This field of possibility, cluttered with all manner of incommensurable items, might seem capable of being homogenized to a certain extent through the currency of *ḥuqūq* into which many of these separate evils could be translated (ingratitude or the failure to return deposits, for example, could be seen as violations of *ḥuqūq*, and thus, further homogenizing, as components of the single category of injustice). But the homogenizing services of this currency should not be overestimated, as the relations in which individual grounds of value stand to each other does not undermine the epistemological and ontological separateness of each. In addition, and as we have seen, evil acts are not exhausted by violations of *ḥuqūq* affecting other human beings (it is on this difference that the distinction between evil acts and offenses rested).

It is not that eventually such a comparison between incommensurable grounds does not lead somewhere. The comparison makes sense indeed if the evil grounds that must be negated are restricted to the category of injustice. An act—specifically one that involves the infliction of pain—is characterized as unjust when either of two things hold: it is undeserved, or it neither leads to greater benefit nor averts greater harm. Provided, in addition, that we could exclude the latter component from consideration as irrelevant to the assessment of blame or punishment—its utilitarian basis making it an inappropriate ground to consider in matters of desert—it seems that we would arrive at the following reasonable position: one should make sure that the act of blame is not undeserved. And indeed injustice, side by side with vain action, form the principal grounds of evil discussed by the Muʿtazilites in connection with the justification of pain, as grounds whose absence one must ensure. While such a restricted domain of evil grounds would make the whole conception accord far better with intuition—barring, perhaps, the tautology that it would reduce to: "an act is good if it is deserved unless it is undeserved"—there is nothing to warrant such a restriction. And on the terms of the conception of goodness canvased by these Baṣrans, the incommensurable comparison class must still remain the frame of reference for any attempts to assess the act of blame administered to the wrongdoer, which will be conducted as an inquiry into what that act is *not* and will have the bearings of a process of elimination.

Yet the final and perhaps prickliest difficulty with this conception that must now be noted is precisely the question of warrant for the restriction I have just touched on. For supposing the warrant for a *first* restriction of domain was granted, and the grounds of evil admitted as relevant in identifying the act as good were confined to injustice, there would then be a further warrant to be granted. This would be a warrant for restricting the aspects weighed against each other *within* the category of injustice, and that one must take into account in identifying an act as an instance of it. For as we have seen, injustice has two possible internal grounds: utilitarian ones, which concern calculations of benefits and harms; and ones relating to desert.

And I said that the evaluative reasoning at work would seem natural if the aspect of injustice considered in determining whether punishment or blame are unjust was that of desert, to the exclusion of the utilitarian component. Natural, yes—but justified? Yet what is there to justify making this decision of relevance? Is one justified, on Muʿtazilite terms, in selecting the aspect that concerns deserts as the only one relevant to the assessment of punishment or blame, to the exclusion of the aspect that refers to utilitarian considerations? Which is to say, how does one decide that the fact that punishment or blame lead to harm that is not offset by any benefit whatsoever—they are final pains, with nothing further to redeem them—does not matter in assessing the value of a pain-inflicting act?

This is the view assumed by the Baṣran Muʿtazilites, which is expressed in the statement that "it is good for us to blame one who offends against us, or who commits great evils, *even if* this blame and desert aggrieves him and harms him and weighs heavily on him"—that is, despite the harm he undergoes, which is itself an aspect giving reason for judging the act unjust.[66] But it would not seem that there is anything in the resources of the theory that authorizes the Baṣrans to judge that desert automatically trumps utilitarian considerations and give the former greater weight than the latter, thereby saying, "The question whether this pain is harmful must not be addressed when it is deserved." For deserved treatments are affirmed to be good only *after* other grounds of evil have been negated—these grounds including injustice, which is affirmed to be present when the pain inflicted is *either* undeserved *or* harm that entails no greater benefit nor averts harm. As ʿAbd al-Jabbār puts it, an act is not unjust "if it is known of [an act] that it is deserved *or* that it leads to benefit or the repulsion of harm."[67] Schematically put, this gives us the following: it is good to give someone pain (if it is deserved and is not unjust)—that is, (if it is deserved and [is deserved *or* does not cause harm without any offsetting benefit]). But what is the meaning of this inscrutable "or" that the Baṣran Muʿtazilites slip into the ground of injustice? Is it an "*or*" or an "*and*"? And can it be stipulated as one or the other without argument? How does one judge the weight of the two grounds when *one* of them is present and the other is absent in the same act—that is, when it is deserved *yet* leads to unmitigated harm, when it exhibits one just-making and one unjust-making ground at the same time? The difference in the truth functor—whether the statement is a disjunction or a conjunction—holds the key to one the prickliest questions in the justification of punishment. Hence, when ʿAbd al-Jabbār remarks that an act's being injustice "is contingent on the absence of all of these grounds [namely, further benefit; averting of harm; being deserved], so when one of them has been affirmed to be present, the act will not fall into the category of injustice," the problem posed by the case where the grounds conflict is not addressed.[68]

There are other facets of this conception of desert that might have been mentioned, but these considerations will suffice to indicate the troublesome and counterintuitive implications of qualifying negative deserts in terms of their goodness. As we are fresh from a discussion of the relation between deserts and injustice, this seems the best place to break a silence that might have come to seem perplexing: Why has the concept of *justice* been so conspicuously absent from the above discussion? Why are deserved treatments characterized solely in terms of their goodness—a characterization that after all does not seem particularly well equipped to bear the burden placed on it? The Muʿtazilites certainly have things to say about the concept of justice (*ʿadl*), and one would not expect otherwise from a theological school that prided itself on their appellation as *ahl al-ʿadl waʾl-tawḥīd.* Yet this concept keeps a low profile in their discussions.

Part of the reason is that one of the principal definitions of the term in circulation gave it too wide a scope, as in the definition by ʿAbd al-Jabbār: the acts qualified as *ʿadl* are those that are "undertaken to benefit or harm another in a way that is good."[69] The domain of beneficial acts that are *just* is narrower than the domain of beneficial acts that are *good*, for the former is confined to other-regarding benefits ("to benefit another"), whereas good acts (are usually said to) include self-regarding benefits. But what makes this definition of justice a surprising one is precisely that its inclusion of other-regarding benefits should be an entirely unconditional one, for while this may include such benefits as rewarding a person who deserves it—a just act—it also includes bestowing benefits on someone who does not. Beneficence is thus paradoxically included in the scope of justice. This is picked up by Māndkīm (from a certain perspective that need not detain us here), who revises the definition to read: "rendering another his right, and exacting one's right [or claim] from another" (*tawfīr ḥaqq al-ghayr wa-istīfāʾ al-ḥaqq minhu*).[70] This definition now makes the concept far more recognizable to us, framed as it is around terms that relate to rights/claims, and therefore deserts and a deontological framework, and much better equipped to be used as a frame of reference for punishment. At the same time, however, it reveals why the concept should have little use within the larger scheme as a separate ground, for it will be recalled that these acts (rendering and exacting rights or claims) are directly subjected to further moral qualifications in the core moral terms of *ḥusn, wujūb,* and so on. Rendering a right is *wājib*; exacting a right is *ḥasan.* As such, the interaction with *ḥuqūq* expressed by the term justice is discussed directly in the core moral qualifications.

But to return to our main track of questioning and take stock: What does all this reveal? Does it reveal anything? What moral is one entitled to draw from identifying the difficulties that beset a scheme of thought? The impulse expressed in such questions is one of the most important revenants that haunt the effort to engage in one scheme of thought while retaining the illuminating perspective of another. To the extent that the latter scheme gives one a vantage point located outside the former, the critical possibilities that it opens up—the possibilities of tracing the bounds of the former—at the same time bring the temptation of standing too far outside the bounds, and seeking large-scale explanations from there for what are perceived as difficulties, flaws, or differences in the target scheme. Of course there are several different explanations it would be possible to offer in response to these questions, whose precise content would depend on whom one was asking. To the question of "what is revealed" by the difficulties traced out above, one of ʿAbd al-Jabbār's Ashʿarite contemporaries would have replied, "The incoherence of ethical rationalism"; a fellow Muʿtazilite might have simply diagnosed the problem as a technical one, to be solved by careful restructuring of the conceptual architecture; one whose hostility encompassed the entire discourse of scholastic theology might have averred the moral to be about the incoherence of *all* rationalism and all attempts to probe the secrets of the divine economy. Yet none of these would quite respond to the request for a moral as this was intended in the above questions, and perhaps the most dissatisfying would be the second, which in presenting the difficulty under the aspect of a mere technical flaw affecting the Muʿtazilite conception of desert, would seem a superficial response indeed. "Surely," one wants to say, "the explanation of such serious trouble must run deeper!"

Such requests for depth need to ensure that they keep in firm view the fact that the notions of "difficulty" they invoke and the very possibility of "identifying" it are contingent on the assumption of a perspective that lies outside the system itself. Thus, it is against *our* intuitions that we measure how counterintuitive it is to think of desert in terms of what blame is *not*. Yet on the other hand, it would be hard to accept a similar judgment for all elements that make up this perspective—hard to accept, for example, that the failure to identify and address the conflict between considerations of desert and considerations of welfare as grounds of punishment (identified above as a considerable weakness in the Baṣran Muʿtazilite justification) is a mere matter of our own particular intuitions as these have contingently emerged from a specific philosophical culture. "How could such a thing have remained unthought?" These are big questions, and here I will not try to sate the impulse to ask them, except by simply underlining the modest yet for all that material observation that they were not; and that they weren't is a reflection of a different perception of what explained itself and what needed to be argued. Beyond this, the most critical question is a practical one, and this is to decide what sort of meaningful interaction is possible given such different perceptions of where explanation must stop.

The Causal Efficacy of Moral Values: Between Sabab *and* ʿIlla

The above discussion has now placed us in a position to put together the Baṣran Muʿtazilite account of the causality involved in the dramaturgy of moral actions, and thereby to interpret those enticing remarks of ʿAbd al-Jabbār's about the causality of desert—cited in chapter 2—that imparted to this study its initial spark: In what way does desert *cause* anything? How far is the account of its causal powers probed?[71] Answering these questions is a matter of taking stock of two different types of conditionality entering the account of desert that we have already met and bringing them into relation.

First, we saw that moral qualities are defined in a conditional way, so that deserts do not automatically accrue on the commission of an act that instantiates an act-description but depend on two sets of conditions, prior (or simultaneous with) and posterior to the act—the agent's moral knowledge, motivation, and liberty; and the agent's other acts, or his repudiation of his past act through regret or repentance. Then we saw that the desert that arises is itself a conditional justification of punishment and blame, as a corollary of the position that goodness is established in a conditional way. And we heard that the principal reason for this position was the desire to preserve a nomological view of the grounds of value: if the grounds of value were to be like necessitating causes (*tajrī majrā al-ʿilal al-mūjiba*), they must be like them in all respects, including the fact that the latter operate unconditionally. When a *ʿilla* is present, it automatically necessitates its effect (*ḥukm*). Thus, as I may put it, desert is a defeasible ground twice over: vertically (its realization is conditional on antecedent factors and defeated by subsequent grounds), and horizontally (the value of actualizing the deserved treatment is defeated by other grounds present in the same act).

Now it may have been noticed already that there is a certain tension between these two areas of Muʿtazilite thinking. For despite the various conditions entering the definitions of moral qualities, the grounds of value are understood in terms of their capacity to *necessitate* an effect (a *ḥukm*). This was an understanding that expressed the Muʿtazilites' desire to provide a rigorous nomological account of moral values in which the meanings of the terms remained stable, and the action of grounds invariable and independent of subjective responses, thus deflecting the specter of voluntarism and founding an objectivist view of moral values.[72] But now what is the effect that act-descriptions necessitate if not the *aḥkām* of desert? And thus, how can one square the presence of multiple conditions on which the rise of such *aḥkām* is dependent with the claim that the act-description from which they arise is a necessitating cause—understood precisely in terms of the independence of its effect on any conditions? When the child given a lavish new toy snatches it and fails to thank the one who brought it, and when the Muslim scholar has a mosque endowed in his name for him to teach in and fails to express thanks to the vizier responsible for the arrangement, the same ground of value is present: ingratitude. In the one case no blame will be due, and in the other blame will be deserved (and no doubt, in this case, duly exacted). The same act-description, different moral consequences. What, then, of causal necessity?

The question would not seem to have an answer on the terms that Ibn Mattawayh insists on in his discussion of the "grounds" of goodness, which as may be recalled were disqualified from the status of grounds because of their conditional nature. For "if there is a ground, it acts in a way akin to necessitating causes, even if it is not in reality a cause."[73] The terms are ones that ʿAbd al-Jabbār for his part propounds even more clearly, as in the following revealing remarks:

> What necessitates the evilness of evil acts, such as the fact that a statement constitutes a lie or a pain constitutes injustice, is akin to necessitating causes [*ʿilal mūjiba*] in that it must necessarily entail this [quality]. Thus, just as it is impossible that a necessitating cause be present without necessitating its proper effect [*ḥukm*], likewise it is impossible that the ground of evil be present without necessitating that the act is evil.[74]

Yet ʿAbd al-Jabbār seems to have been quicker to take stock of the implications of this strong position, going so far as to backtrack from this fundamental tenet by conceding that moral grounds, ultimately, are far less *like* necessitating causes than elsewhere suggested. In a late passage in volume 11 of the *Mughnī* (titled *al-Taklīf* ["The Imposition of the Law"]), having just referred to the fact that the *aḥkām* of an act are affected by whether a person is compos mentis (which is understood in terms of the possession of moral knowledge) and has deserts of the contrary value—two agent-related conditions that affect desert, as we have seen—ʿAbd al-Jabbār goes on to observe, "And [all] this is different from causes that necessitate particular effects [*al-ʿilal al-mūjiba li'l-aḥkām*], so that it would be more appropriate to class [the grounds of value: *wujūh*] with those effects that relate to the choice of agents insofar as they derive from something that has to do with the agent."[75] This statement, it must be said, seems an excessively unguarded one, if one recalls that it was on the platform of an opposition to the claim that moral values depend on the choices of agents, and in particular those of God—spearheaded by Ashʿarite and other voluntarists—that the nomological account of moral values as necessitating causes was promoted. Yet for my purposes, its significance lies in the acute perception of the conditionality of moral consequences that it reveals—dependent as they are on features of the agent—which conflicts with a lawlike conception of the grounds of value.

All of this is directly material to the explicit discussion that the Baṣrans undertake of the causal nature of morally valued acts, and for which Ibn Mattawayh is our most informative ambassador, given the loss of the relevant volumes of ʿAbd al-Jabbār's *Mughnī*. The question, as it is parsed, is raised as one that concerns the causal nature of *acts* (*afʿāl*), and what manner of cause they constitute in generating deserts. But of course if acts are causes of such *aḥkām*, it is insofar as they instantiate act-descriptions (*wujūh*) that themselves entail particular *aḥkām*. The causal nature of *act-descriptions* is thus what imparts to particular *acts* their causal powers.

The Baṣran account of these powers seems to flow naturally from all the preceding. Actions, we hear, "are not causes [*ʿilla*] by way of necessitation [*ʿalā sabīl al-ījāb*] for the things deserved on their account."[76] Why so? For the relation of *ʿilla* and *maʿlūl* is one of mutual entailment: if *ʿilla x* necessitates *ḥukm/maʿlūl y*, both are affirmed and negated together; both must be present or both must be absent. Whereas here, as we have seen, we have several agent-related features acting as conditions (*shurūṭ*) to the effect of deserving. The agent's knowledge of the value of the act; his choosing it *for the sake of* its value; his being able to choose differently; his regretting it at a later point; or his performing actions subsequently that carry the opposite values—all these are pit stops on the career of the value that is stimulated by the commission of a single act that may prevent it from establishing itself with finality.

But there were other alternatives to be elicited from the ontological arsenal of the Baṣran Muʿtazilites. Having rejected this type of causal efficacy, it is with a different model that the Baṣrans proposed to identify the relationship between acting and deserving—and this is the model of causes designated as *asbāb* (sing. *sabab*), casting the relationship between acting and deserving as one between *sabab* and its effect (*musabbab*). The crucial distinction between these two causal models—*sabab* and *ʿilla*—lies in the necessity with which each entails its effect. What distinguishes the former is the contingency of its effect: unlike *ʿilal,* which operate necessarily and directly, without the mediation of other causes or conditions, the *sabab* is a member of a causal sequence that contributes to the production of an effect. The production of the effect is not necessary, and the *sabab* does not uniformly produce a single effect, so that "it is possible for one to exist in the absence of the other under certain conditions." In addition, whereas with *ʿilal* the production of the *maʿlūl* must follow immediately on their presence, this temporal contiguity need not be the case with *asbāb.*[77] Several of these features are encapsulated in the following remark of Ibn Mattawayh's:

> If the grounds [*asbāb*] for the desert of reward and punishment—whether acts of performing or abstaining—are not of the nature of necessitating causes, in which it is impossible that the cause be established while the effect is not realized . . . then it is possible that something may occur that eliminates these deserts even though their grounds continue to exist [*in the sense that an act cannot be undone*], just as it is possible that the act of rendering what is deserved be posterior to the [act that constitutes the] ground of desert, and just as it is possible that what is deserved should diminish even though its ground persists.[78]

Now there are several points in this account that need to be clarified, but perhaps the most important and at the same time most puzzling is this one: If what was said above about the overwhelming tendency of the Baṣrans to talk of grounds of value as virtually necessitating causes was correct—ʿAbd al-Jabbār's moment of clarity constituting rather a deviation from this practice—and if the causal powers of acts are a corollary of the causal powers of the grounds they instantiate, how is it that the model of acts as *asbāb* is maintained even by those, such as Ibn Mattawayh, who seem to keep a consistent line on the grounds of their value and regard them as virtually necessitating? The answer to this question is an interesting yet also a composite one, and in order to be able to present it efficiently, something more needs to be said in order to identify clearly the precise effect that these Muʿtazilites consider as resulting from acts as *asbāb*.

The Muʿtazilites themselves, and not least ʿAbd al-Jabbār, have to shoulder a good measure of blame for obscuring this part of the picture. In a passage of ʿAbd al-Jabbār's *al-Taklīf*, a fascinating discussion of the causal nature of desert takes place when an interlocutor suggests to the author that one who performs an obligatory act deserves praise for it *immediately* on performance, so that the act functions as a necessary cause (*ʿilla*) for the desert of praise (i.e., the *ḥukm*). ʿAbd al-Jabbār denies this causal model, on the grounds we have already seen. If the act was a *ʿilla,* cause and effect would have to be present together. By contrast, the *ḥukm* of desert of praise may be absent even though the act has taken place. "It [that is, praise] is separate from it and therefore may be deserved a long time afterward. This is why it is good for us to praise one whom we know to have done something that makes him deserving of such praise a long time back."[79] Yet desert itself simply *cannot* be what ʿAbd al-Jabbār has in mind as the *ḥukm*: he is in fact thinking of the praise itself, to the *actualized* treatment or act deserved, as what need not immediately follow; it cannot be that it is *deserved* a long time afterward but that it may be *realized* long after.[80]

This appears clearly once we take note of the reason that motivates his rejection of the *ʿilla* model—namely, his fear that this causal model would interfere with the theory of *iḥbāṭ* and *takfīr.* I have already touched on the basic elements involved in the theory when talking about those conditions for deserving that are *posterior* to the performance of an act, in which was included the possibility that acts of the contrary value might be performed. According to the theory of *iḥbāṭ* and *takfīr,* the punishment and the reward one deserves, since they are bound to be of unequal quantities, must "operate" on each other so that one of the two cancels the other out. Deserved reward that exceeds deserved punishment will expiate (*yukaffiru*) the latter; deserved punishment that exceeds deserved reward will frustrate (*yuḥbiṭu*) the latter. But in fact—at least among the version of the theory propounded by Abū Hāshim's followers—the entities entering into relations will be not the actualized treatments but the deserts: "If one were to perform what is evil as well as what is obligatory, frustration and expiation would occur with respect to *what is deserved* through these acts."[81] Thus, ʿAbd al-Jabbār would seem to have conflated here two different orders of causality, the effect (the giving of the deserved treatment) with the cause (that it was deserved), and to be denying that the *latter* follows an act, while it is only the former that he needs to deny.[82]

Yet this conflation must finally be regarded as no more than a lapse; ʿAbd al-Jabbār himself later comfortably refers to the difference between deserving reward in the present and its being granted in the hereafter after a delay (*istiḥqāq* now, *tawfīr* later), and in the same passage shows himself happy to speak of deserving immediately on performing an act of obedience.[83] Ibn Mattawayh's clarity is even crisper, and goes beyond the assertion, sufficient in itself, that "the subject of the Law, *during the time in which he is under the Law*"—and that is to say a person's lifetime—"can either belong to the people of reward and praise, or the people of punishment and blame."[84] His discussion is even clearer in the context of a debate—of which he is again our best informant—revolving around the question of the particular time in which desert arises once an act has been committed. The debate was apparently one stoked by Murji'ite theologians who, in line with their position on grave sinners—whose fate they deferred (*arja'a*) to God's decision on the Day of Judgment—were impressed by the vulnerability of deserts and their liability to be frustrated by later events in a person's life, and refused to grant that these deserts really existed until they were in fact realized—by a person's being rewarded or punished after the Day of Judgment. It is as though the acts and circumstances of one's life were seen as accumulating over a lifetime as raw material that did not yield a final sum until the day when the papers were brought out by the judge and their contents computed; and there was no "real" sum "out there" until the act of calculation took place.

The Baṣran Muʿtazilites we are considering vigorously rejected this idea and insisted that deserts were in fact realized immediately on the commission of the act. The time of deserving, states Ibn Mattawayh, "is the time [*ḥāl*] of the act, and one thereby comes to deserve that [the thing deserved] be done to one in the time that follows the act (*fi'l-thānī*); thus the time that follows the act is the time of the performance of what is deserved."[85] In talking of the time after the act (lit. "the second moment after the act"), Ibn Mattawayh is certainly marking succession and not duration—he must be referring to an extended period marked out as posterior to the act, not to the single moment that immediately succeeds the act, for in fact one will normally need to wait till the Final Day before receiving one's deserts. Thus, at t_1 one acts and deserves, and at t_2 one receives what one deserves. A certain distinction, however, must be drawn—or rather stressed, because it has already been referred to in passing—between the role played by the conditions discussed above, in order to mark the progress of value clearly. The conditions referred to as antecedent or simultaneous—the agent's knowledge, motivation, and liberty—are conditions for *desert* to be realized. The second set of conditions—those posterior to the act—are conditions for the *deserved treatment* to be realized.

Now if Ibn Mattawayh's model seems a bit odd, that's because it fails to mark any temporal separation between the action and the desert. Why not a three-stage model in which one acts at t_1, deserves at t_2, and receives one's deserts at t_3?[86] This oddity in fact does not seem to be an incidental one, and yields the answer to my question that concerned the precise effect of which morally valued acts are causes under their aspect as *asbāb*. For while, as is now evident, desert arises immediately through the act, it is not desert that is the *musabbab* of the act. And this, simply—although this is not quite a reasoning that is explicitly brought out by our sources—seems to be because desert is not an *act* or an *event*—that is, the kind of thing that could fill the placeholder for "effect." It is the reward or punishment, the praise and blame—the deserved treatments—that can fill this slot. And here I can finally bring the above to relate to my starting question, which was expressed as a perplexity about the acceptance of this model of contingent causality for valued acts by those, such as Ibn Mattawayh, who embraced a model of necessary causality for the values of acts. If not an effect that forms the member of a sequence of events, what then *is* desert? The answer to this, in fact, we already know, but it is merely a matter of turning it the right way so that it fits, even though in fitting it may scatter the sense that there is anything to be fitted to and may seem nearly bland: desert is simply a ground of value; it is the ground that makes the action of rewarding and punishing, praising and blaming, a good one—though whether we can speak of it as a "ground" (a *wajh*) depends on which of the two conceptions of goodness we are working with. The fact that someone deserves at a given moment—a point discussed in the context of the Murji'ite debate—is simply the fact that at a given moment, it would be good for one to give them the treatment they deserve. This is captured in Ibn Mattawayh's remark:

> Inasmuch as desert signifies the goodness of a particular action on account of a prior reason [namely, a value-bearing act], it must be the case that it is good for God to punish or reward in the time that succeeds the act of obedience or disobedience. So when we say that the time of deserving is the time of the act, what we mean is what has just been mentioned.[87]

Of course, the more precise description of desert would be in terms of normative constellations of *ḥuqūq* attaching to particular persons, and on this level of analysis, the question could be formulated as one that concerns the ontological status of these *ḥuqūq* and the ontological nature of their attachment to the person. Now *this* is certainly not a bland question; I will be coming around to it from a particular direction in the next chapter when raising a ("counterfactual") question about the legal concept of *dhimma* and its relation to these *ḥuqūq*.

But now it may at last be possible to give one reason why the same author who held that moral *wujūh* must be causes that operate unconditionally could accept that acts bearing *wujūh* are only conditional causes: for to say that these acts *cause* deserved treatments is, in Ibn Mattawayh's view, just to say that they create a "ground"—desert—that would make it good to give these treatments. But as with all good acts, this will be conditional on the privation of other subsequent grounds that reverse the value: "it is good for us to blame and punish as long as nothing arises to change that"—and later events such as a person's regret or other acts constitute precisely such grounds. For example, if one commits an evil act, blame will arise, but if one subsequently comes to regret it, "this regret must influence the goodness of this blame, transforming its status from good to evil . . . so the goodness of one's blame depends on one's persistence and continued acceptance."[88] But even if the moral value of the blame changes because of subsequent grounds that come to compete with the good-making ground of desert, the moral *wujūh* will already have expressed their necessitating action in giving rise to desert in the first place.[89]

As for the challenge posed to the view of *wujūh* as necessitating causes on account of the conditions *prior to* or *simultaneous with* the act, such as the agent's state of knowledge or motivation—conditions that seem to conflict with the model of necessitating causes—that is another story altogether, which certainly the specter of inconsistency would seem to spook. The Baṣrans here seem to have made things difficult for themselves by an unnecessarily austere conception of lawlike action—one that was not, after all, essential to the repulsion of voluntarism, in which what was necessary was not the claim that values were not conditional *simpliciter*, or were not conditional on any features of persons, but more narrowly that their contents and operation were not conditional on the will of any particular person. This, it might be said, is an inconsistency one could easily find ways to remove; but that is a task we can leave to future generations of Muʿtazilites to address, setting them on their way with a brainstorming suggestion: Why not include the so-called conditions into a single complex description of the act?

The Right to Blame, the Fact of Blame: Views of the Person ab Extra

Whether or not this advice is heeded, there are other interesting matters now to which we should turn our attention, in order to pick up the last of the pointers set in place above as signposts of later discussion. In talking about the definitions of moral predicates, we had seen that the ultimate moral facts constituting moral reality—a reality that forms the intellectually perceivable criterion for the application of moral qualities—reduce to the *aḥkām* (rulings, characteristics, consequences) of desert. Tracing out a preparatory move on the chessboard, it was said that more precisely, it is not the deserts entailed by an act that form the primary moral datum for human knowledge; it is the value of giving the person who performed the act the deserved treatment, and more particularly—for evil acts—its goodness. Thus, what you know when you see me stealing something from another, withholding a debt owed, or acting unjustly in various other ways is not that I deserve blame but that it is good to blame me. And of course to know this is to know something about *your own* reactions.

Hence, we hear in no equivocal terms that the object of necessary knowledge is the goodness of the treatment, not the desert: "A person who has reached intellectual maturity knows *the goodness of blame* necessarily."[90] We know by necessity that it is good to blame one who has not performed what was obligatory, and as soon as we know that one has omitted the obligatory, we know it is good to blame them. We know by necessity that it is good to blame a person who commits an offense, and it is a knowledge for which no proof could be given, for "if the goodness of blaming the offender was not known necessarily on his committing the offense, there would be no primary ground from which it could be derived."[91]

Now what is the significance of this conceptual turn? The best way to answer this is by beginning with a crucial clarification: certainly the Baṣran Muʿtazilites did not mean that the knowledge of a person's deserts could be dispensed with. We have all the ingredients in place to see why: if an act possesses a certain value, there must be a ground (*wajh*) for this value. And in the Baṣrans' epistemological template, one cannot know the value of an act without knowing the ground of its value, though they allowed for the interesting possibility that one may know the ground of value without recognizing that *that* is the ground for the value judgment one has made.[92] This meant that I may know an act constitutes a refusal to give back money owed, and thus automatically know that it is evil—which is to say that it deserves blame, which is to say that it is good to blame the agent—without realizing that it is *because* it is a failure to pay back a debt that I judge it good to blame the agent. I may well think (and here we perceive the Muʿtazilites' reason for coining this idea) that it is because God told me to do so that the act is evil and my blame of the agent good. Similarly, then, it would seem that I may know that it is good to blame you for failing in this obligation, without knowing that the reason for its goodness is the fact that you deserve blame. Yet this is what really makes my act good.

Nevertheless, several things must be said here. The first and most important is that on the dominant later conception of goodness, one could not, strictly speaking, describe desert as a ground. A second is that the primacy of our knowledge of the value of the treatment is stressed strongly at places, and desert—as its "ground"—seems rather to be thought of as a conclusion drawn from the first, primary knowledge. Talking about the commission of evil acts and the omission of obligatory ones, ʿAbd al-Jabbār writes, "The knowledge that it is good to blame one who is characterized by these two things is primary in reason [*awwal fi'l-ʿaql*], so if it is good to blame a person for them, *it is thereby established* that he deserves blame for them."[93] Yet a third thing to be said is that at many other places, the epistemology seems to be conceived in a way that bypasses our access to facts about desert even more sharply, by talking of the *action*—one's doing something evil or failing to do what is obligatory—as the ground (the *wajh*) of the goodness of blame or praise. Thus ʿAbd al-Jabbār notes, "This blame is good because the one blamed has not done what was obligatory," or, "His not doing what was obligatory is the ground (*wajh*) for the goodness of blaming him."[94] Of course, strictly speaking, desert and not doing the obligatory should be ordered as different stages of the moral explanation: "X did not do the obligatory" is the reason for deserving blame, and "X deserves blame" is the reason for the goodness of blame. But ʿAbd al-Jabbār's presentation abridges this explanation by omitting the intermediate stage, and what is left is an act explained by another act without the intermediacy of the causal relation that binds the two—namely, desert.

The last feature, one might say, could in part be explained by the focus of the discussion in which it appears—the focus of the book of *Istiḥqāq al-dhamm* is on a debate over *which* is the proper ground or relatum for the desert of blame, and this may slant toward an abbreviated presentation of the explanatory order. Yet taken in combination, these aspects serve to entrench the impression that the role of desert in the epistemological process is—and cannot but be—significantly undercut.

This impression is strengthened even further by a fact that might otherwise have been taken as a merely stylistic idiosyncrasy of the discussions, and this is an overwhelming tendency—found in some writings more than others, and in some writers more than others—to raise issues *not* in the form of statements about desert of blame ("why [or that] X deserves blame") but rather in terms of statements about the goodness of blame ("why [or that] it is good to blame X"). A few examples will suffice to make this idiom clear, most of which derive from ʿAbd al-Jabbār's above-mentioned volume: "Reason attests that if an act is not of this kind [namely, evil], it is not *good to blame* the agent for it, rather it is evil." "Human beings who have reached intellectual maturity (*ʿuqalāʾ*) hold that it is *good to blame* one who commits an offense if they could have guarded against it." "We know necessarily that it is *good to blame* one who is under the obligation to return a deposit . . . [if they do not do so]." "We deny that one who does not know that [a certain person] has committed evil could know that it is *good to blame* them." "Just as it is necessarily known that it is *good to blame* one who commits an offense . . ." "Apologizing [for an offense] changes the state of *blame* from *good* to evil [the blame, that is, that would otherwise be directed to one who committed an offense]."[95] The last statement in particular is embedded in a context in which the term *ḥukm*—the moral quality of an act—is used to characterize blame (*ḥukm al-dhamm*). The fact that the book in which such idiom is found is explicitly signposted as one about *desert* (*istiḥqāq al-dhamm*) makes it all the more interesting that the conceptual matrix widely employed should rather be in terms of the goodness of the deserved treatment.[96]

Now what is one to make of this? Before deciding what we should make of it, we must decide what we should not, by considering a particular interpretation proposed by Hourani of ʿAbd al-Jabbār's discussion of desert. Hourani deemed it to be an important—if not indeed fatal—weakness of the Muʿtazilite concept of desert that its definition did not appear to exclude value terms and hence was liable to the charge of circularity.[97] His examination this problem is framed around a peculiar passage from *al-Luṭf* (volume 13 of the *Mughnī*), in a chapter arguing that desert may be a ground for the goodness of pain. There, Hourani discerned ʿAbd al-Jabbār's awareness of the problem of circularity and his attempt to furnish a solution.

In this passage, the writer is challenged by the objection that "your statement that pain is good because it is deserved is self-defeating, because the meaning of its being deserved is that it is good to do it; thus, when you say that it is good because of this ground [*wajh*], it is as though you were saying, 'it is good because it is good'; and this is self-defeating."[98] 'Abd al-Jabbār's response is to affirm that while the fact that something is deserved includes in its meaning the fact that it is good to do it, this is implicit rather than part of an explicit analysis.[99] A further challenge is then raised to deliver just such an explicit analysis—an analysis that it will be possible to "consider as a cause [*ka'l-'illa*) for its goodness." In 'Abd al-Jabbār's response, a different set of terms make their appearance, bearing the meaning of "requital," "equivalence," or "correspondence":

> It has been established in reason that blame is such [*min ḥaqq al-dhamm*] as to be given for evil acts and offenses as their equivalent [*muqābil*], in such a way as to be requital [*jazā'*] for them, and that praise is such as to be rendered as the equivalent for doing good in the same manner. When this has been affirmed to be the case, we express it by saying that it is deserved, and we make it as a cause in the goodness of doing so [i.e., of blaming or praising].

Hourani does not express complete satisfaction with 'Abd al-Jabbār's attempt to provide a value-free definition but comments that "we can credit him at least with being aware of the problem and struggling to solve it."[100]

The problem for which Hourani attributes to 'Abd al-Jabbār an attempt to solve has certainly been a significant one in the history—especially the more recent episodes—of philosophical ethics, but once again it would seem a mistake to assimilate 'Abd al-Jabbār's concerns to this history. The most important reason for resisting this assimilation is simply that if the concept of desert is not—as it does not appear to be—defined, then Hourani's interpretation seems to fall away: for nowhere, it would seem, has 'Abd al-Jabbār maintained that "the meaning of its being deserved is that it is good to do it."[101] And hasn't he rather maintained in the section under discussion that desert is the *reason* why it is good to exact the deserved treatment (whatever inconsistencies this might engender for his conception of goodness)? That is to say, not only has he not defined desert employing goodness as its term but he has made the former a ground for the latter.

But if Hourani's understanding of the text is set aside, the passage appears even odder. For what view *has* 'Abd al-Jabbār maintained, against which the objection has been conjured? My suggestion, tentative and rather deflationary, is that while 'Abd al-Jabbār has not *defined* desert through goodness, and has kept the two distinct by positing desert as the reason for the goodness of giving the appropriate treatment, this distinctness is after all both incompatible with and endangered by the terms in which goodness is defined (desert, strictly speaking, could *not* be cited as a reason). And even if the two were indeed successfully kept apart on this theoretical level, it is still the case that in practice, the formulation most often encountered concerns the *goodness* of blame, which is the idiom that etches itself in the reader's comprehension the most strongly. It would appear that it is this de facto conflation that ʿAbd al-Jabbār is recognizing in the form of the objector's challenge and undertaking to undo by speaking of desert as a cause. The challenge to tell them apart reflects the tension between, on the one hand, this practice of conflation and the constraints imposed by the theoretical model of goodness, on whose terms desert cannot be spoken of as a reason and made distinct, and on the other hand, the requirements of the discussion under way concerning the things that "make" pain good, in which the ability to speak of reasons is needed most. ʿAbd al-Jabbār, responding to these needs, accedes to the language of *wujūh al-ḥusn*. He does not meet the request for a "cause" of goodness by the stock assertion that "there are not grounds for goodness" but consents to speak of desert as such a cause (*ka'l-ʿilla*), and indeed characterizes its action as one that *necessarily entails* the goodness of the deserved act (*muqtaḍiyan li-ḥusnihi*).[102]

On many levels, then, in the Baṣran scheme, talk about desert gives way to talk about the value of the act of giving these deserts; desert is conceived in terms of the value of an act-description: "it is good to blame," "it is good to punish." Even without the further entanglements that result from the analysis of goodness in terms of the privation of *other* act-descriptions, this conceptual turn would have seemed peculiar enough. With that addition, we are caught in a web of acts from which propositions about desert emerge transformed: it is good to blame unless it is lying, acting in vain, or acting unjustly. The only description—the only ground of value—that is not an *act*-description (desert) is discussed in terms of other act-descriptions.

What are we to make of this singular conceptual woof? We will have taken the most important step in the right direction once the bias toward acts that this woof involves—a bias expressed in reducing desert to the moral evaluation of the act of giving a person what they deserve—has been reversed in order to see what this bias *toward* is a bias *away from*. Yet this is a task that cannot be accomplished without once again regaining our footing in our own moral perspective and the aspect under which the concept of desert presents itself to us. So we may ask ourselves: If desert is not an *act*-description—of receiving the treatment—what *is* it a description of? The most intuitive answer says that desert is a kind of relation holding between a person and something else, something desirable or undesirable to the person. The relation is a normative one, which would actually be instantiated and established if the second term of the relation—the thing deserved—were to be given. But how, whether, and by whom this relation is established in practice and actuality is not an intrinsic aspect of our understanding of desert itself. Since the reason why this relation *ought* to be established in fact lies in certain things to do with the person, with acts one has done or characteristics one possesses, desert is a kind of description of the *person*—it is of that person that it is predicated.[103] It is an evaluation of the person. So the contrast may now be clearer: in the account given thus far of Muʿtazilite ideas, desert is not "attached" to the person. This is what the shift *toward* the act of giving deserved treatments is a shift *away from*: the person.

In tilling the meaning of this shift, our steps lead us back to a theme on which the light has already been sharply trained, and that is the importance of the legal conceptual currency embedded in the Baṣran Muʿtazilites' scheme of values, and in particular, the consequences of the fact that the concept of desert (*istiḥqāq*) is inlaid with the legal concepts of rights and obligations (*ḥuqūq*). In characterizing these concepts above, one point that might have been relevantly made is that the term *ḥaqq al-ʿibād* (or *ḥaqq ādamī*)—translatable as "human right"—cannot be allowed to carry the connotations of the modern concept of "human rights." One reason why such a translation would be unhelpful is that these rights do not seem to accept an interpretation that construes them as *features of a person,* as numerous modern human rights theories tend to consider them. The latter type of theory resists the reduction of rights to the obligations others have to protect and promote these rights. While those of a more modernizing or "appropriating" spirit have argued for the presence of modernlike conceptions of rights in classical Islamic law, the concept of a *ḥaqq* chiefly refers to a relation that holds between persons, rather than to features of persons, and *ḥaqq lahu* is the natural counterpart of *ḥaqq ʿalayhi* on more than a grammatical level.[104]

And now I can at last more clearly draw the consequences of a fact that I touched on in connection with the Baṣran Muʿtazilite construal of deserts in terms of claims attaching to particular persons—reward as a claim of human beings, and punishment as a claim special to God. The more exact picture with respect to bad deserts, which we saw in distinguishing between offenses (*isāʾāt*) and evil acts (*qabāʾiḥ*), is that for offenses, blame is conceived as the right or claim (*ḥaqq*) of the victim; for evil acts, blame is a claim of all rational beings, while the punishment that corresponds to it is a private claim of God's. What is clear is that talk of desert translates into talk of another's claims; one person's *istiḥqāq* is another person's *ḥaqq fīʾl-dhamm* or, correlatively, *ḥaqq fīʾl-ʿiqāb* ("the right to blame," "the right to punish"). It is the relational aspect of the concept that is responsible for the biases we are trying to explain. The translation of a person's *istiḥqāq* into another person's *ḥaqq,* with the stress on the side of "right" (the side of the creditor) rather than that of "obligation" (that of the debtor) in this reciprocal relation, is what seems to explain best why and how this account of desert is biased toward the blamer rather than the blamed, and as a corollary, toward the blame rather than the desert. Desert is something that comes to appear as a possession of and proper to, not the wrongdoer, but rather the one wronged.

The implications of this conceptual matrix are brought out with the most admirable limpidity by Ibn Mattawayh in the context of his discussion of the internal Baṣran debate over the ground for the desert of blame. The more particular context of his remark is too involved to set out concisely, but the following terse remark can be extracted from it without too much violence: "Don't you see," says the author, "that the one deserving blame is not qualified by any attribute or ruling that renews itself on them, but it is rather that it is good for someone else to blame them? So the quality redounds to the blame, not to the blamed."[105] Setting aside the question that concerns the *renewal* of the attribute—which is bound up with the remark's particular context—the seminal significance of this comment lies in its stating clearly what otherwise has to be indirectly deduced. Desert is thought of *not* as an attribute of the agent but in terms of an attribute of the blame it excites, and by extension, the one holding the right to blame.

The features of the picture I have been assembling collude to shift the moral weight away from the acting subject to the responses of the ones who judge or are affected by that subject. The field of value generated by any act comes to arrange itself around other moral beings and not the acting subject. Here we have already begun to trace out the distinctively extrinsic perspective on the moral person that characterizes the Baṣran Muʿtazilite approach to desert, stressing the role in its cultivation of a conceptual currency whose indigenous domain is Islamic law. The following chapters will aim to extend our understanding of how this perspective expresses itself and what it consists of, but it is necessary to pause here in order to say what it does *not* consist of by tracing out yet another way in which the legal framework conditioning the Muʿtazilites' ethical concern seems to contribute to a view of the person *ab extra*.

This contribution can be brought into view by broadly outlining some of the things said by the later Baṣrans concerning the different levels of responsibility that are actualized by an act, and about the ways in which an evil act, once committed (or omitted, in the case of obligations) rearranges the factual world and thus demands to be reversed. The discussion that explores these demands concerns the obligation to undertake repentance (*tawba*), apology (*iʿtidhār*), and the concomitants that are conditions for the validity of these two; having already said some things about these issues, I will need only a few brushstrokes to complete the picture.

It will be recalled that the two main descriptions under which a wrongful act can fall are those of offenses (*isāʾa*) and evil acts (*qabīḥ*), and that the former are subsumed by the latter and distinguished by the fact that they affect others. Apology and repentance correspond to this difference in category; the former is obligatory for offenses, while the latter is obligatory for evil acts—and thus an offense, falling under both descriptions, will require both. Naturally the effects of an offense that require rectification or negation—that is, for which one is considered morally responsible—differ from those of an intransitive evil act. For offenses, the effects considered by ʿAbd al-Jabbār are seen to be threefold: the rearrangement of the material order of goods, in the normative sense specified by *ḥuqūq*—the property one has damaged, the injuries to a person's physical integrity one has caused, and so on; the second effect, which I have already touched on, is the right to special blame on the part of the person wronged that may arise; and the third is the blame incurred for doing what was evil—the two types of blame corresponding to the two descriptions the act exemplifies. For evil *simpliciter*, the effect is mainly confined to the second kind of blame (since it has not affected anybody, there is no harm to be reversed in the material order).

Not every case of offending will require the same normative response, however. A useful way to distinguish the three types of effect and the necessity for reversal that they generate is by the criterion of the dependence of this necessity on the knowledge of the person offended against. The first level is that of material effects, and the need to reverse these is independent of the knowledge of the victim. If I have usurped someone's property, even if the offended party is unaware of the act, it is obligatory that I restore the property.[106] The material balance must be restored, for the material facts created by a past act cannot be undone.

The second level is more interesting for our purposes. The offended party, as we have seen, possesses a special claim to blaming the agent of the deed: *ikhtaṣṣa bi-ḥaqq lā yusāwīhi ghayruhu fīhi.*[107] It is for the elimination of this blame that apology is needed. But this does not mean that one will always have to apologize for an offense, for the obligation to apologize is subject to certain conditions relative to the victim, the most basic of which is that the offended party be a rational being. As such, "one might commit an offense against one who lacks reason of the same sort committed against a rational being and would not incur the obligation to apologize."

To this general condition is superadded another: the offended party must be *aware* of the offense committed against them.[108] Part of the reason for this lies in one of the grounds for this obligation—namely, that one deflect harm from the offended party; apology, we are told, represents "the other's right to have the harm we inflicted on him removed from him."[109] Yet if this is not the material harm, which is the object of a separate obligation, what harm is it? Though this is not said by ʿAbd al-Jabbār in so many words, it seems that the only harm in question can be the sense of *having endured wrong*, having endured an offense, and having been offended.[110] Both English and Arabic capture two meanings in the term translated here as "offending": the word can refer to the violation of a law or rule, to causing injury or difficulty; or it can refer to the subjective feelings of resentment or vexation caused by violations of what is felt to be right and proper—the last sense gestures toward the diminution of one's dignity that is involved. This must be what ʿAbd al-Jabbār has in mind in referring to the need to ensure that "the effect of wrongdoing on the victim's heart is removed."[111]

The other part of the reason for this dependence lies in a second ground for this obligation: one must apologize *to deflect from oneself the harm of being blamed.* If the blame is not actual, the obligation loses (one of) its grounds. Thus,

> if someone had usurped the property of another unbeknownst to him, and then returned it to its original place while the other was unaware, he would not be bound to apologize . . . even though by the act of usurpation he would still be an offender [*musīʾ*]; but since the offense was eliminated without this having been made known, the offense was as though it had never been.[112]

A desert island situation? Do the Muʿtazilites mean to say that moral laws lose their force if nobody comes to know of an infraction—an account seasoned by a utilitarian touch? Hardly: the grounds of this obligation are the harm to both the agent and the victim—actual blame for the first, and offended dignity for the second. An example given in the text will illustrate some of the reasons behind the conditionality of the obligation to apologize. Suppose a doctor applies a painful medical treatment to a patient with the malicious intention of increasing their pain, while the patient continues to believe that their doctor is acting to benefit them. Ought the doctor apologize to the patient in this case? Arguably not, for if anything, a knowledge of the misdeed is calculated to plunge the patient even deeper into misery. What one ought to do instead is expend one's utmost in reversing the damage one has done.[113]

This example may lay to rest some of the worries we might have about making the agent's moral response of apology consequent on another's actual knowledge or reaction of blame. But there are deeper reasons that stand guard against a desert-island scenario. For while the harms of actual blame and offended dignity are contingent on knowledge of the deed, the deed itself is remembered and cataloged in the moral history of the world and the agent in other ways than this one. The memory of the deed is preserved on the next level—at the level of the blame, which is deserved on account of the evilness of the act. While intransitive evil acts incur this type of blame alone and not the special blame of an offended party, transitive acts, as we know, fall under two descriptions: as offenses, by which one may *potentially* incur the special blame, if the act is known; and as evil acts, by which one will simultaneously and *actually* incur the second type of blame—or rather, properly speaking, the desert of blame. The latter type of blame, described as the blame that is associated with or of the nature of punishment (*al-jārī majrā al-ʿiqāb*) must be eliminated not by apology but repentance, the grounds of the obligation to repent being to deflect harm from oneself.[114] As we have seen, two subjects are associated with this type of blame: God, who metes out the punishment that constitutes its counterpart; and *sāʾir al-ʿuqalāʾ*, *jamīʿ al-ʿuqalāʾ*—the larger community or society of people in their capacity as rational beings endowed with a knowledge of moral principles. What is important here is that even if this community should fail to know of misdeeds committed, certainly God would not.

Nevertheless, what the above reveals is the weight carried within the Baṣran scheme by considerations of how one will perform as an object of others' judgments and what appearance one's conduct will make before the latter. The victim's desire to salve their dignity and remove the offense, and the wrongdoer's desire to avoid blame, both express a concern with one's standing before others, or as one might put it, a concern with the preservation of one's honor. The importance of this concern is indicated in the strong conception of blame as a form of harm in the Baṣran Muʿtazilite scheme, where it is included in the harms that arise as the deserved consequences of evil actions and that give one a reason to avoid such actions. And it will be recalled that honor (*ʿirḍ*) was included within the trinity of valuables mentioned in the previous chapter—honor, property, and physical integrity—as goods of the "nonmoral" sort standing at the heart of Islamic law: they are good for a person, not just desirable but desired, and as such, the shadow that social and psychological realities cast on theoretical reflection.

There are several places in the Baṣran Muʿtazilite scheme where this shadow seems to pursue one, where blame and praise strike one less as ideal moral responses than as reflections of actual social practices and socially held values. The "rational beings" that constitute the Muʿtazilites' informants of moral truth contain more than a trace of such shadows. "Rational beings know concerning one who has not done what was obligatory that he deserves blame and that it is good to blame him." "We know that all rational beings, whatever their particular backgrounds, consider [injustice] evil." "Rational beings consider it good to demand compensation and replacements in the case of offense even after one has apologized, and consider it evil to blame [the agent] for the offense itself."[115] The moral propositions and value judgments apostrophized as beliefs of these beings often have an unsettlingly factual ring that challenges the fragile combination of actual and ideal, historically contingent and universal, that is balanced within them. The impression carried by such apostrophizing can be illustrated by juxtaposing two different types of expression: it is the difference between saying "one who robs the poor ought to be punished" and "one who robs the poor is punished by the state"; or between saying "lying is blameworthy" and "people approve of blaming the liar." These phrasings differ in respect to the strength of their reference to the agent or entity that establishes the moral order. In Baṣran Muʿtazilite ethics, the note one seems to hear is less that "one *ought* to blame the wrongdoer," and much more that "one *blames* the wrongdoer." Yet the role of these rational beings in Muʿtazilite ethics, and their foothold between ideal and actual, is a complex one, and I will be returning to it again in the following chapter.

Still, the shadows of social reality are certainly betrayed clearly in a remark such as Ibn Mattawayh's, who says, concerning one who commits grave sin that "we curse him and blame him. . . . There is no dispute that when we see someone committing adultery, we may curse him . . . at that moment."[116] They are betrayed equally as strong in the following passage by ʿAbd al-Jabbār:

> The offender must inform others apart from Zayd ["John Smith," the victim] of his regret about the offense he committed, *in order not to be blamed*. This is necessitated by the *accusation* directed to him; were it only Zayd that knew of his offense[117] it would not be necessary to inform anyone further, but if it was openly known, he must inform them *so that they do not think* that he is persisting in offending against him and *that they may know* that he has desisted.[118]

But what kind of reality is it that is here betrayed? Is there perhaps something more than merely a general concern with social blame that is reflected in this passage? The key here is the word "accusation" (*tuhma*), for it is this that gives away the nature of the concern as, once again, legal provenance. It will be recalled from the previous chapter that one of the most important aspects of the discussion of repentance, in which this passage appears, was the legal cadence that pervades it throughout. I have already discussed one consequence of this—the questions it raises concerning the relation between rational and revealed norms, and between the disciplines of theology and law. Another consequence, however, that we see here is that it serves to bring the discussion into the range of a far more *practical* concern with the legal implications—the *worldly* consequences (*aḥkām*)—of a person's actions and moral conduct.

Moral conduct, it may be said, had never been free from such consequences and never been discussed except under the heat of practical implications: the earliest moments of Islamic theology, in which the status of grave sinners came into dispute, were at the same time the earliest moments of the Islamic state, in which there was an acutely practical concern with the way in which grave sin affected the sinner's status as a believer and thus their relationship to the community of believers. Within this community, Islamic law made extensive provisions for responding to misconduct, and these varied according to the type of right or claim violated. At one end of the spectrum, among the crucial practical consequences carried for a person by their moral actions was their effect on the assessment of their moral character, and more specifically on the ability to affirm someone as a person of honorable record (*ʿadāla*). Such a record was a condition for legal testimony (*shahāda*), acting as a guardian (*walī*), and even more prominently, in the domain of religious studies, transmitting prophetic *ḥadīth*, where the examination of transmitters' character was the subject of a special science (*al-jarḥ wa'l-taʿdīl*, lit. "wounding and declaring just"). The blemish one's record incurs can be seen as the formal analogue of the diffuse social disapprobation depicted in Ibn Mattawayh's remark about the blame directed against the grave sinner. At another, graver end of the practical consequences sustained through one's misdeeds were criminal sanctions, and among the severest were the *ḥadd* penalties administered for grave sins that were recognized as God's claims, such as theft, the consumption of wine, or unlawful sexual relations.

The jurists' concern with repentance is to be read in light of its links to these contexts, inasmuch as repentance was involved in reversing or arresting some of the practical consequences of one's misdeeds.[119] It is in the context of both this type of legal proceeding and an interest in the imposition of sanctions that accusations would be brought forth against a wrongdoer. This connection is made far clearer in another reference by ʿAbd al-Jabbār to accusation, in which he is discussing whether in repenting, an outward expression is required. The fact of the matter, he says, is that it is not, "except if the accusation has been brought before the judge [*qāḍī*], in which case he must show his repentance outwardly in certain circumstances . . . in order to ward off the accusation directed at him."[120]

Of course, it has to be pointed out here that these legal provisions and the practical consequences they stipulated for acts cannot be taken to constitute reflections of actual social realities. Works of substantive law constituted, in Norman Calder's words, "a literary depiction of social reality in *normative* form"—a normative depiction not merely in the sense in which any law represents an ideal whose very need to be formulated derives from the existence and anticipation of actions that conflict with it but also in the additional sense that many of these provisions of Islamic law were not in practice enforced.[121] The gap between theory and practice was narrowest in the regulation of personal affairs such as marriage and inheritance, but perhaps widest in criminal law; *ḥadd* penalties themselves were not often implemented.

But whatever their actual application, such practical concerns introduce a different sense—supplementing the one discussed in connection with *ḥuqūq*—in which to talk about the role played by the legal framework calibrating the Baṣrans' ethics in cultivating an "extrinsic" perspective on the person. It would be extrinsic in a sense that reflects the contrast between the two domains of morality and law. The contrast may be drawn in terms of both the fallibility of judgments belonging to the latter, as an institution practiced by human beings, and the narrower reach that characterizes it: law merely concerns itself with the outer; as for the inner—the *real* object of morality, one might say—it remains out of its reach. The legal character of the Baṣran perspective would seem to align it with the first, extrinsic concern with appearance.

Yet that in this instance, this would be the wrong conclusion to draw should already be indicated by the distinction alluded to above between the bounds of human and the bounds of divine knowledge. These bounds are drawn sharply by ʿAbd al-Jabbār in an example such as the following, in which the evil deed—aptly chosen—is the internal act of unbelief (*kufr*):

> If Zayd committed unbelief in his heart, he would deserve blame *in himself* [*la-kāna fī nafsihi yastaḥiqqu al-dhamm*], yet it would not be good for us to blame him in the absence of a knowledge of that. But once we had come to know that he was committing evil . . . we would know it is good to blame him. Thus, what constitutes the difference between the two cases must lie in the state we are in, and not *the state of the one who is blamed* [*mā ʿalayhi al-madhmūm*], for he deserves blame in both cases alike.[122]

Ibn Mattawayh echoes this example with another of his own, and marks the distinction between appearance and reality even more clearly by means of a contrast between *aḥkām al-dunyā* and *aḥkām al-ākhira*, and hence between human and divine knowledge, insofar as the former—the practical consequences experienced in this world—are determined by human beings, whereas the latter are determined by God, who "knows the innermost thoughts and consciences" (*al-bawāṭin wa'l-ḍamā'ir*) of humankind and has no need for things to be made outward (*iẓhār*).[123] These distinctions decisively liberate the value of human actions from the dependence on human knowledge and judgments, and mollify the implications that the Baṣrans' legal form of concern might seem to trail. In fact, as we will see in the next chapter, the greater difficulty affecting the Baṣran Muʿtazilites' moral scheme in this respect does not lie so much in the strain placed on the judgments of particular human subjects with respect to acts committed by particular persons. It lies far more in the strain placed on the judgments of particular human subjects in their capacity as transcripts of universal moral truths.

Where has all this led us? It is worth pausing a moment to take stock. We have gone from an account of the importance of deserts as reasons for action; to the role of deserts in the definitions of moral qualities and their status as the primary moral facts of the Baṣran Muʿtazilite scheme, notwithstanding their conditional nature; to the asymmetrical attempt to justify punishment and reward—asymmetrical both in justificatory values and the success of the justification; to the more particular problems attaching to the justification of punishment due to its qualification in terms of goodness, which forbids talk of desert as a reason, and in which a conflict between forward- and backward-looking grounds arises without being resolved; through the causal nature attaching to the grounds of value and deserts; and finally the renewed role of the legal framework in calling up a twofold perspective on the person *ab extra,* partly through the worldly practical consequences and human judgments in light of which it considers evil actions, but more fundamentally through the conceptual matrix of *ḥuqūq*—these, in sum, have been the main stops on the way.

Now given what we have picked up between these stops, we already have reason to find the turn of phrase used by ʿAbd al-Jabbār in the passage just cited—in which he spoke of "the state of the one blamed"—a somewhat peculiar one. For in identifying the implications of the language of *ḥuqūq* for the way the Baṣran Muʿtazilites conceptualize desert, my suggestion had been that this language leads to a construction of desert that would seem to disqualify such an idiom. The construction it yields—one that we described as conjuring a distinctively extrinsic perspective on the moral agent—is in terms of *the value of an action or passion (i.e., suffering) that another has the right to exact on account of an action that the agent performed*, and not in terms of *a feature that attaches to the agent himself due to his performance of the act*. So what is one to make of this turn of phrase? And other than for its use in identifying a difference between our own ways of thinking about desert and those of our Muʿtazilite interlocutors, does it *matter*? How important a difference is this? It will be the task of the next chapters to map an answer to these questions—ones that are demanded not so much as a task of exegesis but rather as a continued scrutiny of the Baṣrans' resources and efforts in articulating a satisfactory justification of punishment.

CHAPTER 5

Moral Continuity and the Justification of Punishment

Time and Deserving

In the last chapter, I had little to say about the relation between time and desert except insofar as this was implicit when discussing the causal nature of desert and referring to the possibility of later occurrences that might frustrate or in some way affect the realization of moral consequences flowing out of past acts. The frozen sequence of past acts and the ever-unfolding sequence of present acts are engaged in a constant dialogue over the total value of a person's moral life—a dialogue that extends across the person's life. Our interest in this chapter lies with a different type of revision of a person's acquired deserts that the passage of time may introduce; not merely the revision brought about by novel moral events, trailing new deserts, that may populate such time, but one brought about by the very passage of time itself.

The guiding concern can be brought into focus by first pointing out that desert is a naturally temporal relation—a relation between past and present. The continuation of desert over time means that the person is held accountable and responsible for deeds carried out some time in the past. But how long can this relation extend before extenuating itself—both in the sense of *weakening* the relation and *lessening the seriousness* of the failure to give a person their deserts?

The issues at stake can be sharpened by considering the hesitation we feel, to different degrees in different cases, about holding a person responsible—where this, at its most forceful, means meting out to them an appropriate punishment—for acts submerged in the distant past. The passage of time seems to have an important effect in diminishing the propriety of a moral response to the past. Do we punish the Nazi officer who evaded justice for years, and by now a frail octogenarian pensioner, is caught and tried over acts committed some sixty or more years ago in their youth? Our response to such cases would be calibrated by a variety of factors, such as the weight of the misdeed—the officer's collusion in genocidal crimes commands a revulsion that a burglary or local fraud, discovered decades later, would not—or the fact that the effects of the misdeed have not been entirely extinguished—as in the continued trauma of survivors.

But our response to such cases would also be complicated by the fact that often it is not a purely retributive—desert-based—rationale that dictates it: the Nazi officer would not merely be punished, so late in the day, out of an austere principled sense that "it serves them right" or "they deserve it." There would be a variety of other reasons serving a more utilitarian rationale, such as the significance of the act of punishment as a symbolic means of reaffirming our moral indignation and condemnation of an atrocity of extraordinary proportions posing a threat that has not altogether receded from our horizon. It would take an elimination of such consequentialist considerations from the balance of judgment in order to see more clearly one of the most critical factors on which our response to such prospects of belated retribution naturally depends—and this is the perception of a continued connection between the person who stands before us as a possible object of punishment and the person as they were at the time of committing the acts that constitute the reason for punishing them. Were it not for the consequentialist reasons advocating the punishment of belatedly discovered crimes, we would find it hard to sanction punishing the person who committed them years ago if now we encounter them transformed and morally regenerated. It is hard for me to blame you for something you did if you are no longer the kind of person who did it, if the callous character of long ago has given way to a gentler nature and a more refined moral sensitivity. Even though you are the same person, you are not the same *kind* of person. Here the passage of time is crucial not so much as the scene for different moral acts interacting with the value of previous acts but as the scene for a difference in the moral character from which acts might arise. And the concern with this sort of continuity has its strongest (though not an exclusive) association with a desert-based retributivism.

Already the above formulations show the strong links that such a concern with the justification of deserved treatments has with philosophical questions about the identity of persons over time. It is this concern with linkage between past and present that is shown in the idea, expressed by John Locke in a discussion of personal identity that stresses the role of continued consciousness in sustaining it, that one should not be punished for actions that one cannot recall or associate with oneself—though this must mean: that one *could* recall, under ideal circumstances (including the full self-presence that will occur by God's agency on the Day of Judgment).[1] It is shown, likewise, in the claim that one should be punished only for acts that are characteristic of one's nature at the time of one's act, as in John Stuart Mill's defense of the death penalty in cases where "the attendant circumstances suggest . . . nothing to make it probable that the crime was an exception to [the criminal's] general character rather than a consequence of it."[2] But this stress on a *concurrent* accord between an act and a person's character seems particularly important as supplying the conditions for the subsequent ascription of responsibility to the person for their act on the basis of its having originated in the character that *continues* to be theirs. One finds a good exemplar of this latter stance in David Hume, whose view is worth quoting here a bit more fully as it provides an unusually sharp foil for the discussion that follows:

> Actions are, by their very nature, temporary and perishing; and where they proceed not from some *cause* in the character and disposition of person who performed them, they can neither redound to his honour, if good; nor infamy, if evil. The actions themselves may be blameable . . . but the person is not answerable for them; as they proceeded from nothing in him that is *durable and constant*, and leave nothing of that nature behind them, it is impossible he can, upon their account, become the object of punishment and vengeance.[3]

Durability, of course, is a double-edged blade, and one's discomfort with this notion is linked with the fear of an overly determinate view of human character that would expose moral responsibility as a mirage. While it is necessary that there be something connecting the person to their past that justifies the application of the moral predicate "deserves" to a person over time, for a moral theory that does not subscribe to a deterministic view of human action, this means toeing the line between the extreme of making the object of blame the "person as such" and that of "blaming their acts."

One of the aspects that this account (albeit brief) makes clear is that the duration of desert may be described as a special instance of the broader issue of the duration of the self and the conditions for its identity, and thus that the way one understands the metaphysics of personal endurance is bound to affect how one conceives the endurance of one's moral state. The distance between the two questions was nugatory for Locke, who explicitly signaled his interest in personal identity as deriving from a concern with moral and legal responsibility (the concept of the "person" was in turn understood as a forensic term). And it has been said that "our notions of 'what people are' are to a large extent moral notions."[4] The distance will be much smaller if, as has sometimes been suggested, the project of a philosophical inquiry into personal identity that is self-contained and abstracts from the ends that give the question its significance is as senseless as the insistence that one should be able to determine whether to call something "rain" or merely "drizzle," or to say that someone with half a head of hair is to be called "bald" or not, without any practical reasons that make the choice necessary and impose criteria for choosing. Our purposes then carve out a question of the following form: In what way *must* a person endure through time in order to satisfy the requirements spelled out by the concern with moral responsibility and the justification of punishment? The features of a person that such a question picks out will be inescapably moral ones.

Having set out the ingredients of our own perspective that make such questions necessary, it is important to explain how the specifically Muʿtazilite moral landscape produces them, and intimates the possibility of answering them. If the question of the endurance of desert arises in Muʿtazilite theology at all, it is because the affirmation of the necessity of punishment and reward—on different grounds for Baṣrans and Baghdadis—was coupled with an affirmation of their *perpetuity* (*dawām*). On quitting the present world, heavy with deserts, each person would be assigned to one of the two abodes—paradise or the Fire—to be rewarded or punished. Thereafter, one would continue to be subjected throughout eternity to the treatment one deserved on the moment of death. This position could be stated especially forcefully with regard to reward, as in Ibn Mattawayh's remark in explaining the term "*dawām*":

> What we mean by this is that at every fresh moment, the person rewarding continues to be obliged to do as much as he had done before, and that there is no moment when the person being rewarded ceases to deserve that one do to him as much as was done to him before.[5]

But mutatis mutandis (and among the mutanda would be the value ascribed to the act of giving a person their deserts), the same applied to punishment. Thus, an act committed at a given point in one's life—and as long as its moral consequences had not been reversed by any subsequent actions—constitutes the ground for deserving certain consequences not only over a lifetime but over eternity.

The perpetuity of these treatments accentuates a problem that would have presented itself even on scales of time more modest than this one. What was calculated to make the Baṣran Muʿtazilite position even starker was an additional twist in their eschatological narrative, which theorized the entire annihilation (*fanāʾ*) of the created world after the death of the last human being, so that the *dār al-taklīf*—the abode in which the obedience to law was required—was annihilated as both a physical and a moral state, allowing the fresh re-creation of the world on the Day of Judgment as the scene of the new moral economy, in which one receives the consequences of one's former obedience or disobedience. The stark prospect of a complete annihilation of all beings that this view envisaged added to the steep ontological transitions that a person's identity would have to survive before the person could come into their deserts.[6] The Baṣran claim, then, was that throughout all these transitions, and the duration of one's subsequent experience of deserved suffering or enjoyment, the moral efficacy of one's past actions—actions committed as long ago as in one's youth, or as recently as in one's old age and at the brink of expiring—would not be extinguished, and one's desert would survive throughout nothing less than an eternity.

Yet what suggested the possibility of an answer to the problem this seems to pose was, on the one hand, the set of terms used by the Baṣran Muʿtazilites, as we have already seen, in discussing the concepts of moral evaluation of blame and praise. In the definitions given by both Mānkdīm and Ibn Mattawayh, these were understood as statements descriptive of a person; in particular, they form descriptions of the moral state or status (*ḥāl*) of a person (*yunbi'u ʿan ittiḍāʿ/ʿiẓam ḥāl al-ghayr*). But Ibn Mattawayh performs us a far greater service in the terms he uses to refer to the type of description at issue, talking of blame as "a particular kind of predicative statement" (*khabar makhṣūṣ*).[7] Predicative statements of this sort aim to give information, and are to be judged on the standards of whether they conform to reality or fail to do so, whether they are true or false, as is evident in their definition: "Predicative statements are those that admit of truth or falsehood" (*ammā al-khabar, fa-huwa mā yaṣiḥḥu fīhi al-taṣdīq wa'l-takdhīb*).[8] The moral description involved in blaming clearly must be a true one. What makes it true then? The state of the person, these terms suggest; it is this that gives the reference of the description. If blame endures (and it is desert that would justify blame), the application of the description must endure as well: it must be "enduringly true"; and if its truth endures, so, it would seem, must its reference, which makes it true. How does the moral state of a person endure? What are the criteria that validate the application of this description to a person over time? To these questions, the Baṣran Muʿtazilites' terms seem to intimate the possibility of an answer.

Another intimation does even more to redeem our credentials as listeners rather than conversational partners. For while in part the impetus for questions about the endurance of desert, and the connection between past and present stages of the self that it demands, derives from the concern *we* have that moral desert be intimately connected to the individual, the inspiration is of Muʿtazilite provenance to the extent that it is they who have instructed us always to seek out the mode of "*ikhtiṣāṣ*"—the exclusive possession of an attribute by a being—and taught us likewise that the utmost in such exclusivity (*nihāyat al-ikhtiṣāṣ*) for created beings is that the quality *inhere* in the being as its substrate (*al-ḥulūl fi'l-maḥall*).[9] Our search for something existing in the "substrate" of the person as a continuing ground for desert is in line with this cardinal orientation of Baṣran Muʿtazilite metaphysics.

Yet the expectations arising from these intimations must be carefully balanced by those fostered by what we saw in the previous chapter, where we found several aspects of the Baṣrans' conceptual matrix—and most crucially the role of the legal currency of *ḥuqūq*—discouraging the construction of desert as something *in* the person. In this chapter, one of the main tasks will be to resolve and synthesize these competing pulls, in order to determine what place they allotted in the Baṣran vision to the concept of moral identity and continuity, or to that of character and moral qualities, in the background of an overriding concern with the justification of deserved treatments, and in particular with the special challenge posed by a deferred yet—once realized—eternal punishment. In training the light on questions about the continuity of the moral person, the result—as we will see—will in great part be a study in negation: an account of the sources and resources for the absence of an account of such continuity.

An Eternity of Punishment: The Baṣran Justification of Dawām al-ʿIqāb

If the Baṣran Muʿtazilites' view of the endurance of deserts was up for challenge due to the vast time scales in which it claimed application, there was something additional to be said about the paradoxical amalgam of principles that resulted from their affirmation of the eternal duration of deserved treatments. As we have already seen, it was their claim that according to reason, pardon is good and a right of the one who pardons (*ḥaqq li'l-ʿāfī*), and that God could have pardoned sinners were it not for His once-given, not-to-be-falsified word that He would not do so.[10] The conjunction of these two positions amounted to a claim that punishment is not necessary by virtue of desert (only by virtue of the verbal commitment), but once it has become necessary on other grounds, it is necessary that it be perpetual; and the same rational faculty that judged that pardon is good, judges the perpetuity of punishment to be necessary. This stance may exemplify the Baṣrans' prevarication about the grounds for punishment, and the attempt to find rational grounds may reveal their dissatisfaction with the idea that the verbal commitment itself provides sufficient justification of punishment.

These Muʿtazilites therefore adduced several arguments in an attempt to account for the perpetuity of punishment. One of these was grounded in scripture, and the fact that punishment is deserved in perpetuity (or "eternally": *ʿalā ṭarīqat al-dawām*)—and indeed that it is *good* that it be perpetual—was deduced from the twin premises that God will punish grave sinners for all eternity (a datum of scripture, according to the Baṣrans, though one contested by their opponents) and that He only does what is good (a datum of rational inquiry); thus, it must be good that they be eternally punished.[11]

It is the second argument, however, that holds special interest, as it goes to the heart of the questions I want to ask by making a case for perpetuity in which endurance is assigned to desert as an intrinsic and necessary feature. Here it is asserted that the principles of punishment are the same as those of blame, and that both stand or fall together, for what has a determinant effect (*mu'aththir*) in both is the fact that the person committed acts of disobedience and breached their obligations. And "since it is known that blame is deserved in perpetuity, the same must apply to punishment."[12] But how is it known that blame is perpetually deserved? "This is not something that could be doubted," Mānkdīm continues,

> for it is known that if one strikes his father and persists in this act, it is good that his father as well as others continue to blame him for that act to no end [*dā'iman*), so that even if it was supposed that God took his life and then revived him anew, it would continue to be good that his father blame him, just as it would be good that all rational beings do so.[13]

The same claim, with some interesting conceptual extensions, is echoed by Zamakhsharī, who writes:

> There is no time at which we cease to consider it good to praise one who does good and blame one who commits offenses [*muḥsin, musī'*] barring the annulment of these [deserts], for the grounds of desert are such as are perpetual, namely, one's being a *muḥsin* or a *musī'*—barring annulment of these [deserts]—and this is what has the determinant effect; since the determinant cause is perpetual, its effect must also be perpetual.[14]

The two accounts evidently have several features in common. One is their appeal to necessary or self-evident knowledge, fortified behind the commanding force of the consensual "we" and the "rational beings" whom Mānkdīm and Zamakhsharī, respectively, make the informants for their claims, using their empirical moral judgments as indications of universal rational truths. I will need to say more soon about these beings, and the practice of perceiving and confirming moral truths exclusively through their judgment, when their controversial role in the Muʿtazilites' ethical speculations comes in for closer scrutiny.

Here, our attention must be drawn toward the encouraging finding that these Muʿtazilites had clearly recognized the importance of seeking out an enduring ground that would underlie the endurance of desert. But this finding is hostage to an interpretative task on which the entire cogency of the argument rests: Just *what* are the grounds of desert that are understood as enduring? The response Zamakhsharī gives is seemingly plain—it is the person's being a benefactor or a malefactor. Yet far from being plain, the obvious sense of the words would seem to beg the question being asked. For if to be a benefactor or a malefactor, a *muḥsin* or a *musī'*, indicates the continued performance of good or evil acts, then this would hardly seem a response to the difficulty of explaining how a person continues to deserve certain things after—potentially a *long* time after—the cessation of the acts generating these deserts.

The interpretative possibilities would seem to be foreclosed even more clearly by an aspect of Muʿtazilite ontological theory that directly comes to bear on the application of these moral attributes, and would seem to block the capacity to consider them as *enduring* ones. Here, a brief snapshot of the contents of this theory will be needed in order to situate the issue, anticipating a more detailed discussion soon to come. One of the chief concerns of Muʿtazilite ontology was to give an account of the relations in which entities stood to the attributes they possessed—more properly, of the mode by which entities came to be entitled to their attributes. The word for entitlement we already know—*istiḥqāq*—but in the sense in which it refers to a moral normative relation; in the context of ontology, its sense shifts and comes to denote a normative force of an ontological kind. To say of a being that it "deserves" or "is entitled to" (*yastaḥiqqu*) an attribute is to say that there is a reason or ground for the predication of this attribute of the being. In a terminological twist that was yet again homonymous to the usage of the moral domain, the inquiry into a being's relation to its attribute was framed as an inquiry into the *wajh al-istiḥqāq*—"mode of entitlement"—for that attribute. Attributes are distinguished by the way in which the being of whom they are predicated is entitled to them, and one of the differences between God and created beings is the way in which they are entitled to their attributes: attributes that God possesses by virtue of His essence (e.g., knowledge), created beings like ourselves possess by virtue of certain "accidents" (*maʿānī*).[15]

We will be encountering the diverse *wujūh* of ontological entitlement again below, but here our immediate concern is with identifying the precise ground basing the attribution of the terms at issue. *Muḥsin* and *musīʾ* were diagnosed by the Baṣrans as members of a category of predications that were said to be derived from acts (*ṣifāt/asmāʾ mushtaqqa*). The criterion for predicating such qualities of a person is the existence of the relevant act from their part, and it is the existence of this act that exhausts the signification (*fāʾida*) of the quality. These are predications "to which [one] is entitled on one's performance of particular actions by way of derivation from the act performed."[16] Even within this brief characterization, the implication can be clearly traced: to say that the criterion of attribution is that the agent *be engaged* in the act they denote is to say *currently* engaged ("*on* the performance of the actions"). What ʿAbd al-Jabbār says about the general qualification "acting" (*fāʿil*)—discussed in connection to God—extends just as well to all other predications deriving from specific acts that can also be made of human agents: "If it were said: Do you describe God as never having ceased to be 'acting'? It would be said: This cannot be attributed to Him except on the existence of the act."[17]

Thus, one can predicate "hitting" or "speaking" of an agent only *on* and *for the duration* of their hitting and speaking; similarly with doing good or committing offenses, which confer attributes of this "active" (*fiʿlī*) sort. As this position was one that was articulated with reference to theological ramifications—indeed, it resulted in the denial that act-derived attributes could be said of God throughout eternity and the affirmation that they could *only* be said of God on His performance of the relevant acts, such as "Beneficent" (*mutafaḍḍil*) or "Creating" (*khāliq*) on actions of beneficence or creation—it is unlikely that Zamakhsharī would not have been mindful of it.

One possible account here would be that Zamakhsharī was not really thinking of these predicates at all, as the reference to annulment may suggest: for it is deserts, not acts or act-derived attributes, that can be annulled. This may be an instance of conflation between acts and deserts—though on a different level—where "good doer" and "offender" are used as shorthand for "deserving such as a good doer or an offender deserves." That being the reference, the question why this deservingness endures would still await answer.

Yet the more charitable account would involve attending to a certain crucial distinction between acts that the Baṣran Muʿtazilites did not explicitly make but can be said to imply in several places, and that would provide an obvious way of overcoming the ostensible momentariness of act-derived attributes. Adding to these advantages is the fact that Mānkdīm's argument could cleanly come to dovetail with it. For among the variety of possible actions grouped together as grounds for act-derived attributes, there is a difference to be marked between hitting and speaking, on the one hand, and doing good and committing offenses, on the other, in terms of the temporal duration in which each act is individuated. There is no difficulty identifying when a person started hitting and when they stopped, or when a person started speaking and when they stopped—or what it would mean to *interrupt* these actions—and assigning definite duration to these acts in a way that does not comfortably transfer to an action such as giving money to the poor or stealing a person's belongings. There is a definite moment in which one writes the check of a donation, just as there is a definite moment in which Saint Augustine stole the pears in the story he recounts in his *Confessions.* But how long after that is one to be called a person who gives money to the poor? Until the check is cashed? Until one refuses the next opportunity to give? How does one judge what was the next opportunity? And for how long after he stole and consumed the pears would a Muʿtazilite have described Saint Augustine as "thieving"? Would it be for as long as he would be expected to make reparations for his theft? The same could be asked of all types of offenses, insofar as they violate the *ḥuqūq* of another person that thereafter *remain* violated until righted. If you fail to pay back a debt at the appointed time (this being included in the category of offenses), thereafter you are continually failing to pay back the debt—that is to say, you are continually offending. The *ḥaqq* you owe remains, and its force is not extinguished by the passage of time. Given the Baṣran Muʿtazilite view that reparations for past evil acts were *always* expected and in order, it seems that the duration of the act of offending would have to be construed as extending as long as the balances—moral and material—are not restored and the effects of the act at all levels spoken of above have not been removed. This is to suggest that the end of the act would be coextensive with the agent's act of repentance and/or apology, thereby transcending the instantaneity that would seem to mark the category of act-derived attributes. And while hitting and speaking may differ in this respect, in another, considered under their description as offenses against another person—as in unjustly inflicted pain or words of calumny—these acts too would result in an enduring attribution.

On the face of it, Mānkdīm's example might seem to go no further than merely asserting the claim to be proven ("we blame perpetually"), only supplying detail by furnishing us with a concrete case of wrongdoing. The special strength of the example lies in its representing a violation of the highly prized duty of filial piety (a moral paradigm about which there will be more to say shortly). But read in conjunction with Zamakhsharī's remarks and the above interpretation, Mānkdīm provides a linchpin to an understanding of the reasoning at work by talking of the son's persistence (*iṣrār*) in the act. At first blush, this idea would seem to suffer from the same interpretative impasse as the former theologian's: for if to "persist" means to be *currently* engaged in the act, then the scenario of the refractory son is useless for understanding the survival of desert after the cessation of acting, for acts submerged in the past. Yet once we have introduced the distinction between two types of act—those of definite and indefinite duration—and once we have seen that hitting (the subject of this example) may be viewed under its aspect as an offense, we may see that persistence in the act of hitting would mean (would have to mean) continuing to approve it, which is signified by one's failure to reverse it by apologizing to one's father and repenting of one's terrible act.

This interpretation of the notion of persistence is supported by several passages in ʿAbd al-Jabbār's *Mughnī*, which bring out more sharply the opposition between persistence and repentance, suggesting that one ceases to persist by repenting of one's act. The application of both predicates to a person by calling him a "*muṣirr tā'ib*" ("one who persists and repents") is considered a contradiction in terms, which would have as a consequence "that persistence would not be in all aspects a contrary of repentance"—which our author clearly holds it to be.[18] In addition, ʿAbd al-Jabbār's remarks on the notion of persistence help shore up the view articulated above concerning act-derived attributes of indefinite duration. This emerges via a response he makes to an objector, whose criticism is directed against his view of repentance, and who proposes to construe the person who persists—that is, who has not repented—as one who "continues to perform his act of disobedience" (*yadūmu ʿala'l-maʿṣiyya*). Now *this* concept of "continuing" is clearly understood in terms of an uninterrupted sequence of acts of the first type, modeled on "hitting" or "speaking," as is obvious from ʿAbd al-Jabbār's reply, in which he denies that persistence can be understood in this way:

> On this view, it would not be possible to describe the person as persisting [*muṣirr*] if he stopped committing his act of disobedience in order to eat or drink, so that only the person committing the act of

> usurping [*ghaṣb*] without interruption would be persisting in usurping, and likewise for unlawful intercourse [*zinā*] and theft [*sariqa*]. Thus, a person who turned from unlawful intercourse with one woman to unlawful intercourse with another would not be persisting [in the act] due to the separation between them.[19]

On the one hand, it is important to note that this exchange involves the capacity to consider the act of usurping as an act of definite duration on a par with eating and drinking (and hitting or speaking), which could be interrupted by these acts. But to reject the idea that *persistence* in this action is an act of definite duration is tantamount to rejecting the idea that this *action itself* can be construed as one of definite duration, lasting only as long as one is engaged in the act itself—stealing the pears or filling one's bag with the goods. One would have to be called a usurper (*ghāṣib*) once one has usurped an object over which one had no rights and for as long as one continues to use the usurped object, the return of the object (or its equivalent value) normally marking one's repentance from the deed.[20] Similarly with the terms *sāriq* or *zānī,* for theft and unlawful intercourse.

Where does all this place us in terms of assessing the Baṣran Muʿtazilite answer to the problem posed by an eternally continuing desert? With the above examples, a certain degree of continuity seems to have been set down between the present person and their past deeds. This continuity rides on the obligation to repent, which is generated immediately after an evil act and persists for as long as one has not responded to it. Due to the normative demand to repent, it becomes essentially inadmissible for one to lose one's continuity with—one's relationship to—one's past in the first place after an evil deed has been committed. The failure to respond is considered *by default* a continued endorsement of the act. The conditions set down for repentance and apology, as we will recall, stipulate an experience of regret about committing an evil act under its description as evil and an offense, respectively. One's regret and one's resolution not to return to the act must attach to these descriptions. By default, failure to experience such regret signifies that one continues to identify—as we would put it—with the past act and the larger category of acts in which it belongs. This suggests that the continuity of deserving, and the right to blame and hold responsible, is founded on the continuity of moral (or, that is, immoral) beliefs.

One initial worry with this solution is that as an argument for the duration of desert, it would seem to beg the question. For the reason one has for repenting of a deed—even after an entire lifetime from its commission—is that one wants to avoid the punishment that one deserves. But then our question has been precisely about whether there is enough of a connection between person and past to make him deserve this. To base continuity (which we seek as the basis of desert) on facts about one's moral beliefs *deduced*—by default—from one's violation of the obligation to repent seems to be circular, given that this obligation is founded on the existence of deserts to be eliminated. In addition, it might be questioned whether a solution like this could help us understand why one could attribute desert to a person who is no longer capable of repenting and is at present in the course of experiencing an eternity of punishment.

Yet even should these worries be brushed aside, as a solution it would seem to simultaneously give too much and too little. Too much, in the sense that far surpassing our demands for a basis of continuity between the person and their past act that would be the basis for their desert, it hands us a continuum that is nothing less than a continuous chain of active moral breaches—breaches of the obligation to repent. And the breach of an obligation is an independent ground of desert. But do the Baṣrans thereby deliver us this "something" in the person that we were seeking?

The proposed connection between past and present seems to give too little in being afflicted by a certain emptiness that belies its origins in a charitable interpretation. Something of this emptiness can be felt by noting that while this can be presented as a chain of "active" violations of an obligation, it is not a question of a chain of chosen *acts*. For—as mentioned in chapter 1, in introducing the Baṣran debate over the relatum or ground of blame—not doing the obligatory is not an *act* in the view of Abū Hāshim and his followers. For the latter denied the "plenitude of acts" principle, according to which the agent's being capable of autonomous action (*qādir*) is a necessary and sufficient condition for action, and instead conceived it as a merely necessary one. One might possess the capacity for autonomous action without being "acting" (*fāʿil*). A complement of their ontological position was the view—alluded to above—that it is not necessary that the relatum or reason for blame be a positive act but may be the absence of an act, a simple not-doing. On this model, the failure to repent is not an *act* but the absence of an act.[21] Thus, it is no act continuum that exists. The Baṣrans evidently did not feel that their moral views on desert needed to be complemented by a different ontological position on the continuum of acts.

This negative vision, urging the emptiness of the temporal connection, is reinforced by considering two interrelated points. One is that the content of this failure that seemed the most positive—namely, the continued endorsement of a type of act, which in Baṣran terms would need to be construed as the continuing belief (*iʿtiqād*) that it is good to do—once again seems to lack ontological infrastructure. And here we start to drive our wedge deeper toward the larger metaphysical landscape that forms the backdrop of the Baṣran Muʿtazilites' ethical speculations. We have already gained a glimpse of this landscape in outlining one of its chief characteristics—namely, a concern with identifying the mode of entitlement that grounds entities' possession of their attributes. To predicate belief of a sentient being requires a similar quest for grounds of entitlement, and this time they are to be located in an ontological constituent best translated as an "entitative accident" (*maʿnā*), understood to inhere in the physical body of a person. Anticipating a closer survey of these ontological resources below, here I may simply note that predominantly, no account seems to have been provided by the Baṣran Muʿtazilites for the continuity of these ontological constituents that would form the basis of a continuous attribution of belief to a person.[22]

One reason for this, one suspects, is that their account of the endurance of desert may not have been developed with the sharpest and most disturbing paradigm in mind—that is, the evil act committed once, or episodically, and never again, with an entire lifetime subsequently coming to put distance between the agent and his past deed. In those of ʿAbd al-Jabbār's passages that talk about a person's persistence in evil acts, the revealing word is the "resolve"—*ʿazm, ʿazīma*—to do evil that this theologian sometimes associates with the notion of persisting, and that makes it appropriate to speak of a person as still a usurper or offender. "Resolve . . . is the surest means by which one comes to persist." "People describe the person committing an act of disobedience as one who persists (*muṣirr*), if one continues to engage in it or cling to it, on account of the resolve we have spoken of."[23] And to talk of resolve indicates that one is thinking about a person's acting *again*, in the *future*. That is to say, the guiding paradigm is of a repeated series of evil actions, of a past connected to a future by a consistency in the performance of a certain type of deed.

This was to shy away from the sharper vision of the problem that the Muʿtazilites' Ashʿarite colleagues took special pleasure in brandishing before them, in which it was a *single* lapse—an act not resumed by another—that was dragged throughout eternity and left an inextinguishable trail of desert behind it. Ashʿarites from Juwaynī to Shahrastānī derided their rational-minded coreligionists for the absurdity of their claim that an eternity of punishment could depend on a single act of numinous importance. It is known *necessarily*, Juwaynī affirms, that a single impulsive act or slip (*bādira wāḥida, zalla wāḥida*) cannot warrant eternal punishment: consider a person who has consumed himself in the service of another with the utmost diligence and devotion, for a hundred years and more, and who then gives in to such an impulse and lapses—surely an eternity of retribution is an unreasonable response? Evaluation of one's deservingness should not occur in a saltatory way, through leaps from category to category, but on a continuum, which takes account of the person's life in a more holistic way. This critique was the reverse side of the Ashʿarite position concerning the incommensurability of the divine realm and the human. The Ashʿarites rejected the idea of univocal moral standards that would survive the change of paradigm from "seen" to "unseen"—from *shāhid* to *ghāʾib*—and countered with an alternative paradigm wherein God was cast as sovereign and humankind as subject (*mālik* versus *mamlūk*), taking the difference in status to entail a difference in the principles and concepts applicable to each, and making it difficult to see what standard of commutation could determine such high value for our acts.[24]

One of the most troublesome aspects of this criticism was its way of citing commonsense sentiment and necessary knowledge, thus threatening to raise the dispute to the strident pitch of counterassertions. For did not Muʿtazilites like Mānkdīm and Zamakhsharī invoke our commonsense intuitions as well when they spoke of the perpetuity of blame? Mānkdīm: "It is known that . . ." Zamakhsharī: "There is no time at which we cease to consider . . ." It is on this facet of their arguments and to the difficulties it yields that we must now take a moment to dwell.

Now strictly speaking, the Ashʿarite criticism just referred to could here be dismissed by these Muʿtazilites as an irrelevance, on the grounds that it did not directly pertain to the claim concerning the perpetuity of punishment. To talk about the value of a single act and contrast it with the more continuous evaluation of a lifetime was neither here nor there for this particular claim, due to a distinction the Baṣrans sought to draw between claims about the *duration* of punishment (or reward) and those to do with the *quantity* of punishment and reward deserved for each act. Different acts attracted different quantities (*maqādīr*) of desert, and some were heavier than others. Yet the eternity (*dawām*) of punishment was not conceived as an aggregate of particularly heavy deserts. In a whimsical-sounding claim, the Baṣrans stated that *every* evil act gave rise to deserts of eternal duration, *regardless* of the particular intensity or quantity of the deserved punishment that would be experienced over this duration. It was a feature of acts qua evil that the desert of punishment they attracted was eternal. This is the burden of Ibn Mattawayh's argument when he writes,

> Since we know that minor [*ṣaghā'ir*] and major [*kabā'ir*] sins share with unbelief the quality we mentioned [namely, its evilness], they too must make one deserve punishment. . . . And since it is a characteristic [*ḥukm*] of punishment that it be perpetual, this cannot vary between different evils. . . . As for the difference between minor and major sins, this lies in the quantities of desert that each of them entails.[25]

Unbelief was an act on which there was consensus that it attracted eternal punishment. This view of the perpetuity of desert could be read into Mānkdīm's remarks cited above, where the claim about the eternity of blame is linked to the breach of filial duty, considered as a single act in isolation from anything else one might have done or might do.

And yet of course, it was through the aggregation or interaction of bad and good deserts that one's destiny—whether paradise or the Fire—was decided, as we saw in synopsizing the Baṣran theory of the frustration (*iḥbāṭ*) and expiation (*takfīr*) of deserts. Thus, it would seem that the quantitative aspect determined *whether* one was punished or rewarded (and perhaps also some dimension of intensity, though this is not entirely clear); the durational aspect determined how *long* one was punished or rewarded. One might find the distinction far-fetched and query the possibility of separating these two aspects; for couldn't the son blamed for an eternity legitimately ask, "Why am I being punished *so much*?" But it is important to point out one principal reason why Mānkdīm's and Zamakhsharī's remarks had to be construed as—and confined to—claims about duration. And this was that a number of Baṣran masters insisted that the gravity of an act, and therefore the *quantity* of punishment deserved by it, is not known by reason: only by revelation can one know the difference between a grave sin (*kabīra*) and a minor one (*saghīra*). Left to the devices of reason, we only have a vague insight into the weight of the deserts attracted by different acts.[26] By contrast, those remarks take place within the scope of rational knowledge.

To the extent that the Muʿtazilites responded to the incredulous criticisms of their opponents concerning the commutative principle regulating the quantities of deserved consequences, their most cogent argument derived from a paradigm that we will now be able to recognize. The Baṣrans invoked the disproportion between the benefits human beings have received from God and the evildoing that issues from them to explain why this evildoing should incur such grave consequences; the transgression acquires the character of an act of flagrant ingratitude. The paradigm to which they referred was that of the relationship between father and child. "For we know," writes Ibn Mattawayh, "that the magnitude of the bounty that a father provides magnifies the gravity of [the child's] disobedience and diminishes the value of his obedience. It is the same with the obedience and disobedience that a person displays toward God."[27] The paradigm of the unequal relationship between father and child possesses a significance that is far wider than such limited examples may suggest. It is a paradigm of moral values familiar to us from our this-worldly realm (the realm of the seen, of the *shāhid*) that is used to model the other-worldly realm (the realm of the unseen, the *ghā'ib*)—and more particularly, the relation that obtains between God and humans. A model with a ubiquitous presence in Muʿtazilite ethics, its importance lies in its representing a direct rival of the paradigm espoused widely by the Ashʿarites for describing the relation between God and human beings. This, as we just mentioned, was cast in terms of the sovereign and his subject—a relationship between *mālik* and *mamlūk*, in which the latter had no claims and the former no obligations.

It is this same paradigm—the relation between father and child—that we have seen employed by Mānkdīm in his example supporting the case for perpetual punishment. Now, whatever the other virtues of this paradigm, the use that is made of it on this particular occasion is not free from difficulties—difficulties that have the effect of problematizing the very epistemic basis on which the argument, and by extension the Baṣran moral edifice that it founds, appears to rest. What had the claim been? That the perpetual desert of punishment is proven by our necessary knowledge that the son, having struck his father, is to be blamed perpetually—to be more precise, that he is *in fact* blamed perpetually ("his father as well as others *continue* to blame him for that act to no end"). This claim is in line with the Muʿtazilite programmatic use of empirical moral judgments as the basis of universal moral truths, which is based on their views concerning human beings' necessary or self-evident knowledge (*ʿilm ḍarūrī*) of these truths. These views lead to a habitual conjoining between what people think is good and what is in fact and in itself good, as in the following indicative statement by ʿAbd al-Jabbār: "We have shown that the things that make an act evil cannot occur . . . without the act being evil, so that rational beings (*al-ʿuqalāʾ*) should approve of it and praise the one who does it on the sole basis of their reason; and this is how one distinguishes between evil and good."[28] That is to say, it is the fact that rational beings—human beings of mature reason—disapprove of it that is the basis for distinguishing between good and evil. Here we are picking up a strand left dangling at an earlier point of the discussion, in which it was remarked that the term *ḥukm*—used to refer to the primary moral data about an act; namely, the deserts it carries—can also signify the act of judgment performed by a particular subject, and that it is through the latter, subjective evaluative response that one has access to the former, objective features of an act.

This intuitionist knowledge was the first target of the Muʿtazilites' detractors' fire, and there are many objections that were and could be made to the employment of actual subjective judgments as the basis of the objective truth that it involved. But in this case, the difficulty is one that arises through the very richness and verisimilitude of the moral paradigm in which the Baṣrans deploy this knowledge.

It is ʿAbd al-Jabbār who first makes plain this troublesome richness when in the course of discussing the principles of apology and repentance in volume 14 of the *Mughnī*, he makes certain remarks that discuss and defend the attitude of sustained rejection that a father might show toward his child even after the latter apologizes for a wrongful act. The larger case under defense is the position that there is an obligation to accept a person's repentance, and it is in the course of his argument for this position that an objection is brought forth citing a case where apology (the worldly, interpersonal analogue of repentance) does not reinstate a person after a misdeed, thus appearing to contradict the defended position. "Isn't it the case," it is said, "that a person might offend against his father—the source of great beneficence toward him—so gravely that it is not good that he [the father] should accept his excuses?" ʿAbd al-Jabbār's reply comes as follows:

> Matters are not as you suppose . . . for it is good that the father, when his child offends against him gravely, should continue to shun him or hold back from him, in order to edify him in a way that will serve him in the future [*tahdhīban lahu fi'l-mustaqbal*]—not because his apology did not effect the elimination of what he deserves.

The thought tracked in this remark is expressed again in another context when ʿAbd al-Jabbār asks, Doesn't wisdom sometimes demand that one be lenient with a boy one wants to teach and sometimes harsh?[29] Ibn Mattawayh drives the same point forward in a different way: apart from the paradigm of the relationship between father and child, he introduces a new dimension to the significance of blame as such by classing it with the things that provide "means of assistance and serve one's welfare" (*min bāb al-alṭāf wa'l-maṣāliḥ*). It is an act that is good both for the person blamed, who is thereby deterred, and the person blaming, who is thereby led to "refrain from doing acts similar to those done by [the one blamed]."[30]

All of this marks a new way of regarding responses of blame (and correlatively praise) that departs from the Baṣrans' main formal position. Here, these responses are no longer construed merely as signifying and justified by what a person deserves, and a novel sensitivity is shown to the wider range of reasons—reasons of a forward-looking or consequentialist cast—that may motivate the expression of such evaluations. This is a sensitivity that would have been a welcome refinement of the Baṣran Muʿtazilites' views of punishment had it not been for the fact that it now threatens to wreak an inconsistency in their otherwise hermetically retributive approach, and here sharply undermines the capacity to use actual moral responses as indications of objective truths to draw conclusions about desert that would support this retributivism. For if the son could be exposed by his father and the larger community to severe and unremitting blame for reasons that have nothing to do with desert and far more to do with the father's intention to instruct and edify, what value do these responses possess as reports of moral facts about the son's desert?

This brings into sharp focus the reasons for the dissatisfaction experienced by the Muʿtazilites' opponents at this technique of pulling objective moral facts out of the hat by simply citing the ordinary person (or the ordinary person under a set of normative intellectual conditions) as their quotable authority. This practice came under greater strain the more controversial the moral facts became, and the more the ordinary person—endowed with innate moral knowledge—seemed to put a premature end to debate by a questionable trump card of "I just know." The competing grounds for the value of blame and punishment just mentioned make the weakness of the card clear by creating the need for an evaluation of evaluative judgments that would recognize *some* of them as faithful reports of moral reality, and some not. The controversy that Muʿtazilite views on reward and punishment excited in their religious community made the weakness of this card even clearer and more vexing.

Moral Identity and the Resources of Baṣran Muʿtazilite Ontology

Having paused to consider these questions—questions that go to the heart of the presuppositions on which Muʿtazilite ethics is founded—we can now take stock of our position in connection to my guiding questions. I began the discussion of the endurance of desert tensed between the contradictory pulls exercised by the Baṣrans' suggestive talk of a person's state (*ḥāl*) as the object of blame and their talk—seen in the previous chapter—of a person's desert in terms of another's right to blame and punish—the one pulling toward an intrinsic view and the other toward an extrinsic view of the normative relations generated by a person's moral history (desert as something *in* or *of* the agent, versus desert as something that characterizes another's act). The former seems most urgently required for the purposes of a retributive justification of punishment, and I have been pushing forward into the main breeding ground of Baṣran arguments for the perpetuity of deserved consequences in order to ferret out any further intimations of it. But finally, it must be concluded that the peculiar vacuity distinguishing the connection between past and present that we have come up against is in fact an intimation of a more programmatic indifference on the part of the Baṣrans. It is the extrinsic perspective on the person that gives the Baṣran Muʿtazilite moral perspective its distinctive warp and woof.

The task of the following discussion will be to give content to this perspective from several directions, beginning by tracking down the sources of the Baṣrans' programmatic indifference to any concept of intrinsic moral characteristics attaching to persons or to the continuity of the moral person. Talk of "sources" could express a task of greater ambition than the one I will be attempting here. For there is a variety of levels at which one might seek to explain the overwhelming orientation—for such it is—of Baṣran Muʿtazilite ethics toward the evaluation of acts, not of persons, and its lack of concern for questions of moral continuity. We have already seen one source of this orientation in connection with desert, and this is the influence of the legal conceptual matrix, which encourages the construal of moral desert (*istiḥqāq*) in terms of the right (*ḥaqq*) of the creditor to perform an act—blame, punishment—which in turn attracts the moral quality of goodness (*ḥasan*). This will be an important factor in explaining why the Baṣran repertory of attributes for which grounds of entitlement were sought did not consider the term deserving (*mustaḥiqq*) as an attribute of the agent. Nor, however, did this repertory include any interest in our ability to talk of persons as good or evil (as against their being agents of a particular good or evil act), or indeed to use the wider range of terms signifying morally significant qualities—such as whether a person is courageous or cowardly, generous or miserly, temperate or greedy, cruel or kindhearted, which we find explored with greater imagination by writers in classical Islam working closer to the Greek philosophical tradition, such as Miskawayh (d. 1030) and Naṣīr al-Dīn al-Ṭūṣī (d. 1274), or in a different way, al-Fārābī (d. 950)—to mention some of the most prominent examples—who exhibit a greater concern with a person's intrinsic moral qualifications.[31]

The roots of this exclusion are as complicated as the historical roots of the differences in the metaphysical visions separating the Greek, and especially Aristotelian, thought-world and that of the Muslim *mutakallimūn*. Here, my explanatory aim will not be to provide an account of these roots but will be the more modest one of presenting two types of relatively local accounts of the issue. This account has to be prefaced by distinguishing between two "directions" from which the relationship between morally significant acts and qualities may be viewed: the moral qualities a person possesses may explain why an act was committed; the act committed may explain why a person is described as possessing a certain moral quality. By the first direction, where qualities are *explanatory* of acts, one would explain why a person helped another at a time of need by saying "that person is kind, beneficent, *muḥsin,*" or why a person harmed another by saying "that person is cruel, maleficent, *musī',*" and the causal function of the quality may excite misgivings among libertarians (especially, though not only, where negative moral qualities are concerned); this possible conflict may explain the absence of moral qualities from a given moral theory. It is this sense that dominates in modern virtue ethics, in which character traits are considered as dispositions to act in particular ways (as well as to feel in particular ways and act for particular reasons). This is a conception that goes back to Aristotle, who described virtue as "the sort of state that does the best actions," and the virtuous agent as one who does virtuous actions "from a firm and unchanging state."[32] By the second direction, where acts are explanatory of the *attribution* of qualities, one would explain why the person is considered kind or cruel, *muḥsin* or *musī',* by referring to past acts of this type that they has undertaken. In this direction, the qualities predicated of someone are as *generalizations* of past acts.

It is the first way of viewing moral qualities and character that has been referred to by modern historians of philosophy—notably Alasdair MacIntyre—to explain the wane of the notion of character in post-Kantian ethics, whose desire to repulse the threat of determinism led to a reluctance to recognize the role of established moral traits in determining a person's choices. MacIntyre writes that "the moral agent's character, the structure of his desires and dispositions, became at best a peripheral . . . topic for moral philosophy" in part because the concepts of will and choice entertained by eighteenth-century philosophers such as Immanuel Kant and Thomas Reid required that they be understood as proceeding independently of any psychological or even causal antecedents—and this the concept of character might seem to preclude.[33]

This account does not—could not—find a precise parallel in Muʿtazilite ethics. For one thing, the latter lacks the necessary ingredients of conflict, such as the notion of voluntary action that portrays the agent as a kind of disembodied entity that stands as judge while competing reasons for action are presented to it. Concepts such as those of the reason or the will are not given as distinct entities pitted against the rest of the person, and mind and body are not located on opposite sides of a lurid dualist dichotomy; nor does the term "free will," as it is commonly understood in Western thought, have any exact counterpart in their thought (for reasons too complex to be detailed here, the concept signified by the term *qudra*—power, capacity for autonomous action—could not be taken as such a counterpart, even though it was the flagship of the Muʿtazilite encounter with the determinism of their opponents). But there is something to suggest that to the extent that the Baṣran Muʿtazilites entertained the notion of moral qualities at all as an intellectual option, it was something about the deterministic operation ascribed to them that led them to exclude these qualities from the domain of the morally meritorious.

This reading is encouraged by an interesting set of remarks with which ʿAbd al-Jabbār specifically regales us. In a serendipitous excursus from the principles of praise discussed in the book *al-Taklīf,* an interlocutor steps in to ask ʿAbd al-Jabbār whether his account of the objects or bearers of praise has been exhaustive. In his reply, ʿAbd al-Jabbār makes a rare reference to what approximates to a kind of praise that is directed to the person for features they possess, querying the inclusion of certain "*khiṣāl al-faḍl*" in the objects of praise. These *khiṣāl,* which may be translated as features of excellence or simply excellences, include strength: *quwwa*; intellectual capacities or the faculty of reason: *ʿaql*; knowledge: *maʿrifa*; courage: *shajāʿa*; and most unexpected of all, the fact or attribute of belonging to the house of the Prophet.

This array of characteristics or features of excellence seems to be a rather mixed assortment, for it includes both what we would call nonmoral excellences as well as what we would class as moral ones (particularly courage). Non-moral in two ways: for some of the items on the list, because their content is not moral (e.g., knowledge); for others, because one is not responsible for their existence (belonging to the house of the Prophet as well as intellectual capacities and strength, if these are understood as naturally acquired features).[34] One obvious suggestion about the provenance of these *khiṣāl al-faḍl* would tie them to the vexed theological disputes concerning the comparative merits of the first caliphs (Abū Bakr, ʿUmar, ʿUthmān, and ʿAlī)—a debate charged with weighty political significance. This idea is recommended not only by the strong lexicographical link (which of the caliphs is *afḍal,* the question of *tafḍīl*) but also by the fact that it would explain the inclusion of the genealogical qualification in the list of the above-mentioned *khiṣāl*—belonging to the house of the Prophet was one of the distinctive claims to superiority possessed by the fourth caliph ʿAlī.[35]

Moral or nonmoral, none of the items are deemed by ʿAbd al-Jabbār as relevant to his topic, including the one that seems particularly well placed to be a bearer of value—namely, courage—and the explanation given for the exclusion seems to class courage among the nonmoral items as well. To an extent, ʿAbd al-Jabbār seems to assert the exclusion axiomatically, saying simply that these items do not belong to the type of praise he has been considering, which concerns acts. To the degree that he offers an explanation, it is by way of an analogy. These characteristics, ʿAbd al-Jabbār notes, signify ways in which one person excels over another (is "*afḍal min ghayrihi*"), and one is *honored* and *extolled* on their account (the word is *taʿẓīm*)—and this sense is different from the moral type of praise. What sense is it instead? It is that by which "we honor God Almighty because He is knowing by His essence and powerful by His essence."[36]

The analogy is striking, for it compares the qualities on the list with the honor given to a being for qualities possessed essentially and, one may add, enduringly. What this shows, on the one hand, is that a tertium quid that bears the structure of the concept of personal qualities—and the structure of moral qualities in particular, in its inclusion of courage among the excellences—is indeed available to ʿAbd al-Jabbār. On the other hand, by alluding to essential predications, the conception draws these qualities in such a *close* relation to the person they are predicated of that their exclusion seems to stem from consigning them to the extreme end of the character-acts continuum, where in speaking of certain qualities, one is speaking of the person *as such*. Between the qualities (or dispositions) and the person, there is not sufficient distance for responsibility by voluntary causation to be interposed. Such qualities, we are left to assume, are ones that the person has not brought into existence. This is a partial analysis of the reasons, of course; the other part, nonanalyzable, consists of the axiomatic assertion of their irrelevance.

The above picture seems to receive confirmation in another set of interesting remarks made by ʿAbd al-Jabbār in a different context, in which he is dealing with the question of divine compensation due to created beings on account of undeserved suffering. Deciding whether suffering is deserved or undeserved rests on making certain kinds of judgments as to the causes of the suffering in question, and the extent to which its occurrence was within the control of the sufferer. If on my way to work on a fine morning, absorbed in a flight of fancy, I stumble and earn myself a sprained ankle, I will only have myself and my flighty moods to blame. But if my absent mind came over me because my night's sleep had been disrupted by my neighbors' rambunctious partying, in an ideal world I would be compensated for the suffering that resulted. The puzzles that burgeon around the question of control and responsibility can be glimpsed even in such a simple and relatively painless example. How finely does one draw the limits between what can and cannot be helped, between what is internal and external with regard to causation? Could I perhaps have had a better night's sleep had my resentment at my neighbors' insensitivity not doubled my sleep difficulties? And do I have any control over these paroxysms of passion, these moral habits of thinking and feeling? Questions about responsibility for suffering inevitably lead to captious debates about the scope of the voluntary.

Such questions need to be kept in the background as a foil for ʿAbd al-Jabbār's remarks in this connection. Discussing the compensation due to a person for grief experienced over uncontrollable events, ʿAbd al-Jabbār is arrested by another prompter-questioner who raises the following point:

> Different people respond with different degrees of grief [*ghamm*] when faced with adversities and harm. Thus the miser's grief will be great, and will exceed that which is experienced by one who is generous.... So is your view that all this requires compensation, or are there certain instances that would be judged to have been caused by the person who experiences the grief himself, thereby eliminating the need for compensation?

In his reply, ʿAbd al-Jabbār seems to categorically exclude this pair of character traits—miserliness and generosity—from the pale of the voluntary.

> If the difference between the degrees of grief is a result of divine action [*min fiʿlihi Taʿālā*], then this does not affect the necessity of receiving compensation in return for all of it. And it is God who effected in the miser (*faʿala biʾl-bakhīl*) the vexation that makes it onerous for him to give and increases the grief he experiences on the loss of a benefit, and it is He that effected in the generous person the magnanimity that makes it easy for him to do so.[37]

Having excluded these traits from the voluntary, he has also excluded them from the meritorious. The type of questions concerning responsibility that were raised above were answered by a stark denial of voluntary control.

Thus, it is partly a deterministic view of moral qualities that might account—in a local sense of "accounting"—for the Baṣran Muʿtazilites' indifference to these. But a second and more substantial account for the absence of a developed view of moral qualities must be traced in the resources that the Baṣrans' developed to describe ontological reality. This account, once again, will be a local one, in that the question will not be one of the historical origins that led to the formation of the Baṣran Muʿtazilites' metaphysics as much as one of describing the ways in which, in the stage of formation represented by the Jubbāʾites and their followers, it in fact programmatically excluded a concern with moral qualities and moral identity.

The first step in this direction must be made by limning the essential character of this metaphysics that conditioned the way in which the diverse subjects forming its syllabus were articulated—and that is its atomistic structure. Atoms (*jawāhir*) and accidents (*aʿrāḍ*) provided the main ontological joints of the metaphysics shared by most Muslim *mutakallimūn* as an account of the composition of the created world. Conceived as entities whose essential nature was to occupy space, atoms were the indivisible elements from which all bodies (*ajsām*)—all macroscopic objects—were composed. Seen from the perspective of a larger taxonomy, there were three broad categories into which being was divided: on the first division, things were classed into the existent and the nonexistent. Existents then subdivided into the class of existents that have a beginning in time and those that do not, the latter being a class with a single member—the divine Creator. Temporally originated existents once again subdivided into those whose nature it is to occupy space and those that do not, atoms composing the former class and accidents the latter.[38] The relationship between the two types of entities was seen as one of inherence: if the nature of atoms is to occupy space, that of accidents is to inhere in atoms, and in doing so to perform their main ontological function, which is at the same time the reason for their postulation: namely, to confer to their atomic substrates—whether individually or in aggregates—the qualities that we know them to possess. Atoms and the material aggregates they produce constitute the proper subjects of predications.

This, in broad strokes, was the background for the main enterprise engrossing the Muʿtazilites' ontological interest, which was to map the variety of ways in which beings related to their attributes. Originally stimulated by a strong theological concern—one never entirely lost, and only extended toward a less derivative interest in questions of physics and metaphysics—that aimed at furthering a particular view of God's attributes (sketched out in chapter 1), in its mature form the Baṣrans' ontological scheme recognized a definite number of relationships of entitlement (*wajh al-istiḥqāq*) between entities and attributes. For the purposes that guide us—in which we are concerned with the ontological resources relevant to a moral characterization of persons—the attributes that are of immediate interest are three: those whose grounds are the essence of a being, those whose grounds consist of an entitative accident, and those grounded in the action of an agent.[39]

The interest of the first lies mainly in the foil and perspective it creates for us; for it provides the basis for saying what the type of human features we are concerned with *cannot* be. The highest form of exclusive relation between a being and its attributes is realized when the being's essence (*dhāt* or *nafs*) supplies the grounds for its attributes. God's knowledge, power, or life are attributes of this sort, grounded in the divine essence, whose designation as "essential" (*dhātiyya*) signifies this relation of entitlement (and is therefore far from the sense ascribed to this word in the context of a philosophical concern with a being's definition and the identification of the attributes that it cannot lose without ceasing to exist). While human beings can share in the same qualities and be knowing, powerful, or living, the difference between God and human beings lies in the mode by which their qualification is achieved. Attributes that belong to God by virtue of the way He is in Himself (*mā huwa ʿalayhi*) and are thus necessary to Him (*wājiba*), are merely contingent (*jā'iza*) for human beings, and depend on two main grounds that entitle human beings to attributes: accidents, and actions performed by the agent.[40]

Accidents—in this connection specified as *maʿānī* (sing. *maʿnā*), which I follow Richard Frank in translating as "entitative" accidents—were responsible for conferring on beings a variety of different attributes. Again in Frank's words, an accident is "an intrinsic, determinant cause of some real aspect of the being of the subject," and its presence functions as a necessary cause for the being's possession of the corresponding attribute.[41] "Locative" characteristics such as an atom's being in motion (*mutaḥarrik*), at rest (*sākin*), or contiguous to or separate from another (*mujāwir, muftariq*) are explained through the inherence of the accident of motion (*ḥaraka*), rest (*sukūn*), and so on, in the substrate of the atom. Similarly with animate beings: the entity's being living (*ḥayy*) or knowing (*ʿālim*) is dependent on the inherence of particular accidents of life (*ḥayāt*) or knowledge (*ʿilm*) (the term "entitative" captures the reifying logic that led to the postulation of corresponding accidents).

But here a crucial distinction was marked by the later Baṣrans between two different types of predication that could be generated by the inherence of an entitative accident: the predications specific to animate beings—particularly human beings—and those specific to atomic composites that were not characterized by life. This distinction was introduced by Abū Hāshim through his theory of states, which offered a way of incorporating into Muʿtazilite ontology the "intuition"—which the atomistic point of departure could not automatically accommodate—that attributes predicated of human beings, while they are caused by the inherence of accidents in *atomic parts* of such beings, do not seem to redound to the atomic substrate but to the being as a whole. If Zayd is "knowing" or "willing," this is the result of corresponding entitative accidents of knowledge and will that inhere in specific atoms or atomic clusters within the composite whole—as, for example, knowledge may inhere in the single organ of the heart or some atoms therein. But the attribute of being knowing is predicated of the human being as a whole—of Zayd as a single entity. One does not say that the *atom* knows but that the *person* knows.

Abū Hāshim's theory pressed the claim that the accident of life (*ḥayāt*) has the function of conferring unity to the being in whom (or in which: for it is not yet a "who") it inheres, imparting to it "the status of a single thing" (it becomes *fī ḥukm al-shay' al-wāḥid*).[42] A corollary of this was the claim that any attributes that require life as their ontological precondition are in turn predicated of the being-as-whole as this has been unified by the presence of life, and not of any of its particular parts, even though the accidents that generate them similarly inhere in a limited atomic segment of the living whole. This analysis extended to attributes such as willing, intending, knowing, capable of autonomous action, and so on, which were identified as "states" (*ḥāl*, pl. *aḥwāl*) effected as attributes of the composite whole and represented "the way the thing is" (*mā huwa ʿalayhi*)—more precisely, the way the person is.[43]

For our purposes, what is important about this category of attributes is that its discussion unfolds on a level where the object of concern is constituted by generic attributes. The question concerns the ground for predicating knowledge, will, the capacity for autonomous action, or intention, as properties not yet individuated by their objects—by *what* one knows, *what* one wills, or *what* one intends, and thus by whether, for example, one wills evil or knows that one ought to choose a given act, whether one intends to lie or tell the truth, whether one regrets a past injustice, or whether one's beliefs about one's past actions are unchanged. Where an interest in the varieties of particularization enters the field, it is of a sort that has little connection to matters that concern value. For example, among the questions that engaged the energies of the Baṣran Muʿtazilites was the way in which the objects or "relata" of various attributes were differentiated through the kind of substrate in which the accidents generating them inhered. In this context, the Baṣrans explored the ways in which the object of the power of autonomous action (*qudra*) is specified by the structure of the organ in which it subsists—for instance, the *qudra* inhering in the hand has a different type of action as its object or relatum from that of the *qudra* inhering in the foot.[44] Another expression of this sort of interest—one that may seem to inch closer to our desideratum—could be traced in the discussion of the way in which accidents (such as the accident of knowing or willing) are differentiated by virtue of their relevant objects. Here, some held that the *qudra* for knowing, walking, or speaking are different in kind, and it was further debated whether, for example, the "quanta" (borrowing Frank's apt expression) of *qudra* for knowledge were differentiated according to the different objects known.[45]

But these shapes of questioning are still far from encouraging any attention to ontological particularizations of accidents and attributes that would be of moral significance, and individuation arising through moral and voluntary action. Although the attributes of this category—and in particular those predicated of living beings—are formulated in terms reminiscent of those we encountered above in connection with desert, in ʿAbd al-Jabbār's reference to *mā ʿalayhi al-madhmūm,* and Mānkdīm's and Ibn Mattawayh's references to praise and blame as describing the "*ḥāl*" of the person, this interesting link yields nothing further. The most that can be said about any connection of "being deserving" to this category of attributes is that praise and blame are said to be predicated of the living whole. The reason for this is that the attributes that gave rise to the act—whether as preconditions, such as the power of autonomous action, or as causes, such as motivation (understood as a type of knowledge)—are predicated of the whole, and the subject of predication is inherited by the responses that are deserved through the act.[46] But no entitative accident is shown to ground this attribute—deserving—nor perhaps could any have been expected on this generic level of ontological qualification. And it is not that one could not succeed in eliciting a response to the shape of one's questions by way of an exercise of laborious exegesis that would unveil the potential of the Muʿtazilite scheme for developing answers to such concerns. It is that it is unlikely that this could be accomplished without becoming a Muʿtazilite oneself, and if conversion was the cost of conversation, the latter would certainly have gone too far, losing sight of the important fact that the questions it raises were ones that the thinkers it addresses did not attempt to answer.

It is to the second category of contingent attributes mentioned above that we must next turn our interest. This category includes those attributes that can be brought into being through an agent's voluntary action. Every act that is undertaken by a person carries several kinds of ontological fecundity, bringing about conspicuous rearrangements of the world, whether by conferring predicates to things that did not possess them before or engendering new entities. The latter are confined to accidents, this forming the only order of beings that can fall within the scope of human agency, for the origination of bodies is restricted to the agency of God.[47] In this light, ontological analysis of human actions can be said to exhibit two orders, which represent the reverse sides of causality. On the side of causes, we have the states of the agent that cause the act to exist, among which those of principal relevance are the agent's being capable, knowing, and willing. On the side of effects, one must distinguish between two different types of ontological novelty: the actualization of *accidents,* and the effectuation of new *attributes.* The latter type of effect—yet further subdivisions—moves in two directions: the attributes that the act confers on other than the agent, and the attributes that it confers on the agent himself.

In shaking the coins out of my wallet, I create the accident of motion in the coins and the wallet. The part of the event that can be ascribed to me as "my act" is primarily my bringing this accident into existence. Once I have done so, ontological laws take over, and the accident becomes the ground by which the coins and wallet acquire the attribute "moving"—strictly speaking, it would be wrong to describe me as bringing the *attribute* into existence (attributes are not *existents* such that they can be conceived as objects of *anyone's* creative power). While this is the primary effect, the brute existence of an act does not exhaust the scope of my agency. Brute existence is effected through my state of being capable of autonomous action. It is the other states of an agent that one must refer to in order to explain the further determination of the features of the act: Why was the object moved at this speed? Why did I skip instead of run? Why was the sound I uttered a statement (*khabar*) instead of a command (*amr*)? Why a false statement rather than a true one? It is the agent's will and knowledge—that is, their states of being willing and knowing—that determine *which* act it will be and *which* features it will possess, though here again distinctions are drawn between the scope of voluntary agency and natural predicative laws: while I may choose to utter a false statement, I do not confer falsehood on it, for it is the relation of the statement to what it describes that determines this feature. Similarly, I do not confer on an act its moral property, since the description of the act itself is the ontological ground that entitles it to its moral attribute: I choose to utter a false statement, but the attribute "evil" is attracted by natural ontological mechanisms, as it were.

The second direction of attributes generated by an act holds special interest for us, for it would seem to hold out an answer—and the glimmer of a certain possibility—to some key questions concerning the moral characterization of agents. What kind of attributes attach to an agent by virtue of their act? And more to the point, how are the attributes that an agent attracts specified by the particular nature or character of the act that agent chooses to perform?

Now in fact, I have already had occasion to preempt some of the salient aspects of this category of attributes—the act-derived ones (*al-asmāʾ al-mushtaqqa*)—in commenting on Zamakhsharī's and Mānkdīm's arguments for the perpetuity of deserts, and the use of the terms *muḥsin* and *musīʾ*—benefactor and offender—made by them. There I had remarked that predications such as these derived from the agent's performance of the relevant actions. In undertaking an act, one takes the "name" of the act and acquires a predication specified by the type of act: if an offense, one is an offender; if one is speaking, one is a speaker; if writing, one is a writer. But the predication ceases with the cessation of the act, and does not outlast its cause: *while* one is speaking, it is true to say that one is a speaker. A first suspicion had been that such a category was ill equipped to bear the burden of continuity that the justification of punishment demanded that it carry, for the predication of act-derived attributes appears to be an ephemeral one. Yet I drew a distinction between acts of definite and indefinite duration, with the former including acts such as speaking or hitting, and the latter including acts such as offending, in which one continues to engage in the act by default and on a *normative* criterion of what would constitute its termination—namely, the obligation to repent that prevents the act from finishing because it *ought* not to have finished.

This distinction seemed to do the greatest justice to the argument of these Baṣrans. Nevertheless, it did not remain altogether trouble free, especially due to the peculiar emptiness that seems to haunt it as a proposal about something that would carry the brunt of the agent's moral continuity. In amplifying our picture of this type of attributes, I will need to pick out a different type "emptiness" by which they are beset and that affects their capacity to form the ground of a person's moral identity. A concrete example may help focus our vision here. A cross-section of the ontological facts in a given act—say, crying out "Help!" in a loud voice while being hustled into a van by one's abductors—would yield something like the following agent-centered description. The agent is characterized by the state or attribute of the capacity of autonomous action (*qudra*) through the inherence of the accidents of this capacity in the relevant parts of their body—a capacity that ranges over crying out as well as not crying out.[48] The agent wills to create sound, and by the inherence of the entitative accident of willing (*irāda*) and that of the knowledge (*ʿilm*) of the relevant linguistic form, the agent's combined states of capacity, willing, and knowledge bring the sound into existence, creating the accident of sound in the substrate of the relevant bodily organ—that is, the throat. Having caused this act to exist, the agent is called "one-who-cries-out."

Thus, there is a circuit of predication that begins from the agent and is then resumed back into them: an act is produced from *non-act-derived* attributes such as capacity, willing, and knowledge, and the act then redounds to the agent as a further predication of an *act-derived* attribute. One point to note is that the agent's states of willing and knowing appear to enjoy a double ontological membership: the "reason" why an agent is willing or knowing is that these states are grounded in relevant entitative accidents, but it is *also* that the agent has performed an act, for an agent is considered as "doing an act of knowledge" and "doing an act of will" (*yafʿalu al-ʿilm/ al-irāda*). This double membership would seem to be explained as a difference in the orders of causation: the first order is the object of a metaphysical description, and the latter of an intentional or voluntary one (though the Muʿtazilites do not emphasize this double membership in their discussions of act-derived attributes and mainly examine external acts).[49]

A far more apposite point that needs to be raised, however, in connection with the above example is as follows. There are many possible descriptions one might make of the same act: *mustanjid*—"calling out for help"—would have done just as well as *ṣārikh*—"shouting"—in describing the person crying for help. "Obnoxious," "waking up everyone in the neighborhood," or "threatening to botch our operation" would illuminate further the multiplicity of perspectives from which the act could be conceived, since no qualification is set down to restrict the descriptions to ones the *agent* intended or distinguish intended from accidental effects. Indeed, with offenses and other evil acts, it is irrelevant to the description whether the agent intended to commit the act qua offense and in order to offend.

Such a plurality of descriptions, however, raises none of the questions and poses none of the problems one might anticipate, for the following reason: in the case of act-derived attributes, the linguistic predication *does not reflect an ontological reality*. Since language is not being used to deduce metaphysical reality, the problem of ontological relativity that multiple descriptions might have posed drops away. Act-derived predicates are *predications* in the root sense of the word: they are what is *said* of a person, "names" (*asmāʾ*), and by no means indicate a real ontological property of the agent. This is the meaning of ʿAbd al-Jabbar's assertion that "as for the qualities of the agent [*ṣifāt al-fāʿil*, here used in the sense of act-derived qualities], they all denote that an act has occurred on his part, and do not signify his being in a state [*ḥāl*]."[50] In contrast to attributes grounded in the being's essence or an entitative accident, in making such attributions one is not referring to any *real state or characteristic of the agent*, nor does the fact that the agent is named after their act mean that the act "effects" any change in the agent. The predication merely informs one that the act has been brought about through the agency of the person. "The basis of attribution," in Richard Frank's words, "remains the reality of the act whose being and reality are fully distinct and separate from that of the agent."[51] Hence, whether one described a thief in flight as running, fleeing from the police, breaking the law, or trying to keep the stolen goods, all descriptions might do equally well, since the act has no ontological correlate that must be made to correspond to the expression we use and that makes the discovery of the primary referent an exigency. What this means is that the kind of attributes that redound to an agent by virtue of his acts are, again, not *in* the agent. Thus, the set of qualities that seemed to have the closest connection to the agent's moral actions and hold the greatest promise as a foundation for moral identity, turn out to be signifiers that are "empty" in the sense that they lack a referent in the person that would help them outlast the cessation of his act.

This survey may be reckoned as a relatively local account of the ways in which Baṣran Muʿtazilite ontology, in its mature form, failed to accommodate any notion of moral qualities that attach to agents. The recidivist offender or the persistent good doer never becomes "such a person who does good" or "does evil." A cross-section of the ontological dramatics that begins from a morally significant act and ends with an act of retribution or recompense would at no moment in time involve the ascription of a real moral quality to the agent, except perhaps for the particularized states of willing and knowledge that are not followed up by the Muʿtazilites given the generic qualities that are at the center of their metaphysics.[52]

And through the above, and in the formulation just given, we have implicitly given an answer to the second half of the questions guiding these explorations, which began both from an interest in moral qualities—in the moral *particularization* of ontology—but also in the possibility of their *continuity*, which from our own perspective seem crucial for affirming a person's continued responsibility and liability for their past acts. For if the dramatics of action would "at no moment in time" involve the ascription of a real moral quality to the agent, inevitably the search for moral qualities *surviving* the passage of time is already recognized as a fruitless one in advance. "Ineluctably so!" one might here interject. "For how could one have expected things to be otherwise in a system of such inveterate atomistic persuasions? What expectations of continuity could such a scheme legitimately invite?" And yet here it would have to be responded that the Muʿtazilite theological system was a scene in which different aims competed over the shape of the overall scheme within the scope of possible intellectual directions circumscribed by the historical setting. The expectations guiding the above quest for a basis of desert—and therefore the investigation of the loud absence of moral qualities in Baṣran metaphysics—are ones whose partial dependence on our own ethical perspective I have not tried to conceal, but that Baṣran Muʿtazilite claims do plenty to compel us to raise, and in places suggest the possibility of answering.

It is instructive in this connection to return here to the language of the starting remarks that staked out the ground of this chapter, where the project of a "self-contained" philosophical inquiry into the conditions of personal identity was contrasted with one in which the inquiry is conducted with an eye to the practical purposes that primarily motivate one's interest in the question and also supply criteria for answering it. The primary concern for us was the ability to predicate desert over time ("In what way would a person *have* to endure through time in order to satisfy the requirements spelled out by those concerns?"). What the above ("local") investigation revealed is certain features of Muʿtazilite ontology that hamper the formation of a concept of moral identity and continuity that would discharge the needed functions. This finding is particularly interesting when juxtaposed with an observation made independently by a variety of readers of Muʿtazilite works concerning the link between the Muʿtazilites' anthropology and their theological aims. It has been suggested that there is a "logical correlation between the problem of human nature and that of moral and religious obligation (*taklīf*)" in the Baṣran Muʿtazilites' approach.[53] Their view of the nature of human beings and their characterization of the features of persons is functional and practical indeed, and the primary concern to which it is made subordinate is that of establishing the conditions under which God's imposition of obligations can be judged good.

Jan Peters puts the matter strikingly when he writes that ʿAbd al-Jabbār "*deduces* the qualities of man from his being charged by God": capacity for action, knowledge, perception, life, and will are among the principal qualities thus deduced. For "a responsible subject must be able to perform the act he is charged with, he must know how it is (its *kayfiyya*), and he must be willing to produce that act in a certain way." As for the other two qualities mentioned, they are preconditions for the realization of the ability to act: "In order to be able he has to be living . . . and a living being can only be distinguished from other beings by its being perceiving." This conjunction of properties grounds the moral responsibility of human beings, and by doing so, ensures that the imposition of duties will be good. Had it been imposed on agents who could not be judged responsible, it would have been either vain or unjust on the part of the divine *Mukallif*.[54]

So the concept of the person is developed functionally; but the end it serves is other than the one we were pursuing above. Both ends have in common a concern with moral responsibility. But in the former one asks, "How can *taklīf* be good? The person must be responsible for their acts. In order for the person to be responsible, they must have the following features." In the latter one asks, "How can punishment be good?" And part of the response consists of saying, "The person must have been responsible." But the answer cannot be concluded here, in great part because of the difference in tense (the agent *had been* responsible—that is, at the moment of acting the agent was free to choose whether or not to do so, and had full knowledge of its value, or if not, was responsible for their ignorance). One demands something further, something that would establish the relation of the person to their acts—of the present person to acts committed in the past—and as such justify the continued attribution of these acts to them and explain why they ought to be made to suffer. The Muʿtazilites concerned themselves with the former question, and accordingly adjusted their conception of the person to meet its demands; the second question, while in a strong sense a necessary complement of the first, does not seem to have interested them. And yet it was the fact that it was a necessary complement of the first, and that the concept of the person was developed in subservience to the Muʿtazilites' moral concern, that makes it legitimate to look for it, responding to the expectations raised by this concern—even if, finally, the Muʿtazilite concept of the person turns out to have been hostage to the fragmenting tendencies of their atomism.

And fragmenting this atomism certainly was; Abū Hāshim's theory of states—which founded the unity of persons on the properties of life—might have met the need for a kind of unification, but this was a project that yielded unity rather than continuity. The currency of time in which the unity of a person's features was conceptualized could at best be seen as that of a momentary instant (if it was to be seen in these terms at all: such temporal dimensions seem to have been far from the Baṣran Muʿtazilites' minds when casting the issues). The unambitious level on which the unity of persons was considered was in great part symptomatic of the luxuriant and expansive contents that marked the Muʿtazilites' atomistic metaphysics. The plurality of entities it postulated stood in need of a centripetal force that would gather them in and relate them to the person in a more holistic way. The hierarchical approach to being typical of Aristotelian philosophy, based on principles exercising an organizing and unifying effect, existed in a galaxy that was far from the Muʿtazilite horizon. "Many *mutakallimūn* comprehended things as mere conglomerates of accidents, without any substance of their own," writes Josef van Ess, picking up on points previously made by Frank in connection with the early Muʿtazilite Abu'l-Hudhayl's metaphysics. Frank had captured one of the chief aspects of this metaphysics in his felicitous description of the "particulate or granular quality of the body" and his remark that

> there can . . . be no question of "essences." . . . The being of the thing . . . has no essence, nature, or intrinsic principle, by and of itself in its being what it is, that determines the individual qualities and attributes which characterise its being that which it is.

And again:

> The person, in the final analysis, is the totality of his "accidents" at a given moment within their unity of inherence in the body which is itself, in its own reality as a body, a function of a set of defined "accidents."[55]

While Baṣran metaphysics may have left several elements of Abu'l-Hudhayl's thinking behind once the theory that concerned the unity of living beings was elaborated, many elements—such as their lack of interest in ordering principles—remained unchanged. The point of departure, then, was one of such high fragmentation that the possibilities of travel were prejudiced from the start, and Abū Hāshim's theory was only the shortest of journeys on the road to personal unification.[56] What surprises the Baṣrans—a surprise that their metaphysics both departs from and then continues to foster—would seem to be the fact that entities are united, that they are composite or hold together at all, that this pullulating plurality of atomic elements—which their metaphysics perpetually invites one to imagine and remember as being the foundation of visible reality—constitutes a single, spatially continuous whole. The fact that beings constitute *temporally* continuous wholes does not yet seem to have rivaled the hold of this overriding fascination and succeeded in surprising them.

Thus, as I already noted above (in "An Eternity of Punishment" in this chapter)—in connection with the possibility of construing the failure to repent in terms of an enduring moral belief about one's past act—no ontological infrastructure is provided that would support such endurance. In light of the sketch of Baṣran ontology given above, we are now in a position to say what this infrastructure would have looked like. It would have taken the form of the endurance of the entitative accident (*maʿnā*) that is the ground of the person's "state" (*ḥāl*) or attribute of being "believing." Yet this interesting ontological possibility was not pursued by the Baṣrans—or more accurately, with the line of thought that prevailed among the post-Jubbāʾite members of the school. For while they indeed occupied themselves with the question of the continuity or endurance (*baqāʾ*) of accidents—which were the subject of long and fractious debates both between Muʿtazilites and between themselves and their Ashʿarite opponents, who refused to recognize enduring accidents—and while they affirmed the endurance of several accidents, the range of the latter seems to have been confined to ones that bore little relation to human qualities of relevance to our concerns.[57] A view of greater promise had fought for ascendancy among the earlier Baṣrans, and in particular among the two Jubbāʾīs, who had both affirmed that some forms of knowledge and belief should be included among enduring accidents. But beginning with Abū Isḥāq ibn ʿAyyāsh, this view was rejected by the Baṣrans, and henceforth the only enduring accidents with a special interest for human agents included in Alnoor Dhanani's list are the power of autonomous action (*qudra*) and life (*ḥayāt*)—and these do not hold an interest for moral agents of the kind we are seeking, as both are to be seen merely as conditions for action that the agent does not himself bring about.[58]

Some of these last points will receive greater light in the next chapter, where I will be taking a closer look at the endurance of accidents in connection with the view of human identity evolved by the Baṣran Muʿtazilites in the context of their eschatology. There I will also have occasion to partially track some of the important contrasts distinguishing the Aristotelian and atomistic views of the person. But at this juncture, one last task still lies ahead as an indispensable last step for a complete understanding of the Baṣrans' account of the endurance of desert.

The Primacy of Revealed Names: Al-Asmā' wa'l-Aḥkām

One of the things that could be said about the foregoing discussion is that its main tenor—and the main cast of the results it has yielded—has been predominantly a negative one. Beginning from a set of questions rooted in our own sense of the strategic importance of locating in the agent a bearer of continuity that would join past and present, and justify ascriptions of responsibility and punitive responses, we found that such continuity is not realized in terms of an ontologically articulated moral identity. There is nothing *in* or *of* the person that grounds their desert. This finding is illuminated and interpreted further when we switch to the part of the account where the positive tenor comes out strongest, and we discover, if not natural ontological entitlement, what other principles of entitlement were associated with the preservation of desert.

We encounter these principles immediately on making the transition from one part of their theological syllabus to another—when we move from the contents of the Muʿtazilite rubric of *al-waʿd wa'l-waʿīd* (the promise and the threat) to those of the rubric *al-manzila bayna al-manzilatayn* (the intermediate position), or *al-asmā' wa'l-aḥkām* (the names and the rulings or judgments) as it also came to be designated. These are two of the five cardinal principles of Muʿtazilite theology that share a great deal of their subject matter. Yet the difference lies in the fact that whereas the former rubric lends its space to the articulation of the general principles of reward and punishment, in the latter desert and its cognates are discussed in the context of and mediated by a special class of "names" that had been the subject of great controversy since the earliest days of theological speculation in Islam.

Three principal names comprised this class: "believer" (*mu'min*), "grave sinner" (*fāsiq*), and "infidel" or "unbeliever" (*kāfir*). In understanding the controversy that these names had caused among early Islamic groupings, it is important to note the vantage point that gave it its point of departure. This was a vantage point of an exegetical nature: the names were received from scripture; and it was a task of exegesis to identify the criteria that had to be fulfilled for a person to be recognized as belonging to their class. It is this exegetical starting point that is captured in Toshihiko Izutsu's observation of the peculiar form in which the question was cast. One asked, "*Who* is a believer?" rather than, "What does belief consist in?"[59] The fact that the stand point was an exegetical one meant that the words were not "empty," for otherwise the debate would not have focused so intently on these names, and might have dispensed with the rubric of "*al-asmā' wa'l-aḥkām*." It would have been sufficient to discuss the criteria for posthumous treatments directly and qualitatively, without mediating this by inquiring into the name that applies to one by virtue of one's acts or beliefs; one could have simply asked, Will one be rewarded or punished for such acts or beliefs? Textual references fixed the entailments or *aḥkām* of the names insofar as they predicated certain posthumous treatments of the classes of individuals designated by these names, and so part of the controversy over the identity of believers, grave sinners, and unbelievers was conducted through debate about these scriptural references. But the names, while demanding exegesis, were invested with sufficient significance by scripture to give them the air of "titles" rather than names. It was important to "qualify" for these titles.[60]

It was mainly the first two names that formed the linchpin of theological disagreements, as the case of unbelievers admitted little doubt, whether in the criteria of applying the name or the treatment reserved for people identified as belonging to this class. The relevant Qur'ānic references left no room for doubt that those who deviated from strict monotheism and associated any other entity with God would be consigned to eternal punishment, as in 5:72: "Whoever joins other gods with God, God will forbid him the garden, and the Fire will be his abode."

It was with respect to the believer and the grave sinner that the profoundest differences arose. The methodology of the dispute centered on the definition of belief, and what each party included in the definition decided how the category of the grave sinner was to be dealt with. The Murji'ites defined belief by verbal confession of one's faith, and thus accorded the status of believer to grave sinners who made such confession, whatever their other acts might be, deferring the judgment about the posthumous destiny of such persons to God. The Khārijites gave such an emphasis to acts as a criterion for belief that the grave sinner was excluded from the class of believers, and the verdict they pronounced on such sinners was eternal punishment. The Ash'arites made the inner act of belief constitutive of it and affirmed that knowledge of God could trump acts of disobedience in the final appraisal—hence, like the Murji'ites, including grave sinners in the community of believers, citing in support verses such as 4:48: "God forgives not that partners should be set up with Him; but He forgives anything else, to whom He pleases." With regard to their posthumous treatment by God, they asserted that God is not obliged to punish them (God can have no obligations), and may pardon them if He so wishes, though if He punishes them this will be just, and if He pardons them it will be out of His gratuitous bounty.

Against these views, the Mu'tazilites maintained that the grave sinner was in an intermediate position, and was to be designated neither as a believer nor an unbeliever; the name or title of "believer" was denied to the grave sinner on the Mu'tazilite definition of belief, in which external acts of obedience were paramount (in just what manner, will be shortly explained). Yet while grave sinners were not classed as unbelievers, they would share the fate of the latter and be confined to eternal punishment if they died without repenting of their sin. The Qur'ānic verses from which they drew their support included, among others, 4:14: "But those who disobey Allah and His Messenger and transgress His limits will be admitted to a Fire, to abide therein: And they shall have a humiliating punishment." And again, from 27:90: "And if any do evil, their faces will be thrown headlong into the Fire: 'Do ye receive a reward other than that which ye have earned by your deeds?' "[61]

While the Muʿtazilites did not dispense with the special rubric that dealt with these names, their approach ostensibly rendered it redundant. For they reversed the direction of the inquiry, and without ever severing their positions from scriptural bases, made the exegetical part to an extent a secondary one by employing rational moral truths as the primary basis of their position on names. Instead of beginning by the name and asking about its criteria, they began from moral criteria and arrived at the name. Given this, the typical rubric dealing with "the intermediate position" reiterates material found in the rubric of "the promise and the threat," such as the definition of blame and praise, reward and punishment, and continues with a classification of persons according to the magnitude of their deserts. Those who deserve a "great amount" of punishment and those who deserve less than that amount; those who deserve a "great amount" of reward and those who deserve less than that. Those deserving great punishment are called "unbelievers"; those who deserve less than that are called "grave sinners"; those who deserve great reward are labeled angels or prophets; and those who deserve less are named believers or "pious" and "upright."[62]

These names were identified by the Baṣran Muʿtazilites as terms of praise or blame; but they were not to be seen as terms obeying a "natural"—or "rational"—rule of application. Rather, they constituted a special class of terms designated as "revealed" or "legal" names (*asmā' sharʿiyya*), which were distinguished by the fact that their signification was one promulgated and instituted by scripture. In this case, the terms of praise or blame in question had been instituted as names whose reference consisted of those who possessed specific kinds of deserts, thereby making the latter primary as criteria that determine attribution. The *aḥkām* (the entailments, consequences) of these revealed predicates are identical to the *aḥkām* of desert accruing from past acts. Recast in familiar terminology, it is sometimes said that one is "entitled" to (*yastaḥiqqu*) the revealed attribute by virtue of one's deserts (*istiḥqāq*).[63] The relationship of entitlement here is one of signification: the latter is the moral reality that forms the criterion—the ground of entitlement, as it were—for the application of the name; and the former is, once again, a mere word.

"Once again," one says, for what comes to mind is the similar characterization only recently given for the category of act-derived attributes (*asmā' mushtaqqa*), which seemed to hold the greatest promise for an ontology of moral qualities. And yet what must be immediately remarked here is a fact that carries not a small degree of perplexity; for according to the Baṣran

Muʿtazilites, these revealed predicates are specifically to be distinguished from attributes derived from acts. The motivation behind this claim was no great secret to divine. As we have just seen, in the Muʿtazilite definition of belief (*īmān*), belief is constituted by external acts of obedience over and against the cognitive act of belief. Yet lexically—and as long as one keeps to the *natural* application of linguistic terms—the attribute believer could be said to derive from the *act* of belief (I am called a believer because I believe in the one God); which is just what the Ashʿarites and, with their own variant views, the Murjiʾites maintained as the criterion of application. This went hand in hand with a vociferous rejection of the Muʿtazilite claim about the transfer of these terms to a specifically scriptural domain of usage that refracted their natural signification. In the words of the Ashʿarite Ibn Fūrak (d. 1015),

> The terms current in the domain of religion are the [same as the] terms current in the domain of language, for God—may He be exalted—addressed the Arabs in their language. . . . The revealed Law did not change the language from its original condition nor did it invent a term that had not existed before.[64]

Against this, the Muʿtazilites clung to their position that these names had been assigned a different meaning by revelation and were no longer governed by the principles of natural linguistic usage. Accordingly, the names are not classified as act-derived ones, and the predicate is a "revealed" one that supervenes on moral deserts, which are in turn acquired through external acts. I act, I acquire deserts, I acquire a name. Acts; desert; the name: this is the process of attribution.

Yet the perplexity attaching to this claim becomes evident when we turn to look at one of the arguments used to urge the exclusion of revealed names from the class of act-derived predicates. There, both ʿAbd al-Jabbār and Mānkdīm point out that the latter cease to apply to a person once one's act has ceased, whereas one can cease to commit acts of grave sin or unbelief yet still be called a grave sinner and an unbeliever. It is also pointed out that repentance does not invalidate the application of act-derived predicates, while it invalidates that of these names.[65] Presumably "to cease committing unbelief" means desisting from an active or "conscious" denial of God; thus both the grave sinner and the unbeliever are understood to deserve their names even in the absence of acts.

But on the interpretation suggested above in commenting on Zamakhsharī's and Mānkdīm's arguments for perpetual deserts, we saw that the greatest justice (or indeed charity) to their position would involve an admission that a certain class of act-derived attributes—such as offending or doing beneficent acts, but not hitting or speaking—must have the capacity to endure through time, until their application is terminated by the kind of actions involved in repentance and apology. Without this admission, the main argument for the endurance of desert would fall through due to the ephemerality of the act-descriptions that were given as its grounds. ʿAbd al-Jabbār himself had made remarks that clearly lent themselves to supporting this distinction between types of act-derived attributes.

So what are we to make of the present conflict? Here I must admit my own perplexity. Perhaps at this point the impulses of charity and justice would lead to opposing interpretations. Once again, then, this may be a question best left to future generations of Muʿtazilites to puzzle over.

Whatever we might make of this conflict, however, it is clear that the two types of names—revealed and act-derived—share one crucial feature in common. This is a feature that has already been brought out for notice: both are "mere" names—though this is true in each case in a slightly different sense. For revealed names, the case seems to resemble the one discussed in chapter 4 in connection with moral terms such as "obligatory," "evil," or "good," which we discerned as names whose criteria of application—the *reality* grounding the use of the word—were the rulings of desert. Similarly in this case: the terms "believer," "unbeliever," and "grave sinner" are names whose criteria are a person's deserts. What this suggests is that this aspect of the Baṣran Muʿtazilite account could give us little help in explaining the endurance of desert or its grounds, for the existence of deserts is *presupposed* as a basis for the application of the revealed names.[66] Short of an account explaining why and how deserts endure, the use of revealed names glosses over the difficulty in a way that presents these names in light of the very means for the endurance of desert—as though it is *only* through these names that deserts were being preserved. Through a signifying relationship established by the divine Lawgiver between deserts and the names of belief, unbelief, and grave sin, the bearer of a name is a bearer of a title of deed—of the values to which all one's previous deeds entitle one, and for which the name serves as historical record. This title is liable to be replaced or torn up at any moment through the actions that the person chooses to do, but until that time, it serves as a form of encryption of one's past acts. Yet since one's past is never posited in one through an intrinsic ground, these names linger over one as extraneous judgments or descriptions that form one's only link to these acts. These judgments, of course, are partly a human practice—but also a divine one; both because the criterion for forming them was set up by the divine Lawgiver but also because, short of any other account, one is left by default with the only option of considering the Lawgiver's bookmaking memory as the main support for the moral continuity of a person's life—and *that* memory is certainly something that endures.

Why Not Dhimma?

Having sounded several counterfactual notes—notes resulting in a negative description—throughout the foregoing, the impulse to strike a final one can here be indulged in order to resolve a remaining source of wonderment.

Much of the above analysis of the absence of a qualitative account of the person or an ontological grounding of desert that would attach it to the person may be said to have been prefigured in a handful of simple remarks made in the last chapter. There, it was suggested that it is the analysis of desert (*istiḥqāq*) into relations of rights and obligations (*ḥuqūq*) that lies behind the fact that desert may not be conceived as something belonging to the agent. It is rather something belonging to the agent's victim, creditor, or otherwise holder of a claim. The most natural way to inquire about the preservation of desert might thus have been in terms of a question about the preservation of these rights and claims. It is interesting, then, to speculate on the reasons that discouraged the Muʿtazilites from appropriating a certain concept developed by Muslim jurists, whose function in part seems to be precisely that—namely, the preservation of *ḥuqūq*.

This is the concept of "*dhimma*," which in its function within theoretical legal discussions, can be translated as "capacity"—that is, the capacity of an individual to be a proper subject of the Law, to be the subject of rights and obligations (*maʿnan yaṣīru bi-sababihi al-ādamī . . . ahlan li-wujūb al-ḥuqūq lahu wa-ʿalayhi*). This "faculty" comes into existence with the birth of the person, though in early life one can contract rights (e.g., one can inherit and acquire property) but not obligations. In its function in substantive legal discussions, it lies at the heart of the central categorization of liabilities within Islamic law, whereby two different types of liability are distinguished: liabilities that relate to a *specific object* (*ʿayn*)—as when one borrows a certain item or leaves it with someone for safekeeping—and liabilities that relate to "*debts*" (*dayn*), which are those involving money or fungible objects. "Debts" is apostrophized since this sort of liability is not confined to what we normally term a debt, but covers any number of moral obligations resulting from such actions as the destruction or usurpation of another's property, selling, oaths, pledges or gifts, and wills and bequests, as long as these do not involve specific objects.[67]

Before proceeding to mine the distinction, one comment should be made concerning the relation between the substantive and theoretical manifestations of the concept. The usage of the concept in the sphere of substantive law (*fiqh*) has been described as distinct from that of the sphere of legal theory (*uṣūl al-fiqh*); yet the two are evidently closely related, on terms that might be described as that of potential to actual, or a disposition to its exercise.[68] Just as the fragility of an object is realized when it happens to break, so the eligibility for legal consideration and the exercise of moral personhood is realized when moral relations are acquired in the form of *ḥuqūq*—such as the ones involved in the generation of liabilities. This double function of the concept within juridical thought—as eligibility for moral relations ("*capacity*") and substrate for moral relations ("*capaciousness*")—is what must explain the discordant sounds that reach one as concerns the ontological order within which this feature or faculty must be classed. The range of views displays a disconcerting diversity, with one individual identifying it as a subject of predication while another identifies it as a predicable quality. Some jurists understand *dhimma* as the subject of attribution, as the person, self, or being—the *dhāt* or *nafs*—that is legally responsible, while others see it as the attribute, as the *waṣf* ("description") by which a person becomes responsible. The diversity of opinion may in part be explained through the different functions this feature is invoked to play; its description as a "self" or being would seem to grow out of its function as a location or substrate for moral relations; its description as a quality or attribute seems to grow out of its function as the quality of legal personhood.[69]

Two features of the substantive function of *dhimma* stand out as particularly interesting for our purposes. The first is that this conceptual category appears to arise out of the impulse to seek a location or "substrate" to attach pending or unresolved moral (legal) relations. While in the case where an object exists—as, for example, when a specific article has been lent from one party to another, or a deposit has been left with a person—the *ḥaqq* of the creditor "attaches" (*taʿalluq* is Sanhūrī's term, with all its resonance for the conceptual field of *kalām*) to the object, in cases where, for instance, a sum of money has been borrowed, there is no such "locus" for the claim to reside, and the claim has to attach to the *person*. *Al-ḥaqq yathbutu fī dhimmat fūlān*: obligation becomes an "incorporeal right in the *dhimma* of the debtor," existing "in the seat of rights that is the person." *Dhimma* has thus been described alternately as a seat, a "repository" (*mustaqarr wa-mustawdaʿ*), and a locus or substrate (*maḥall*) that throughout a lifetime comes to be populated with *ḥuqūq*. The locative or spatial connotations of the concept are emblematized in the way one speaks of *dhimma* as empty or full (*shaghl/farāgh*). Note this interesting facet: while the *ḥaqq* is a reciprocal relation, and therefore exists as a right for one person and a claim for another, it attaches to the *obligated* party. This contrasts with the phenomenon I noted in Baṣran Muʿtazilite discussions, in which the moral relation of desert was conceptualized as *another's* right to blame or punish, and in which it was not the party from whom something ought to be exacted who was made the principal term of the relation and the center of moral gravity.

The second feature follows from the first. *Dhimma* is an entity postulated to explain how an unfinished moral dynamic is preserved in the world and "where" it is to be found, but a broader function it seems to possess is to explain the ascription of responsibility—not just *where* responsibility exists but *that it does* exist. This appears at its clearest in posthumous responsibility. If having dug a well, death soon overtakes me, and subsequently a hapless passerby falls into it, who is responsible for the misadventure? If *dhimma* survives my physical death, I will be responsible and the wrong will attach to my *dhimma*. Were someone to sell an object to a buyer who subsequently discovered it to be faulty, under normal circumstances they would have been able to return it to the seller and recover the price. Yet what if the seller has passed away in the meantime? The answer mediated by this concept is that the seller's *dhimma* is then "occupied" by the price of the object, unless that person has left behind property that the *ḥaqq* can attach to.[70] There was not, to be sure, unanimity among jurists concerning all aspects of the continuation of this faculty after death, but the majority of them seem to have agreed on different versions of the claim that it survived.

This, then, is the resource that could have made itself available for the Muʿtazilites in their theorizing of desert. It is clearly concerned with responsibility, offers a facility for the endurance of obligations, and uses the person as the substrate; also, it revolves around the concept of *ḥaqq*, which as we have seen, lies at the root of the concept of desert as *istiḥqāq*. It matters little that—as one must observe—in its use in the legal sphere, the "moral facts" or *ḥuqūq* enduring there may be in some respects narrow, covering as it does only a limited category of liabilities or moral relations. In fact, the concept of *dhimma* was linked to broader desert-related contexts by thinkers standing nearer to the center of the Islamic tradition, as suggested in the reference by the latter-day encyclopedist Jalāl al-Dīn al-Suyūṭī (d. 1505) to repentance as a "clearing of one's *dhimma*" (*barāʾa* or *khalāṣ al-dhimma*).[71] Repentance, of course, is what clears the decks of desert in the Muʿtazilite account. Finally, the types of concerns that are dealt with through this faculty are close to the issues—central to Muʿtazilite concerns with justice, and debated among Muʿtazilite theologians from an early date—raised in connection to the famous quandary about the person who initiates an action that produces its evil consequences only after the agent's death (the common example was the archer whose arrow kills its target after the death of the one who shot it). These examples raise questions about posthumous ascriptions of responsibility and blame that are contiguous to those that occupied the jurists in the notion of *dhimma*. Yet for all these associations and recommendations, the Muʿtazilites all but ignore the existence of the concept of *dhimma*, and even ʿAbd al-Jabbār at his most juridical maintains a mysterious oblivion with regard to it.[72] Why did the Muʿtazilites pass by this offer of *taʿalluq* or relation, though their reasoning is groomed on this conceptual turn, and though its concerns would seem to dovetail with their own?

One possible answer might have to do with the fact that the concept of *dhimma* appears to be intimately linked to notions of a covenant or pledge (*ʿahd*), as attested by jurists and lexicographers alike. In one of the juridical interpretations of *dhimma* as subject rather than predication, it is defined as "a person under pledge (or covenant)" (*nafs lahā ʿahd*).[73] This feature reveals the concept of *dhimma* as one affianced to the conceptual paradigm of revelation. This is supported by its description as a *revealed* or *legal designation*. In Sanhūrī's words, *dhimma* is "a revealed/legal description (*waṣf sharʿī*) that is postulated by the Lawgiver as existing in a human being, and by which he becomes . . . capable of contracting rights and obligations."[74] Insofar as the postulant is the divine Being, we would once again be dealing with a revealed or "institutional" ontology, not one of natural moral attributions.

Was it this link to revelation that discouraged the Muʿtazilites from appropriating the concept? But how plausible is this, given what we have seen of their generous reliance on the traditional resources of law and scripture? Having humored the impulse to wedge this question open, we may be hard-pressed to close it with fruitful speculations. One may speculate that the determining factor was a chronological one, and that by the time the concept of *dhimma* had been established within the edifice of Islamic law, theological debates had already received their formative cast, which was arranged around the axis of revealed names and the treatments reserved for and deserved by their bearers. The Muʿtazilites' theory of desert that relied on the revealed predications—believer, unbeliever, and grave sinner—may have satisfied existing needs, and so this concept never entered the synthesis between their theology and the legal sciences.

CHAPTER 6

The Identity of Beings in Baṣran Muʿtazilite Eschatology

Resurrection and the Criterion of Identity

The picture of Baṣran Muʿtazilite thinking about desert and its relation to the person as it now stands before us makes clear in what sense one may talk of the absence of any concern with the person as a moral and temporally extended being. This picture will be touched up with fresh color—though its main contours will not be radically altered—in this last stop, in which our interesting task will be that of seeking to enrich it by holding it up to the Baṣrans' eschatological vision, and a particular aspect of this vision that seems especially well poised to make a contribution.

This vision was one that numerous Qur'ānic verses and prophetic traditions articulated with vivid and graphic detail, creating powerful impressions of the delights of paradise and the torments of the Fire lying in store for their rightful recipients. Here, our interest will not lie with the concrete imaginings giving content to the eschatological events as much as with certain questions of metaphysics that in fact possess conceptual and indeed moral priority over these concrete descriptions.[1] For if these descriptions served a purpose for the believers who made use of them in their devotional lives, a great part of this purpose lay in their capacity to give human beings the necessary impetus to choose good and avoid evil, by evoking desire for (*targhīb*) the pleasures of paradise and evoking fear of (*tarhīb*) the torments of hell. The protreptics of *al-targhīb wa'l-tarhīb*, however, were premised on one implicit assumption. And this was that the particular person who performed certain acts in the present life would be the same person who would be reaping their consequences in the hereafter. The principle is no less familiar to us now than it was then: one point that modern philosophers puzzling over the nature of personal identity have underscored with special force is that assumptions about identity form the basis of prudential concern—of decisions to do something now so as to be benefited later. For if the person who will stand to benefit in old age from the prudent self-denials and restraints endured in youth will not be the same person who bore these denials—if, as some have maintained, the connections between youth and old age are such as to undermine our capacity to validate claims of identity between these temporal stages—then what motive do *I* have now to limit my pleasures, if it will not really be *I* who will be harvesting their fruits?

This point was equally urgent with respect to the rewards and punishments giving content to the Islamic eschatological vision, and for the Muʿtazilites, it was made even more pressing by the particular construal they placed on the connection holding between acts and otherworldly treatments. For not only did they, like all their fellow believers, stress the importance of these treatments as a motivation to action but they justified their occurrence by reference to a person's acquired deserts. One was rewarded or punished *because* one had done certain acts by which to deserve these things. Without this relationship of desert, any act of rewarding or punishing would be rendered unjust. This moral position lent an even more numinous significance to the ability to identify the person acting as the person receiving the deserts of the acts performed.

The Muʿtazilites had understood this point from early on, and with the Baṣrans this understanding was rendered with a perspicuity that left nothing to be desired, with Ibn Mattawayh talking plainly of the epistemic goal of securing "the knowledge that Zayd is the person who offended some time ago or who was obedient some time ago, so that the things he deserves for doing so may be rightly applied to him in the other world [*li-taṣiḥḥa ākhiran al-aḥkām allatī yastaḥiqquhā ʿalayhi*]."[2] The moral cadence that conditions their thinking on these matters is advertised clearly in the fact that the divine act of resurrecting or re-creating (*iʿāda*) the person on the Day of Judgment derived its value from the value of the act of rewarding and punishing. If it was necessary to resurrect a person at all, it was because they had deserts pending that needed to be rendered to them. As a consequence, it is *obligatory* to resurrect those who deserve reward or compensation (because reward is obligatory), whereas it is *merely good* (*ḥasan*) to resurrect those who deserve punishment.[3]

It was under the rubric of an inquiry into the metaphysics of resurrection that most of the Baṣran Muʿtazilites did their thinking on the topic of the nature of the human beings that would live and experience the afterlife. That human beings would be resurrected at all was a fundamental premise of the Islamic faith with its stress on moral accountability. That this would take the form of a *bodily* resurrection was an article of faith that had caught the limelight after Ghazālī's eleventh-century polemic in his *Tahāfut al-falāsifa* ("The Incoherence of the Philosophers") against the practitioners of Islamic philosophy—and especially Avicenna (d. 1037)—when he included it among three fundamental tenets of the faith that placed the philosophers outside the pale, due to their espousal of an eschatological vision based on the survival of immaterial souls, which alone experienced joy or suffering. The philosophical view of the afterlife (*ma'ād*) was one of several intellectual options threshed out by Muslim thinkers, which Ghazālī detailed in his renowned religious compendium, *Iḥyā' 'ulūm al-dīn* ("The Revival of the Religious Sciences"). The prominent tendencies that he described as rivals to the philosophical one included the view that death signifies the separation of the human spirit or soul from the body, which it may then later rejoin, and the view that the person does not survive their bodily death, and that death signifies the complete cessation of consciousness and privation of experience, which is only restored with a restoration of the body on the Day of Judgment.[4]

Now if the Baṣran Mu'tazilites had a special reason (to do with their ethical views) that made the question of identity one of extra urgency, they also had special reasons that made for extra difficulty in answering it—and this was the fact that the view they took of death and resurrection was unequivocally represented by this last description. After an intellectual tension that gave a bright flame in the early history of *kalām* but did not take long to fade out, the atomistic metaphysics that formed its hallmark settled on an overwhelmingly materialist interpretation. Feeding that earlier flame had been theologians such as Mu'ammar ibn 'Abbād al-Sulamī (d. 830) and al-Naẓẓām (d. circa 835–45), who had been among the most notable advocates of an anthropology that made room for a more diverse ontological repertory, which would include different kinds of ontological constituents directly affecting the type of anthropology that could be developed. Naẓẓām had identified man as a spiritual substance (*rūḥ*) interpenetrating the material body, while Mu'ammar had advocated a description of man as an indivisible atom to which spatial or corporeal attributes do not apply.[5] But the metaphysics that prevailed among the majority of *mutakallimūn* consisted in an atomism understood in uncompromisingly material and spatial terms.

Shareholders in this broader intellectual background, the Baṣran Mu'tazilites conceptualized human beings as purely physical entities, exhausted in their description as atomic aggregates serving as substrates for the inherence of accidents. The corollary was obvious: for these atomists, no understanding of resurrection other than an entirely physical one was possible. Death (*mawt*) was conceived as occurring with the dissolution (*tafrīq*) of the atoms of the body to an extent that led to the impairment of the structure (*binya*) necessary for accidents of life to inhere in the body. When this occurred, it marked the cessation of the conscious experience expressed in such psychological occurrences as knowing, willing, or believing, for the accidents responsible for these occurrences depended on the prior inherence of accidents of life. No spirit or soul survived the person's physical destruction. The Baṣrans conceived spirit (*rūḥ*) as signifying little more than breath, which was essential for the being to be alive, but in no way the separable carrier of one's being.[6] The body once dissolved, the person thus ceased to exist until the Day of Judgment, when they would be resurrected by God. Resurrection was in the main a matter of putting back together the atomic bits that had once constituted a person (though there was an additional twist of the ontological narrative to be explained shortly).

The difficulties that were posed by such a materialist view of human beings—and thus of death and resurrection—for the possibility of establishing the identity of resurrected beings are not trivial ones, as modern philosophers combining a religious concern with a materialist view of the person have discovered in trying to ground a philosophically sensitive account of resurrection. One of the interesting recent discussions of the question that aims to heighten our feel for these difficulties—and the resulting implausibility of identity claims—is that of the Christian philosopher Peter van Inwagen, who invites us to consider a manuscript originally written by Saint Augustine that is kept in a monastery until one day it is burned in a fire. Suppose, then, that God were to create a parchment possessing the exact same set of qualities as the one that was destroyed. Van Inwagen's claim is that this would and could not be the identical object but only a likeness that bears the exactly identical qualities, and not even the almighty God, he insists, has the power to make it the same object. How *could* it be the same when clearly there was a period when it did not exist except in charred cinders? And equally important, nothing can make it the case that the second sculpture was *written by Saint Augustine*.[7]

One response that has been compellingly made to these arguments is that they invoke the wrong kind of model in considering claims about human identity. There are many different kinds of "scattered objects"—composite objects whose component parts exist for a period of time in a state of distribution that lacks physical contiguity and are at a later point reassembled. As an alternative, it has been suggested that we look on the resurrection of human beings as analogous with the reassembly of a watch taken apart on the repairman's table, the reassembly of a gun dismantled to be stored, or even the modern artwork that can be assembled on-site.[8] Just as these objects do not, in a sense, lose their identity due to the "intermittent" existence they lead, so with human beings whose material parts disintegrate and are scattered abroad following their death. One's intuitions about identity cultivated and extended by such analogies, one is brought closer to perceiving how human beings suffering decay and the dissolution of their atomic constituents on death could have their parts recalled from the ends of the universe in order to be put back together.

In the Islamic context, this idea would have been a helpful one if one subscribed to one of the two options identified by Muslim theologians as competing ways of imagining the apocalyptic final events that would occur on the Day of Judgment. In the first option, the resurrection of human beings was a matter of gathering together (*ḥashr*) parts existing in a state of dispersion (*tafriqa*) throughout the created world. In his discussion of this view, Fakhr al-Dīn al-Rāzī gave a graphic account of it in which he named its main presupposition—namely, God's sustained knowledge of the particular parts that belonged to each being. This meant that

> even if the atoms [*ajzā'*] forming one's body turn into dust and get mixed up with one another, since God knows all things that can be known—both universals and particulars—He knows that the atom that lies at the bottom of this particular sea and the atom that lies at the top of this particular mountain taken in combination constitute the heart of Zayd, who had obeyed God during his lifetime.[9]

This was a view that evidently rested on the claim—contested by Islamic philosophers—that God has knowledge of particulars. The second account of eschatological events, however, foreclosed this possibility; for it envisaged the complete annihilation (*fanā'*) of created being before the Day of Judgment and its creation anew.

Looking at the works of Ash'arite writers such as Rāzī, Āmidī, or Jurjānī, one concludes that the later consensus was that the question was moot—there were grounds to support both the idea that cosmic annihilation would occur and the idea that it wouldn't. In part, the question was one of textual interpretation. For there was a handful of Qur'ānic verses that could be taken to indicate that the world will be destroyed in its entirety and then created again prior to God's resurrection and judgment of human beings. One of these verses was 28:88, which announced that "everything that exists will perish except God's face" (*kullu shay'in hālikun illā wajhahu*); another was 55:26: "All that is on earth will perish" (*kullu man 'alayhā fānin*); yet another—whose implications had to elicited with greater effort—was 57:3: "He is the first and the last" (*huwa al-awwal wa'l-ākhir*).[10] But Rāzī's view was that these verses were general ones (*'umūmāt*), and they could be interpreted in a narrower sense if good reasons existed. And this, in his opinion, was precisely the case here; for if their sense was taken at face value and left unrestricted, the resulting account had the grave disadvantage that it would make the doctrine of the identity of resurrected beings a difficult one to sustain. These were among the reasons that fed into Rāzī's own views concerning the separability of the spirit and its survival of death—beliefs that naturally liquidated any difficulties about a person's identity, as they involved the continued survival of an element that constituted its basis.[11]

But in the Mu'tazilite scheme, one was unable to draw great profit from the idea of the divine mind tracking the individual's atoms through cosmic time across its states of dispersion. For as we already saw in passing in the last chapter, the Baṣran Mu'tazilites—apparently considering the strength of the scriptural evidence decisive—affirmed the occurrence of a comprehensive annihilation of created being prior to the Day of Judgment. This position was theorized by a stark and rather startling metaphysics. On the death of the last human being subject to the Law (*mukallaf*), God released a single quantum of the accident of annihilation (*fanā'*), whose fundamental property was that it constituted the contrary (*ḍidd*) of atoms. As a corollary of this property, it was also one of the few accidents that could not inhere in atoms; that it did not inhere in any one atom entailed that it lacked an exclusive relation (*ikhtiṣāṣ*) to any particular atom; this, in turn, meant that it bore a relation to *all* atoms without distinction. Thus, a single quantum of annihilation stood to sweep every single atom out of existence. Nothingness would succeed with a deafening silence and within the twinkle of an eye. It did not matter whether this deep gash in the continuity of being were to last for a single moment (as our sources seem to suggest) or longer, for the damage—so to speak—would already have been wrought: this temporal gap would have rent the fabric of spatiotemporal continuity of individual elements that might have supported the identity of their aggregates. If the identity of particular watches, guns, or artwork could be plausibly said to survive their dismantlement, the same could certainly not be said with comparable intuitiveness if one posited that their atomic parts did not merely scatter, perhaps entering into new combinations to form new complex objects, but were wholly annihilated, as were all other existing objects.[12]

The starkly imagined temporal gap that Baṣran Muʿtazilite eschatology envisaged is one that needs to be constantly held in mind in order to appreciate the challenge that the Baṣran view of identity had to tackle. How, then, did the Baṣran Muʿtazilites confront these redoubtable difficulties? To clear the ground for their response, I want to call to mind here the options that their metaphysics—whose rudiments we now know—made available to them. The entities constituting created reality were exhausted in two kinds: atoms and accidents. Nothing but these two kinds of entities were candidates for grounding the identity of human beings. And it was, in fact, the former—the atomic elements that constituted a person—that the Baṣran Muʿtazilites came to invest with the capacity to underwrite the identity of persons. The order of exposition that will allow us to make the most of the Baṣran answer involves first clarifying the reasoning on which this view rested; the next goal will be to lead this answer gradually back toward the center of our concern by holding it up to the evaluative purposes that give identity its importance both in our view and, as we have seen, that of our Muʿtazilite thinkers.

In the Baṣran account of the identity holding between persons between this world and the next, two aspects stand out as especially worthy of mention. One is that this account was explicitly signaled as one modeled on the nature of personal identity that was realized in the worldly domain and the temporal order applicable to it. The second is that it found its anchor in a cardinal theorem of Muʿtazilite epistemology.

The first aspect was revealed in the fact that formed the point of departure for the discussions, and this was the simple fact of our ability to make ordinary judgments of identity—one that any account of the conditions constitutive of identity should be able to explain. For "it is necessary," ʿAbd al-Jabbār writes, "that a person should know on a given day that he is the one who previously willed something, and that the old man should know that he is the one who was a child and then a youth." And this, he claims, we do in fact know—by immediate or self-evident (*ḍarūrī*) knowledge: "The knowledge that one is the [same] person who was willing yesterday is a necessary one."[13] What this point of departure clearly disclosed was that if the question of identity was problematized, this would *only* be in connection to the transition between this world and the next. If the worldly domain was eligible to be used for eliciting the criteria constitutive of identity, this was because it posed no questions of its own.

The ordinary judgments of identity referred to by the Baṣrans are mainly cast in a first-person form. In considering the judgment a person might make that at t_1, one is the same person who had willed something at t_2, we will go to the heart of the matter if we abstract from the judgment of identity itself and focus on the simple judgment "I will"—or keeping closer to their conceptual matrix, "I am willing": *anā murīd*—that it involves. Now a general but critical fact about Baṣran epistemology was that the knowledge represented by ascriptions of attributes to entities ("I am willing" and "you are knowing" just as much as "this ball is moving" or "the atom is black") was analyzed in terms that posited the entity (or "the entity's essence or self": *dhāt*) as the strict object of knowledge. The real object of my knowledge when I know that *x* is *F* is *x*—it is "I," "you," "the atom," or "the ball," which forms the subject of predications. ʿAbd al-Jabbār puts this by saying that as concerns "the attribute that one knows a person to have [*al-ṣifa allatī yaʿlamuhu ʿalayhā*] . . . one's knowledge attaches to the qualified subject [*al-mawṣūf*] rather than to [the attribute]." Hence also, he says, "the knowledge of a thing's state requires the knowledge of the thing's self [*dhāt*]." The entity qualified has conceptual priority over the qualification.[14]

The next step, though, in grasping the Baṣran Muʿtazilite analysis requires us to summarize a vast leap of Baṣran thought and, condensing it into a single drop, simply state as a bald fact: in statements that concern living beings—primarily human beings—such as "I am willing," "You are knowing," or "we believe," the Baṣrans identified the subject contained in these statements with the material totality of atoms (*jumla*). The "I" in some way *was* the material substrate, so that to say "I am willing" was at the same time to predicate "willing" of the atomic totality that constituted a person. This is expressed fairly clearly in ʿAbd al-Jabbār's words that "the knowledge that one is willing and living is a knowledge of his parts [or atoms: *ajzāʾ*], even if this is not at the particular level"—though it remains to be added that one's knowledge was understood to attach to these parts, not qua individual atoms, but considered as a structured totality (*jumla*).[15] Once this leap was accomplished (a leap between what to us may seem to be two different categories: mental and physical), the corollary for their account of identity was only a stone's throw away. For if present ascriptions of attributes to human beings involve reference to this material substrate, then the capacity to make judgments of identity—to ascribe attributions made at different times as referring to the same subject—depends on the continuity of the material parts that compose this totality. Should these parts change, we would no longer know that this was the same person who had been qualified by certain attributes in the past or acted in certain ways.[16]

Or so the Baṣrans averred. Thus, God only had to re-create the same parts that had constituted a person during their lifetime in order to ensure that it was the same person, and that identity held between the worldly person and their otherworldly continuation. Thus Ibn Mattawayh:

> [A person's] fundamental parts themselves cannot admit change, and God must re-create the identical parts, which He knows despite their state of dispersion, and which it is not impossible for Him to gather together and return to their former condition. . . . For were it permissible that other than these parts be re-created, the one obeying would not be identical to the one being rewarded, or the one disobeying to the one being punished.[17]

The main qualification that nuanced this account is indicated in the terms "fundamental parts" (*ajzā' al-aṣl*), which were taken to indicate those parts that were necessary for a person to be alive, and given this, the more precise claim was that "what must be re-created is the quantity that is necessary for a person to be alive."[18] It was this material minimum that—certain internal controversies aside—was said to form the nucleus of identity, and its constancy throughout a person's life was assumed as an empirical fact, as was its exclusive possession by one and only one individual throughout cosmic history. As for the threat posed to the latter claim by the prospect of cannibalism—in which one person's parts were subsumed into another's—the Baṣrans' speculations terminated in a view of empirical facts that was essentially a posture of faith: no one individual's fundamental parts could ever (be permitted to) overlap with another's.[19]

This, then, was the Baṣran theory, synoptically put. It does not take long to observe that the chief and not inconsequential difficulty that this theory had to face had to do, very simply, with its point of departure—that is to say, the transfer of worldly criteria of identity to the otherworldly domain. For even supposing that the empirical facts about the worldly continuity of one's atomic parts had been in the Muʿtazilites' favor (a view of the facts that not only posterity but already also contemporaries—such as Avicenna—would refuse to credit), the difficulty that was posed by the exhaustive annihilation of the atoms constituting human beings *could* not be addressed by using a paradigm that was predicated on their evident continuity.[20] Whatever other problems the theory might face, this would seem to be the gravest.

At this point in the narrative, there is one particularly formidable page of Muʿtazilite metaphysics that one wishes one could delicately attempt to turn in order to see whether the writing on the other side might shed light on the present question. Heavy with controversy as with metaphysical import, this was the page inscribed with the contentious metaphysical tenet that many (though not all) Muʿtazilites became famous for among the circles of their fellow theologians. This was the tenet that "the nonexistent is a thing" (*al-maʿdūm shayʾ*). Put in a nutshell, the Muʿtazilite view of nonexistents involved the claim that the broadest category in reality was "thing," and it included as subdivisions the categories of "existent" and "nonexistent." And to say that thing is a category in *reality* meant that it was not merely to be understood as a mental object. The reasons why the Muʿtazilites came to profess this view were partly exegetical, and revolved around several Qurʾānic proof texts in which God is portrayed as giving the command "Be!" to a *thing* that He wants to create (e.g., 16:40, *innamā qawlunā li-shayʾin idhā aradnāhu an naqūla lahu 'kun' fa-yakūnu*; cf. also 36:82). God's creative act takes the form of the command "Be!" addressed to a thing that does not yet exist. In the more developed forms of the theory, the nonexistent was closely identified with the possible, which would include both possibles that have not yet been actualized, and those that were actualized in the past but have passed out of existence. In formulating their claims, the Muʿtazilites were very much guided by a concern to establish nonexistents as objects of divine knowledge and power (indeed, power [*qudra*] was understood to range *only* over nonexistent objects—for the function of power was precisely to make something exist).[21]

We will now recall that in the above quote of Ibn Mattawayh's, there was an allusion to God's knowledge of each person's parts "despite their state of dispersion"—and if the account was to explain what it was meant to explain (namely, how identity survived the *annihilation* of all existents), this must also mean, "despite their state of nonexistence" once annihilation occurs. A similar allusion coruscates fleetingly in the writings of ʿAbd al-Jabbār's, who remarks that "if God annihilates the world, He has the power to re-create those who deserve reward, and has knowledge of their [constitutive atomic] parts, and therefore it is possible for Him to re-create them."[22] These intimations to divine knowledge are here especially tantalizing, and they suggest the following interesting query: Could it be that it is this metaphysical theorem that implicitly underpins the Baṣrans' parsimonious references to God's knowledge of the material parts? Was it then the metaphysics of nonexistent things that came to the rescue of the identity of nonexistent human beings?

This seems to be what later theologians and philosophers made of the issue, by whom the connection between these two questions—the topic of resurrection and that of nonexistents—was explicitly traced out. The Ashʿarite al-Jurjānī (d. 1413), with his *Sharḥ al-mawāqif*, is a late but limpid example of this trend. Discussing the possibility of resurrecting human beings after the annihilation of the world (a possibility that had to be considered even by those who, unlike the Baṣrans, did not unequivocally affirm that it would take place), he states that according to the Muʿtazilites, "if an existent ceases to exist, its particular self or essence [*dhāt*] remains, and *this makes it possible* for [human beings] to be re-created." A bit further, responding to an objection that the identity of persons across this temporal gap would demand that the person be distinguished (*tamayyaza*) during this gap of nonexistence, he remarks: "On the principle of the Muʿtazilites that the nonexistent is a thing . . . this possibility would be evident."[23] Rāzī's discussion of the afterlife marks the connection equally well by parsing the question about personal identity across the gap of annihilation in terms of a question about the possibility of re-creating the nonexistent (*iʿādat al-maʿdūm*).[24]

These writers—who are certainly not alone in this trend—are joined by contemporary commentators. Thus, Michael Marmura names the Muʿtazilite justification for the claim that the re-created being is identical to the previous existent as one that "rests on their doctrine that the non-existent is a 'thing' or an 'essence' (*dhāt*)." And that the Muʿtazilite doctrine in question extends to this case is implicitly assumed by Rob Wisnovsky, who uses the example of particular human beings in illustrating his discussion of it.[25]

As the contexts of the discussions—both modern and ancient—suggest, the connection between the two theses has plenty to do with a discussion broached by Avicenna on the topic of nonexistents and the possibility of their re-creation. First in the *Metaphysics* of his *al-Shifāʾ* and then resuming those earlier remarks in his *Mubāḥathāt,* Avicenna declared the impossibility of re-creating something that no longer exists ("*al-maʿdūm lā yuʿādu,*" as the formulation went). It was in the latter work that he delivered himself of the following interesting comment:

> If the view is sound of those who claim that a thing exists and then ceases to be qua existent, but insofar as its particular self [or essence, substance: *dhāt*] is concerned, it continues to be a self and does not perish qua self, and then existence is given back to it, then one might affirm the possibility of recreation [*iʿāda*].[26]

This drew a clear link between the way one conceived of nonexistents and the view of re-creation one could support. And while the sort of re-creation at issue was not as clear in the *Metaphysics* (whose context was far removed from concerns with the afterlife), it seemed clearer in the *Mubāḥathāt* given the concern with the soul situating the remark in question, and it was spelled out plainly by Ghazālī when, in a posture of rebuttal, he picked up these remarks in his *Tahāfut al-falāsifa* and addressed them as an objection made by the philosophers (and Avicenna in particular) to the possibility of a physical resurrection.[27]

The doctrine of nonexistent things being a distinctive Muʿtazilite position, one would naturally assume that Avicenna's interlocutors are Muʿtazilites throughout the relevant texts, even though, as Marmura points out, Avicenna never clearly refers to the Muʿtazilites in his discussion. And in denying the view that nonexistents can be re-created, he certainly treats it as one that was actually held, as in pronouncing on "the falsehood of the view of one who says that nonexistents can be re-created."[28] The context would suggest that there is *somebody* who says this, and that this *must* be the Muʿtazilites.

Yet what is curious is that while the doctrine of nonexistents Avicenna was targeting was clearly a Muʿtazilite specialty, this link between the two issues cannot be traced in the prime location where one would expect to find it—namely, in the Muʿtazilite discussions of bodily resurrection. This, despite the fact that a reference to nonexistents turns up—as how could it not?—in the very definition of resurrection or re-creation (*iʿāda*), which is explained as "the creation of a nonexistent that had existed before" (*ḥaqīqat al-iʿāda lā takūnu illā ījād li-maʿdūm kāna mawjūd min qablu*).[29] One is therefore compelled to wonder whether the soldering of the two issues was a beneficent service that Avicenna performed on behalf of the Muʿtazilites unbeknownst to them, though one performed too late for them to profit from it by developing the idea in greater detail.

Surveying the doctrine of nonexistent things, in fact, one finds no evidence to suggest that it was oriented by a desire to cater for an account of the preservation of the identity of human beings during the period of their nonexistence. Given the account of personal identity described above, it would seem that the least that would have been required would have been a concern with the individuation of nonexistent atoms—something that would distinguish *these* nonexistent atoms as having once belonged to Zayd from *those* as having once belonged to ʿAmr. But for one thing, even though nonexistents included both possibles that had never been unactualized, and those that had been actualized in the past and had then ceased to exist, the focus of the Muʿtazilite interest seems to be sharply slanted toward the former. This was remarked by Frank when he noted that "the status and reality of the once but now no more existent was a topic of scant concern for the theologians of the *kalām*."[30]

For another, we can say—without going into too much detail—that the resources of the Baṣran theory in its developed state only seem to enable us to distinguish nonexistents on the level of *classes* of things, such as the quality of being an atom ("an atom's being an atom") or that of being black (which Rāzī parses as "*ṣifāt al-ajnās*," referring to *jawhariyya* and *sawādiyya*), and not on the level of *particular individuals*, which is what we need here.[31] In addition, the Baṣrans seem far more interested in classes of nonexistents on the *atomic* level than on the level of complex atomic aggregates such as human beings—for whom the "*dhāt*" (the subject of predications, the essence of the being) is *not* an individual atom but the material totality of atoms unified by life. Short of an account of how isolated atoms were individuated by the history of their relations to a larger whole, it would seem that they would have to be individuated by a continued membership in the material totality, and that the entire totality constituting a particular human individual would have to be picked out as a single nonexistent object. Yet in the terms of the Baṣran scheme, this totality was realized through an accident of "composition" (*taʾlīf*) that held the atoms together, and subsequently through an accident of life that unified it into a single thing. This meant that the aggregate itself could not be realized as a single entity in a state of nonexistence, for it was a basic ontological thesis that relationships of inherence could only be realized on the plane of existence.[32]

All of this suggests that the page of Muʿtazilite metaphysics that so cryptically retains its back turned to us has little of interest inscribed on the other side, as far as our particular purposes are concerned. As things stand, the concept of divine knowledge that the Baṣran Muʿtazilites deploy in speaking of the identity of re-created beings seems to be one unsupported by the technical sophistications spearheaded under the doctrine of nonexistent things. Which is not the same as saying that it *couldn't* have been supported by extending these sophistications, or that it wasn't rather a *nontechnical* conception of this doctrine—a reliance on the basic intuition inspiring it—that might have seemed to the Baṣrans to provide an adequate answer making sophisticated inquiries redundant.

By this basic intuition, I have in mind the Baṣrans' core idea about the nonexistent as that which is necessary in order to provide our true judgments with their referents—or to put it in their idiom, to provide our knowledge with its relatum or *mutaʿallaq*. For one principal point of departure in thinking about nonexistents seems to have been this: first one knows something about something, and then one postulates an object to serve as its *mutaʿallaq*, for knowledge without one is impossible. This starting point can be clarified by asking the paradoxical-sounding question, How it is that we know about a nonexistent that it is a nonexistent in the first place? In a sense, there is no space for such a question to be asked, for we make no discovery, nor do we seek to make one; we begin from the point at which the nonexistent has already been manifested in our speech and figured as the subject of our thought.[33]

From this perspective, as long as one can say something (true) about an entity, this entity will be realized as a nonexistent, and one identifies nonexistents precisely through the predications one makes of them. For human beings, it will be sufficient to make true statements about them in order to identify them, such as statements referring to their historical past. One may say of a person now deceased that "Abū Muḥammad was a man of great piety" or "Abū Muḥammad would have been outraged had he known his sons would sell the family business after his death." I take it that on the broad intuition of the Muʿtazilite view of nonexistents, by virtue of the sheer fact of making such statements (which, let us suppose, constitute true knowledge) one would be picking out a nonexistent subject—a *dhāt*—whose function would be to form the relatum or *mutaʿallaq* of such statements, and that here would have to be the entire atomic totality that is the person who once existed. Thus, it is never a matter of our statements having to confront the entire undifferentiated mass of nonexistent atoms and rifle through them in order to locate the particular atoms making up a complex referent like Abū Muḥammad. Our statements meet Abū Muḥammad already in one piece, as it were.

Of course, to make one's statements the starting point in this way may well seem like placing the cart before the horse. Yet this would be an account not of why the view was a good or plausible one—for this particular expression of it was never after all defended—but why the intuitive basis underlying the sophisticated articulations of the Baṣran doctrine of nonexistents may have made the space for a question about nonexistent human beings less visible, and how on an intuitive level the matter may have appeared. Certainly, left merely at this level, and shorn of the technical elaborations enjoyed by other aspects of the doctrine of nonexistents, this would come closer to being a *merely* intuitive posture, and at that, one reminiscent of a posture of faith. The affirmation of God's knowledge of the nonexistent human being's parts strikes one as nothing more than that: a simple profession of faith—and as such, as the point at which justification comes to an end.

Accidents and the Formal Reality of Resurrected Beings

Yet now it is time for me to lead these questions back to our point of departure and reorient them around the pivot of our concern—one that we share with the Muʿtazilites, whose interest in criteria of identity was derivative to their interest in the moral consequences that flowed from success or failure in establishing it. This would be a failure that would mean nothing less than the injustice of punishing and rewarding persons who are other than those who had acted in a way to deserve this. Now the above-mentioned difficulties confronting the criterion of identity articulated by the Baṣran Muʿtazilites are ones formulated from a point of view not marked by any particular concern with these momentous moral consequences. Still, as we said in the last chapter, criteria of identity depend on the purposes that dictate one's interest in them, and they would seem to vary in content or stringency depending on these purposes. In particular, we care to establish a thicker view of identity when the concern is with desert and moral accountability (or more precisely, with deserts of this magnitude; we would be less stringent if the desert claim was over a pat on the back and a smile of approbation, or a mere frown of discontent). With this order of desert, it is not enough to judge that $person_1$ at t_1 is identical to $person_2$ at t_{100}, where the two instants are separated by a few decades, and that $person_1$ committed an act of cruelty in order to justify punishing the person. There has to be a continuity of a thicker sort that permits us to hold the person responsible for the past act *now*.

These are notes that essentially rehearse the perspective set at anchor in the previous chapter, and so, in effect, does the answer to the question—a question separate from the one pursued earlier in this chapter—about how the Baṣran Muʿtazilites' criterion of identity served their moral concern. The answer seems to be that it simply did not; for insofar as the Muʿtazilite angle of questioning was a distinctively moral one, a purely physical criterion for personal identity seems inadequate unless it could be seen to correlate with psychological attributes that would enter into the thicker notion of identity required by moral desert. What could be the use of affirming, on the basis of an argument concerning the reconstitution of scattered objects, that the body that stands before us at the time of re-creation is numerically identical with the same body that raised the knife unless it is also established that there is a corresponding *psychological* continuity that makes it possible to continue to ascribe to me at the time of re-creation the murderous intentions I had at the time I wielded it? Yet the material substrate, as it was conceived by the Baṣrans, had no such essential correlation with continuities of a formal sort. It was nothing more than a bare locus to which accidents "merely" occurred (the term *ʿaraḍa*—to befall, to occur—which stands at the root of the term for accidents—*ʿaraḍ*—itself partly betrays the transient and extraneous relationship that held between an accident and its substrate).[34] It takes little more to conclude that the Baṣran Muʿtazilite conception of the identity of persons between this world and the next is perfectly in keeping with their conception of persons within the present world, in exhibiting a similar indifference to psychological—and more important, moral—aspects of the person.

But the above exploration of identity has not quite exhausted the Baṣran Muʿtazilite attention to matters of eschatology (to put it more cumbersomely, of "eschatological anthropology"). For on the one hand, there is no doubt that the criterion of identity purveyed was a primarily physical one, and accidents were excluded from the criteria of identity after a short skirmish between the Baṣrans and several changes of mind on the part of Abū Hāshim, who at different times proposed that the accidents of life (*ḥayāt*) and composition (*ta'līf*) should be included among the elements of the person to be re-created along with their parts, as conditions necessary for their identity. Interestingly enough, his reasoning for the inclusion of the latter accident—"composition"—had to do with its role in helping us distinguish between individuals. Abū Hāshim, we are told,

> identified as the reason for the necessity of re-creating *ta'līf* that this is what differentiates one particular totality [which a living being consists in] from others. For the distinction between Zayd and ʿAmr occurs on the basis of their appearance [or form: *ṣūra*], whereas material parts are all of the same kind.[35]

The last part of this remark is an interesting reprise of the point made above—namely, that the Baṣrans did not articulate a conception of physical parts in terms that took them past the generic and individuated them by reference to their bearers. But what is important here is that ultimately opinion came down strongly in favor of denying any role to accidents in the constitution of a being's identity. Thus, "the living being . . . is the totality constituted by those [fundamental atomic] parts, and *not* the accidents that inhere in it," and therefore "it is the material parts of the living being that must be re-created, not the accidents that inhere in them." And this was as much as to say that neither is identity to be located in the attributes that derive from these accidents (*mā yakhtaṣṣu bihi min al-ṣifa*).[36]

Yet on the other hand, and while ultimately it was the material locus that prevailed as a criterion, this could not remain merely a bare locus wholly bereft of attributes and the accidents that ground them. What would a bare atom be except a mere noumenon—a thing lacking in all phenomenal qualities that would enable it to appear as something perceivable or intelligible? For it is accidents that are responsible for conferring to an entity all the properties that make it visible—its color, its movement, its size (through the accident of composition that makes it possible for invisible and indivisible atoms to unite into a visible body). Passing on to living creatures, it is accidents that confer to them all the properties that make them living creatures at all, distinguished from inanimate matter, by the inherence of the accident of life. And life, in turn, is the ontological precondition for the inherence of the accidents of knowing or willing that distinguish a human being from other animal beings.

The inclusion of these ontological constituents in the vision of the otherworldly person was thus an inescapable necessity. And in fact, while accidents were not discussed by the Baṣran Muʿtazilites under the aspect of those things that *had* to be re-created (*wajaba*)—obligatory if it was to be the same entity—accidents came to the fore when the discussion turned to those things that *could* be re-created (*ṣaḥḥa*). And here we may take note of the perhaps paradoxical point that while the latter were not included in a conception of identity, nonetheless the question the Baṣrans debated was not merely about the creation but about the *re*-creation of these entities—that is to say, about the re-creation of the very same accidents that had been carried by a person in the past. The question that then engaged them was: *Which* accidents could be re-created? Given its focus, this aspect of the Baṣran Muʿtazilites' account would seem the prime location in which to look for the fuller conception of the person that populates their eschatological vision. It is here that we may hope to hear more about the presence, in this vision (even if not as criteria of identity), of those attributes that we previously identified as the most natural objects of a specifically moral concern—above all, motivation (construed as a form of knowledge) and will, whose ontological ground was provided by entitative accidents.

What must be remarked here to connect the discussion of the two types of ontological constituent—atoms and accidents—is a certain significant feature of the Baṣran Muʿtazilites' conception of indivisible atoms, which at the same time represents a crucial reprieve from, and adjustment of, the vision of a disjointed and discontinuous reality that we have stressed up to this point as the result of their atomistic metaphysics. The Baṣran scheme recognized in atoms a basic capacity to endure (*baqāʾ*). Once an atom had been created, it would continue to exist until and unless its existence was interrupted by its contrary—in the case of atoms, the accident of annihilation. It is crucial to stress the fundamental stability of the created world that flowed from this basic ontological thesis as its immediate corollary. For our purposes, an even more strategic importance attaches to spelling out more clearly the conception of continuation or endurance that this thesis involved. For as we will now see, one of the principal three conditions laid down by the Baṣrans for identifying those accidents that could be re-created was that they should likewise possess the capacity to endure. And it is the conception of endurance—equally applicable to atoms and accidents—that was in part responsible for the poverty of the conception of the person that emerged once the Baṣran conditions for re-creation were accounted for.

These three conditions are enumerated by Ibn Mattawayh in the following concise words: "In our view, that which may be re-created [*mā taṣiḥḥu i'ādatuhu*] must be enduring [*bāqī*], must be an act of God as against the act of any other being, and must be initiated in the immediate substrate of one's power [*mubtada'*].[37] The last condition is meant to distinguish these acts from acts whose effect depends on a mediating cause (*sabab*)—designated as "generated" acts (*muwallada*). But this last condition will not be engaging us here because, while many interesting human features would not violate it and thus pass this first test—with the (not insignificant) exception of knowledge generated by inquiry (*naẓar*)—the restrictiveness introduced by the other two conditions is such as to render redundant counterfactual speculations about the wider range of accidents and hence attributes that would have been admitted on the first.[38]

Both of the other two conditions had one principal feature in common that was catalytic in disqualifying them from the possibility of re-creation. This consisted in certain austere—and in their austerity fairly baffling—criteria of temporal individuation or time specificity articulated by the Baṣran Mu'tazilites for the relevant accidents. Starting with the criterion of endurance, the most important point to clarify is what it meant *not* to be able to endure. The Baṣrans construed the latter not merely in terms of an inability to continue in existence through two successive moments; the far stronger claim that the Baṣrans seem to have made is that the accidents in question could not exist except at a *particular moment in time*. And it was this time specificity that was designated as the chief reason for the exclusion of non-enduring accidents from the class of those to be re-created on the Day of Judgment. As Ibn Mattawayh explains,

> If something is such that it is not possible for it to endure, its re-creation is impossible for the reason that if it cannot endure, its existence is confined to one moment in time [*mukhtaṣṣ bi-waqt wāḥid*], whereas to admit the possibility of its re-creation entails the possibility of its existing in two moments in time.[39]

The reasoning is singular; to lack the capacity to endure thus seems to mean *not*: "to endure for no more than one moment," but rather: "to endure for no more than one moment that is a *particular* moment in objective or absolute time." Whatever the singularity of this reasoning, it is this same conception that underlies the inclusion only of enduring accidents and atoms—likewise marked by endurance—in the range of re-creatable entities.

Yet this turn of reasoning was replicated in the second condition used to sift accidents for potential re-creation—namely, that they should be acts of God as against any other being. One interpretative remark is in order here to dispel a possible source of puzzlement: How are we to understand this talk of accidents as *acts*?[40] The reason for this is simple: every accident (and indeed atom) is created and forms the object of *somebody's* power (*qudra*)—whether divine power or the power of living beings like ourselves. Now the chief difference between the nature of our power and that of God's is that, as we saw in chapter 5, the latter is grounded in the divine essence, whereas human power is grounded in the inherence of a corresponding entitative accident (*maʿnā*). It is, in fact, this very feature of human power that is implicated in the rationale that undergirds the third restrictive condition about what can and cannot be re-created. For once again, the Baṣrans seem to have described these accidents in terms of an austere criterion of temporal individuation. This criterion is indicated in the following comment by Ibn Mattawayh, who having pointed out that the objects of human power include *both* enduring and nonenduring accidents, goes on to assert that re-creation is possible for neither type of object, as long as the power through which they have originated is one grounded in an accident of *qudra*.

> For even though [the objects of *qudra*] include things whose *existence* [*wujūd*] is not restricted to a particular time, the *origination* [*ḥudūth*] of all of them will be restricted to a particular time. . . . The basic principle here is that it is a characteristic [or ruling: *ḥukm*] of a single [accident of] power that it may only attach at a single time, in a single substrate, to a single quantum of an act, belonging to a single class. So were we to deem it possible that the object of this power be re-created, this ruling would be violated, for it would have to be re-created by means of that same power, since another power may not attach to this same object, nor may the power of another agent do so.[41]

This extended quote reveals the special asperity that marked the Baṣran Muʿtazilites' views about the time specificity of the ontological constituents in question. Its logic is clarified by one further remark, in which Ibn Mattawayh points out that accidents whose existence is restricted to a particular time "cannot be re-created because re-creating them involves the possibility that it exist earlier or later," re-creation constituting, in a sense, "a deferred creation" (*ta'khīr al-ījād*).[42] Once again, then, it seems that the temporal specification that the Baṣrans have in mind when they talk of "a single time" is understood not merely in the sense that "there cannot be more than one instant of time at which the accident can exist" but in terms of a *determinate* moment in objective time that cannot occur earlier or later. Such a concept of individuation evidently sets up criteria for identity of unusual stringency—indeed criteria that *by definition* made it impossible to establish identity *over time*.[43]

Taken together, the consequences of these conditions for the vision of the person to be re-created (or "resurrected") on the Day of Judgment seem to be rather sweeping. For if none of the things that had been created by human power could be re-created, this immediately excluded all the morally significant acts of knowing and willing that would have issued by virtue of it over a lifetime.[44] Ibn Mattawayh's list of human objects of power (*maqdūrāt*) includes features such as willing (*irāda*), not willing (or aversion: *karāha*), belief (*iʿtiqād*), opinion (*ẓann*), and thought (*fikr*).[45] The consequence of the condition excluding all human *maqdūrāt* was that no single act of willing or believing sustained over a lifetime would cross the threshold of eternity to be reexperienced by—to be restored to—its erstwhile bearer. The person who emerged from the reassembly of their selfsame atoms would only carry over the threshold of eternity the things with which they first crossed the threshold of life as well as whatever other ontological enrichments God might have dispensed to them throughout their life. This, we may speculate, would include innate moral knowledge, which was created in a person by God directly. More obviously, this view would accommodate certain physical characteristics—such as a person's color (*lawn*). As Ibn Mattawayh's inventories once again inform us, this was classed among the accidents capable of endurance, along with a number of other items contained in the following list: tastes, smells, heat, cold, moisture, dryness, life, the capacity for autonomous action, locative accidents such as motion and rest, and composition.[46] As will be observed, nothing in this inventory betrays a concern for characteristics that relate to human cognition or volition.

To state this, of course, is to do no more than rehearse an observation already made in the previous chapter in the context of a question about the Muʿtazilites' concern with personal continuity. What can thus be said is that the indifference to personal continuity in the otherworldly domain mirrors the indifference to such continuity in the worldly one, as does the indifference to any conception of distinctive psychological attributes that result from one's own voluntary efforts (and a fortiori, specifically moral ones). Through the double effect of *both* conditions combined, any such attributes are left out of their view of the resurrected beings that will inhabit eternity. The above remarks, then, yield no revisions to our existing picture of the Baṣran Muʿtazilites' conception of the human person, and only extend it by presenting it in light of a more programmatic commitment.

The vision to which such conception tempts one to succumb is that of a robotic army of generic human beings summoned out of nothingness to undergo experiences of pleasure and pain, whose only moral basis consists in a past act whose main basis, in turn, lies in the identity of a material body that once committed them, yet that is shorn of all moral marks that would register its historical connection to them. The robotic aspect of these beings is heightened by observing that if the theory of afterlife metaphysics that these Baṣrans articulated made little room for individuating psychological features, neither did it seem to make any for individuating features of bodily appearance. For the only condition involved in their account that pertained to appearance was essentially a structural one, which flowed from the ontological necessity that atoms be structured in a particular way (*mabnī binya makhṣūṣa*) in order for life to be able to inhere. But this was a structure that, we must conclude, would be common between different kinds of living beings, and far from distinguishing Zayd from ʿAmr, would hardly go so far as to distinguish human beings from nonhuman animals.[47] Once Abū Hāshim dropped his proposal for including in the constitutive criteria for identity the accident of composition (*ta'līf*) that a person had possessed during their life—a proposal motivated, as we have seen, by the fact that this accident was responsible for the form that distinguished one individual from another—any questions about the phenomenal differentiation between persons seem to have fallen away. Thus, for all that the theory allowed, the psychological uniformity of resurrected beings would only be matched by the uniformity of their appearance, and the only reprieve from this prospect came from scriptural evidence alluded to by the Baṣrans that promised looks of glowing beauty to those rewarded and terrible disfigurement to those punished.[48]

Nevertheless, before we entirely succumb to this unsettling vision, we should take a moment to make a second remark—one that may provide it with a merciful mitigation. For perhaps in this case it is our fault to have been dazzled by an excessively scrupulous attention to our sources and have failed to consider the possibility that the type of identity that our theologians demand—one whose satisfaction seems nothing less than a conceptual impossibility—may after all be one that is unnecessarily austere. Unnecessarily so, in the sense that the failure to satisfy it need not entail the absence of the features that seem to us to have the greatest interest and significance.

For we will recall that the debate, as it was cast by the Baṣran Muʿtazilites, concerned the possibility of re-creating the exactly identical ontological constituents that had animated—more prosaically, inhered in—a person's body in the past. Yet the impossibility of doing so, in Baṣran terms, is an impossibility of creating what one would call the identical "tokens"—the same particular accident of power, life, will, or knowledge that had inhered in my body in the past, and was annihilated along with the rest of created beings at the end of the world. This, however, would by no means amount to the impossibility of creating something that belongs to the same "type"—the same *type* of willing, knowing, thought, or opinion. The distinction between type and token is certainly not an imported piece of ingenuity, for the Muʿtazilites naturally recognized a distinction between particular things and the classes (*jins*, in the present context) to which they belong. Nor is the inspiration for deploying it here an exogenous one. It is suggested, for example, by Ibn Mattawayh's remark in discussing the condition that excludes accidents generated by a secondary cause (*sabab*) that even if one could not create the precisely identical effect (*al-ʿayn al-musabbaba*), "it is possible to re-create what belongs to the same class [*jins*]."[49]

Indeed, this distinction maps on to a difference between the phenomenal and the metaphysical that is central to the Baṣran view of the relation between what is ordinary, common sense, and self-evident, and the ontological foundations of the ordinary that must be elicited by studious inquiry (an inquiry that takes ordinary knowledge as its starting point). For we know that a person is alive, that one knows something or wants something, without knowing that the metaphysical basis of these qualities are these things identified inquiry as "accidents," which act as necessary causes of these phenomenally available qualities. This, our theologians urge, is the precise reason why those—such as the Ashʿarites—who believe, however misguidedly, that *no* accidents endure for more than an instant, can at the same time hold that the person remains the same living being.

> If we were to suppose that a person's [accidents of] life did not endure but were created anew at every moment, it would not undermine our knowledge that this is the same living being. This is why it is possible for one who believes that accidents cannot endure to know that Zayd is the same person who existed yesterday, even if he believes that all of the entitative accidents within him are created anew.[50]

Similarly with the accidents of composition—several remarks imply that one may *look* the same (remain the same at a *phenomenal* level) even while the tokens of composition that produce this appearance (its *metaphysical* underpinning) are replaced by others of the same type.[51]

What the possibility of drawing this distinction entails is, at the very least, that the person to be resurrected might be granted the same range of qualities—corresponding to the same type of accidents—which they had once possessed during their earthly life. For in its absence, and if for a type of attribute-corresponding accident not to be re-created means not to be created at all (which the Baṣran silence on this question forces one to conclude), interesting psychological features would seem to be entirely excluded from the conception of the resurrected person, who looms before us an entity altogether psychologically bald. And there is at least *one* such feature that the Muʿtazilites would certainly wish to claim for human beings in the afterlife—and that is the knowledge of God, gained in this world as an effect generated by inquiry, and thus on the strict conditions we have seen (which exclude generated accidents) not susceptible to re-creation. Yet this knowledge is unequivocally included in the otherworldly script; only—as ʿAbd al-Jabbār's words reveal—it will be produced by a process different from the one that had caused it in the present world: for "God will create a knowledge of Himself in our hearts in the hereafter without the need to witness miraculous signs."[52] Here we must understand that a different cause will produce the same effect—that is to say, the same *type* of knowledge, which will be realized through a different token of the accident that corresponds to it.

As to whether these qualities are distinctive and individuating in a way that spares us the vision of an army of robotic beings subjected to punishment or reward—here we should not expect the depiction of distinctiveness to go beyond the one developed to describe human beings in their worldly circumstances. This distinction between types and tokens recognizes the possibility of re-creating only the types of willing, knowing, motivation, and so on, that the overall theory allows for. At the same time, it is worth pointing out what is perhaps too evident to merit mention: these mitigating considerations are the result of an exercise of exegesis, and the Baṣran Muʿtazilites themselves do not seem to have been explicitly concerned about reflecting on the overall, global vision of the person that their local ontological positions colluded to produce.[53]

At this point it is worth retracing our steps, in order to make one last remark before concluding. Beginning from the Muʿtazilite concern with moral desert, we pursued the Baṣran account of personal identity across the gap of individual death and cosmic annihilation. This account, as we saw, stipulated an exclusively physical criterion of identity based on the identity of a person's core atomic substrate. Accidents—responsible for both physical appearance and psychological features—were of no concern for identity, and of marginal concern for the overall picture of the human person to be created on the Day of Judgment, though on the basis of the distinction just drawn between metaphysical and phenomenal, not categorically excluded.

In making the criterion of identity a material one, and in making this material basis a mere aggregation of homogeneous atomic parts, the Baṣran Muʿtazilite account contrasted sharply with the account of identity that began to prevail among later theologians once the seepage of Greek philosophical influence had transformed the practice of *kalām* from the eleventh and twelfth centuries onward, bringing with it an ontology that challenged the materialistic atomism of *kalām* metaphysics. It will be instructive to juxtapose the two worldviews here by observing that among the results of the increasing dominance of the former was a tendency to look away from the material basis of beings and toward their formal reality as a ground for identity. Rāzī provides us with a clear example of this trend when he writes, in his work *al-Arbaʿīn fī uṣūl al-dīn*, that "the particular individual cannot be equated merely with these material parts [*ajzāʾ*] . . . but with those parts as characterized by particular qualities. If this is so, then those qualities form part of the essence [*māhiyya*] of that individual insofar as he is that individual."[54] An equally clear exemplar is found in Jurjānī, who affirms that "what is necessary in re-creating the same thing is the re-creation of its individuating accidental properties" (*iʿādat ʿawāriḍihi al-mushakhkhiṣa*). The stress embodied in these statements echoes Avicenna's typically Aristotelian affirmation that "a man is not a man by virtue of his matter but by virtue of his form, which exists in his matter."[55]

From another aspect, though, and without underestimating the vast differences in intellectual outlook that separates the Aristotelian orientation of these views and the Muʿtazilites' atomistic materialism, Jurjānī's discussion is potent in situating the contrast between these worldviews within a broader horizon of similarity that informs them on a different level. This horizon can be seen if we pause to consider two of the arguments raised and discussed by Jurjānī against the possibility of preserving the identity of resurrected beings. The first of these moves on a plane best described as that of conceptual necessity. It is condensed in the following claim: the being resurrected in the afterlife *cannot* be identical to a being that existed at some previous time because that would mean that nonexistence intervenes between a thing and itself; but in order for the concept of "betweenness" or "something intervening" to be realized, there must be two different things involved. "It is necessarily impossible that nonexistence should intervene between a thing and itself, because 'intervening' [*takhallul*] requires that there be two parts that are distinct from one another [*ṭarafayn mutaghāyirayn*]."[56]

One possible response to this challenge might have been to point out that while the claim sounds intuitive, it all depends on the examples one chooses to model it on and the way one describes them. A river that runs through a single country might be described as intervening between a thing and itself, since it's England on one side and England on the other. In another sense, of course, it is no doubt true that the two sides—considered from a "purely physical" point of view—*aren't* identical; there's simply *two* of them. What this would demonstrate is that we should show great circumspection over the cases we select for use as models for the identity of persons (who are far more likely to be compared to legal entities like England than to the banks of a river considered "from a purely physical point of view").

As for Jurjānī, his tactic is to rephrase the claim so that it removes the offending idea of nonexistence as something that "intervenes." The claim *just means* that first "the thing existed for a time, then existence was withdrawn from it at another time, and then at a third time it was again characterized by existence."[57] Yet what is important to notice here is that whatever its virtues, this rephrasing perpetrates a strategic misstep. In talking about an "it" that survives as the subject of these different statements, it *presupposes* the identity of the thing in question—which was the very point that needed to be established. This move, it may be hazarded, is not too dissimilar to the one performed by the Muʿtazilites in their unself-conscious transition over the gap that interrupts the continuity of the material basis of identity. In different ways, both moves involve a rather cavalier—as it seems to us—stance on the problem and a rather dim—as it seems to us—appreciation of its depth, leading them to a reasoning that on analysis, proves a circular one, presupposing what it sets out to prove.

Of course, it could be said here that this has been the most famous means of getting personal identity (or indeed, *any* philosophical question) wrong in the history of its philosophical investigation. If this turn of thought seems more reminiscent of a generic flaw in argumentation than of a meaningful similarity, Jurjānī's second argument does a little better in tracing out a more substantive resemblance. It is the second argument that connects more immediately to Jurjānī's view about the criterion of identity (which he locates in individuating attributes), confronting it with the challenge posed by the possibility of duplicates—which here signifies duplicate sets of attributes. Suppose, the challenge goes, that God indeed resurrects a given individual, and suppose, as you wish to claim, that the individual is identical to the one that had existed before. Nevertheless, it must then be possible that God should create another individual whose attributes are exactly identical to those of the first; yet this means that it is possible that there should be two individuals who are distinct from one another even though all their attributes are the same. The absurdity of this conclusion demands the rejection of the first premise.

The fractious idea on which this objection rests concerns the identity of indiscernibles. Jurjānī's response to the problem is first to point out—no doubt rightly—that if this were a problem, it would arise not just with respect to resurrected beings but also with respect to beings existing in this life. The main thrust of his response, however, is to say that as a matter of fact it is not possible that an entity should exist that would be qualitatively indistinguishable from another; their essential attributes would be in common, but their individuating features would have to differ. "If it was said: what we mean by a likeness [of the original being] created ab initio is that it would not be distinguished from the re-created being by any aspect [*wajh*], then we would say: the possibility of its existing in this manner is not granted."[58] "The possibility is not granted" must here mean: it would not be permitted to happen—presumably by God.

The shift of emphasis—from the Muʿtazilite claim that the material substrate underwrites identity, to Jurjānī's that it is a person's attributes that do so—should not obscure the common ground that unites these two positions—namely, a basic posture of fideism enlisted to shield the ground of identity against the vagaries of empirical reality. For all his different philosophical horizon, Jurjānī relies on divine intervention in securing the identity of persons no less than the Muʿtazilites did, within their own terms. Yet whereas their fideism took the form of an assumption that God would not permit a single human being to share their fundamental, identity-constituting material parts with another, Jurjānī's faith seems to express itself in the presumption that God would not permit a single entity to share its individuating and identifying attributes with any other. None of this should be taken to deny the real and significant differences that divide the two horizons of thought represented by Jurjānī and Rāzī, on the one hand, and the Baṣran Muʿtazilites, on the other.

The muted but indubitable presence of divine agency in the Baṣran Muʿtazilites' moral and metaphysical scheme is an important feature to consider in mapping its overall character. In several of the issues pursued above, the examination of the Baṣran view has often culminated in a perception that a demand for explanation was either dimly perceived or only thinly filled by our theologians. This was the case with the need to explain the continuation of desert across time, as it was with the preservation of identity across time and the steep existential gaps it had to traverse. The same could be said, though on a different level, about several of the issues discussed in chapter 4, such as the conflict between the grounds of utility and the grounds of desert in justifying punishment—and the examination of these issues has been mostly filtered by a primary interest in the justification of punishment. The role implicitly assigned to God in filling the spaces where a demand for explanation is felt has been a recurrent theme in this discussion. Short of an articulate view of how desert attaches or relates to the person ontologically, we are left with the idea of God—the master bookkeeper—retaining the facts about one's past actions and the values of one's deeds, and storing them up as legal titles of deed in an otherworldly chancery, whose worldly counterparts are scriptural names such as "believer," "unbeliever," or "grave sinner." Short of an enunciated ontology for nonexistent persons, we face a primitive notion of God's knowledge that keeps track of one's identity-bearing material parts.

At the same time, it must be kept in mind that in constructing this account, there has been a constant tension between the sources from which to take the questions that drive the direction of inquiry—our questions or the Muʿtazilites'? Our demands for justification or their own perception of the appropriate limits of explanation? Whether—to resume a running theme—this dulled response to explanatory gaps, and the invocation of a theological postulate to fill them, disposes us to treat the Muʿtazilites as philosophers or theologians, as partners in conversation or lifeless exhibits in a historical display beyond reach—and whether this constitutes a difference between how we treat them and how we treat later Muslim theologians such as Rāzī and Jurjānī—what is more important is to be self-conscious about why one does so, and about the notions of an "explanatory need" or a "problem" that one deploys in the process and the sources for the questions from which one begins. For the depth of philosophical problems against which one solution or another is measured is one whose measure is in turn set by particular practices of reflection. The main task of this study will have been accomplished if the balance between listening and conversing—between letting the thinkers speak, and making them speak in one's language and to one's measures—has been fruitfully struck, and with a self-consciousness that has forced neither party to mask the needs that guide them.

APPENDIX

Translation from Mānkdīm Shāshdīw, "The Promise and the Threat," in *Sharḥ al-uṣūl al-khamsa*

The text translated below consists of three passages excerpted from the section "The Promise and the Threat" in Mānkdīm Shāshdīw's *Sharḥ al-uṣūl al-khamsa,* which presents us with one of the most continuous Baṣran Muʿtazilite discussions of questions related to desert in the course of an exposition of the five characteristic Muʿtazilite principles. In selecting these texts from Mānkdīm's lengthy work, my aim has been to include ones that would convey as full and representative a picture as possible of the views of the Baṣran Muʿtazilites. Yet this has had to be balanced with a concern to preserve as much as possible of the integrity of the discussion, respecting its natural beginnings and ends, and resisting the temptation to cull at will passages that seem richer in content than the fractious and fastidious ending ("if one says . . . we will say") of a discussion dwindling toward its conclusion. Following this alternative policy might have given a meatier text, but at the cost of presenting nothing more than a sequence of disjointed quotations. Thus, I have often preferred to keep thematically unified sections intact with the hope that this will give a more faithful representation not only of *what* these Muʿtazilites were saying but of *how* they were saying it. (The passages translated are from ʿAbd al-Karīm ʿUthmān's edition [Cairo, 1965], 611–23, 642–47, 666–72).

The Third of the Five Principles: The Promise and the Threat

Here what should have been mentioned, following established custom, is the meaning of the promise and the threat, but as we have already spoken of this, there is no reason to repeat it and we may occupy ourselves with what is of distinctive concern for the present discussion.[1] The investigation of the issues in this domain falls in three parts. The first concerns the discussion of that which is deserved (*mustaḥaqq*) on account of acts. The second, the discussion of the conditions on which it is deserved. And the third, the discussion of the modality [*kayfiyya*] of desert, and whether it is perpetual or has a determinate duration.

That Which Is Deserved on Account of Acts

As for that which is deserved on account of acts, this consists of praise and blame, and the reward and punishment that follow them. And each of these terms bears a particular meaning.

As for blame [*dhamm*], this is an utterance [*qawl*] that expresses the low status of a person, and it is of two types. One type is followed by punishment [*ʿiqāb*] on the part of God, and this is only deserved for acts of disobedience [or sins: *maʿṣiyya*]. An act of disobedience consists of doing what another does not will, involving a certain kind of standing—namely, that the one who disobeys is beneath the one who is disobeyed; hence the fact that one cannot say "the prince disobeyed so-and-so," although one may say "so-and-so disobeyed the prince." When used in the absolute, this word exclusively refers to disobedience toward God, so that if you want to convey something else you would qualify it and say, for example, "so-and-so disobeyed his father, his grandfather, or the prince," and so on. And then there is another type [of blame] that is not followed by punishment on the part of God.

As for praise [*madḥ*], it denotes an utterance that expresses the elevated status of a person, and it also subdivides into a type that is followed by reward [*thawāb*] on the part of God, and this is only deserved for acts of obedience [*ṭāʿa*], the meaning of which has already been set out in several places. As for the type that is not followed by reward, this is the praise deserved in response to beneficence. So this is the meaning of these terms.

The Conditions for Desert

As concerns the conditions on which these deserts[2] are established: we have already mentioned the division of blame into one that is followed by punishment on the part of God and one that is not. Now for the one that is followed by punishment, the conditions for desert are two: one of them relates to the act, while the other relates to the agent. The one that relates to the act is that this should be evil [*qabīḥ*], and the one that relates to the agent is that he should know that it is evil or be in a position to know it. This is why we have said that children do not deserve blame for doing evil acts, because they do not know that they are evil nor are they in a position to know that. Yet on the other hand, we have said that Khārijites deserve blame for killing Muslims even if they believe their action to be good, because they are in a position to know that this is evil. This is how things stand with respect to the blame that is followed by punishment from God.

For the blame that is not followed by punishment from God, there are likewise two conditions for deserving it: one relating to the act—and this is that it should be an offense [*isāʾa*]; and another relating to the agent—and this is that he should have intended to commit an offense in doing that.

As we have said, blame divides into two types, one followed by punishment and one not; likewise also with praise, which divides into two types. One is followed by reward from God, and the conditions for deserving it are twofold: one relates to the act—and this is that it should involve a benefit over and above its goodness; while the other relates to the agent—and this is that he should know that it has a quality over and above its goodness [*ḥusn*]. And these two must both be observed, as with blame. This is why we say that children do not deserve praise for their actions, inasmuch as they do not know that they have a quality additional to goodness. As for the type that is not followed by reward from God, once again two conditions apply—one relating to the act, and the other to the agent. The one relating to the act is that it should constitute beneficence [*iḥsān*], and the one relating to the agent is that he should intend to perform an act of beneficence in doing it. These, then, are the conditions for deserving praise and blame for one's acts.

As for the conditions for the desert of reward and punishment on account of acts, they are like the conditions for the desert of praise and blame, except that a further condition must be additionally observed, and this is that the agent should be such that it is possible for him to be rewarded and punished. Or if you wish, you might say that the condition is that the agent be such that his actions are the result of desire or deficient opinion [*shahwa aw-shubha*]. This is why we say that Hindus deserve to be punished by God for burning themselves even though they do not do so out of desire but rather on account of a deficient opinion—namely, that by means of this they are liberated from the world of darkness into the world of light. But indeed this condition has to be taken into account because otherwise it would follow that God could deserve punishment; yet it is known that were it supposed that an evil action was to issue from Him, He would not deserve punishment, even though He would deserve blame—exalted far above this be He! So these, in sum, are the conditions that must be taken into account in this respect.

If it was said: If these are the conditions governing the desert of praise and blame, and reward and punishment, what is it that has the determinant effect [*mu'aththir*] in the matter? It would be said: One's doing evil is what has the determinant effect, and everything else is a condition. And we say this because it is not possible that one's knowledge of the evilness of the evil act or one's capacity to know this [that were identified as conditions for desert] should be what possesses the determinant effect in the desert of punishment, because that is something that is given by God, and it is not possible that one should deserve punishment for an act of God's but rather one will deserve punishment exclusively for what he himself does. This is how the case stands as far as blame and punishment are concerned. As for what has the determinant effect in the desert of praise and reward, it consists in one's performing what is obligatory, and avoiding evil and the like, while everything else is a condition.

The Desert of Reward

With these basic facts behind us, know that if God enjoins on us acts involving hardship [*shāqqa*], there must be a reward in return for them that corresponds to it [*yuqābiluhu*]. Indeed, this amount would not suffice unless it reaches a degree such that it could not be given as an independent gesture and by way of beneficence, for otherwise it would not be good to impose the Law as a means to gain it. This we say because if these strenuous acts were not met by what we have mentioned, God would be acting unjustly and vainly, as was explained when discussing pain and compensation.

If it were said: Could it not suffice that one should deserve praise in return for these strenuous acts? It would be said to him: No, for praise is of little consequence if it is devoid of accompanying benefits. Moreover, praise is not something that is deserved exclusively from God, for one may deserve praise from someone other than God just as much as from God, whereas what is deserved as the corresponding equivalent for fulfilling the Law must be performed by God. And if they say: Could praise given by God not suffice then? We will say: This, as we have said, is of little consequence.

If it were said: How can your claim stand when it is well-known that one will exert himself to the utmost in order to obtain the sovereign's approbation and praise, disregarding the hardship one endures in the attempt? It would be said: The reason he desires this is because of the rank and retinue [he thereby attains], so that, were this praise to stand alone, he would not content himself with it and would not choose it.

If it were said: Yet did the Arabs not disdain their lives and fortunes in seeking after praise and honorable repute, deeming such repute a second life span? We would say: This is one of the pieces of ignorant foolishness ascribed to them, and at any rate they must have believed that this was a good that outweighed the strains they had to suffer for it. This resembles their habit of asking that a camel be slaughtered, or a horse or a male camel confined at their graves, and that spears should be raised and swords placed over them—all this, for the great benefit they believed themselves to derive from it.

Moreover, if these acts had not involved hardship, and we performed obligatory acts and avoided evil ones, we would still deserve praise. And should you be disposed to doubt this in our case, there is surely no doubt that God deserves praise for doing what is obligatory and refraining from what is evil, even though there is no hardship for Him in doing so. There must therefore be something that corresponds to this hardship, and this consists of reward, as we say.

Furthermore, praise is the kind of thing that can be given to the one who deserves it without the need to resurrect him [*iʿāda*], and thus there would be no reason to affirm that the dead will be brought back to life after dying. Yet the fact that we know that God will certainly bring people back to life after they have died is a proof that reward must be deserved, this being impossible to give to people unless they are resurrected. This is an additional ground [supporting our view].

And it is on this same basis that one would respond should they say: Couldn't what is deserved for these strenuous acts belong to the class of joy? For when joy is separated from any benefit, it is of little consequence, as we have said.

Were it said: How can your claim stand that reward is deserved for strenuous acts, when we know that one deserves reward for things that involve no hardship, such as the knowledge of God or other things? Likewise, the upright pious man may not experience much hardship in performing these acts of obedience, having accustomed himself to them and become used to them, and yet all the same he still deserves reward for them, in your view.

It would be said: We did not stipulate that there should be hardship in the act itself; it might be in the act itself, in its causes or preliminaries, or in what accompanies it and is connected with it. And there is no doubt that the knowledge of God is of this sort, for even if it does not involve hardship in itself, its cause—namely, reflection—involves an undeniable degree of hardship. Also, the effort to preserve it, and the resolve to dispel sophistries and doubts, and to fend off one's adversaries involve great strains. Indeed, were it to be said that the hardship involved in the knowledge of God is greater than that involved in any other act, it would be nearer the truth—so how can their assertion hold?

As for their statement that the pious, god-fearing man might not suffer any hardship in performing these acts of obedience and avoiding sinful acts, so how could he deserve reward for this—it carries no force. For these acts are not free from hardship, whether in themselves or what connects to them, as we have said. Yet insofar as he [the pious man] exercised himself over their performance by never letting out of his sight the punishment he will deserve should he occupy himself with the contrary acts and the reward he will deserve for performing them, it became easier for him to act this way. He thereby became like the merchant who sets his sights firmly on the profit he will gain through that trade; under these circumstances, the strains to which he is exposed—traveling and the like—become easier for him to bear. It is no different in this case. This is the sense in which God said [referring to prayer]: "It is indeed hard, except to those who bring a lowly spirit" (2:45).

And it is in the same manner that one would respond should they say: Haven't you reported that the Prophet—peace be on him—said that one will be recompensed for satisfying his [sexual] desire with [the woman that] is lawful to him? Yet it is obvious that there is no hardship involved in *that*. For we say: It is not necessary that the hardship should be contained in the act itself but is enough that it should attach to his resolution to confine himself to her, and not to pass her over and turn to one that is more desirable to him.

So this is the view we affirm as regards the reward one deserves from God.

Yet our master Abu'l-Qāsim [al-Balkhī] took issue with this overall account and said: Rather, the truth is that God imposed these strenuous acts on us due to the debt we bear toward Him for the great blessings we have received from Him. And that is hardly an improbable view; for everybody would acknowledge that if a person was to pick up another from the street and bring him up in the best possible way, generously providing for him and bestowing on him all manner of favors, it would be permissible for him to enjoin him to do an act that involves some hardship for him, such as to say "hand me this jug" or "complete this line for me," without the need to indemnify him with anything further in return for it. Likewise with God; His blessings on us can hardly be counted and His assistance toward us can hardly be encompassed. And having taken the view just described, he [al-Balkhī] said that the reward[3] He gives to the obedient is not because they deserve it but out of generosity.

The centerpiece of our response to him is to say: If God made these acts strenuous to us[4] even though it was possible for Him not to make them that way, this must involve the reward we have spoken of. As for the case he cites—that if among us a person bestowed on another all manner of favors, then it would be permissible for him to enjoin on him an act involving some hardship for him, such as to say "hand me this jug" or the like—this is not valid. For it is permissible for him to do so in matters where the hardship a person undergoes does not appear too great. Yet this is not how things are with the obligations God has imposed on us, for some of them demand willing self-sacrifice and the placing of one's very life in jeopardy, so there is no comparison to be made with the situations he adduces. Thus, if the benefactor he describes was to enjoin on the beneficiary something that involves great hardship, such as to labor arduously in his service, and stand on call all day and all night or the like, he would not be acting beneficently toward him. Indeed, the beneficiary would be entitled to say: You should not have bestowed these benefits on me in the first place so as not to hold me to these obligations afterward.

As for his claim concerning reward—namely, that it must [*yajibu*] be given to those who obey as an act of generosity—its incoherence is plain. For generosity constitutes beneficence [*tafaḍḍul*], and beneficence is that which it is permissible for an agent either to do or not to do, whereas obligation is that which it is not permissible for him not to do. So how can it be said: "This is obligatory as an act of generosity"? And is this any different from saying: "It is obligatory that it be done and it is not obligatory that it be done"—which is absurd?

These aspects having been clarified, [the next thing to say is that] what we know concerning the reward deserved from God is the general fact that it must consist of pleasures. As for the fact that it will involve food and drink and women, this is known by revelation, though we could also know it on the basis of God's seeking to rouse our motives toward it [*targhīb*], for one might say: If [these pleasures] were not of the same kind as what we desire in this world, it would not be possible for our motives to be roused. This, then, is what we say concerning reward.

The Desert of Punishment

When it comes to the desert of punishment, both reason and revelation indicate that it will take place. As for the indication of reason, it is twofold. One is that God made it obligatory on us to perform obligatory acts and refrain from evil ones, and informed us about what is obligatory and what is evil, so there must necessarily be a reason why this information was given and this obligation imposed. And there is no other reason save that if we were to infringe it or do other acts that are opposed to it—evil and the like—we would deserve to suffer great harm [*ḍarar*] from Him.

And if it were said: Why isn't it possible that the reason for that should be that, if we were to infringe it and do its opposite, we would deserve blame from God and other beings possessed of mature reason [or "rational beings": *ʿuqalāʾ*]? It would be said: Blame that does not involve harm is not such as to be heeded; this is why we do not trouble about the blame of those who disagree with us, since no harm comes of it.

And if it were said: Couldn't the reason for the imposition of obligation rather be that one might thereby deserve reward from Him? It would be said to him: No, for reward is a benefit [*nafʿ*] and the pursuit of benefit is not an obligation, and therefore it would not be good to impose an obligation for its sake. Otherwise, it would be equally good that He should make supererogatory acts [*nawāfil*] obligatory, for they, too, make one deserve reward—but we know that this is not the case.[5]

If it were said: Couldn't His imposition of obligation be good due to the fact that these obligatory acts are obligatory? It would be said to him: A thing's being obligatory in itself does not suffice to make the imposition of obligation good. Thus, if the sovereign was to threaten a person that he would cut off one of his limbs if he did not give him half his money, it would be obligatory on this person to give him half his money, even though it is not good on the part of the sovereign to make this obligatory.

If one were to say: This entails that it is possible that God should make acts that are evil obligatory and make acts that are obligatory evil; but if you resist this entailment, that is because the imposition of obligation is rendered permissible and good insofar as a thing is obligatory in itself. It would be said to him: The entailment you mention does not affect us, for we have said that a thing's being obligatory in itself does not suffice to make the imposition of obligation good, but rather a further aspect has to be taken into account—and this is the harm we would deserve should we infringe it. This entailment would follow had we said instead that what God makes obligatory does not have to be obligatory in the first place—and this we haven't said. This, then, is one indication.

The second indication [of reason] is what our master Abū Hāshim said, whose precise formulation is that God created in us a desire for evil and an aversion for the good, so there must be an amount of punishment to counter it that restrains us from committing evil acts and motivates us to perform obligatory ones. Otherwise, the Imposer of the Law would be tempting us with evil, and it is not possible that God should tempt with evil.

If it were said: It is through blame that temptation is removed and fear induced. It would be said: We have already said things that serve as a response to this, for we remarked that blame alone is of little consequence.

If it were said: It is the *supposition* that punishment will occur and the fear of it that removes temptation, so why do you categorically assert that one deserves to be punished by God? It would be said: The supposition that punishment will take place only results in the removal of temptation if one *knows* that one deserves punishment and one then *supposes* that one will in fact be punished. In that case, it results in the removal of temptation—but not in any other way. Thus, if a person was informed that there is a wild animal on a particular road, he would be afraid to take that road if he knew categorically the harm wild beasts cause, and that they are the kind [of animal] that causes injury, and if he supposed that if he were to take that road, harm might befall him. In that case, this would avert him from taking that road. If, however,[6] the animal did not belong to the harmful and injurious kind, and if there was no known harm, it would not avert him from taking that road. It would be similar in the present case. This sums up the knowledge afforded by reason.

As for the revealed indication, this is that God promised reward to the obedient and threatened the disobedient with punishment, and were it not that [these things] must be done, it would not have been good that promises and threats should be made about them. This is the approach adopted by Abu'l-Qāsim al-Mūsawī, who said that no other approach should be employed in this question. By contrast, we have said that one may employ the indication of reason just as much as the indication of revelation in this domain.

Objections of the Heretics

There are several sophistic objections to which the heretics cling in this question, such as to say: God's purpose in imposing the Law [*taklīf*] is to benefit the subject of the Law [*mukallaf*], so if the subject does not benefit from God's imposing the Law on him, he should not be punished; for at most, all there is in the matter is that he caused himself to forfeit this benefit—yet how could it be good for God to punish him for that? His situation is like that of a hired hand who caused himself to forfeit his wages by abandoning his work; just as it would not be good for his employer to subject him to flagellation because he caused himself to forfeit his wages, likewise in this case.

Our response to this is that God does not punish the subject of the Law for the fact that he caused himself to forfeit the benefit [he would have gained] through the Law; rather, He punishes him for his committing evil acts and violating obligatory ones. This is the ground for the desert of punishment, as with blame. Don't you see that rational beings do not blame one who violates obligations and commits evils for causing himself to forfeit benefits [he would have gained] through obligations, and that they rather blame him for his violating obligations and committing evils? Likewise with punishment. But in fact, their analogy with the worldly domain [*al-shāhid*] is not valid, for human beings do not deserve punishment from one another.

Among the ideas to which they also cling here is that punishment consists of harm undertaken by God, and that to inflict harm on another is good by way of appeasing one's wrath, or benefiting the person punished or the person punishing. Whichever of these grounds it might be, they are [all] lacking in the present case. So one must conclude that punishment given by God is evil.

The response is that this is not a comprehensive division such that one's options are exhausted in either affirming or denying it, and therefore it cannot be used as an argument. These grounds that you have mentioned have no bearing indeed on the goodness of punishment, for the appeasement of wrath does not contain a ground that renders it good to inflict harm on another, and the same thing applies with regard to benefiting the one punished. Moreover, this division omits the adversary's view [i.e., the one supported by Mānkdīm's school], for the view of those dissenting over this question is that the reason why it is good for God to punish the subject of the Law is rather that he deserves this through his commission of evil acts and violation of obligatory ones—a possibility that [the opponent] did not include in the division he produced, thereby rendering his case void. But this division could also be turned against them in the case of blame, so that one might say: Blame too constitutes harm, so it should not be good except by way of appeasing wrath or causing benefit, according to what you have said; yet we know that this is not the case. And if they say: [It is good] rather by way of being deserved, we will say: Then content yourselves with the same when we claim a similar ground for punishment. With the above account, the desert of reward and punishment has thus been established.[7]

The Annulment of Reward and Punishment

We have now discussed the fact that praise and reward, and blame and punishment, may be deserved because one has not done an action just as they may be deserved for one's having done an act of obedience or a sin, and we have discussed the ground for this according as the present context admits. What must be discussed next are the conditions that have a determinant effect on the annulment [*isqāṭ*] of reward and punishment.

Know that reward is annulled in either of two ways: through one's regretting [*nadm*] the acts of obedience one has performed, or one's commission of a sin that is greater than [the reward deserved]. We say that reward is annulled through regret of one's act of obedience, because the case here is similar to that in which one does good to another and then regrets his beneficence. His regret over that annuls what he had deserved, and it is likewise in the present case.

As for its annulment through a greater act of disobedience, that too is patent. For it is as though one were to do to a person some degree of good and then commit an offense against him that was far greater than that. Everybody knows that under these circumstances, he will not deserve praise or thanks as he did prior to his offense. Likewise in the question at hand.

This sums up the factors that annul deserved reward, and there is no third beyond the two mentioned, for it is absolutely clear that reward cannot be annulled through God's annulling it.

As for punishment deserved from God, it can be annulled through one's regretting the acts of disobedience one has committed, or by an act of obedience that is greater than it [i.e., the punishment deserved]. The ground here is the same as in reward, for the counterpart of regret in the worldly domain is apology. And it is well-known that if a person commits an offense against another and then apologizes properly, the blame he deserves is annulled so that it thenceforth ceases to be good that the offended party should blame him. The same thing holds for repentance [*tawba*] in connection with punishment. This much concerns regret.

As for acts of obedience exceeding it, they effect the annulment of deserved punishment because matters here are as they would be in the case in which one offended against another by breaking the tip of a pencil, but then followed this by giving him princely amounts of money that one would normally balk at parting with and would not permit himself to spend. Under these circumstances, he would not deserve blame from [the offended party] for that trivial offense[8] due to the handsome gift he had made. Likewise in the question at hand. So these are two grounds that effect the annulment of deserved punishment in a way similar to reward. However, the number of acts of obedience has an effect on the annulment of the punishment one deserves if it is minor evils [*ṣaghā'ir*] that are concerned. The punishment deserved for grave sins [*kabā'ir*], by contrast, cannot be removed by doing many acts of obedience in lives such as [i.e., as short as] ours, as will be explained at a later point, God willing.

But here there is a further ground that is such as to effect the annulment of punishment deserved from God, and that is God's decision to annul it and forgive one's sins—a ground that does not apply in the case of reward, as we have already explained.

And if it were said: So is it then good for God to annul the punishment deserved by unbelievers and grave sinners? What view is one to take of the matter? We would say: The community of scholars has been divided over this question. Our position is that it is good for God to forgive sinners and not to punish them, but He has informed us that He will do to them what they deserve. The Baghdadis, on the other hand, said: It is not good that God should annul this, but indeed He is under an inescapable obligation to punish one who deserves punishment, as we will explain, God willing.

The Disagreement over Punishment

Know that our Baghdadi fellows have placed God under an inescapable obligation to do to sinners what they deserve, saying that it is not permissible that He should forgive them. They have thereby assigned a higher status to the obligation to punish than to reward, for according to them, reward is only obligatory insofar as it constitutes generosity—which is not their view with respect to punishment; for that has to take place under all circumstances.

Yet what shows this view of theirs to be false and validates our own is that punishment is God's private right [*ḥaqq Allāh ʿala'l-khuṣūṣ*], to waive which does not involve the waiving of a right that is not among its concomitants, and which He may choose to exact.[9] Thus, He can waive it as one may waive a debt; for since that is a pure right of its holder, does not involve the waiving of a right that is not among its concomitants, and is one that he may choose to exact, he may waive it just as he may exact it. Likewise in the present question.

And we say "to waive which does not involve the waiving of a right that is not among its concomitants" in order to make room in our account for blame, for it is annulled through the annulment of punishment because it belongs to its concomitants, like the term of repayment [*ajal*] in the case of debts [i.e., the former drops away when the latter does].

If it were said: A right is something from which its holder may derive benefit, yet it is impossible for God to be benefited, so how can you say that punishment is a right of God's? It would be said to him: What we mean in saying this is that proof shows us that God may forgive sinners or He may choose to punish them, contrary to what the Baghdadis claim.

If it were said: Isn't it the case that blame is a right belonging to the one against whom an offense is committed? Yet for all that he does not have the right to waive it. So couldn't punishment be a right of God's even though He cannot waive it? It would be said: What we have already discussed eliminates this objection, for we have said that blame is a private right of God's. This is not true of blame, for just as it is a right of the one offended, it is no less a right of the one who offended him and of all rational beings, for if they are certain that they will be blamed for an offense they will not commit it, or will be less likely to do so.

It is in the same way that one should respond if they say: Thanking is a right of the benefactor, yet he does not have the right to waive it; it is likewise with punishment. For just as thanking is a right of the benefactor, it is a right of the beneficiary; this is why he deserves reward from God and praise from rational beings. So how can it be claimed that it is a right of the benefactor?

If it were said: Isn't reward a right of human beings, just as punishment is a right of God? Yet at the same time a human being cannot waive the reward he deserves. So isn't it possible that the same should hold with respect to punishment? It would be said: Someone who[10] possesses a right may only waive it if it also possible for him to exact it, and if he is not like a minor under guardianship (*maḥjūr ʿalayhi*). It is for this reason that a child is not capable of waiving his right, even though the right belongs to him, inasmuch as he cannot exact it. This being clearly established, we may say that our situation with respect to reward is like the situation of a child with respect to the rights he possesses. For just as he may not waive any of his rights given that he may not exact them and that he is under guardianship, similarly in this case. This may be clarified by adding that a human being would be like one compelled [*mulja'*] not to waive the reward he deserves. So this objection falls away entirely.

As for the sophistic objections brought forth by the Baghdadis on this issue, they said, for example: Punishment is a form of assistance [*luṭf*] given by God [for the fulfillment of duties], and divine assistance must be given to the subject of the Law in the most efficient way possible, and it will only be so if punishment is obligatory on God. For if the subject of the Law knows that he will receive what he deserves under all circumstances, he will be more likely to perform obligatory acts and avoid grave sins. And they also reinforce this [objection] by saying: If punishment is a form of assistance to the subject of the Law, God must inform him that He will carry it out, otherwise He would be violating an obligation He is under.

The centerpiece of our response here is to say to them: Assistance must be given to the subject of the Law in the most efficient way possible, as you have said, but only if that is possible. And here that is not possible, because there is always a chance that a grave sinner might repent and turn back to God, regretting the acts he has done and desisting from them. So how can he be informed that he will definitely be punished? This account must be sound, for otherwise he would have to be informed that his repentance will not be accepted if he performs a grave sin, even if he does his utmost in turning toward God and striving to rectify the results of his actions. And yet it is evident that this would constitute a stronger form of assistance. And if it were said: This is not possible, so it cannot happen; we would say: In that case, why can't you accept a similar response from us? Moreover, assistance consists of those things that have a motivating or deterrent effect [*lahu ḥaẓẓ al-duʿā' wa'l-ṣarf*] yet punishment has no such effect, and that which has this effect is rather the knowledge that punishment is deserved—so how can their claim stand?[11]

The Punishment of Grave Sinners

Having finished with this account, he [ʿAbd al-Jabbār, whose work is the basis of Mānkdīm's] proceeded to discuss the position that grave sinners [*fāsiq*] remain in the Fire for ever, and are subjected to torment for all eternity without surcease, following this with a discussion of the fact that they deserve punishment eternally [*ʿalā ṭarīq al-dawām*]. The correct order would have been to discuss the fact that grave sinners deserve punishment eternally first, and then to use this as a base for discussing the fact that they will be subjected to torment in the Fire for ever. But we shall keep to his practice and follow his procedure, and thus use the same starting place.

What proves that grave sinners remain in the Fire for ever and are subjected to torment for all eternity is the set of general statements expressing threat [*ʿumūmāt al-waʿīd*], for just as they show that the grave sinner will suffer the punishment he deserves, they show that his sojourn [in the Fire] will be perpetual, for there is no verse among those we have enumerated that does not also speak of a perpetual sojourn, of being consigned eternally, and the like.

And here there is another route one may follow, which involves a compound of revelation [and reason], and which can be formulated by saying that a sinner can be in either of two situations: either he will be forgiven or he will not be forgiven. If he is not forgiven, then he will remain in the Fire forever—which is our position. If he is forgiven, then he cannot but[12] enter paradise from the first—for if he did not enter paradise, it could not be, as there is no intermediate place between paradise and the Fire; so if he is not in the Fire, there is no other possibility but that he should be in paradise. And if he enters paradise, either of two situations may hold: either he will enter as one who is being rewarded, or as one who is receiving something out of beneficence. Yet it is not possible that he should enter paradise as one receiving something out of beneficence, for the entire community is agreed that if the subject of the Law enters paradise, there must be something to distinguish his situation from that of the "youths of perpetual freshness" [*al-wildān al-mukhalladīn* (mentioned in the Qur'ān in 56:17)] and that of children and the insane [who did not fulfill conditions of responsibility, and therefore could not acquire desert]. And it is not possible that he should enter paradise as one being rewarded, for he does not deserve that, and to reward one who does not deserve reward is an evil act; but God does not do evil.

If it were said: Why is it evil to reward one who does not deserve reward? It would be said: Because reward is deserved by way of honoring and exalting, and it is not good to give a thing of this kind in the absence of desert. Thus, it is not good for a person to honor a person who is not related to him in the way he honors his father, or to honor his father in the way he honors the Prophet—peace be on him—or to honor the Prophet in the way he honors the Almighty.

This sums up the discussion that concerns the grave sinner's eternal torment in the Fire.

The Duration of Punishment

As for the discussion of the fact that punishment is deserved eternally, it consists of saying that if it wasn't deserved eternally, it would not be good that God should torment grave sinners with the Fire and consign them to it for all eternity. Yet we have shown that God will punish the grave sinner for all eternity; so this shows that punishment is deserved eternally.

Another proof[13]—the one to be relied on in this question—can be formulated by saying that punishment is like blame: they are deserved together and they are eliminated together, so that one cannot be standing while the other has been annulled. Yet it is known that blame is deserved by way of perpetuity; so the same must hold for punishment.

If it were said: Yet why do you say that blame and punishment are established and eliminated together, so that one cannot continue to stand while the other is annulled? It would be said: This is because the same thing that establishes the one establishes the other, and the same thing that annuls the one also annuls the other. Don't you see that the thing that establishes blame and has a determinant effect on its desert is the commission of sins and the violation of obligatory acts—the very thing that establishes punishment? Similarly, what annuls blame is repentance or an act of obedience that is greater than the sin, and it is this that also annuls punishment. So it is clear that what effects their desert is one and the same. Since this is the case, then if one of the two is deserved eternally, the other must also be deserved eternally. For it is not possible that for two things deserved in the same manner, and in which the cause determining the establishment or annulment of one is the same as the cause determining the establishment or annulment of the other, one of the two should be deserved eternally, while the other is deserved for a limited duration [*munqaṭiʿan*]. Rather both must be deserved either for a limited duration or eternally. But that one should be deserved eternally and the other for a limited duration—that is impossible. Once this has been established, and given that it is known that blame is deserved in perpetuity, the same must hold with respect to punishment.

If it were said: How is it that we know that blame is deserved for eternity? It would be said: This is not something that could be doubted. For it is known that if one strikes his father and persists in this act, it is good that his father as well as others continue to blame him for that act to no end, so that even if it was supposed that God took his life and then revived him anew, it would continue to be good that his father blame him, just as it would be good that all rational beings do so.

And if it were said: How can you rightly claim that punishment follows blame and that they are established and eliminated together, when we know that were God to commit an evil act, He would deserve[14] blame—may He be exalted above such a thing!—Hethough He would not deserve punishment. Our response to that is that we have not claimed that they are established and eliminated together under all conditions, and that there are no circumstances in which the one is found separate from the other. Rather, what we said is that if both of them are established and deserved, then they are established and eliminated together, because what has the determinant effect for the desert of the one is what has this effect for the desert of the other, and what has the determinant effect for the annulment of the one is what has this effect for the desert of the other. If these things hold true of them, they must be deserved in the same way: either both will be deserved eternally, or both for a limited duration. But that one should be for eternity, while the other for a limited duration—that cannot be.

If it were said: How can you rightly say that blame is deserved for eternity, then extending the same principle to punishment by analogy, when we know that if a person who has committed an offense and the person he has offended against were to die, the blame would be annulled? It would be said: If anything is annulled through their dying, it is the act of blaming—not the desert—that is annulled [i.e., presumably "ceases"], and our discussion is concerned with desert. And there is no time at which it ceases to be good for the victim of the offense to blame the offender, even if God should take their life many times over and revive them anew many times over. Moreover, if punishment was not deserved eternally, this would apply equally to unbelievers [*kāfir*] and grave sinners [*fāsiq*], so it would not be good for God to punish unbelievers for an eternal duration. And since we know that it is good for Him to do that, this constitutes a proof that punishment is deserved from Him eternally, whether we are considering unbelievers or grave sinners.

If it were said: There is a difference between these two, for a grave sinner's obedient act changes the punishment [he deserves] for his sins from having an eternal duration to having a limited one—something that does not hold with respect to the unbeliever. It would be said: This claim is unsound, for a grave sinner's obedient acts have no effect on changing his chastisement from an eternal to a limited duration; otherwise an unbeliever's chastisement would also have to be limited, for his acts also include obedient ones.

If it were said: This is predicated on the assumption that an unbeliever can have obedient acts—an assumption we do not concede. It would be said: An obedient act consists of nothing more than one's doing what God wills, and [the unbeliever's] acts may include things that God wills, such as returning deposits, thanking the benefactor, honoring one's parents, and so on. So this should change the punishment of his sins from being eternal to being limited in time, as with acts of obedience performed by the grave sinner. Yet we know that this is not the case.

And if it were said: It is a condition for an act to be an act of obedience that the one obeyed should know the one being obeyed; yet this is not the case with unbelievers. We would say: There are unbelievers who know God and acknowledge Him, such as the Jews and the Christians. So their punishment should shift to a limited duration; yet we know that this is not the case. Moreover, one might describe the unbeliever as obeying the Devil when he commits grave sins and performs depravities, even though he does not know or acknowledge him. Furthermore, if the grave sinner's acts of obedience changed the punishment of his sins from being eternal to being limited, they would also have to change his blame from being eternal to being limited in time. But since we know that he deserves blame perpetually and that his acts of obedience have no effect whatsoever on the blame, this is a proof that the punishment for an act of disobedience is not changed from being eternal to being limited by being accompanied by an act of obedience, as was said by [Ibn Shihāb] al-Khālidī.

As for what al-Khālidī says on this head, his view is that obedient acts have an advantage over disobedient ones insofar as what is deserved for obedient acts must be performed and it is not permissible that one should fail to carry it out. This is not the case with what is deserved for disobedient acts; for one may annul this out of beneficence and grant pardon. This is why a grave sinner's acts of obedience can change the punishment of his sins from being eternal to being limited in time. Yet it would be said to him: The advantage you speak of is one that all other acts of obedience have over all other acts of disobedience, and there is no difference between a grave sinner's acts of obedience and an unbeliever's. So why shouldn't [the latter's] punishment be changed from an eternal duration to a limited one?

One would also say to him: An act of obedience does not have an effect on its own, for we know that if one did not deserve reward for it, it would have no effect whatsoever. The same is true of reward; for reward has an effect through aggregate quantity, so that if one's punishment was greater, the reward would be annulled, and if they were both of equal quantity, they would both be annulled. So nothing remains here except the advantage that he [al-Khālidī] attributes to an obedient act over a disobedient one—namely, the obligation to give the person what he deserves for his obedient act, and the goodness of beneficently annulling what he deserves for his disobedient act. But this advantage is the same with respect to an obedient act as it is with another disobedient one, so if one disobedient act was accompanied by another, it should change the punishment [of the former] from being eternal to being limited in time. Indeed, it should be the case that another person's obedient acts changed the punishment of his own sins from an eternal to a limited duration, given what we have said—that this advantage has the same relation to his own acts of obedience as to another's act of obedience. Yet we know that this is not the case.

If it were said: Isn't your position that the reward for one's obedient acts affects the punishment for one's disobedient acts, whereas another's reward does not affect it? So why couldn't the same apply in the present question? We would say: There is a patent difference between the two, for one's reward must inevitably affect one's punishment inasmuch as one cannot deserve them together. For [the possibility of] deserving the two is predicated on the possibility of combining them, and it is not possible to combine them. For one is deserved by way of requital and retribution, while the other is deserved by way of honor and exaltation—and these two are contraries. But this is not so in the case you spoke of, for it is not impossible for one person to deserve reward while the other deserves punishment. So his objection falls away.

NOTES

CHAPTER 1
The Framework: The Muʿtazilites

1. Adopting the editor's addition of *bihā: fa-yuṭīʿū bihā.*
2. The text appears in the excerpt from his *Maqālāt al-Islāmiyyīn,* in *Faḍl al-Iʿtizāl wa-ṭabaqāt al-Muʿtazila,* ed. Ayman Fu'ād Sayyid (Tunis, 1974), 63–64 (listed under al-Balkhī in the bibliography).
3. A gateway to these principles is provided in William M. Watt, *The Formative Period of Islamic Thought* (Oxford, 1998), 228–49. For a discussion of the ordering of the five principles, see Ibn Mattawayh, *al-Muḥīṭ bi'l-taklīf,* ed. ʿUmar al-Sayyid ʿAzmī (Cairo, [1965]), 19–22. A note on citation: throughout this study, I use the edition of the first volume of Ibn Mattawayh's work edited by ʿAzmī, and keeping to his title, I cite as *Muḥīṭ.* This makes the different editions easier to signal; where volumes 2 and 3 are referenced, they will be cited as *Majmūʿ,* vol. 2 and vol. 3. Vol. 2 is *Kitāb al-Majmūʿ fī l-Muḥīṭ bi-l-Taklīf (Paraphrase du* Muḥīṭ *du Qāḍī ʿAbd al-Jabbār),* ed. J. J. Houben, rev. D. Gimaret (Beirut, 1981). Vol. 3 is J. Peters, ed. (Beirut, 1999).
4. Watt, *Formative Period,* 179.
5. Mānkdīm Shashdīw, *Sharḥ al-uṣūl al-khamsa,* ed. ʿAbd al-Karīm ʿUthmān (Cairo, 1965), 133.
6. The last principle that ranges itself within the subject matter of the general principle of justice—though perhaps less of a celebrity than the other two—is that of *al-amr bi'l-maʿrūf wa'l-nahy ʿan al-munkar* ("commanding the right and forbidding the wrong"), which recognized a duty to actively exhort to righteous conduct and forbid or exhort against the unrighteous. This principle is the topic of a comprehensive discussion in Michael Cook, *Commanding Right and Forbidding Wrong in Islamic Thought* (Cambridge, 2000).
7. This spirit of computation was common to theologians of different schools, despite the fact, remarked by Louis Gardet, that many of them did not recognize a notion of desert intrinsic to acts that would cohere with the idea of computing acts' values (Gardet, *Dieu et la destinée de l'homme,* [Paris, 1967], 299). But

it was more pronounced in the Muʿtazilite scheme—which did recognize such a notion—and is exemplified in their discussions of the concepts of *iḥbāṭ* and *takfīr,* the processes whereby bad and good deserts cancel each other out (more on this below).

8. Abu'l-Ḥasan al-Ashʿarī, *al-Ibāna ʿan uṣūl al-diyāna* (Beirut, 1990), 104.
9. Ashʿarī, *Kitāb al-Lumaʿ fi'l-radd ʿalā ahl al-zaygh wa'l-bidaʿ,* ed. Ḥammūda Ghurāba ([Cairo], 1955), 117.
10. ʿAbd al-Qāhir al-Baghdādī, *al-Farq bayna al-firaq,* ed. Muḥammad Muḥyī al-Dīn ʿAbd al-Ḥamīd (Beirut, n.d.), 125. Ashʿarī had suggested this already by saying, "Evil [*sharr*] may proceed from God—may He be exalted—by way of creation, but He will be just notwithstanding" (*Ibāna,* 121). When al-Baghdādī speaks of inherence, he is presupposing a certain ontology that the Muʿtazilites would have recognized. Human acts might be created by God, but they would not inhere in Him; the human being committing the act is the locus or substrate of inherence.
11. ʿAbd al-Karīm al-Shahrastānī, *Nihāyat al-iqdām fī ʿilm al-kalām,* ed. al-Fard Jayūm (Cairo, n.d.), 370.
12. Respectively, ʿAbd al-Malik al-Juwaynī, *Kitāb al-Irshād ilā qawāṭiʿ al-adilla fī uṣūl al-iʿtiqād,* ed. Asʿad Tamīm, 3rd ed. (Beirut, 1996), 236, 321; Fakhr al-Dīn al-Rāzī, *al-Arbaʿīn fī uṣūl al-dīn* (Hyderabad, AH 1353), 389.
13. Abū Rashīd al-Nīsābūrī, *al-Masāʾil fi'l-khilāf bayna al-Baṣriyyīn wa'l-Baghdādiyyīn,* ed. Maʿn Ziyāda and Riḍwān al-Sayyid (Tripoli, 1979), editors' introduction, 11. The list is hardly meant to be exhaustive.
14. A good introduction to the major figures of Baṣran Muʿtazilism—and in particular, those among them who associated themselves with Abū Hāshim—can be found in Margaretha J. Heemskerk, *Suffering in the Muʿtazilite Theology: ʿAbd al-Jabbār's Teaching on Pain and Divine Justice* (Leiden, 2000), 13–71.
15. Here a brief note should be made concerning two of the sources to be used—the later scholar al-Zamakhsharī (d. 1144), with his *al-Minhāj fī uṣūl al-dīn,* and the Zaydite Mānkdīm, with his *Sharḥ al-uṣūl al-khamsa.* The former does not belong squarely to the tradition constituted by the followers of Abū Hāshim which most other sources used here carry forward, influenced as he was by the philosophically cadenced views of Abu'l-Ḥusayn al-Baṣrī. In my use of his writings, I will be confining myself to areas undisturbed by controversy, and most of the material cited is seconded by other sources. As concerns the latter, it should simply be noted that while Imāmite Shīʿites generally did not accept the Muʿtazilite view of the unconditional punishment of the sinner, Zaydites, by contrast—to whom Mānkdīm belongs—gave their assent to the entire range of Muʿtazilite principles, and thus a study of Baṣran views of desert need not attend to these differences in sectarian loyalties. For a discussion of the relationship between Muʿtazilite thought and Imāmism, with comments on the Zaydites, see Wilfred Madelung, "Imâmism and Muʿtazilite Theology," in *Le Shiʿisme imâmite. Colloque de Strasbourg (6–9 mai 1968),* ed. T. Fahd (Paris, 1970), 13–30. For the attribution of *Sharḥ al-uṣūl al-khamsa* to Mānkdīm, see Daniel Gimaret, "Les *uṣūl al-hamsa* du Qāḍī ʿAbd al-Ğabbār et leurs commentaires," *Annales Islamologiques* 15 (1979): 47–96.
16. This analogy is suggested in Richard C. Martin, Mark R. Woodward, and Dwi S. Atmaja, *Defenders of Reason in Islam: Muʿtazilism from Medieval School to Modern Symbol* (Oxford, 1997), 53.

17. The term *muta'allaq* is a multipurpose word that appears in a wide range of contexts. If one keeps to the core contexts, the base meaning of the expression "the *muta'allaq* of x" seems to be "that which x connects, attaches, or relates to," or "the object of x." One speaks of the *muta'allaq* of one's power of autonomous action (*qudra*), to denote the actions one can do with one's power; one speaks of the *muta'allaq* of knowledge or will, to denote the thing known or willed, that to which knowledge or will attaches. And in this use, the *muta'allaq* would seem synonymous with the terms *maqdūr, ma'lūm,* and *murād*. Similarly, when one speaks of the *muta'allaq* of repentance or blame, one would be referring to the object of one's repentance (what one repents of) and the object of blame (what one blames). In the latter context, to ask about the relatum of blame is tantamount to asking about the reason for blaming. For a brief comment on this concept, see also Dhanani, *The Physical Theory,* 22n17; Daniel Gimaret, *Théories de l'acte humain en théologie musulmane* (Paris, 1980), index, 411.
18. Baghdādī, *Farq,* 186; cf. Mānkdīm, *Sharḥ,* 424–26; cf. Gimaret's reference to the argument in his *La doctrine d'al-Ash'arī* (Paris, 1990), 138–39.

CHAPTER 2
Reading Mu'tazilite Ethics

1. "How," Rāzī asks in the course of narrating his Transoxanian disputations, without entering into disputation with certain scholars, "could [one] know about their lack of knowledge?" (Fakhr al-Dīn al-Rāzī, *Munāẓarāt jarat fī bilād mā warā' al-nahr fi'l-ḥikma wa'l-khilāf wa-ghayrihimā bayna al-Imām Fakhr al-Dīn al-Rāzī wa-ghayrihi* [Hyderabad, AH 1355], 7). The records of his own disputations provide ample evidence of the social meanings—and especially the politics of shame and honor—that displays of dialectical prowess could command.
2. The Mu'tazilite view of the chains of transmission of their doctrine are discussed in Heemskerk, *Suffering in the Mu'tazilite Theology,* 14–21.
3. For discussion of the importance of dialectic within the Islamic sciences, with special emphasis on the legal sciences, see George Makdisi, *The Rise of Colleges* (Edinburgh, 1981); on a historical note, also his "The Scholastic Method in Medieval Education: An Inquiry into Its Origins in Law and Theology," *Speculum* 49 (1974): 640–61; E. Wagner, "Munāẓara," in *EI*², 7:565–68, references. Indeed, Makdisi's assessment of the role of dialectic was such as to make him declare that "without it, Islam would not have remained Islamic" ("The Scholastic Method," 649; a judgment that he refers to the role of dialectic in the determination of legal orthodoxy by means of consensus [*ijmā'*]).
4. This is the dilemma as adumbrated in Richard Rorty, "The Historiography of Philosophy: Four Genres," in *Philosophy in History,* ed. R. Rorty, B. Schneewind, and Q. Skinner (Cambridge, 1984), 49. For my insight into the questions discussed here, I am indebted to John Marenbon for his unstintingly generous suggestions and remarks; this debt must be hedged in the usual way: all deficiencies of insight are my own.
5. Richard W. Bulliet, "Orientalism and Medieval Islamic Studies," in *The Past and Future of Medieval Studies,* ed. J. Van Engen (Notre Dame, 1994), 97.

6. For a good starting point to explore the appropriation of Muʿtazilism in modern Islam, see Martin, Woodward, and Atmaja, *Defenders of Reason in Islam.*
7. See Daniel Gimaret, "Muʿtazila," in *EI*², 7:783–93.
8. Mānkdīm, *Sharḥ,* 48. Note that necessary knowledge need not be innate—the question whether moral principles themselves are intended by the Muʿtazilites to be innate could be made the subject of lengthy discussion, though one that would be hampered by the opacity of central passages bearing on this point given by Mānkdīm and ʿAbd al-Jabbār. For a discussion of ʿAbd al-Jabbār's epistemological views (though not, unfortunately, of this particular aspect of his account), see Marie Bernand, *Le problème de la connaissance d'après le Muġnī du cadi ʿAbd al-Ǧabbār* (Algiers, 1982).
9. This is expressed most clearly by Ibn Mattawayh, *Muḥīṭ,* 235. Cf. ʿAbd al-Jabbār, *al-Mughnī, VI/1: al-Taʿdīl wa'l-tajwīr,* ed. Aḥmad Fu'ād al-Ahwānī (Cairo, 1962), 66; ʿAbd al-Jabbār, *al-Mughnī, XIV: al-Aṣlaḥ/Istiḥqāq al-dhamm/al-Tawba,* ed. Muṣṭafā al-Saqā (Cairo, 1965), 156, 241. (Note that this tripartite volume will be abbreviated to *al-Aṣlaḥ*. Abbreviations for other volumes are easy to identify.)
10. The translation of *wajh* as "(act-) description" is not the one that has been generally preferred by other scholars. "Ground" has been used by George F. Hourani (*Islamic Rationalism* [Oxford, 1971], index), and "aspect" or "way" by Jan R.T.M. Peters (*God's Created Speech* [Leiden, 1976], index; for a wider conspectus of the various translations proposed in the scholarly literature, see Heemskerk, *Suffering in the Muʿtazilite Theology,* 116–17n12). It may seem that "description" carries none of the causal overtones that *wajh* suggests—overtones that emerge more clearly in the term *ʿilla*, which sometimes replaces it and are revealed in such passages as in *Taʿdīl,* "lying is evil because it is lying, injustice because it is injustice" (61), "willing may be evil because of its being a will to evil [*li-kawnihā* . . .]" (62; most of the terms set out above are gathered together on these same pages). But the description is the ground; the causality involved is that of the logical relation holding between a universal and its particular instantiation; and the term "description" captures the necessity of identifying what the act is—of describing, categorizing it—as a preliminary to ascertaining its value. Throughout this study, I will be rendering *wajh* either as ground or as (act-) description, depending on what the context renders preferable.
11. ʿAbd al-Jabbār, *Taʿdīl,* 18, 185.
12. Sherman A. Jackson, "The Alchemy of Domination? Some Ashʿarite Responses to Muʿtazilite Ethics," *International Journal of Middle East Studies* 31 (1999): 187.
13. See, for example, ʿAbd al-Jabbār, *Taʿdīl,* 22. For an interesting and more detailed exposition of the Muʿtazilite response to those who deny their ethical views, see ʿAbd al-Jabbār, *Luṭf,* 280–81, 302–5. For a good example of the kind of critique directed to Muʿtazilite epistemological claims, see Juwaynī, *Irshād,* 229ff.
14. ʿAbd al-Jabbār, *Taʿdīl,* 214–15; reading *bi-fiʿl* for *yafʿalu,* ibid., 214.
15. For the sort of psychological introspection ʿAbd al-Jabbār envisages, see especially ibid., 185. Introspective knowledge of one's internal states is one of the divisions of necessary knowledge listed by Mānkdīm in his exposition in *Sharḥ,* 50–51. An expanded treatment of this argument is given in my 'Equal before

the Law: The Evilness of Human and Divine Lies," *Arabic Sciences and Philosophy* 13 (2003): 243–68. See also Michael Marmura, "A Medieval Islamic Argument for the Intrinsic Value of the Moral Act," in *Corolla Torontonensis: Studies in Honour of R. M. Smith,* ed. E. Robbins and S. Sandahl (Toronto, 1994), 113–31.

16. Thus, my interest here does not entirely intersect with the question raised with increasing vigor as to the philosophical status of *kalām*—a vigor that may partly derive from the understanding of "philosophical" as, precisely, a kind of status or honorific. Even if this status was granted, it would still be a separate task to determine the relation between reason and revelation, or the modes of argument specific to each. Richard M. Frank has offered sensitive reflections on the qualities of *kalām* and its philosophical character throughout his work; see, for example, his introduction to *Beings and Their Attributes* (Albany, NY, 1978), addressed to the status of the earlier period of *kalām* before its "aristotelianization" in the Ash'arite tradition from Ghazālī onward. See also his "Reason and Revealed Law: A Sample of Parallels and Divergences in Kalâm and Falsafa," in *Recherches d'Islamologie: Recueil d'articles offert à Georges C. Anawati et Louis Gardet par leurs collègues et amis* (Leuven, 1977), 123–38; "*Kalām* and Philosophy, a Perspective from One Problem," in *Islamic Philosophical Theology,* ed. P. Morewedge (Albany, NY, 1979), 71–95. For a more general discussion of the features of *kalām,* see his "The Science of *Kalām,*" *Arabic Sciences and Philosophy* 2 (1992): 7–37. The *kalām* of the later period and its philosophical claims are addressed in Robert Wisnovsky, "The Nature and Scope of Arabic Philosophical Commentary in Post-classical (ca. 1200–1900 AD) Islamic Intellectual History: Some Preliminary Observations," in *Philosophy, Science, and Exegesis in Greek, Arabic, and Latin Commentaries,* ed. P. Adamson, H. Baltussen, and M.W.F. Stone (London, 2004), 2:149–91.
17. Alnoor Dhanani, *The Physical Theory of Kalām: Atoms, Space, and Void in Basrian Mu'tazilī Cosmology* (Leiden, 1994), 3; for the distinction between *daqīq* (or *laṭīf/ghāmiḍ*) and *jalīl* areas of *kalām,* see ibid., 3–4. Dhanani's spirit is echoed in part in the remarks with which Frank introduces his study of Abu'l-Hudhayl's metaphysics; see Richard M. Frank, *The Metaphysics of Created Being according to Abû l-Hudhayl al-'Allâf* (Istanbul, 1966).
18. 'Abd al-Jabbār, *Ta'dīl,* 3–4.
19. The notion of *wujūh* will be discussed in greater detail in chapter 3.
20. 'Abd al-Jabbār, *Ta'dīl,* 57.
21. For the use of this method in establishing the existence of entitative accidents (*ma'ānī*), see Ibn Mattawayh's *Muḥīṭ,* 40ff. The importance of this particular claim lies in the role it plays in the Mu'tazilite proof of the temporal origination of the world. And here one might remark—without intending it as a remark of disparagement—that the sense of contingency used in argumentation is already present in the conclusion that is sought (one cannot get something out of nothing).
22. 'Abd al-Jabbār, *Ta'dīl,* 61.
23. Aristotle's "magnanimous" man has often been cited as corresponding to a particular ideal of the Greek gentleman, and therefore a conspicuous historical particularity arresting and belying the universality of his account of the good. Moore's inclusion of aesthetic pleasure has likewise been taken by Alasdair MacIntyre as a reflection of the values of the Bloomsbury circle to which

he belonged, and thus once again, as a particularity presented in the form of objective moral truth (*After Virtue* [London, 1981], 15–16).

24. ʿAbd al-Jabbār, *Taʿdīl,* 13, with reference to the acts that are neutral in value on account of the absence of intentional or conscious states in their agents (e.g., in those who are asleep); God, of course, could never fail to be in a state of knowing.
25. Ibid, 98: "*istiḥqāq mā yastaḥīlu fiʿluhu lā yaṣiḥḥu.*" Cf. Mānkdīm, *Sharḥ,* 613–14. The passage from *Taʿdīl* continues, "*min ḥaythu kāna ḥusn al-shay' yatbaʿu ṣiḥḥatahu,*" providing an interesting instance of the analysis of desert into goodness in Baṣran Muʿtazilite thought, which will be discussed in detail in chapter 4. Cf. Ibn Mattawayh's brief remarks in *Majmūʿ*, 3:303, 308.
26. This way of referring to *qudra*—which should not be confused with the metaphysical possibility of contemporary philosophical idiom—takes its lead from the range of expressions that have been used to translate the term by a variety of scholars. This range includes Frank's translation as "objective possibility" or "the original ontological possibility," seconded by Peters, who also refers to it as "ontological" or "metaphysical" (for Frank's view, see Peters, *God's Created Speech,* 67n166; for Peter's view, see ibid., 235n56, 367n205), and Gimaret's rendition as "logical possibility" ("La notion d''impulsion irrésistible' (*ilǧâʾ*) dans l'éthique Muʿtazilite," *Journal Asiatique* 259 [1971]: 30, 46). However we decide to translate it, the important contrast that needs to be marked is between the possibility represented by *qudra* (which is the ontological constituent that makes action possible: *tuṣaḥḥiḥu al-fiʿl*) and the possibility that is determined on the level of a person's motives (*dāʿī*). Possibility granted on the first level does not, crucially, entail possibility on the second, and "one's motives to perform an act might be so strong that no other act in fact issues from one, *even if* one is capable of it *[qādir]*" (ʿAbd al-Jabbār, *al-Mughnī, VIII: al-Makhlūq,* ed. Tawfīq al-Ṭawīl and Saʿīd Zāyed [Cairo, n.d], 59). For discussion of the specter of determinism haunting Muʿtazilite thought—which this distinction particularly raises—see Gimaret, "Impulsion," 25–62, esp. 46ff. (and cf. *Théories,* e.g., 47–49); Peters, *God's Created Speech,* esp. 412–14; Frank, "The Autonomy of the Human Agent in the Teaching of ʿAbd al-Ğabbār," *Le Muséon* 95 (1982): 323–55.
27. Blame is also normally considered a form of harm, so that it would not seem possible to predicate that of God either, but the Muʿtazilites worked out a way of considering blame that abstracted from the experience of harm (its details are not wholly transparent to me: as a starting place, see ʿAbd al-Jabbār, *Taʿdīl,* 98; see also ibid., 14, amending line 11 from "*lā yastaḥiqqu*" to "*la-istaḥaqqa*").
28. Ibid., 82: "one cannot deserve blame for acts that one cannot guard against." This constraint is implicated in the other conditions for the realization of desert articulated by the Baṣrans, discussed in greater detail in chapter 4.
29. One might anticipate one type of response to this position, which would be that the true ends of Muʿtazilite moral reflection were not theological ones insofar as their greatest concern was to establish the human liberty to act (this suggestion seems to be carried by Hourani's remarks in "Divine Justice and Human Reason in Muʿtazilite Ethical Theology," in *Ethics in Islam,* ed. R. G. Hovannisian [Malibu, CA, 1985], 73). Short of getting embroiled in rather fruitless discussions concerning the order of intellectual priorities and relations of dependence, here I will have to content myself with ʿAbd al-Jabbār's concise statement of purpose given at the start of this discussion and with remarking

that the theological ends are inscribed in bold in the substance of the moral positions put forward, making it difficult to read their ethics in any other way than as an ancillary creed.

30. Hourani, *Islamic Rationalism,* 2, 5.
31. Ibid., 2.
32. Ibid., 15.
33. Ibid., 145, 81, 34, 50.
34. Hourani, "Divine Justice," 73.
35. These aspects of Muʿtazilite ethics will be discussed a bit more fully below.
36. Hourani, *Islamic Rationalism,* 3. For the discussion of lying, see ibid., 76–81.
37. For further discussion of this position, see Marmura, "A Medieval Islamic Argument"; Vasalou, "Equal before the Law."
38. Hourani, *Islamic Rationalism,* 123–26. Several more examples could have been mentioned, but it is hard to discuss them at this stage without presupposing ground that has not been covered yet. One such example—to be read in light of what will be said below—is Hourani's discussion of the definition of evil and of a conditional clause inserted by ʿAbd al-Jabbār to provide for the possibility that the agent will not deserve blame for a minor sin (*ṣaghīr:* translated as "peccadillo" by Hourani). "The peccadillo [minor sin] is embraced in the definition, because it is not deserving of blame only when there is a restricting reason [or preventive factor: *māniʿ*]." Hourani comments that "the reason *he has in mind* is the general record of good conduct of the agent" (ibid., 51; italics added). But the use of such terms obscures the theological context in which this statement should be read, and which is less about "the record of good conduct," and much more about the theologoumena of minor and major sins and of the operations of mutual cancellation between the deserts of an agent (the operations of *iḥbāṭ* and *takfīr*), to enter into the details of which would be to evoke the concern with posthumous destinies that underlies the theory and belies its aims. See chapter 4 for more about this theologoumenon.
39. Hourani does indeed devote a section to divine obligations, which is placed *after* his general treatment of the category of the obligatory on these terms. His choice of the order of his own exposition would seem to reflect his perception of the ordering of the stages of Muʿtazilite inquiry and understanding of the direction in which this moves. "*Starting* from a conviction that we can know some principles of ethical value with certainty through intuitive reason . . . [they] worked out what the principles and their consequences were," he says of the Muʿtazilites in *Islamic Rationalism* (145; italics added). As I've already noted, the issue here cannot be reduced to a question of classification, and whether one ought to categorize Muʿtazilite thought as theological or philosophical; it is not the terms themselves but their construction that is problematic. Despite the decided slant in *Islamic Rationalism* toward the presentation of ʿAbd al-Jabbār as a philosophical thinker, this question about the status of his (and the Muʿtazilites') thought was only raised directly in the works that followed, where Hourani (somewhat tentatively) proposed to describe Muʿtazilite reasoning as philosophical, on the basis of criteria that concern their intellectual means—namely, the degree to which they relied on scriptural resources for the justification of their positions. See his "Divine justice"; the collection of essays in *Reason and Tradition in Islamic Ethics* (Cambridge, 1985), esp. "Ethics in Classical Islam: A Conspectus," 19–20.

40. See George Makdisi, "Ethics in Islamic Traditionalist Doctrine," in *Ethics in Islam,* ed. R. G. Hovannisian (Malibu, CA, 1985), 47. As a definition of the scope of ethics, it will appear somewhat too narrow—or at least, his conception of the "practical" may need to be enlarged—as it would exclude from the scope of ethics inquiries into the ontology or epistemology of value, whereas this, too, is an integral part of the ethical quest, even though there might be different ways of drawing the connection between the "first-order" inquiries into substantive moral questions that Makdisi has in mind and "second-order" levels. One way of drawing it would be to stress how results in the latter affect a person's motivation to lead an ethical life: what makes the second-order view that values lack objectivity an upsetting one is that it seems to undermine our reasons for realizing it. Similar comments apply to Reinhart's statement that "because ethics is basically a practical science that studies normative action, the purely theoretical efforts of Islamic theologians (such as Muʿtazilites and Ashʿarites) to describe, for example, whether God creates and is responsible for human actions, is arguably not part of Islamic ethics either" (A. Kevin Reinhart, "Islamic Law as Islamic Ethics," *Journal of Religious Ethics* 11 [1983]: 186).
41. Hourani, *Islamic Rationalism,* 15.
42. Ibid., 8, 53.
43. Loose, for the informality of the structures of learning through which *kalām*—among other traditional sciences—was practiced is usually contrasted with institutional forms of learning familiar, for example, in the medieval Latin West. For discussion of medieval Islamic education and its formal and informal characteristics, see Michael Chamberlain, *Knowledge and Social Practice in Medieval Damascus, 1190–1350* (Cambridge, 1994); Jonathan Berkey, *The Transmission of Knowledge in Medieval Cairo* (Princeton, NJ, 1992).
44. See my "Equal before the Law."
45. Within my confines it would be impossible to do full justice to Hourani's approach, and inevitably the present account has placed the emphasis on certain features and not others. It should be read in conjunction with the last section of *Islamic Rationalism* (chapter 7: "Significance"), which displays Hourani's awareness of a number of problems attendant to his approach.
46. Hourani, *Islamic Rationalism,* 75. Mānkdīm's definition is cited by Peters (*God's Created Speech,* 89–90), who judges it to be the best all around.
47. Oliver Leaman, "ʿAbd al-Jabbār and the Concept of Uselessness," *Journal of the History of Ideas* 41 (1980): 129; italics added.
48. This view is reported by Ashʿarī as a position of unanimous agreement among the Muʿtazilites: "The Muʿtazilites unanimously affirm that God—may He be exalted!—created His servants to benefit them and not to harm them" (Abu'l-Hasan al-Ashʿarī, *Maqālāt al-Islāmiyyīn wa-ikhtilāf al-muṣallīn,* ed. Muḥammad Muḥyī al-Dīn ʿAbd al-Ḥamīd, [Beirut, 1999], 1:317); cf. Abu'l-Ḥusayn al-Khayyāṭ, *Kitāb al-Intiṣār,* ed. H. S. Nyberg, 2nd ed. (Beirut, 1993), 25; cf. Shahrastānī's discussion (and rejection) of this view in *Nihāyat al-iqdām,* 397ff. And cf. Jār Allāh al-Zamakhsharī, *A Muʿtazilite Creed of az-Zamahšarî (d. 538/1144) (al-Minhâǧ fî uṣûl ad-dîn),* ed. S. Schmidtke (Stuttgart, 1997), 62–63, where the connection between the beneficent purpose of God and vain action is quite explicit.
49. ʿAbd al-Jabbār, *Taʿdīl,* 34.

50. Hence Mānkdīm's treatment of *'abath* in the context of discussing the challenge posed to this conception of the purpose of *taklīf* by the existence of persons of whom God knows that they will not believe (Mānkdīm, *Sharḥ*, 511ff.).
51. For the view on compensation—and Abū 'Alī's disagreement with the majority view—see Zamakhsharī, *A Mu'tazilite Creed*, 68–70; cf., more fully, Mānkdīm, *Sharḥ*, 485ff. This type of view seems to be closely connected to another majority Mu'tazilite position concerning the necessity of imposing the Law (*taklīf*) as a condition for being rewarded. Most Mu'tazilites agreed that the order of benefits in which reward consists could *only* be attained through undergoing the hardships of *taklīf* and through *deserving*, and could not have been given through an act of sheer beneficence (*tafaḍḍul*). See, for example, Zamakhsharī, *A Mu'tazilite Creed*, 64; cf. Mānkdīm, *Sharḥ*, 510–11.
52. Leaman, "The Concept of Uselessness," 129. Referring to *al-Mughnī, XIII: al-Luṭf*, ed. Abū al-'Alā' al-'Afīfī (Cairo, 1962), 312.
53. Hourani, *Islamic Rationalism*, 76. Peters, on his side, has pointed out that Hourani's discussion is constrained by the limited textual bases employed; for fuller references and a brief discussion of the concept, see his *God's Created Speech*, 89–90.
54. Both quotes from Hourani, *Islamic Rationalism*, 76.
55. Heemskerk, *Suffering in the Mu'tazilite Theology*, 1.
56. Apropos the question of how pain is perceived. Ibid., 81.
57. Ibid., 74, 81; italics added.
58. Ibid., 112.
59. See his review of the book in *Journal of Islamic Studies* 13 (2002): 58–59.
60. In the middle of the range, and combining the virtues of Hourani's engaging approach and those of Heemskerk's descriptive one, one could place Michael Marmura's contribution ("A Medieval Islamic Argument") about the debate over the deontological prohibition of lies, defended by Mu'tazilites and denied by their Ash'arite colleagues. Marmura is careful to stress the tension between the Mu'tazilites' "rationalism" and their dogmatism—that is, their use of reason for theological ends—and while providing context, its detachment is not that of a descriptive project, and the commentator's judgments strike a balance between observer and participant. Scholars engaging with Mu'tazilite ethics with reference to the Ash'arite response are in general less prone to misidentifications of its aims, as this brings theological context clearly into view. Richard Frank's faithfulness to the Mu'tazilite perspective in his "Moral Obligation in Classical Muslim Theology" (*Journal of Religious Ethics* 11 [1983]: 204–23) has a lot to do with his aim, which was "to view the two contemporaneous ethical systems . . . in their broadest theological contexts" (204). The same remarks could be applied to other works undertaken in this spirit. Similar sensitivity is cultivated by attention to the interconnections holding between the various Mu'tazilite positions and the unifying concerns that undergird them. An example of this kind of attention is Albert Nader's *Le système philosophique des Mu'tazila* (Beirut, 1956), which while published before the edition of the works of the later Baṣran Mu'tazilites (such as *al-Mughnī, Sharḥ*, and *Majmū'*), is still valuable for certain of its observations concerning the ways in which the various building blocks of Mu'tazilite thought give each other mutual support. A useful and concise comment on some of the most salient works on Mu'tazilite

thought can be found in A. Kevin Reinhart, *Before Revelation: The Boundaries of Muslim Moral Thought* (Albany, NY, 1995), 217.

61. ʿAbd al-Jabbār, *al-Aṣlaḥ*, 41.

CHAPTER 3
Theology as Law

1. See, for instance, Ṣalāḥ al-Dīn al-Ṣafadī, *al-Wāfī bi'l-wafayāt*, ed. O. Weintritt (Beirut, 1997), 27: 218.
2. ʿAbd al-Jabbār, *al-Aṣlaḥ*, 355. And see Mānkdīm's more manageable account of the disputed question in *Sharḥ*, 794–98.
3. ʿAbd al-Jabbār, *al-Aṣlaḥ*, 350; for general discussion, 350 ff. Cf. Ibn Mattawayh's discussion in *Majmūʿ*, 3:399–405.
4. For a particularly rich discussion with many references to Ashʿarite and Muʿtazilite perspectives on the disputed questions, see Ibn Ḥajar al-Haytamī, *al-Zawājir ʿan iqtirāf al-kabāʾir*, (Beirut, 1988), 2:217–30 (and for the rather extreme particularism ascribed to Abū Isḥāq—probably al-Shīrāzī—that was ultimately rejected by the majority, see 220). This majority view was that of Ashʿarī, as Ibn Fūrak reports it: *Mujarrad maqālāt al-shaykh Abi'l-Ḥasan al-Ashʿarī*, ed. D. Gimaret (Beirut, 1987), 166. It is interesting to note that the Muʿtazilite view was not the preserve of these rationalist theologians, and the severity of their position—which here appears as the severity of an exacting conceptual rigor—could just as easily appear as the severity of an exacting piety and spiritual rigor. This is the case when a view like Abū Hāshim's is attributed to an authority as weighty and hostile to a rationalistic spirit as Aḥmad ibn Ḥanbal. See Ibn Mufliḥ, *al-Ādāb al-sharʿiyya wa'l-minaḥ al-marʿiyya*, ed. Muḥammad Rashīd Riḍā (Cairo, AH 1348), 1:65.
5. In describing it as juridical, he was referring to the fact that "they were mainly interested in man and his responsibility" rather than in the explanation of natural phenomena; "they started from man's obligation toward God" rather than from metaphysical questions. Josef van Ess, "Muʿtazilah," in *Encyclopedia of Religion*, ed. M. Eliade (New York, 1987), 10:227. Quotation in main text, 228.
6. Mānkdīm, *Sharḥ*, 792 (cf. Ibn Mattawayh, *Majmūʿ*, 3:400); ʿAbd al-Jabbār, *al-Aṣlaḥ*, 317, 327.
7. Al-Sharīf al-Murtaḍā, *Rasāʾil al-Sharīf al-Murtaḍā*, ed. Aḥmad al-Ḥusaynī (Qom, AH 1405), 2:268. The "good" mentioned in the definition presumably refers to the "genre" of moral values that may include obligation (i.e., *ḥasan*; this generic type of value is discussed further in what follows).
8. These terms are sampled in ʿAbd al-Jabbār, *al-Aṣlaḥ*, 436.
9. Most clearly, in the division drawn in ibid. (162), which will be discussed below.
10. Ibid., 451.
11. To this, some writers add a fourth: "*qulūb*"—in which the harm would be confined to its effects on a person's mind, heart, or spirit. See Badr al-Dīn al-Zarkashī, *al-Manthūr fi'l-qawāʿid*, ed. Taysīr Fāʾiq Aḥmad Maḥmūd (Kuwait, 1982), 1:423. The above may be found diffusely in the literature on repentance. See, for example, Haytamī, *Zawājir*, loc. cit., and "al-Tawba," in *al-Mawsūʿa al-fiqhiyya* (Kuwait, 1988), 14:119–33. As concerns the definition of repentance,

writers on the topic register a debate about the relation between the three elements referred to above—regret, resolution, and desistance—and whether one (regret) was a constitutive element with the other two as conditions, or whether they were jointly constitutive. Haytamī's remark in *Zawājir* (219) appears to associate the former view with *fiqhī* writings—which moved closer to *ḥadīth*, such as the well-known *ḥadīth*, "*al-tawba nadm*"—and the latter with theological circles.

12. ʿAbd al-Jabbār, *al-Aṣlaḥ*, 436–38.
13. C. van Arendonk-(J. Schacht), "Ibn Ḥadjar al-Haytamī', *EI*², 3:779.
14. Mānkdīm, the scope of whose work is evidently narrower than that of the *Mughnī*, provides a succinct reference to these conditions of repentance in *Sharḥ*, 798–99 (itself a useful guide for the structure of ʿAbd al-Jabbār's longer discussion), with a brief remark to say that there is another place where such questions received greater attention. No doubt he would have a work of legal nature in mind. Ibn Mattawayh's reference is even more laconic: *Majmūʿ*, 3:410. Like Mānkdīm, he too alludes to another place where such details are discussed at further length.
15. As we hear from the Muʿtazilites' biographical literature, al-Karkhī was a figure with strong connections to Muʿtazilite theologians, a number of whom read law with him (including Abū ʿAbd Allāh al-Baṣrī). They are mentioned in concentration in the tenth *ṭabaqa* in Ibn al-Murtaḍā, *Ṭabaqāt al-Muʿtazila*, ed. S. Diwald-Wilzer (Wiesbaden, 1961). Abū Hāshim himself is said to have held disputes with him on questions of law (ibid., 94–95).
16. The question of *ijtihād* was one that both Jubbāʾīs, Abū Hāshim and Abū ʿAlī, had an expressed interest in, and it seems to be one of the few matters of law to which they devoted special works. For a helpful bibliography of the Jubbāʾīs, see Daniel Gimaret, "Matériaux pour une bibliographie des Ǧubbāʾī," *Journal Asiatique* 264 (1976): 277–332. The works just mentioned are referred to in ibid., 280, 305.
17. The scope is explicitly marked at the conclusion of volume 14 (*al-Aṣlaḥ*, 461), where ʿAbd al-Jabbār states that he will be going on to talk about matters concerning prophecy (*nubuwwāt*), "as we have now covered those things that concern the rationally known Law [*al-taklīf al-ʿaqlī*]". Implicitly it is indicated in *al-Aṣlaḥ*, 164, talking about blood money—"but this has nothing to do with rationally known obligations"—or talking about bodily harm—"considerations [*badal*] for it are determined by the Law, and this is why we have not discussed them in this section" (reading *yataqqadaru* for *yataʿadhdharu*).
18. One of the clearest presentations here is Ibn Mattawayh, *Muḥīṭ*, 241. ʿAbd al-Jabbār's organization in *Taʿdīl* is unevenly balanced, and the discussion of the grounds of evil holds the field.
19. ʿAbd al-Jabbār, *al-Aṣlaḥ*, 162. Ibn Mattawayh rehearses an abridged version of this scheme in *Majmūʿ*, 3:418, yet without using the term *ḥaqq*, instead ranging the scheme around the different kinds of grounds (*asbāb*) that give rise to obligations. Mānkdīm gives a similar account in *Sharḥ*, 327–29, while also mentioning other models of classification.
20. *Al-Aṣlaḥ*, 166: "*wa-mā yalzamuhu min shukr al-ʿibād yajrī majrā al-ḥaqq lahum*."
21. For the reference to necessary knowledge (the passage suggests that for some *ḥuqūq*, the knowledge will be an acquired one), see ibid., 165. *Ḥuqūq ʿaqliyya: al-Mughnī, XVII: al-Sharʿiyyāt*, ed. Amīn al-Khūlī (Cairo, 1963), 120 (alas, one

of few coveted references to rationally known moral truths that one extracts from this work). The interpretation of the term *'aqlī* is in *Shar'iyyāt,* 101, where it is said of the qualities of acts, "if their knowledge is gained by reason, one qualifies them by it and refers to them as 'rational qualities' [*aḥkām 'aqliyya*], whereas if they are known by revelation one refers to them as 'revealed qualities' [*aḥkām sam'iyya*]."

22. Ibn Qayyim al-Jawziyya, *I'lām al-muwaqqi'īn 'an rabb al-'ālamīn,* ed. Ṭaha 'Abd al-Ra'ūf Sa'd (Beirut, 1973), 1:108–9. For a discussion of God's rights in the context of penal law, see Joseph Schacht, *An Introduction to Islamic Law* (Oxford, 1991), 175–87; see also index, under *ḥaqq*. For a further discussion of the concept, see Mohammad H. Kamali, "Fundamental Rights of the Individual: An Analysis of *Ḥaqq* (Right) in Islamic Law," *American Journal of Islamic Social Sciences* 10 (1993): 340–66; one may take issue with the author for being rather unhelpful with his incomplete citations (to confine citation to the author of a work and the date of its publication when the work in question runs into a good many thick volumes is not to cite at all), and thus not permitting us to ascertain the accuracy of the citation when the modernizing aims of the author render him prey to distrust (does one find "equality" and "freedom" in classical expositions of *ḥuqūq*? Kamali suggests so: 347). See also "*Ḥaqq*," in *al-Mawsū'a al-fiqhiyya* (Kuwait, 1990), 18:7–47.
23. The anthropocentric view will receive additional support by a fact to be discussed later in this chapter—namely, that rights and claims were understood predominantly in terms of benefits, thereby embodying a clear anthropocentric focus (God, the Self-Sufficient, being above benefits and harms). And it is this understanding that will be employed by opponents of the Mu'tazilite view of punishment that construed the latter as a claim (*ḥaqq*) belonging to God (Mānkdīm, *Sharḥ,* 645: "A right is something from which its holder may derive benefit [*al-ḥaqq mā li-ṣāḥibihi an yantafi'a bihi*] yet it is impossible for God to be benefited"). Cf. Ibn Mattawayh, *Majmū',* 3:411. See the next chapter for details on this view, especially the "Justifying Reward and Punishment" section.
24. The concept of *dhimma* will receive further attention in chapter 5, in the "Why Not *Dhimma*?" section.
25. Respectively, *al-Aṣlaḥ,* 440, 443, 458.
26. A good synopsis of the challenges that gave the Baṣran account of revelation its formative focus can be found in Ibn Mattawayh, *Majmū',* 3:419.
27. For slightly further detail on the concept of *luṭf* and its agent neutrality, see Heemskerk, *Suffering in the Mu'tazilite Theology,* 148–51. This is an assistance that God is *obliged* to provide once He has chosen—of His own accord and out of His bounty—to create beings possessed of attributes that necessitate placing them under *taklīf.*
28. 'Abd al-Jabbār, *al-Mughnī, XV: al-Tanabbu'āt wa'l-mu'jizāt,* ed. Maḥmūd al-Khuḍayrī and Maḥmūd Muḥammad Qāsim (Cairo, 1965), 23; cf. 42: "The reason why [these laws: *sharā'i'*] serve one's welfare is the ground of obligation that is realized in them—namely, that one chooses to perform one's rational obligations because of them, and but for these laws, would not have done so." Note that the title of this work is given as *Tanabbu'āt* in the edition; but it is to be wondered whether the correct title should not rather be *Nubuwwāt,* which is in fact the form in which 'Abd al-Jabbār refers to it in one of the volumes that follows it—namely, *Shar'iyyāt,* 289.

29. ʿAbd al-Jabbār, *Tanabbu'āt,* 65. For the reference to reward, see ibid., 45.
30. Ibid., 33.
31. By contrast, while his father Abū ʿAlī had agreed that revelation was rendered good as a *luṭf* serving the welfare of the subjects of the Law, he believed that this condition was realized even in the case where revelation conveyed truths accessible to reason, but came to impress them more forcefully, rouse one to a keener awareness of them by admonition, and warn (*ta'kīd, tanbīh, taḥdhīr*). See ibid., 20–21.
32. Ibid., 26.
33. Ibid., 27.
34. Mānkdīm, *Sharḥ,* 565. Cf. ʿAbd al-Jabbār, *Tanabbu'āt,* 45: "Revelation [*al-samʿ*] . . . reveals the particulars of qualities known by reason."
35. Mānkdīm, *Sharḥ,* 564–565. Cf. the discussion in *Tanabbu'āt,* 36ff.
36. ʿAbd al-Jabbār, *Sharʿiyyāt,* 330: "*al-ʿilla fi'l-sharʿiyyāt tajrī majrā al-dawāʿī wa-mā yakshifu ʿan kawn al-fiʿl luṭfan*"; see also chapter 4, the "To Deserve" section.
37. ʿAbd al-Jabbār, *Sharʿiyyāt,* 286.
38. ʿAbd al-Jabbār, *Tanabbu'āt,* 33. Cf. Ibn Mattawayh, *Majmūʿ*, 3:434.
39. The story is slightly more complex owing to the use of the term *dayn,* translated here as "debt." This encompasses not merely the obligation of payment to defray a debt acquired through an act of borrowing but the obligation of payment arising through consumption (*istihlāk*) or the destruction (*itlāf*) of an object, or through contracts or employment. See *al-Aṣlaḥ,* 163. Schacht defines *dayn* as "a claim or debt, primarily of money but also of fungible things in general" (*Introduction to Islamic Law,* 144–45).
40. Abu'l-Ḥusayn al-Baṣrī, *Sharḥ al-ʿumad,* ed. ʿAbd al-Ḥamīd bin ʿAlī Abū Zunayd (Medina, AH 1410), 2:41.
41. Ibid., 55–58.
42. For example, the succinct instance of this view found in ʿAbd al-Jabbār, *Taʿdīl,* 122: "That which necessarily entails [*yaqtaḍī*] the evilness of an evil act—such as the fact that a statement is a lie, or a pain is unjust—functions in the manner of necessary causes [*yajrī . . . majrā al-ʿilal al-mūjiba*]." Cf. *Tanabbu'āt,* 48: "The ground of obligation [*wajh al-wujūb*] is as the necessary cause [*ʿilla*] to the quality [*ḥukm*] in that it necessarily entails that the act in which it obtains is obligatory." This conception of the operation of grounds of value will be discussed and qualified in the following chapter.
43. *Tanabbu'āt,* 125; see also 48–49, 122. The term "consequentialism" employed in the text is a cumbersome one, but is preferable to alternatives such as "utilitarianism," which is burdened by negative evaluative connotations in ordinary usage and its association with a particular school of ethics in philosophical usage. Note that despite the distinction drawn, ʿAbd al-Jabbār feels comfortable at places employing the term *ṣifa* and *wajh*—the standard term used in the Baṣrans' ethical expositions to refer to grounds of value, normally understood as necessitating causes of value—in talking about consequentialist grounds (e.g., *Tanabbu'āt,* 47: "*qad yaḥsunu li-baʿḍ al-wujūh allatī dhakarnāhā, min dafʿ maḍarra wa-ijtilāb manfaʿa*"; *al-Aṣlaḥ,* 161: "*al-taḥarruz min al-maḍārr aḥad al-ṣifāt alladhī* [*sic*] *yajibu lahu al-fiʿl*"). Clearly a language of reason giving is still required, but this does not prevent us from marking the distinction between the two types of reason.

44. This principle of priority is expressed in the notions of *ʿazīma* and *rukhṣa* in Islamic law. The former indicates the original binding force of a ruling whose observance is demanded of the subject, and the latter the mitigation of the ruling and its substitution by a more lenient one in cases of hardship—a distinction closely connected to the conception of the aims of the Law (*maqāṣid al-sharīʿa*) as elaborated by legal theoreticians. An example of such *rukhṣa* (lit. "license"), in which pressing need can nullify or mitigate obligation, concerns ablution, which one must normally perform using water; in cases where water is not available, earth or sand can be used instead. The Ḥanafite jurist al-Kāsānī (d. 1189), who discusses this question in the context of *kaffārāt* (acts of expiation) to illustrate how need affects the expiation one is obliged to undertake, states that if there is a certain amount of water available that is needed for purposes of drinking, it is "as though it did not exist" and sand may be used instead. And here he uses an interesting turn of phrase, saying that it is *mustaḥaqq al-ṣarf ila'l-ḥāja* ("it is deserved [in the sense of 'rightly designated or reserved'] for the satisfaction of need" ('Alā' al-Dīn al-Kāsānī, *Kitāb Badāʾiʿ al-ṣanāʾiʿ fī tartīb al-sharāʾiʿ* [Cairo, 1910], 5:97). For a discussion of the dichotomy between *ʿazīma* and *rukhṣa*, see Wael B. Hallaq, *A History of Islamic Legal Theories* (Cambridge, 1999), 177ff. This idea is intimately linked to the legal principles that "*al-ḍarūrāt tubīḥu al-maḥẓūrāt*" or "*al-mashaqqa tajlibu al-taysīr*" (see the discussion of the principles in Jalāl al-Dīn al-Ṣuyūṭī,' *Kitāb al-Ashbāh wa'l-naẓāʾir fī qawāʿid wa-furūʿ fiqh al-Shāfiʿiyya*, ed. ʿAbd al-Karīm al-Fuḍaylī [Beirut, 2001] 106–20). A brief reference to *rukhṣa* is found in ʿAbd al-Jabbār, *Sharʿiyyāt*, 100.
45. What about the last example mentioned at the start, concerning the garment blown by the wind into one's house, where reason was said not to demand that one declare the discovery, whereas revelation does? Unless ʿAbd al-Jabbār has in mind here the general legal principle that a stronger legal ruling is always to be preferred to a laxer one (cf. the remarks in *Sharʿiyyāt*, 350—e.g., in saying that a legal cause that results in prohibition is to be preferred to one that does not, because the former is "*adkhal fīmā yaqtaḍī al-sharʿ wa-ashadd muṭābaqatan lahu*"; cf. the spirit animating the legal principle that where two rulings are possible, one of which is permission and the other prohibition, the latter is to be preferred: see Zarkashī, *al-Manthūr*, 1: 125–33), he is probably referring to the generally agreed *fiqhī* ruling concerning property adventitiously found by a person (*luqṭa*), according to which the items must be publicly acknowledged by the one who finds them, and the claim implicit in the contrast might be the ethically important and contentious view that *aṣl al-ashyā' ʿala'l-ibāḥa* (the presumption that the value of acts that benefit a person prior to the advent of the law is "permissibility": e.g., *Tanabbu'āt*, 103. For details of this crucial debate, see Reinhart, *Before Revelation*).
46. ʿAbd al-Jabbār, *al-Aṣlaḥ*, 441.
47. The last-mentioned condition is actually transported from a related passage in ibid., 162; the context is the obligation to return deposits.
48. This seems clear, for example, in ʿAbd al-Jabbār, ibid., 445, where a conditional statement appears ("*idhā lazimahu radd al-ḥaqq ʿala'l-jamāʿa*") and the context indicates that ʿAbd al-Jabbār is speaking about the domain of rationally known truths. Another passage in *Sharʿiyyāt* (49) suggests this even more pointedly by stating that the obligation to return a deposit "is only obligatory on particular conditions and on [the owner's] demand." Yet this is one of the occasions

in which the disputational context in which these views are articulated makes it hard for one to be confident about one's use and interpretation of a given passage that appears as a brief aside in a larger disputational whole, especially when the relation between the claim it makes seems to beg for reconciliation with the claim made about such an obligation in more focused sections—as in the passages already cited in the main text in which rational (including moral) grounds are described as unconditional and unvarying. (And that it must beg does not mean that it is difficult for what it begs to be given.)

49. Ibn Mattawayh, *Majmūʿ*, 3:185–86, in connection with the obligation to thank the benefactor.
50. This impression is reinforced in passages in which the possibility of conflict between reason and revelation is referred to but passed over without comment, such as in the transition from the discussion of rationally known principles in ʿAbd al-Jabbār, *al-Aṣlaḥ*, 445: "As concerns what obtains after the advent of revelation, if the latter conveys something that is at variance with what the dictate of reason demands, then this [i.e., the revealed ruling] is what must be adhered to, otherwise it is the claims [*ḥuqūq*] we mentioned that are obligatory."
51. George Makdisi, "Ashʿari and the Ashʿarites in Islamic Religious History," *Studia Islamica* 17 (1962): 37–80, and 18 (1963): 19–39. Makdisi pursues this theme in his subsequent works, such as *The Rise of Humanism in Classical Islam and the Christian West* (Edinburgh, 1990), and *The Rise of Colleges* (Edinburgh, 1981), from whence the quotation that follows is taken (8).
52. Al-Ḥākim al-Jushamī, *Sharḥ al-ʿuyūn* (in *Faḍl al-Iʿtizāl wa-ṭabaqāt al-Muʿtazila*), 382–83.
53. See *Luṭf*, 566, reading *jadd* for *ḥadd*. A work published under the title *Fiʾl-Tawḥīd*, (ed. Muḥammad Abū Rīda [Cairo, 1969]), whose editor proposed to identify as the lost work by Nīsābūrī, unfortunately does not seem to fit the bill, if we follow Gimaret (as it seems we should) in his conclusion that it is a commentary by a later author on Abū ʿAlī ibn Khallād's *Sharḥ al-uṣūl* (see his "Les *uṣūl al-hamsa*," 73).
54. Makdisi explicitly seconds this conjecture in *Rise of Colleges*, 125–26.
55. In explaining why in the revealed Law one may enter into ownership after one's death, see, for example, ʿAbd al-Jabbār, *al-Aṣlaḥ*, 447 cf. ibid., 439, with reference to the loss of an individual object: "this is why the jurists [*fuqahāʾ*] have said . . ."
56. See Bernard G. Weiss, *The Spirit of Islamic Law* (Athens, GA, 1998), 66–87. The connection drawn between this practice of particularism and a voluntarist theory of value is no doubt an important one (Daniel Brown, "Islamic Ethics in Comparative Perspective," *Muslim World* 89 [1999], 185).
57. ʿAbd al-Jabbār, *Sharʿiyyāt*, 332.
58. It should be remarked here that the Muʿtazilites were not alone in using legal concepts and material in *kalām* discussions. Concerning the normative currency of *ḥuqūq*, for example—said above to invoke a legal frame—one notes its presence, even if the references are but brief, in Ashʿarī's remarks on repentance (Ibn Fūrak, *Mujarrad maqālāt*, 167), and also in Juwaynī's (*Irshād*, 339–40), where the contrast between human and divine claims is an organizing principle. But clearly for those who held that the values of acts were imparted to them by revelation, the issues raised by the use of revealed resources are of

a different order than for those, like the Mu'tazilites, who had two domains of evaluative knowledge to reconcile.

59. 'Abd al-Jabbār, *al-Aṣlaḥ*, 454.
60. Ibn Nujaym, *Al-Baḥr al-rā'iq sharḥ kanz al-daqā'iq* (Cairo, n.d.), 6:148.
61. 'Abd al-Jabbār, *Ta'dīl*, 32: "*mattā qulnā innahu 'ḥaqq lahu,' afāda istiḥqāqa fi'lin 'ala'l-ghayr.*" See below for further comment on this formulation.
62. 'Abd al-Jabbār, *al-Aṣlaḥ*, 165.
63. The context of the remark is an attempt to explain why an obligation to compensate—that is, to grant a person particular benefits—arises when one takes a person's possessions (*amlāk*) away from them: "It is obligatory to give compensation for the removal of a person's possessions because this involves preventing a person from benefiting from them, for here what matters is not particular objects per se [*a'yān*] but rather benefits and harms." *Luṭf*, 555.
64. *Luṭf*, 555 (Zayd-on-'Amr example), 557 (book example). On the other hand, and while the violation of rights constitutes an injustice, 'Abd al-Jabbār resists the idea that the obligation to desist from injustice be understood as deriving from any "right not to be subjected to injustice"; for *ḥuqūq* are set up by antecedent grounds, and such a right has no ground of this sort. This, at least, is how I understand 'Abd al-Jabbār's somewhat opaque remarks in *al-Aṣlaḥ*, 165.
65. The distinction, we may recall, was framed around obligations in the relevant passage of *al-Aṣlaḥ*; but obligatory and evil acts are as contraries: if it is obligatory to return a deposit, it is evil not to. In the main text I speak of "moral principles" for the sake of simplicity. Note, further, that while the moral acts in question are other-regarding, self-regarding acts can also be seen to reduce to the conceptual category of *ḥuqūq*. The reason for this will be indicated shortly, and it concerns the interpretation of the concept of *ḥuqūq* in terms of welfare. When it is said that in acting contrary to moral requirements one is "perpetrating injustice against oneself" (*yaẓlimu nafsahu*)—a widely used idea that ultimately harks back to the Qur'ān (e.g., 3:117, 16:33, et al.)—the description of the act as a form of injustice is due to its not leading to greater benefit in the future but rather to "final harm," since such a conduct will lead to posthumous punishment.
66. 'Abd al-Jabbār, *Luṭf*, 23, 495. One may also, however, refer to the objects themselves as what the claim is over, as in, for example, Ibn Mattawayh, *Majmū'*, 3:369: "*qad tustaḥaqqu al-duyūn wa-yata'akhkharu qaḍā'uhā*'.
67. Unlike reward, punishment can also be extracted in this world, and thus there is also a *worldly* use of *istiḥqāq* that concerns the adjustment of moral balances, as in a case referred to by Ibn Mattawayh in which it is said that the person responsible for avenging the blood of a victim of homicide (*walī al-dam*) "has a claim over the killer to kill him in retaliation" (*yastaḥiqqu 'ala'l-qatīl an yaqtulahu qawadan*). Ibid., 346; though note that in this context, Ibn Mattawayh is disputing the precise interpretation of this legal norm, and whether it *is* punishment or, as Ibn Mattawayh holds, may constitute a tribulation (*miḥna*).
68. As in 'Abd al-Jabbār, *al-Mughnī, XI: al-Taklīf*, ed. Muḥammad 'Alī al-Najjār and 'Abd al-Ḥalīm al-Najjār (Cairo, 1965), 522: *ta'khīr al-ḥaqq, zawāl al-ḥaqq*, speaking of reward (cf. ibid., 464ff.); cf. *Muḥīṭ*, 241: *tawfiyat al-ghayr ḥaqqahu, wa-yadkhulu fīhi al-thawāb wa'l-ta'wīḍ*, for reward and compensation (cf. *Majmū'*, 2:310–11). Also Ibn Mattawayh, *al-Tadhkira fī aḥkām al-jawāhir*

wa'l-a'rāḍ, ed. Sāmī Naṣr Luṭf and Fayṣal Budayr 'Awn (Cairo, 1975), 209: *tawfīr al-ḥuqūq 'alā man yastaḥiqquhā,* alluding to otherworldly treatments, followed by a reference to "*al-thawāb wa-ghayrihi min al-ḥuqūq.*" Cf. Ibn Mattawayh, *Majmū',* 3:370: "*al-ḥuqūq al-mustaḥaqqa,*" referring again to reward and punishment. Punishment is also construed as a claim, but a divine one; more will be said on this below. The Baṣrans' discussion of compensation in particular is replete with the vocabulary of *ḥaqq* and *istiḥqāq,* and an excellent place to look for clarification of the relations between these terms. It is worth noting here that the concept of justice (*'adl*) is not as unproblematically understood in terms of rights or claims. Certainly there is one definition in currency among our theologians in which this is the case, as in Mānkdīm: justice is "rendering a *ḥaqq* unto another and exacting a *ḥaqq* from him" (*Sharḥ,* 301). But the story here is more complex. For further detail, see chapter 4, the "Justifying Punishment" section.

69. 'Abd al-Jabbār, *al-Aṣlaḥ,* 334. Conversely, the person for whom there is a *ḥaqq 'alayhi* will suffer harm in giving the right holder their due; cf. Ibn Mattawayh, *Majmū',* 3:411: "*ma'nā qawlinā 'ḥaqq 'alayhi' yufīdu annahu min bāb mā yaḍurruhu 'inda al-istīfā'.*"
70. Shihāb al-Dīn al-Qarāfī, *Kitāb al-Furūq* (Cairo, AH 1344), 1:140. And for a discussion of the relation of *ḥuqūq* to benefits, see Kamali, "Fundamental Rights."
71. This fact—namely, our wish "to contrast what a man deserves with what others are justified in giving him or obligated to give him"—is taken by Laurence Stern to be a central aspect of our concept of desert that is "common to all of the uses which we do make or might be tempted to make of the term." See his "Deserved Punishment, Deserved Harm, Deserved Blame," *Philosophy* 45 (1970): 317–29.
72. Reinhart, *Before Revelation,* 154.
73. These scholars would include Hourani, Peters (*God's Created Speech*), Frank (e.g., "Moral Obligation"), Heemskerk (*Suffering in the Mu'tazilite Theology*), Marmura ("A Medieval Islamic Argument"), Gimaret ("Impulsion," *Théories*), Gardet (*Dieu et la destinée de l'homme,* 297), Chamberlain (*Knowledge and Social Practice,* 79-n47, it is translated as "merit," though in the context of the usage with which he is concerned, *istiḥqāq* is rendered more often as "suitability," "adequacy," or "eligibility," themselves evaluative terms [see 64]), and so on. Most of these scholars simply use this translation without comment.
74. Reinhart, *Before Revelation,* 154–55; cf. 'Abd al-Jabbār, *Luṭf,* 345. It is perhaps peculiar in light of his view that Reinhart still renders *istiḥqāq* as desert in the passages he translates. Perhaps he intends the term to be understood under a different meaning—but that would be to enjoy without warrant the benefits of a sensible-sounding translation, sidestepping the problems that arise once the English term is substituted by one closer to the meaning he suggests.
75. Makdisi, *The Rise of Colleges,* 62, in the context of his discussion of the principles of charitable endowments (*awqāf*).
76. Frank's own rendition of the term *istaḥaqqa* (*Beings and Their Attributes,* index of Arabic terms) should have been instructive: "'to deserve,' i.e., *appropriately* or *necessarily* to be *such* as to have [a given perfection or state of being]."

CHAPTER 4
The Baṣran Muʿtazilite Approach to Desert

1. James P. Sterba offers a definition of this kind in "Justice and the Concept of Desert," *Personalist* 57 (1976): 188–97. Cf. Joel Feinberg, "Justice and Personal Desert," in *Doing and Deserving* (Princeton, 1970), 56: "To say that a person deserves something is to say that there is a certain sort of propriety in his having it."
2. See, for example, John Kleinig, "The Concept of Desert," *American Philosophical Quarterly* 8 (1971): 76.
3. Steven Sverdlik, "The Nature of Desert," *Southern Journal of Philosophy* 21 (1983): 586. Cf. Ted Honderich's related remark in *Punishment: The Supposed Justifications* (Cambridge, 1989), 26: "Any desert claim that reduces to the assertion that it is obligatory or permissible to impose a penalty cannot, of course, be offered as a reason for the proposition in dispute, that it is obligatory or permissible to impose the penalty. This is a simple fallacy where the supposed reason is identical with the supposed conclusion."
4. The distinction is drawn in this context in Sterba, "Justice and the Concept of Desert," 189. Thus, for example, the claim that heaven will be "boring"—a claim whose spirit is echoed by Bernard Williams in "The Makropulos Case: Reflections on the Tedium of Immortality" (in *The Metaphysics of Death*, ed. J. M. Fischer [Stanford, 1993]), 73–92, where he discusses the idea of eternal life and commends death as a happy escape from a predicted eternal life of ennui—involves the assumption of certain unpleasant facts about these possible objects of desert.
5. See the definitions of obligation in Ghazālī, *al-Mustaṣfā min ʿilm al-uṣūl,* ed. Ibrāhīm Muḥammad Ramaḍān (Beirut, [1994]), 1:69–73; Abū ʿAbd Allāh al-Iṣfahānī, *Al-Kāshif ʿan al-maḥṣūl fī ʿilm al-uṣūl,* ed. ʿĀdil Aḥmad ʿAbd al-Mawjūd and ʿAlī Muḥammad Muʿawwaḍ (Beirut, 1998), 1:237–44; Sayf al-Dīn al-Āmidī, *al-Iḥkām fī uṣūl al-aḥkām,* Sayyid al-Jumaylī (Beirut, 1984), 1:138–39 (whence the first quotation). For all their divergence from Muʿtazilite positions, these definitions are striking in their terminological and conceptual similarity to those of their Muʿtazilite peers. The legal and the theological were indeed closely intertwined. The quotation from Bāqillānī is from *Kitāb al-Tamhīd,* ed. R. J. McCarthy (Beirut, 1957), 251; cf. his *Kitāb al-Inṣāf fīmā yajibu iʿtiqāduhu wa-lā yajūzu al-jahl bihi,* ed. ʿIzzat al-ʿAṭṭār al-Ḥusaynī (Cairo, 1950), 43.
6. ʿAbd al-Jabbār, *Sharʿiyyāt,* 96. The word *tabiʿa* is a good correspondence for my "moral consequences" (it appears on several of the pages that follow: e.g., 97, 98).
7. For the *luṭf* connection, see Ibn Mattawayh, *Muḥīṭ,* 18, 19. Cf. *Majmūʿ*, 3: 178–79, 299; Mānkdīm, *Sharḥ,* 620; ʿAbd al-Jabbār, *Taʿdīl,* 187.
8. *Sharḥ,* 495. The Baṣran Muʿtazilites frustrate their students by perpetrating a strategic equivocation in this particular point through the disjunctive formula that they often use in referring to the motives one ought to act from. One ought to perform an obligatory act, they say, "*li-wujūbihi* ***aw****-wajh wujūbihi*" ("because it is obligatory or because of the ground that makes it obligatory"; e.g., Ibn Mattawayh, *Majmūʿ*, 3:195, 307). But this seems to be the difference between returning a deposit *because it constitutes a return of a deposit,* and returning a deposit *because one will deserve praise and reward for doing so* (which,

as we will see, obligation reduces to)—that is to say, it is the difference between acting for the sake of duty (to use a different expression) and for the sake of one's welfare.

9. ʿAbd al-Jabbār, *Taklīf,* 515.
10. For definitions of the concepts, see Abu'l-Ḥusayn al-Baṣrī, *Kitāb al-Muʿtamad fī uṣūl al-fiqh,* ed. Muḥammad Ḥamīd Allāh (Damascus, 1964), 1:363ff.; ʿAbd al-Jabbār, *Taʿdīl,* 7ff.; Zamakhsharī, *A Muʿtazilite Creed,* 59; Ibn Mattawayh, *Muḥīṭ,* 232ff.
11. ʿAbd al-Jabbār, *al-Aṣlaḥ,* 7, and *Taʿdīl,* 18.
12. *Taʿdīl,* 25; cf. 43: "*tasmiyyat ahl al-lugha mā ṣifatuhu mā dhakarnāhu bi-annahu wājib,*" and so on. The *ahl al-lugha* can be interpreted either in terms of the philologists of the Arabic language or the Arabs who provide these philologists with the canon of authoritative linguistic usage in their capacity as master speakers of the language. Cf. Hourani, *Islamic Rationalism,* 27–29.
13. Ibn Mattawayh, *Muḥīṭ,* 306. This is a topic that would take us out of our remit to go in to; for a discussion of some of the issues raised here in connection with the Baṣrans' view of language, see my "'Their Intention Was Shown by Their Bodily Movements': The Baṣran Muʿtazilites on the Institution of Language," *in the Age of al-Fārābī: Arabic Thought in the 4th–10th Century,* ed. P. Adamson (forthcoming).
14. ʿAbd al-Jabbār, *al-Aṣlaḥ,* 21. For the distinction between the two types of disagreements, see ibid., 7–8, and *Taʿdīl,* 18–30.
15. A further condition for the desert of *reward* in particular was said to be the hardship involved in performing an act that was obligatory or avoiding an act that was evil (e.g., Ibn Mattawayh, *Majmūʿ,* 3:303). Yet strictly speaking, this is not an extra condition but something intrinsic to the character of these acts (or more precisely, to *our* character as agents of these acts). I'll be discussing this condition in the next section, in connection with the justification of reward or punishment. Yet another condition has already been explored in chapter 2 as the impossibility of deserving something that cannot be received. For discussion of the conditions of desert, see, for example, ʿAbd al-Jabbār, *Taklīf,* 501–2, 511–16; Ibn Mattawayh, *Majmūʿ,* 3:301–12; Mānkdīm, *Sharḥ,* 612–14; Zamakhsharī, *A Muʿtazilite Creed,* 73–74. As to compulsion (or constraint: *iljāʾ*), a succinct definition is found in *Taʿdīl,* 13: "One is compelled to performance of an act either because it involves benefit for him and no [offsetting] harm, or because he thereby escapes from a great harm—whether this harm is known or believed to be the case—or because he knows that, were he to attempt not to do it, he would be prevented." For a fuller characterization, see Gimaret, "Impulsion."
16. ʿAbd al-Jabbār, *Taʿdīl,* 188; cf. Hourani, *Islamic Rationalism,* 82: "Motives are defined entirely as intellectual states."
17. This condition is mentioned briefly in Ibn Mattawayh, *Majmūʿ,* 3:304; it will be discussed again in "The Causal Efficacy of Moral Values."
18. ʿAbd al-Jabbār, *Taʿdīl,* 26. "Under a certain description": or, "in a certain way"; the reference here is to the conditions required for the realization of desert.
19. Cf. *Taʿdīl,* 19: "Blame is deserved [for an evil act] if it is performed by those capable of guarding against it; as for those who are not, they cannot deserve blame for it, yet it does not cease to be an act for which blame is deserved under certain conditions." References to acts as *madkhal* and *taʾthīr* abound, but see, for example, Zamakhsharī (who employs the former; *A Muʿtazilite Creed,*

59); Abu'l-Ḥusayn al-Baṣrī (who employs both; *Mu'tamad,* 1:364ff.); Ibn Mattawayh (who uses the former; *Muḥīṭ,* 233); 'Abd al-Jabbār (likewise; *al-Aṣlaḥ,* 7).

20. Ibn Mattawayh, *Muḥīṭ,* 232: "*lā ḥukma lahu . . . wa-in wuṣifa bi-annahu ḥasan aw-qabīḥ.*" This was a point of dispute among the Baṣrans, and both Jubbā'īs disagreed with the view reported above. Even those who accepted this view drew a distinction between acts whose value depends on a particular intention and those whose value depends on their consequences regardless of intention. For an outline of the dispute, see Heemskerk, *Suffering in the Mu'tazilite Theology,* 118–19.
21. There is, though, a distinction drawn by the Baṣrans between two types of blame, only one of which is considered to be the counterpart of punishment (*al-jārī majrā al-'iqāb*). This will be discussed shortly.
22. Mānkdīm, *Sharḥ,* 611–12, 698–700; Ibn Mattawayh, *Majmū',* 3:305–6, 339–40.
23. Mānkdīm, *Sharḥ,* 699. The distinction between dispraise and blame as denoting different kinds of objects is J. J. C. Smart's ("Free-will, Praise, and Blame," *Mind* 70 [1961]: 303–4), and it may be seen as a useful one.
24. *Istikhfāf, ihāna*: see, for example, Ibn Mattawayh, *Muḥīṭ,* 14; Mānkdīm, *Sharḥ,* 698–99. In another passage, 'Abd al-Jabbār associates desert of blame with a license to curse the person (*al-Mughnī, XII: al-Naẓar wa'l-ma'ārif,* ed. Ibrāhīm Madkūr [Cairo, n.d.], 473), and cf. Ibn Mattawayh, *Majmū',* 3:367—a remark made more interesting if read against the practice of public cursing in which the rivalry between conflicting theological and legal schools often expressed itself.
25. See, for instance, Heemskerk, *Suffering in the Mu'tazilite Theology,* 176, 182, in connection with the compensation owed for verbal insults and slander. Note that there were tendencies to interpret the notion of *qadhf* widely, construing any assault against a person's honor as an instance of it. See, for example, Ibn Mufliḥ, *al-Ādāb al-shar'iyya,* 1:73–74; "Every transgression against a person's honor—be it the spread of veracious rumors or mendacious claims—falls under the category of *qadhf.*"
26. Murtaḍā al-Zabīdī, *Tāj al-'arūs min jawāhir al-Qāmūs,* ed. 'Alī Shīrī (Beirut, 1994), 10:81–82; cf. Edward W. Lane, *An Arabic-English Lexicon* (Beirut, 1968), 5:2008.
27. See Bishr Farès, "'Irḍ," *EI²*, 4:77–78.
28. Thus, given the main focus of this study on the desert arising from moral actions, compensation will not be receiving much attention. For details, see Heemskerk, *Suffering in the Mu'tazilite Theology.* For reward and punishment, see the above references in the previous notes. For a more concerted discussion of the nature of honor and dishonor that they involve, see also Ibn Mattawayh, *Majmū',* 3:352–59, 376–81.
29. Ibn Mattawayh, *Majmū',* 3:357.
30. This stance on punishment ties in with the Baghdadi position on the question of *al-aṣlaḥ* (the optimal or most beneficial), already adumbrated above, where they held that God is obliged to do the best for human beings in what pertains to both worldly matters and matters of religion—a position, rejected by the Baṣrans, that assumed that provision of benefit is a ground of obligation.
31. See Mānkdīm, *Sharḥ,* 617–19, 642–47. For a concise exposition, cf. Zamakhsharī, *A Mu'tazilite Creed,* 73–76.

32. Ibn Mattawayh, *Majmūʿ*, 3:303.
33. ʿAbd al-Jabbār, *Makhlūq*, 175. The grounds for reward and the integral role of *mashaqqa/kulfa* in desert are discussed widely by Muʿtazilites. See, for example, Mānkdīm, *Sharḥ*, 613–19; Ibn Mattawayh, *Muḥīṭ*, 11–15 (as well as the vicinity of the above-quoted remark in *Majmūʿ*, vol. 3); ʿAbd al-Jabbār, *Taklīf*, e.g., 509, 515. It is worth noting, however, that the principles that hold for the desert of praise and blame differ in certain respects from those that obtain for reward and punishment. One such difference is that hardship is a condition for the desert of reward, but not for the desert of praise (as pointed out in Gimaret, "Impulsion," 61n42); were it a condition, God could not deserve praise for His acts.
34. The second quote is from ʿAbd al-Jabbār, *Taʿdīl*, 98 (cf. Ibn Mattawayh, *Majmūʿ*, 3:309). The first quote is from ʿAbd al-Jabbār, *Luṭf*, 295–96, and is situated in an interesting discussion of the whimsical-sounding question, "Is punishment harm?" But the question is not a preposterous one, for harm is specified as obtaining when *in the overall balance of pain and pleasure*, pain preponderates (see ibid., 295). Thus the question—one of great relevance for the issue under discussion here—is whether the pain suffered in punishment might be outweighed by the pleasure one took in the acts that made one deserve punishment, so that the pleasures might be seen as a sort of "advance payment" (*ka'l-ujra al-mutaqaddima*). This is denied not just because the pains of punishment are so great that no amount of advance pleasure could possibly balance them out but also for the reason indicated in the passage quoted.
35. Heemskerk, *Suffering in the Muʿtazilite Theology*, 178; for the account on which most of this section draws, see 142ff.
36. Ibid., 178–79. Cf. Mānkdīm, *Sharḥ*, 505.
37. ʿAbd al-Jabbār, *Luṭf*, 473.
38. Heemskerk, *Suffering in the Muʿtazilite Theology*, 162–63. ʿAbd al-Jabbār, *Luṭf*, 558. The separation of punishment from compensation finds resonance with contemporary retributivist attitudes, as in Alan H. Goldman's statement that "punishment justly imposed is distinct from compensation owed to victims" ("The Paradox of Punishment," in *Punishment*, ed. A. J. Simmons et al. [Princeton, 1995], 35).
39. Ibn Mattawayh, *Majmūʿ*, 3:343; cf. Mānkdīm, *Sharḥ*, 619–21.
40. ʿAlī ibn Muḥammad al-Jurjānī, *Sharḥ al-mawāqif li'l-Qāḍī ʿAḍud al-Dīn ʿAbd al-Raḥmān al-Ījī*, ed. Maḥmūd ʿAmr al-Dimyāṭī [Beirut, 1998], 8:331): *ẓann al-wafāʾ bi'l-waʿīd fīhi min al-zajr wa'l-radʿ mā lā yakhfā*. Mānkdīm makes a remark that attempts to meet this problem (*Sharḥ*, 621), but unpersuasively.
41. Ibn Mattawayh, *Majmūʿ*, 3:345; for the other arguments, see 344–48. Note that Abū ʿAlī appears to have disagreed with this identification of the right holder of punishment. The same fundamental assumption is carried in Ibn Mattawayh's remark that one cannot deserve anything from oneself, and that desert "must be affirmed of someone other than the agent, so that the one who deserves should be other than the one from whom desert is due" (ibid., 299). One necessarily deserves something *from someone*.
42. This section draws chiefly on ʿAbd al-Jabbār, *al-Aṣlaḥ*, 311ff.
43. See, for instance, the summary in ibid., 334, to be read in its larger context.
44. Examples of intransitive evil are mentioned in ibid., 435–36; examples of offenses are given in ibid., 312ff.

45. Ibid., 316. Ibn Mattawayh mentions the distinction in *Majmūʿ* 3:409, and it is to be understood in ibid., 191–92.
46. This second level of blame is referred to as "the blame that is good for the rest of rational beings [to direct to the offender]" in *al-Aṣlaḥ*, 316. The term *ʿuqalāʾ* should be taken to refer not to all human beings but to those who have reached intellectual maturity and come to know the fundamentals of moral truth (unlike, for example, minors and the insane). "Rational beings" should be understood as an abbreviation of this lengthier denotation.
47. Ibn Mattawayh, *Majmūʿ*, 3:307 (reading *naffara* for [the typographic mistake] *naqqara*), 309. Cf. ʿAbd al-Jabbār, *Taklīf*, 484–85.
48. The quotes are from Ibn Fūrak, *Mujarrad maqālāt*, 163. And just as reward was an instance of *ibtidāʾ faḍl*, punishment was one of *ibtidāʾ ʿadl*.
49. Mānkdīm, *Sharḥ*, 645. Cf. Ibn Mattawayh, *Majmūʿ*, 3:357.
50. Mānkdīm, *Sharḥ*, 644. Cf. Ibn Mattawayh's discussion in *Majmūʿ*, 3:411–13.
51. This is a rather problematic point, for reasons that led me to the opposite conclusion in my "Equal before the Law"; revelation is only an indicant (*dalīl*, *dalāla*) of objective moral truths, and according to ʿAbd al-Jabbār's frequent affirmations, what is deserved does not become so by virtue of statements promising or threatening to respond to actions with particular treatments (e.g., with respect to reward, it is said that "*min ḥaqq al-thawāb an yakūna mustaḥaqqan wa-biʾl-khabar lā yadkhulu fī hādhihi al-ṣifa*"; *al-Aṣlaḥ*, 265). Yet clearly this principle is qualified—however problematic this move may be—by the logic of "private claims" by which God would have had a right to pardon punishment (though not to waive reward), were it not for the threat.
52. For this distinction, see Ibn Mattawayh, *Majmūʿ*, 2:310–11. Jurjānī's point is equally much Ījī's, on whose lines he is commenting. See *Sharḥ al-mawāqif*, 8:331.
53. For more detail on this point, see my "Equal before the Law."
54. What may not be evident in the assignment of the same moral value of *ḥusn* to both the remission and exaction is the fact that the former would in fact constitute an act of *beneficence* and not a *plain* good act. This point is touched on in the main text in what follows. ʿAbd al-Jabbār's list of the *wujūh al-muḥassanāt* in *Taʿdīl* (73) does not mention the remission of claims, only their exaction (desert is given as a ground). For a rather different discussion of the category of *ḥusn*, see also Hourani, *Islamic Rationalism*, 110–12. A significant omission on the part of Hourani—who expressed a certain, and justifiable, puzzlement over the nature and grounds of this category—is the exclusion of deontological grounds such as the ones mentioned above that pertain to rights/claims and desert; this omission led him to (mis)diagnose the contents of this category as mainly consisting of acts beneficial to their agents.
55. ʿAbd al-Jabbār, *Taʿdīl*, 122.
56. For all the above, see Ibn Mattawayh, *Muḥīṭ*, 239–40; ʿAbd al-Jabbār, *Taʿdīl*, 70ff.
57. ʿAbd al-Jabbār, *Taʿdīl*, 11, and *al-Aṣlaḥ*, 17–18. ʿAbd al-Jabbār's ambivalence will emerge again in the main text below. The distance between Ibn Mattawayh's view and ʿAbd al-Jabbār's seems to depend on how one construes the two elements mentioned by the latter as requisites for *ḥusn:* one of them is the negation of evil grounds (as in Ibn Mattawayh), while the other is that the act must have a further quality or state (*ḥāl zāʾida*) that brings the act out of the basic qualities of mere existence or nonexistence, and as one might say, into the

realm of value (e.g., *Ta'dīl*, 59). Is this quality the same as the *gharaḍ* spoken of by his later colleague? That it is so, is suggested by a passage in 'Abd al-Jabbār, *Luṭf*, 317, where *gharaḍ* is the term employed; and here his allegiance to the revised conception is clearly stated (316–17).

58. The use of *wujūh* can thus be confusing, as it might be taken either as a sign of inconsistency or an expression of support for the Jubbā'īs' conception of *ḥusn*. But one must assume that the term is nontechnical when it is used by an author who has gained the reader's trust by his overall clarity, and one feels he can place such trust in Ibn Mattawayh, who while denying *wujūh al-ḥusn*, nonetheless employs the term himself in certain contexts; see, for example, *Muḥīṭ*, 262, speaking of the "*wajh ḥusn*" of permissible acts.
59. The coextensiveness of the two terms is suggested in, for instance, Mānkdīm, *Sharḥ*, 327; 'Abd al-Jabbār, *Ta'dīl*, 7. But this is not uniformly sustained across all Mu'tazilites or even in the work of individual thinkers. For example, Ibn Mattawayh speaks of the *mubāḥ* as being a *type* of *ḥasan: Muḥīṭ*, 233; cf. the implication of *Ta'dīl*, 31: "*ammā al-mubāḥ, fa-huwa kulluhu ḥasan*." As concerns the semantic charges of *mubāḥ*: the condition that a person has been informed of the act's value is mentioned in *Sharḥ*, 327; *Ta'dīl*, 31. *Muḥīṭ*, 243–44; (most clearly) Baṣrī, *Mu'tamad*, 1: 366. Ibn Mattawayh's further specification is in *Muḥīṭ*, 262; yet 'Abd al-Jabbār's definition in *Shar'iyyāt*, 146, seems to speak directly against it by including self-regarding benefits.
60. On the consensus, see, for example, Mānkdīm, *Sharḥ*, 327; 'Abd al-Jabbār, *Ta'dīl*, 15; Ibn Mattawayh, *Muḥīṭ*, 243–44.
61. 'Abd al-Jabbār, *Ta'dīl*, 31; for the second point, 34. It is unclear whether 'Abd al-Jabbār here felt compelled to acknowledge an entailment of his definition (which would then make it right to speak of a *problem* in the definition); but the case of punishment certainly makes it difficult for him to support his claim (ibid., just above the passage on *ibāḥa*) that all of God's acts are not just *ḥasana* but indeed will always have a quality above mere goodness, and will only consist either of self-imposed obligations or beneficence.
62. Ibn Mattawayh, *Muḥīṭ*, 234.
63. An in-depth discussion of pain can be found in 'Abd al-Jabbār's *al-Luṭf*; the grounds of the goodness of pain are treated in concentration from 316ff. See also Mānkdīm, *Sharḥ*, 483ff.
64. 'Abd al-Jabbār, *al-Aṣlaḥ*, 242–43.
65. Though I speak of a "wrongdoer," this policy is more for the purposes of abbreviation, and should not obscure the differences dividing Abū Hāshim and Abū 'Alī concerning whether being a "doer" must be the ground of the goodness of blame, as already mentioned.
66. 'Abd al-Jabbār, *Luṭf*, 344. Note here that the translation for this passage given by Reinhart in *Before Revelation* is unsound, reversing the subject-object relations expressed in the text. Referring us to this passage, he writes that "according to the Baṣrans, instinctively one is offended, filled with pain, and one's mind is affected by the detestable thing in such a way that harm is seen as deserved for the blameworthy and detestable act" (153). The reaction is here presented as belonging to the one who is confronted by evil acts ("detestable" being his choice of term for the translation of *qabīḥ*); but in fact, the passage speaks of the pain experienced by one *committing* evil acts when one is subjected to blame, and not by the one *blaming* the committing agent.

67. ʿAbd al-Jabbār, *Taʿdīl*, 66 (*idhā ʿulima kawnuhu mustaḥaqqan aw-muʾaddiyan ilā nafʿ aw-dafʿ ḍarar*).
68. ʿAbd al-Jabbār, *Luṭf*, 317; cf. *Taʿdīl*, 72, 90.
69. Ibid., 48; *yaḥsunu* is meant to qualify both the benefit and harm, as is obvious from the text that follows.
70. Mānkdīm, *Sharḥ*, 301; cf. 132. The term *inṣāf*, which appears here and there, though not too frequently, would seem to correspond to the second half of this definition—that is to say, to the rendering of another's right (*qaḍāʾ/tawfīr al-ḥaqq*). Thus reward is a matter of *inṣāf*; ʿAbd al-Jabbār, *Taklīf*, 531. (Analogously, the notion of *intiṣāf* refers to a person's exaction of the claims that individuals have on others on their behalf; this is the ground of obligation for God's mediating in the distribution of compensation owed by one person to another. See, for example, ʿAbd al-Jabbār, *Luṭf*, 526–27.)
71. See chapter 2, "Approaches to the Study of Muʿtazilite Ethics" section.
72. In Hourani's statement of Muʿtazilite objectivism: "By 'objective' is meant that there are real qualities or relations of acts that make them right, so that statements about the rightness of acts are true if the required qualities or relations are present and false if they are absent, independently of the opinions or desires of the person who judges them right or wrong" (*Reason and Tradition*, 23).
73. Ibn Mattawayh, *Muḥīṭ*, 239.
74. ʿAbd al-Jabbār, *Taʿdīl*, 122; see also the formulations in ibid., 123.
75. ʿAbd al-Jabbār, *Taklīf*, 529–30.
76. ʿAbd al-Jabbār, *Makhlūq*, 169.
77. The remark comes from ʿAbd al-Jabbār, *al-Mughnī, VII: Khalq al-Qurʾān*, ed. Ibrāhīm al-Ibyārī (Cairo, 1961), 21. See Richard M. Frank, "*Al-Maʾnà:* Some Reflections on the Technical Meanings of the Term in the Kalâm and Its Use in the Physics of Muʾammar," *Journal of the American Oriental Society* 87 (1967): 251; For an explication of the term *sabab*, cf. Peters, *God's Created Speech*, 208–9, index.
78. Ibn Mattawayh, *Majmūʿ*, 3:382.
79. ʿAbd al-Jabbār, *Taklīf*, 507. Note, however, that Abū Hāshim goes on record with a view that utilizes the language of *ījāb*, and asserts a necessary causal nexus between the moral quality of an act and the desert it engenders. ʿAbd al-Jabbār, *Taʿdīl*, 122: "Were we to deem it possible that an evil act might be committed [adopting the reading of *yaqaʿa* instead of *yaqbuḥa*] by an agent who knows it is evil and yet that he might not deserve blame for it, this would lead to his never deserving blame . . . because what *necessitated* his desert would be present but desert would be absent." Abū Hāshim's adoption of such a view (one that would have to meet with disapprobation on ʿAbd al-Jabbār's part) may have to do with the fact that for him, the distinction between an act's being wrong and the agent's deserving blame is much narrower, owing to his exclusion of the acts of those who do not satisfy conditions of responsibility (minors, etc.) from the realm of value. ʿAbd al-Jabbār, by contrast, would hold that (many of) the acts of minors have moral value and yet do not engender desert, and so for him the distinction between these two things is much wider.
80. The same conflation seems to be carried out in ibid., 26, where in explaining that his definition of evil covers venial or minor sins (*ṣaghāʾir*) as well, ʿAbd al-Jabbār says, "Venial evil acts are included in the definition, because it is only due to a preventive factor that one does not deserve blame for them" (cf. 30,

217). Ibn Mattawayh seems similarly inattentive in *Majmūʿ*, 3:393, when he talks of *istiḥqāq al-ʿiqāb* as the conditioned subject, as against the punishment itself.

81. Ibn Mattawayh, *Majmūʿ*, 3:325. Abū ʿAlī held a somewhat different opinion: see ibid., 386–91; Mānkdīm, *Sharḥ*, 624ff. At the same time, it was maintained that the two types of desert could not simultaneously hold (*lam yajuz an yastaḥiqqahumā maʿan, Majmūʿ*, 3:386), and yet also that the two deserts acted on one another (*azāla aḥadu al-mustaḥaqqayni ṣāḥibahu*, 388) and that both are existent (*mawjūdayni, ḥāṣilayni*). The precise details of this metaphysical operation would clearly challenge the sharpest minds.
82. The above passage raises other interesting issues that will be discussed in connection to my next question, which will occupy the next chapter ("Why does desert endure through time?").
83. ʿAbd al-Jabbār, *Taklīf*, 522–23. And the distinction between one's not receiving, rather than not deserving, blame seems to be set out clearly in ʿAbd al-Jabbār, *al-Aṣlaḥ*, 175, where he contrasts *taqarrur al-istiḥqāq* with *aṣl al-istiḥqāq*; I take the former to refer to the actualization of deserts, and the latter to deserts themselves. See also ibid., 174.
84. Ibn Mattawayh, *Majmūʿ*, 3:320.
85. Ibid., 358; see also the discussion in ibid., 363–69.
86. This stage seems to be rejected outright just after the passage cited. Note that there is a slight question as to whether ʿAbd al-Jabbār meant to disagree with the model when talking of desert as transpiring "*after* the time of the act" (*baʿda ḥāl al-ṭāʿa*—specifically an act of obedience); *Taklīf*, 522. The loss of the relevant volumes of the *Mughnī* makes it harder to answer such questions, but in any event, the area of agreement—namely, that desert "exists" for some time before it is actualized by deserved actions—is more important than the area of disagreement, if any.
87. Ibn Mattawayh, *Majmūʿ*, 3:363. Cf. 364: Desert "refers to an act whose future occurrence will be good, which would not have been good had it not been for the prior ground"—that is, the act. Thus, the theory of *iḥbāṭ* and *takfīr* is not to be understood in terms of complex metaphysical operations taking place between two entities but in terms of the evaluation of the giving of a treatment that they produce. This is evident in the passage from Mānkdīm, *Sharḥ*, 628: "When we say that the greatest [desert; *mustaḥaqq*] negates the lesser one . . . we mean nothing else but that it is not good that God carry it out on the subjects of the Law [i.e., human beings] whereas it had been formerly good to do so—we do not mean that there is a relation such as that between cause and effect."
88. Ibn Mattawayh, *Majmūʿ*, 3:364; previous quote from 369. Cf. 363: "*yushtaraṭu ḥusnu dhālika* [i.e., the deserved treatment] *fi'l-thānī bi-an lā yakūna min al-ʿabd mā yuḥbiṭu wa-yukaffiru*."
89. One thing that is not entirely clear to me is whether the proposed explanation would account *only* for negative deserts and not for positive ones, which are qualified as obligatory. This again may be a matter for future generations of Muʿtazilite prodigies to solve.
90. ʿAbd al-Jabbār, *al-Aṣlaḥ*, 186. This is also noted by Peters, who observes (apropos a view of Hourani's that will be discussed shortly) that the "goodness of . . ." is used instead of "deserves . . ." in ʿAbd al-Jabbār's inventory of objects apprehended by the human intellect; *God's Created Speech*, 86n260.

91. ʿAbd al-Jabbār, *al-Aṣlaḥ,* 313. The *wajh* of the goodness of blame, within the context of the aims of this book, is discussed in concentration in ibid., 235ff. While generally it is the goodness of blame that is made the object of necessary knowledge, this is not an exceptionless rule. Such exceptions include the passage in *Luṭf,* 346, where what is described as the principle "established in reason" is that "blame is such [*min ḥaqq al-dhamm*] as to be [given] for evil acts and offenses as their equivalent [*muqābil*], in such a way as to be requital [*jazāʾ*] for them, and that praise is such as to be rendered as the equivalent for doing good in the same manner." (Hourani translates: "It is characteristic of blame . . ." [*Islamic Rationalism,* 46]; Reinhart translates: "It is right that blame . . ." [*Before Revelation,* 154]). The passage in which this phrase occurs is discussed below. And there certainly are instances in which desert is made the direct object of knowledge, as in Mānkdīm, *Sharḥ,* 425: "We know that he deserves blame . . ." (*naʿlamu istiḥqāqahu liʾl-dhamm*), or *al-Aṣlaḥ,* 232: "Those who have reached intellectual maturity know that one who did not do what was obligatory deserves blame . . ." (*al-ʿuqalāʾ yaʿlamūna . . . annahu yastaḥiqqu al-dhamm . . .*).
92. See, for example, Ibn Mattawayh, *Muḥīṭ,* 239; ʿAbd al-Jabbār, *al-Aṣlaḥ,* 154.
93. ʿAbd al-Jabbār, *Taklīf,* 510.
94. ʿAbd al-Jabbār, *al-Aṣlaḥ,* 243, 256. Cf. ibid., 236, with the "illegitimate" language of causes: ***ʿillat*** *ḥusnihi kawn(u)hu ghayr fāʿil li-mā wajaba ʿalayhi.*
95. ʿAbd al-Jabbār, *al-Aṣlaḥ,* 173, 176 (reading ***ḥusn*** *dhamm al-musīʾ*), 233 (syntactic structure slightly smoothed), 312.
96. It is most noticeably in this book, and most noticeably in ʿAbd al-Jabbār's work, that one finds this idiom at its strongest. Ibn Mattawayh's discussion of the same issues in *Majmūʿ* exhibits both stylistic practices. Yet as will be clear from the main text, even the latter reduces desert into the terms of the goodness of a treatment, as attested to most strongly in a passage from *Majmūʿ,* 3:336, to be discussed shortly.
97. Hourani, *Islamic Rationalism;* cf. his later remarks in "Divine Justice," 79–80.
98. ʿAbd al-Jabbār, *Luṭf,* 346.
99. The terms employed here are far from satisfactory, and it is hard to improve on them given the ambiguities this passage is shrouded in. The contrast between implicit and explicit meaning is conveyed by the terms "*yataḍammanu fiʾl-maʿnā*" and "*yufīduhu taṣrīḥuhu.*" Hourani translates the former as "contains implicitly" versus "the analytical explanation states" (*Islamic Rationalism,* 46). Reinhart translates the pair as "includes as part of its meaning" versus "is useful as an explanation [of the full scope of the term]" (*Before Revelation,* 154). While I make a suggestion below about how this passage ought to be read overall, this particular component does not give up all of its mystery.
100. Hourani, *Islamic Rationalism,* 47.
101. This is not entirely precise: one *does* find statements worded precisely in these terms in the work of the Baṣrans. See, for example, Ibn Mattawayh, *Majmūʿ,* 3:344: "*maʿnā al-istiḥqāq ḥusn al-fiʿl li-sabab mutaqaddim.*" But here it would seem wrong to take the word *maʿnā* as carrying an intention to explain the meaning of the word—rather, what is being indicated is the evaluative force it has as a ground, even if this involves the "illegitimate" language of grounds as causes (cf. ibid., 356, talking of punishment: "*lā wajha li-ḥusnihi illā al-istiḥqāq*").

102. ʿAbd al-Jabbār, *Luṭf*, 346.

103. Cf. Feinberg: "In general, the facts which constitute the basis of a subject's desert must be facts about that subject" ("Justice and Personal Desert," 58–59).

104. Thus Aḥmad Abū Sinna, in his "Naẓariyyat al-ḥaqq," defines the term *ḥaqq* as that which is affirmed by the Law *for* a human being or God *on* another, and identifies four principles that must all be satisfied for the presence of a *ḥaqq* that include a person who bears the right and a person who bears the obligation. Abū Sinna, like Kamali, does not take enough care to distinguish between the concepts of classical Islamic law and contemporary concepts, and refers to such "modern" rights as liberty and equality; but he translates the latter into the structure of the Islamic model insofar as he construes the latter rights in terms of the obligation of other human beings to respect them (see Aḥmad Fahmī Abū Sinna, "Naẓariyyat al-ḥaqq," in *al-Fiqh al-Islāmī, asās al-tashrīʿ*, ed. Muḥammad Tawfīq ʿUwayḍa [Cairo, 1971], 175–234).

105. Ibn Mattawayh, *Majmūʿ*, 3:336: *allā tarā annahu lam tatajaddad liʾl-mustaḥiqq liʾl-dhamm ṣifa wa-lā ḥukm, wa-innamā ḥasuna min ghayrihi an yadhummahu, faʾl-waṣf yarjiʿu ilaʾl-dhamm dūna al-madhmūm.*

106. "When one has offended against another, whether by usurping his property or the like, apology does not annul the obligation to return the specific object or its equivalent [or substitute: *mithl*] whereas it annuls the blame"; ʿAbd al-Jabbār, *al-Aṣlaḥ*, 314.

107. Ibid., 316.

108. Ibid., 326. These two aspects—*ʿaql* and *ʿilm*—may be construed, respectively, as the condition that it be *possible* for one to know the offense and the condition that one *actually* know the offense.

109. Ibid., 318.

110. By way of parallel: Arthur Schopenhauer picks out the "feeling of enduring wrong" as a separate harm that contributes to the suffering caused by an unjust action, being the feeling that one has been made to endure someone else's superior strength (*On the Basis of Morality*, trans. E.F.J. Payne [Indianapolis, IN, 1995], 150). This "feeling" might be seen as corresponding to the notion of "grievance" as discussed in contemporary theories of punishment, which results from offenses and satisfaction of which is obtained by the infliction of punishment; grievances are to be understood as "feelings, not injuries" (Honderich, *Punishment*, 28 ff.).

111. ʿAbd al-Jabbār, *al-Aṣlaḥ*, 450.

112. Ibid., 326–27. More accurately, the obligation to apologize is realized not just in case the offended party actually knows of the offense and directs blame to the agent but when the agent has good reason to believe this will obtain.

113. Ibid., 327. The structure of the text is somewhat problematic; instead of "*biʾl-majrūḥ, yaẓunnu dhālika nafʿan*" read "*waʾl-majrūḥ yaẓunnu dhālika nafʿan.*" Compare another illustration of these reasons in ibid., 328.

114. Ibid., 316: Apology "only eliminates the blame that is the exclusive claim of the one against whom the offense was committed and not the blame that [the offending party] deserves for what he did insofar as it was evil—and not insofar as it was an offense." Note that there was not unanimous agreement on this point. Abū Hāshim is reported as maintaining that apology eliminates both types of blame (e.g., ibid., 339).

115. Ibid., 232–33; *Luṭf*, 301; *al-Aṣlaḥ*, 314.

116. Ibn Mattawayh, *Majmūʿ*, 3:367. The context of the remark is the dispute over the Murjiʾite position mentioned in the main text concerning the time of deserving. Here the reality of blame is taken as an indication that desert of blame—as its good-making ground—has been realized.
117. Reading *sūʾ* or *isāʾa* instead of *siwāhu*.
118. ʿAbd al-Jabbār, *al-Aṣlaḥ*, 324–25.
119. This is evident in the discussions of repentance found in the legal works referred to in the previous chapter. See especially Zarkashī, *Manthūr*, 1:413ff.; Haytamī, *Zawājir*, 2:216ff.
120. ʿAbd al-Jabbār, *al-Aṣlaḥ*, 315.
121. Norman Calder, "Sharīʿa," in *EI*[2], 9:323; italics added.
122. ʿAbd al-Jabbār, *al-Aṣlaḥ*, 240.
123. Ibn Mattawayh, *Majmūʿ*, 3:398; for the example by which he marks the distinction between types of *aḥkām*, ibid., 402. Cf. the discussion of the need for the outward expression of repentance in Haytamī, *Zawājir*, 2:221: "Inward repentance [*al-tawba fi'l-bāṭin*] . . . may take place . . . when the wrongdoing does not relate to a *ḥadd* penalty, property, or claims belonging to human beings."

CHAPTER 5
Moral Continuity and the Justification of Punishment

1. See John Locke, *An Essay concerning Human Understanding*, ed. Peter H. Nidditch (Oxford, 1975), bk. II, ch. 27; §26 makes clear the ideal character of the relevant memory. Cf. Jerrold Seigel, *The Idea of the Self* (Cambridge, 2005), 96–97. Construed as the position that "if we forget our crimes we deserve no punishment," this view has been decried as "morally repugnant" by modern philosophers such as P. Geach (quoted in Derek Parfit, *Reasons and Persons* [Oxford, 1986], 325).
2. John S. Mill, "Speech in Favour of Capital Punishment (1868)," in *Applied Ethics*, ed. P. Singer (Oxford, 1986), 98.
3. David Hume, *Enquiries concerning Human Understanding and concerning the Principles of Morals*, ed. L. A. Selby-Bigge, 3rd ed. (Oxford, 2000), 98 (and also 98ff.); second set of italics added.
4. Bob Brecher, *Getting What You Want? A Critique of Liberal Morality* (London, 1998), 10. The importance of the connection between conceptions of the self and those of the good lies at the heart of Charles Taylor's project in *Sources of the Self: The Making of Modern Identity* (Cambridge, 1992).
5. Ibn Mattawayh, *Majmūʿ*, 3:354.
6. For a more detailed exposition of this question, see chapter 6.
7. Ibn Mattawayh, *Majmūʿ*, 3:318 (and see references in chapter 4).
8. Ibn Mattawayh, *Tadhkira*, 384.
9. Ibn Mattawayh, *Muḥīṭ*, 50.
10. The phrase here is from Zamakhsharī, *A Muʿtazilite Creed*, 75; the background to this view has already been given in chapter 4, in the "Justifying Reward and Punishment" section.
11. Mānkdīm, *Sharḥ*, 667. The condition of God's goodness is suppressed but clearly implied.

12. Ibid., 667–68. The same extrapolation works for positive deserts; see, for example, ʿAbd al-Jabbār, *Luṭf,* 510: "With regard to reward, we say [that it is perpetual] on the basis [*bi-dalīl*] of the perpetuity of praise, and we have shown that the former is deserved in the same way as the latter." Cf. Ibn Mattawayh, *Majmūʿ*, 3:354–55.
13. The translation of *ḥasan* by the English *good* is not entirely satisfactory, for reasons already seen in chapter 4: good has a stronger normative value than that which the Muʿtazilites assign to *ḥasan*. The sense of the latter tends toward that of (mere) "legitimacy," lacking the protreptic tone of "it is good to help those in need." Mānkdīm, *Sharḥ,* 668.
14. For the sake of a wielder terminology, I will also be loosely translating *muḥsin* as "benefactor" and *musīʾ* as "malefactor" below. Zamakhsharī, *A Muʿtazilite Creed,* 74. Ibn Mattawayh here disappoints with the brevity of his discussion in *Majmūʿ*, 3:357.
15. The various modes of *istiḥqāq al-ṣifāt* are succinctly though not completely set out in *Muḥīṭ,* 107. For a fuller discussion, see Frank, *Beings and Attributes,* and below in the present chapter.
16. ʿAbd al-Jabbār, *Al-Mughnī, XX: Fiʾl-imāma,* ed. ʿAbd al-Ḥalīm Maḥmūd and Sulaymān Dunyā (Cairo, n.d.), 2:186. Two notes are in order here: one is that the subject of the quotation is in fact God (not my "one"), as it is taken from the remarks opening the discussion of God's act-derived attributes; but it was an essential part of the Muʿtazilite position that a univocal semantic account must be given for divine and human attributes, and that "reason and language" (*al-ʿaql waʾl-lugha*) provide the stable standard for their application (succinctly put: ibid., 188, referring to a longer discussion of language in *al-Mughnī, V: Al-Firaq ghayr al-Islāmiyya*, ed. Maḥmūd Muḥammad al-Khuḍayrī [Cairo, 1965], 160–203, esp. 179ff.); indeed, this is true even more clearly with respect to act-derived attributes than it is with essential attributes, where the grounds of metaphysical entitlement to an attribute differ between the divine and created order. The second note, connected to the first, is that since the Muʿtazilite concern was primarily with divine attributes, predicates of disvalue—such as *musīʾ*—in fact do not appear in their relevant discussions. Thus, my inclusion of *musīʾ* in this class is a speculative one, albeit one that seems justified (and it is, for example, included as the contrary of *muḥsin* in Ashʿarī's report of Abū ʿAlī's view of act-derived attributes: *Maqālāt al-Islāmiyyīn*, 1:258, 264). As for the term *muḥsin,* it appears in the discussion of act-derived attributes of *Fiʾl-imāma* (194), though it is given only passing attention as ʿAbd al-Jabbār has already discussed its meaning elsewhere, as in, for instance, *Taʿdīl,* 34, and *al-Firaq ghayr al-Islāmiyya*, 180, where the basis of predication is put clearly: "When [God] performs a beneficent action, [it is necessary] that He be qualified as 'beneficent'" (*mattā faʿala al-iḥsān [wajaba] an yūṣafa bi-annahu muḥsin*). Cf. ʿAbd al-Jabbār, *Khalq al-Qurʾān,* 58, 181. For comment on the Muʿtazilite distinction between essential and active attributes, see Michel Allard, *Le problème des attributs divins dans la doctrine d'al-Ašʿarī et de ses premiers grands disciples* (Beirut, 1965), 115–19; for the treatment of the term *muḥ sin*, see also Daniel Gimaret, *Les noms divins en Islam* (Paris, 1988), 387–89.
17. ʿAbd al-Jabbār, *Fiʾl-imāma*, 188, adding *bi-* to *dhālika.*
18. ʿAbd al-Jabbār, *al-Aṣlaḥ,* 388; cf. 345.

19. Ibid., 345. Compare ibid., 411, in connection with the application of the term *muṣirr* to those committing grave sins.
20. But for an uncertainty in the text, a passage in ibid., 409, would provide even clearer support for the idea, in making reference to the need of the person who repents to "cease . . . to be a usurper" (*an yufāriqa . . . kawnahu ghāṣiban*). But the text is not entirely convincing as it stands, due to an interpolation that divides these words ("*idhā dāma*").
21. In addition to the references given in chapter 1, see Nīsābūrī, *Masā'il,* 266ff.
22. For further detail, see the next section in this chapter.
23. ʿAbd al-Jabbār, *al-Aṣlaḥ,* 345; the "on account of the resolve" explains people's description. Cf. ibid., 411.
24. Juwaynī, *Irshād,* 321–28 (for the particular point mentioned in the main text, 325). Cf. Shahrastānī's remarks in *Nihāyat al-iqdām,* 475-76.
25. Ibn Mattawayh, *Majmūʿ,* 3:360. Among the many peculiarities of the distinction is that the operations of *iḥbāṭ* and *takfīr* between different deserts then seem to take on the mind-boggling aspect of the mathematics of multiple infinites, if all the "quanta" of desert are infinite, with some smaller and others larger.
26. Mānkdīm, *Sharḥ,* 332–34; cf. ʿAbd al-Jabbār, *al-Aṣlaḥ,* 393. Ibn Mattawayh recognizes a basic intuitive knowledge of the qualities that make some acts graver than others, but adheres to the claim that this does not entail knowledge of the distinction between major and minor sins. *Majmūʿ,* 3:415–16.
27. Ibn Mattawayh, *Majmūʿ,* 3:414. And cf. ʿAbd al-Jabbār's remarks in *Faḍl al-Iʿtizāl wa-ṭabaqāt al-Muʿtazila*, 209–11, where he addresses Ashʿarite criticisms concerning the standard of commutation determining the value of deserts, invoking the disproportion between benefits received and evils committed. This seems to be the light in which we should understand Mānkdīm's claim concerning the blame that is followed by punishment "that is only deserved for an act of disobedience [*maʿṣiyya*], and an act of disobedience consists of doing what another does not will, involving a certain kind of standing—namely, that the one who disobeys is beneath the one who is disobeyed [in status/standing]" (*Sharḥ,* 611). Mānkdīm's view would seem paradoxical in light of the Muʿtazilite insistence that the qualities of acts are not affected by the identity of their agents, but it would seem explicable if the difference in the status—that is, the identity—of the agents is understood to involve the receipt of benefits on the side of the being lesser in status, affecting the value of acts.

    More interesting than both the voluntarism of the Ashʿarites and the Muʿtazilite account of the value of acts, and better equipped to account for the commutative standard involved in the correlation of acts with their posthumous treatments, was the view that stressed the value of *intention* over the performance of external acts. In his work on legal principles that deals with the notion of intention (*niyya,* cf. *maqāṣid*: aims), al-Suyūṭī writes, "The believer dwells in paradise for eternity even though he obeyed God only for the duration of his lifetime because it is his intention that had he remained [in his earthly life] forever, he would have continued to believe, and would be requited for this by dwelling in paradise for eternity" (Jalāl al-Dīn al-Suyūṭī, *al-Ashbāh wa'l-naẓā'ir,* 26–27).
28. ʿAbd al-Jabbār, *Tanabbu'āt,* 120.
29. ʿAbd al-Jabbār, *al-Aṣlaḥ,* 374 (reading *yaḥsunu li'l-wālid* in line 10), and *Tanabbu'āt,* 49.

30. Ibn Mattawayh, *Majmū'*, 3:380, 409; cf. ibid., 412, where he says that blame is a right that belongs to both the blamer and the blamed insofar as it serves the welfare of both. This idea is echoed in Mānkdīm, *Sharḥ*, 646. Cf. 'Abd al-Jabbār's remark on the utilitarian purposes served by praise in *Taklīf*, 508.
31. A gateway to these figures is provided in Majid Fakhry, *Ethical Theories in Islam* (Leiden, 1991).
32. Aristotle, *Nicomachean Ethics*, trans. Terence Irwin (Indianapolis, IN, 1985), 1104b25, 1105a30; cf. ibid., 1114b25, talking about the virtues: "Certain actions produce them, and they cause us to do these same actions." The idea that character traits and virtues are dispositions that can be used to explain behavior is one commonly found in the tradition of virtue ethics. See, for example, MacIntyre, *After Virtue*, 149; Richard B. Brandt, "The Structure of Virtue," in *Midwest Studies in Philosophy, Volume XIII. Ethical Theory: Character and Virtue*, ed. P. French et al. (Notre Dame, 1988), 64, 64–82 (generally). But a more qualified characterization of these traits or virtues would be in terms of "multitrack" dispositions that concern patterns of emotional response, choice, and action.
33. See Alasdair MacIntyre, "How Moral Agents Became Ghosts *or* Why the History of Ethics Diverged from That of the Philosophy of Mind," *Synthese* 53 (1982): 295.
34. In qualifying knowledge as nonmoral, I am referring to the kind of classification *we* would make (knowledge is a good, but a nonmoral good), in order to sidestep a puzzle that I am unsure how to resolve: knowledge *does* possess a distinctively moral status in the Mu'tazilite scheme, though the emphasis, of course, is on knowledge conducive to salvation. Ignorance is one of the grounds of evil contained in Mu'tazilite lists (indeed it is one of the few *nontransitive* evils mentioned). But then what kind of knowledge does 'Abd al-Jabbār have in mind here? Perhaps knowledge that lacks religious utility? If so, then our qualifications and theirs might coincide at this point.
35. The expression *khiṣāl al-faḍl* occurs precisely and suggestively in this kind of context in Ibn al-Murtaḍā, *Ṭabaqāt al-Mu'tazila*, 86. Cf. Mānkdīm, *Sharḥ*, 766–67, where the term *khaṣla* is employed in the same context though not in the recognizable conjunction *khiṣāl al-faḍl*. In identifying 'Alī's merits, Mānkdīm mentions knowledge and courage. The term also appears in various places in the volume of the *Mughnī* dedicated to discussion of the imamate and the question of *tafḍīl*; see, for example, *Fi'l-imāma*, 2:119, 134, 137, though note that on 134 the scope of the term seems to be more inclusive and to contain desert-generating features as well; and for mention of 'Alī's merits, which includes knowledge and courage, see ibid., 141. In broader usage, however, the expression does not seem to have been confined to this kind of context. For example, Ibn Qayyim al-Jawziyya employs the term to convey a wide spectrum of meritorious features, ranging from knowledge and a solemn comportment, to humility and long-suffering: *'Uddat al-ṣābirīn wa-dhakhīrat al-shākirīn*, ed. Zakariyā 'Alī Yūsuf (Cairo, n.d.), 229–31.
36. 'Abd al-Jabbār, *Taklīf*, 508. The analogy is offered immediately on mention of the first two characteristics: strength and intellectual capacities; if it is meant to apply just to these and not to the ones that follow, the latter would simply be excluded without explanation. These first two features seem best poised to be considered in the analogy, being natural features of the person rather than acquired

(as knowledge and, presumably, courage) or relational ones (belonging to the house of the Prophet); still, the comparison seems designed to relate to all of the examples. Compare Ibn Mattawayh's discussion of the varieties of honoring and dishonoring, and the distinction between deserved and undeserved honor, in *Majmū'*, 3:379–81.

37. 'Abd al-Jabbār, *Luṭf*, 438; cf. Heemskerk, *Suffering in the Mu'tazilite Theology*, 173.
38. For this threefold division, see Dhanani, *The Physical Theory*, 15–16; for Dhanani's commentary, see ibid., 16ff.
39. The types of attribute excluded from the discussion are the following two: the attribute of the Essence, as Frank calls it, which signifies the attribute whereby a being is identical to itself, and the attributes whose grounds are neither essence nor an entitative accident, which are exemplified by unity (*wāḥid*), temporal origination (*muḥdath*), and so on. See Frank, *Beings and Attributes*, under the relevant chapters. The following sections draw generously on the foundations that Frank has set down.
40. Ibn Mattawayh, *Muḥīṭ*, 176.
41. Frank, "*Al-Ma'nà*," 252; for a discussion of this term, see also Heemskerk, *Suffering in the Mu'tazilite Theology*, 75–78.
42. The unity of the living substrate is discussed in the context of the debate over man in 'Abd al-Jabbār, *Taklīf*, 328–29; Ibn Mattawayh, *Majmū'*, 2: 245–46.
43. For a discussion of this theory, see Richard Frank's earlier "Abū Hāshim's Theory of 'States': Its Structure and Function," in *Actas do IV Congresso de Estudos Árabes e Islâmicos, Coimbra-Lisboa 1 a 8 de setembro de 1968* (Leiden, 1971), 85–100, and *Beings and Their Attributes, chapter 2*; Ahmed Alami, *L'ontologie modale: Étude de la théorie des modes d'Abū Hāšim al-Ğubbā'i* (Paris, 2001).
44. Frank, *Beings and Their Attributes*, 108 (a reference that must be judged in great part as an ornamental one, in light of my overall indebtedness to Frank's work).
45. This is rather summarily put: see Nīsābūrī, *Masā'il*, 243–50; cf. Frank, *Beings and Their Attributes*, 72–79.
46. Frank, *Beings and Their Attributes*, 45.
47. Ibn Mattawayh, *Muḥīṭ*, 87ff.
48. It was a strategic part of the Mu'tazilite platform on free will that the *qudra* for an action was also a *qudra* for its opposite. The object or relatum (*muta'allaq, maqdūr*) of the inhering accident of *qudra* is not determined to attach to a specific object, as the Ash'arites maintained. One can use the currency of the ability to realize either of two contraries constituting a type of act: the same ability can be used to believe or disbelieve, to move an object or keep it in rest. For a discussion of the concept, see Peters, *God's Created Speech*, 200–206; Frank, "Autonomy."
49. The case of willing seems to have been a subtle one: while the Baṣran Mu'tazilites classed it with active attributes (*ṣifāt al-af'āl*), they did not include it in act-derived attributes (*asmā' mushtaqqa*—which here are distinguished as a subcategory within the broader class of active attributes), on the ground that the basis for attributing to a person that that person is "willing" is not that they engaged in an *act* of willing (something to which we have no ready epistemic access) but that the person is in a *state* of willing (something to which the Baṣran believe we do have immediate access). See 'Abd al-Jabbār, *Fi'l-imāma*, 2: 226–

28; cf. Nīsābūrī, *Masā'il*, 352–53. But the same reasoning would apply in fact to knowledge. The more precise picture would thus seem to be the following: while indeed one performs acts of knowledge and willing (and it is necessary that they be described as acts if one is to be responsible for them and deserve praise or blame for them, as one does), nevertheless these acts are not the *ground of entitlement* for the qualities "knowing" or "willing."

50. ʿAbd al-Jabbār, *Khalq al-Qur'ān*, 53.
51. Frank, *Beings and Their Attributes*, 136; for these attributes, see ibid., 135–38. Cf. Peters, *God's Created Speech*, 209–10. And cf. Gimaret, *Théories*, 275: "La 'qualification de l'agent' . . . n'est vraiment qu'un nom, un mot. L' 'état,' en revanche, est plus qu'un mot, il a une certaine réalité." The interesting context in which this remark is made concerns the application of the term unjust (*ẓālim*) to God; like *musī'* and *muḥsin*, this too is a term that the Muʿtazilites subsume in the class of act-derived attributes, and thus does not denote a real state of the agent.
52. In light of all the above, it is unclear to me what Louis Gardet had in mind when he alluded (albeit in a tentative way) to the Muʿtazilites' conceiving of evil acts as creating in their agent something like "an intrinsic state of moral evil," a conception that would belong to the plane of nature (*Dieu et la destinée de l'homme*, 297).
53. Majid Fakhry, "The Muʿtazilite View of Man," in *Recherches d'Islamologie: Recueil d'articles offert à Georges C. Anawati et Louis Gardet par leurs collègues et amis* (Leuven, 1977), 108. While according to Fakhry this relation reached its clearest expression at the hands of ʿAbd al-Jabbār, Albert Nader had already remarked on this general phenomenon in his work on the Muʿtazilites, where he notes that "le souci moral conduisait les investigations psychologiques des mu'tazila"; "toute leur étude de l'homme est soumise au problème moral" (*Système*, 285, 281), though his perspective and characterization of this relationship of subordination is rather different from the one discussed in the main text. For a more detailed discussion of ʿAbd al-Jabbār's views on the imposition of the Law, see ʿAbd al-Karīm ʿUthmān, *Naẓariyyat al-taklīf* (Beirut, 1971).
54. Peters, *God's Created Speech*, 159; see also ibid., 159ff. Peters points out the importance of the fact that the context in which ʿAbd al-Jabbār discusses the nature of human beings is his treatise on *taklīf* (the imposition of the Law).
55. Josef van Ess, "The Logical Structure of Islamic Theology," in *Logic in Classical Islamic Culture*, ed. G. E. von Grunebaum (Wiesbaden, 1970), 37–38 (the context is his discussion of definition in *kalām* and the ways in which it differs from Aristotelian definition); Frank, *The Metaphysics of Created Being*, 14–15, 35. And if the Muʿtazilite view of the person was thus fragmented, it was a fortiori even more so in the Ashʿarite account, as Frank makes plain in his "Currents and Counter-currents," in *Islam: Essays on Scripture, Thought, and Society: A Festschrift in Honour of Anthony H. Johns*, ed. P. G. Riddell and T. Street (Leiden, 1997), 123.
56. And cf. van Ess, "Mu'tazilah," 227: "Continuity was a factor that never came first in this model. . . . With respect to human existence, this lack of continuity comes to the fore in the Mu'tazili concept of person." Van Ess observes that life itself in the Muʿtazilite scheme is "only an 'accident,' a quality added to the conglomerate of atoms which form the body," which "God adds . . . to the atoms that form [human beings] when God creates them; God withdraws this

accident when he makes them die; and adds it again when he resurrects them." As the handmaiden of divine power, the Mu'tazilites' atomism engenders an emphasis on dependence and transience that is reflected in the fragmented view of the person.

57. For this aspect of Ash'arī's view, see Gimaret, *La doctrine d'al-Ash'arī,* 89–91. For broader discussion of Ash'arite ontology, see generally part 1 of the same work; Richard Frank, "The Aš'arite Ontology: I Primary Entities," *Arabic Sciences and Philosophy* 9 (1999): 160–61, 163–231, and "Bodies and Atoms: The Ash'arite Analysis," in *Islamic Theology and Philosophy: Studies in Honor of George F. Hourani*, ed. M. Marmura (Albany, NY, 1984), 39–53.
58. Dhanani, *The Physical Theory,* 47. Other accidents mentioned are color, taste, odor, heat and cold, humidity and dryness, and so on. For the question of the endurance of belief and knowledge, see Gimaret's references in *La doctrine d'al-Ash'arī,* 90; especially Ibn Mattawayh, *Majmū',* 2:143. This is the background to Ibn Mattawayh's passing reference, in his catalog of the accidents that endure, to some thinkers (who remain unnamed) who place knowledge in this class: *Tadhkira,* 42.
59. Toshihiko Izutsu, *The Concept of Belief in Islamic Theology* (Tokyo, 1965), 4.
60. There is no innovation involved in referring to them in this way. See, for example, Sarah Stroumsa's reference to "the title of a believer" in "The Beginnings of the Mu'tazila Reconsidered," *Jerusalem Studies in Arabic and Islam* 13 (1990): 276.
61. A useful index of the main verses around which the debate revolved can be found in Ibn Ḥazm's discussion of it, *al-Faṣl fi'l-milal wa'l-ahwā' wa'l-niḥal,* ed. 'Abd al-Raḥmān Khalīfa (Cairo, AH 1347), 4:36–48.
62. Mānkdīm, *Sharḥ,* 697–98.
63. The use of the term *istiḥqāq* for the revealed names is exemplified in ibid., 717: "[These names] should not be applied save to those who deserve them" (*lā yajūzu ijrā'uhā illā 'alā mustaḥiqqīhā*).
64. Ibn Fūrak, *Mujarrad maqālāt,* 149; cf. Bāqillānī, *Tamhīd,* 346–47.
65. 'Abd al-Jabbār, *al-Aṣlaḥ,* 301–2; Mānkdīm, *Sharḥ,* 703–4.
66. This, however, is not to say that one could operate epistemically solely on the basis of these deserts and independently of revelation. For although the Baṣran Mu'tazilites appeal to the bases of desert in a way that lends them conceptual primacy and seems to render the rubric on revealed predicates otiose, it does not in fact become so, due to an epistemological point registered in passing above: the value of an act—that is, the value of the deserts it entails—is not known by our rational faculty alone. In what seems to have been the dominant opinion among the Baṣrans, one does not distinguish what is a minor or grave sin by reason. Yet the differential values of deserts are to a great extent based on this distinction. Thus the criterion of greater or lesser punishment, which decides the attribution of a revealed name in the Mu'tazilite scheme, is formally empty: one cannot learn to apply the name by looking at the bases of desert. So how does one know? From the resources of revelation and tradition.
67. 'Abd al-Razzāq al-Sanhūrī, *Maṣādir al-ḥaqq fi'l-fiqh al-Islāmī* ([Cairo], 1954), 1:9ff.; "Dhimma," *al-Mawsū'a al-fiqhiyya* (Kuwait, 1992), 21: 274–79; Chafik Chehata, "Dhimma," *EI*², 2:231. The following discussion is largely based on these sources. It is rather vexing for the student of these legal concepts to attempt even such basic categorizations, since the sources—both classical and

modern—seem to point in a multitude of directions that are not always susceptible to a unifying interpretation. Hence my categorization here is an amalgam of the data presented in the above sources, taking the division into theoretical/substantive from Chehata, and the division into *ʿayn/dayn* from Sanhūrī.

68. Here I must seem to be riding roughshod over the distinction drawn by the author of the article in the *Mawsūʿa* between the concept of *ahliyyat al-wujūb* and *dhimma* as that between a capacity/receptivity (*qābiliyya*) and a substrate (*maḥall*) (276). The messages one gets in this piece about the meaning of *dhimma* can be rather confusing—in turn a reflection of the confusing diversity of opinion among jurists and the different functions of the concept. (I presume it is the second function that gives rise to the characterization of *dhimma* in this distinction.) Despite these complexities, our purposes permit us to keep the discussion on a level of generality that hopefully sidesteps them.

69. On the other hand, we may note that there is a similar tendency to collapse the person into their capacity as a moral being or a morally appraisable one in the case of *ʿirḍ* as well, which is defined both as a being (*nafs*) *and* those aspects of the being susceptible of praise and blame (see al-Zabīdī's definition referenced above in chapter 4). A further way of interpreting this phenomenon would be as an indication of the crucial role that moral evaluations play in constituting the concept of the person.

70. And as with harms, so with benefits: if you set up a trap before you die and an animal is caught after your death, who does the animal belong to?

71. Jalāl al-Dīn al-Suyūṭī, *al-Ḥāwī liʾl-fatāwī* ([Cairo], AH 1352), 1:109–11, with reference to the kind of repentance required for calumny or malicious slander. This discussion unfolds in the paradigm of the division between *ḥaqq Allāh* and *ḥaqq ādamī.*

72. Two of the few occasions on which ʿAbd al-Jabbār refers to *dhimma* are found in *al-Aṣlaḥ,* 454, 457; a rather unremarkable instance of its substantive legal function. A similar silence, it may be noted, seems to reign with respect to the notion of honor or *ʿirḍ,* even though it could be said to constitute the background of Muʿtazilite thinking in several ways, emerging in their arguments about the perpetuity of praise and blame, the conception of blame as a harm, and more generally the ubiquity of the not-quite-so-ideal *ʿuqalāʾ*.

73. "Dhimma," *Mawsūʿa,* 274, 276; cf. Ibn Manẓūr, *Lisān al-ʿArab* (Cairo, 1303/1886), 15:111. The relation between the terms *dhimma* and *dhamm* (blame) may furnish food for thought; in what ways can *dhimma* be regarded as a religious/legal counterpart of *ʿirḍ*?

74. Sanhūrī, *Maṣādir,* 16; cf. "Dhimma," *Mawsūʿa,* 276, where we are given the generous choice between *either* a legal *or* a natural ontology (*ṣifa ḥukmiyya* or *ṣifa ḥaqīqiyya*), but where the legal interpretation would *seem* to be made preponderant in the description of the faculty further down as a *ẓarf iʿtibārī*—the latter presumably meaning "legal" (as in "*shakhṣiyya iʿtibāriyya*").

CHAPTER 6
The Identity of Beings in Baṣran Muʿtazilite Eschatology

1. For a helpful introduction to the more descriptive aspects of the eschatological narrative, see Jane I. Smith and Yvonne Y. Haddad, *The Islamic Understanding*

of Death and Resurrection (Oxford, 2002). See also Louis Gardet, "Ḳiyāma," in *EI*², 5:235–38; Roger Arnaldez, "Maʿād," in *EI*², 5:892–94.

2. Ibn Mattawayh, *Majmūʿ*, 2:315.
3. Ibid., 310–11. Cf. ʿAbd al-Jabbār, *Taklīf*, 464–67. On the other hand, the gulf between Ashʿarites and Muʿtazilites should not be carved too deeply here. Despite the disavowal of desert on the part of the former, the late Ashʿarite al-Bājūrī (d. 1860) likewise grounds the importance of identity in the unacceptable consequence that would otherwise follow that the person compensated or punished would not be the one who had been obedient or disobedient (Gardet, *Dieu et la destinée de l'homme*, 270).
4. See Richard Frank, *Al-Ghazālī and the Ashʿarite School* (Durham, NC, 1994), 57–58. Cf. Rāzī's more analytic précis in *Arbaʿīn*, 287–88. For an overview of Islamic thinking about the soul, see also Michael Marmura, "Soul: Islamic Concepts," *Encyclopaedia of Religion* (New York, 1987), ed. M. Eliade, 13:460–65. Ghazālī's thought on the subject of the afterlife forms a particularly interesting case because of the position it occupied at the crossroads of a variety of different intellectual fields and accompanying anthropologies—the philosophical, the theological, and the mystical—and is thus especially useful for gaining a perspective on these different fields. This crossroad position, let it be said, results in a high degree of ambiguity from which Frank's above-cited passage of the *Ihyāʾ ʿulūm al-dīn* itself is not exempt. An excellent introduction to this aspect of Ghazālī's thought is Timothy Gianotti, *Al-Ghazālī's Unspeakable Doctrine of the Soul: Unveiling the Esoteric Psychology and Eschatology of the* Iḥyāʾ (Leiden, 2001). See also Michael Marmura's more local discussion in "Al-Ghazālī on Bodily Resurrection and Causality in *Tahāfut* and the *Iqtiṣād*," *Aligarh Journal of Islamic Thought* 2 (1989): 46–75.
5. For the views of Naẓẓām and Muʿammar, see Ashʿarī, *Maqālāt al-Islāmiyyīn*, 2:26–27; for Muʿammar's view of man, see Baghdādī, *Farq*, 154–55; for Naẓẓām's, see 135–36. These views are described by the Baṣrans in the context of their anthropological discussions: see Ibn Mattawayh, *Majmūʿ*, 2:241ff.; ʿAbd al-Jabbār, *Taklīf*, 309ff.
6. For the basic position on the spirit, see ʿAbd al-Jabbār, *Taklīf*, 334, 338; Ibn Mattawayh, *Majmūʿ*, 2:247. Cf. Ashʿarī's position as reported by Ibn Fūrak, briefly described in Tariq Jaffer, "Bodies, Souls, and Resurrection in Avicenna's *ar-Risāla al-Aḍḥawīya fī amr al-maʿād*', in ed. D. C. Reisman, *Before and After Avicenna* (Leiden, 2003), 167. The account of death given above is cobbled together from a mosaic of texts—most concisely, from the implication of the view that the inherence of life requires a particular structure on the part of the substrate (*binya*, which corresponds to the accident of *taʾlīf*, whose contrary is *iftirāq*). See, for example, ʿAbd al-Jabbār, *Taklīf*, 333, 338, 353, where a brief reference to the nature of death also can be found. And see also Nīsābūrī, *Masāʾil*, 235: "Separation [*tafrīq*] negates that which life needs in order to exist, and therefore negates it [i.e., life] by mediation," referring to the loss of structure, as is plainer in the discussion that follows on 239–40.
7. Peter van Inwagen, "The Possibility of Resurrection," *International Journal for Philosophy of Religion* 9 (1978): 114–21.
8. See David B. Hershenov, "Van Inwagen, Zimmerman, and the Materialist Conception of Resurrection," *Religious Studies: An International Journal for the Philosophy of Religion* 38 (2002): 451–69, and "The Metaphysical Problem of In-

termittent Existence and the Possibility of Resurrection," *Faith and Philosophy* 20 (2003): 24–36. And see also more broadly the collection of papers in K. Corcoran, ed., *Soul, Body, and Survival* (Ithaca, NY, 2001).

9. Rāzī, *Arbaʿīn*, 288. Note that *ajzāʾ* has been elsewhere translated as "parts"; in the terms of *kalām* atomism, there is no inconsistency in this, as a person's parts consist of atoms.
10. Ibn Mattawayh discusses these verses in *Majmūʿ*, 2:287. Cf. ʿAbd al-Jabbār, *Taklīf*, 437–41. And for the above, see also generally the discussions of the afterlife and resurrection in Rāzī, *Arbaʿīn*, 284ff.; Jurjānī, *Sharḥ al-mawāqif*, 8:316ff.; Sayf al-Dīn al-Āmidī, *Ghāyat al-marām fī ʿilm al-kalām*, ed. Ḥasan Maḥmūd ʿAbd al-Laṭīf (Cairo, 1971), 283–314; Gardet, *Dieu et la destinée de l'homme*, 259–89.
11. See Rāzī, *Arbaʿīn*, 292; see also the views expressed in *al-Tafsīr al-kabīr* (Cairo, n.d.), 21:36ff., commenting on verse 17:85 (*"yasʾalūnaka ʿan al-rūḥ . . ."*).
12. The above description is distilled from the chief Baṣran discussions of the topic: Ibn Mattawayh, in *Tadhkira*, 208ff.; and *Majmūʿ*, 2:285ff.; ʿAbd al-Jabbār, *Taklīf*, 432ff.
13. ʿAbd al-Jabbār, *Taklīf*, 467, 443. Cf. Ibn Mattawayh, *Majmūʿ*, 2:312: *"yajibu an yurāʿa fī bab al-iʿāda mā yurāʿā fī ḥāl al-tabqiya"* (cf. *Taklīf*, 467, where the Baṣran position on identity—to be immediately discussed in the main text—is spelled out: "*lā budda min an tuʿtabara ajzāʾuhu fiʾl-iʿāda kamā lā budda min iʿtibārihā fiʾl-baqāʾ*"). Note here Mānkdīm's inclusion of "the fact that Zayd is the [same] person we had seen before" in the contents of necessary knowledge: *Sharḥ*, 50.
14. ʿAbd al-Jabbār, *Taklīf*, 470, and *Khalq al-Qurʾān*, 38. See also, for example, *Taklīf*, 312; Ibn Mattawayh, *Majmūʿ*, 2:241. Cf. Frank's discussion in *Beings and Their Attributes*, 26–27. With respect to the examples of subjects referred to above, note that strictly speaking, only atomic aggregates that have been unified by accidents of life can be picked out as single entities; thus, a human being can be considered as a single subject of predications in a way in which a ball cannot.
15. ʿAbd al-Jabbār, *Taklīf*, 468. For a more comprehensive discussion of this baffling epistemological leap, see my "Subject and Body in Baṣran Muʿtazilism, or: Muʿtazilite *Kalām* and the Fear of Triviality," *Arabic Sciences and Philosophy* 17 (2007): 267–98.
16. The argument in Ibn Mattawayh, *Majmūʿ*, 2:315, makes this crisply clear.
17. Ibn Mattawayh, *Majmūʿ*, 2:313. Cf. ʿAbd al-Jabbār, *Taklīf*, 476, which is clearer in naming the totality (*jumla*) of these parts as the basis of identity. The references for the Baṣran view supplied in these notes are intended to be indicative and not exhaustive.
18. Ibn Mattawayh, *Tadhkira*, 246. The meaning of *ajzāʾ al-aṣl* is explained in e.g., *Majmūʿ*, 2:312. Cf. ʿAbd al-Jabbār, *Taklīf*, 478: "What must be re-created is the minimum [amount of parts] required for a person to be alive."
19. For more on the Baṣran speculations on cannibalism or the more innocent case of consumption by nonhuman animals, see ʿAbd al-Jabbār, *Taklīf*, 379–81; Ibn Mattawayh's brief note in *Majmūʿ*, 2:314. Cf. Rāzī, *Arbaʿīn*, 290–91; Jurjānī, *Sharḥ al-mawāqif*, 8:322–23. Cf. Avicenna's objections to the possibility of a physical resurrection in his *al-Risāla al-aḍḥawiyya fī amr al-maʿād*, ed. Sulaymān Dunyā (Cairo, 1949), 56. Naturally the above account rounds out

certain controversies that divided the Baṣrans, and especially Abū ʿAlī and Abū Hāshim, discussed most concisely in *Majmūʿ*, 2:312–16. One of the differences between the two masters was that Abū ʿAlī stipulated the re-creation of parts that went beyond this fundamental minimum. Finally, note that given the above, Deborah Black's description of the *kalām* view of personal identity as a "bundle theory" does not seem to be a sound one insofar as it applies to the Muʿtazilites (in "Psychology: Soul and intellect," in *Cambridge Companion to Arabic Philosophy*, ed. P. Adamson and R. C. Taylor [Cambridge, 2004], 308)—unsound, unless a bundle theory is understood to include any theory that denies the survival of a unified *immaterial* something, and to exclude theories that affirm the survival of a unified *material* something.

20. See Michael Marmura, "Ghazali and the Avicennan Proof from Personal Identity for an Immaterial Self," in *A Straight Path: Studies in Medieval Philosophy and Culture*, ed. J. Hackett et al. (Washington, DC, ca. 1988), 195–205, in which facts about bodily change supply a main cog to the wheelwork of Avicenna's views about identity.
21. Cf. the brief reference in *Tadhkira*, 44. For discussion of the Muʿtazilite doctrine of the nonexistent, see Richard Frank, "Al-Maʿdum wal-Mawjud: The Non-existent, The Existent, and the Possible in the Teaching of Abū Hāshim and His Followers," *Mélanges—Institut dominicain d'études orientales du Caire (MIDEO)* 14 (1980): 185–209; Robert Wisnovksy, "Avicenna and the Avicennian Tradition", in *Cambridge Companion to Arabic Philosophy*, ed. P. Adamson and R. C. Taylor, 105–6, and *Avicenna's Metaphysics in Context* (Ithaca, NY, 2003), 145ff.; Peter Adamson, "Al-Kindî and the Muʿtazila," *Arabic Sciences and Philosophy* 13 (2003): 57–66; Peters, *God's Created Speech*, 107–9; Alami, *L'ontologie modale*, 35–53.
22. ʿAbd al-Jabbār, *Taklīf*, 456.
23. Jurjānī, *Sharḥ al-mawāqif*, 8:316, 321.
24. Rāzī, *Arbaʿīn*, 285. Note, however, that the use of the term *maʿdūm* was afflicted with a strategic ambiguity in many of the discussions of *maʿād*. It was used often—though not always—indiscriminately to signify the entity whose parts are in a state of dispersion *as well as* the entity whose parts have been annihilated—uses that it is important to distinguish. For example, while in the reference just given Rāzī uses the term *maʿdūm* to refer to the case of annihilation, elsewhere—for example, 290—the term *maʿdūm* is used to cover the case of dispersion (*tafrīq*) as well; and Rāzī is not alone among our writers in perpetrating this ambiguity. Note, also, that despite the special possibilities that the doctrine of nonexistent things opened up to the Muʿtazilites for their view of resurrection, it is interesting that their fellow Ashʿarites did not deny themselves the right to make similar claims about God's knowledge of the individual's component parts during their nonexistence—claims that sound fairly surprising given their denial of the Muʿtazilite doctrine. See, for instance, Jurjānī, *Sharḥ al-mawāqif*, 8:322 ("God knows those parts . . ."); Ghazālī, *al-Iqtiṣād fi'l-iʿtiqād*, ed. I. A. Çubukçu and H. Atay (Ankara, 1962), 214.
25. Michael Marmura, "Avicenna on Primary Concepts in the *Metaphysics* of His *al-Shifa*,'" in *Logos Islamikos: Studia Islamica in Honorem Georgii Michaelis Wickens*, ed. R. M. Savory and D. A. Agius (Toronto, 1984), 220, and cf. "Soul: Islamic Concepts," 462. Wisnovsky, *Avicenna's Metaphysics*, 148; he is careful, though, to signal the fact that his account is partly a conjectural one (149). Cf.

Gardet, *Dieu et la destinée de l'homme,* 271–272, picking up on Jurjānī's remarks.

26. Avicenna, *Kitāb al-Mubāḥathāt,* in *Arisṭū 'inda al-'Arab,* ed. 'Abd al-Raḥmān Badawī (Cairo, 1947), 1:131. And cf. his remarks in *al-Shifā': al-Ilāhiyyāt,* ed. G. C. Anawati and Sa'īd Zāyed (Cairo, 1960), 1:36, to which he refers in the former work. (These passages contain the germ of several key positions one finds later *mutakallimūn* engaging with in their defense of the afterlife, and especially where the question of nonexistents turns up.) Note that Avicenna's works will appear under his Arabic name (Ibn Sīnā) in the bibliography.
27. Ghazālī, *Tahāfut al-falāsifa,* ed. M. Bouyges (Beirut, 1962), 243–44.
28. See Marmura, "Primary Concepts," 221, 235; Avicenna, *Ilāhiyyāt,* 36 ("On the basis of our understanding of these things, you may clearly perceive the falsehood of the view of one who says that nonexistents can be re-created.")
29. Ibn Mattawayh, *Majmū',* 2:287.
30. Frank, "Al-Ma'dum wal-Mawjud," 190.
31. Rāzī, *Muḥaṣṣal afkār al-mutaqaddimīn wa'l-muta'akhkhirīn min al-'ulamā' wa'l-ḥukamā' wa'l-mutakallimīn,* ed. Ṭaha 'Abd al-Ra'ūf Sa'd (Cairo, n.d.), 59. Cf. his discussion of the nonexistent in *Arba'īn,* 53–68. It must be noted, though, that Rāzī's philosophical influences make him liable to translate the Mu'tazilite conceptual apparatus into terms not altogether faithful to their idiom. That idiom could be more faithfully expressed by saying that with respect to atoms, for example, the attribute of their essence (*ṣifat al-dhāt*) precedes their attribute of existence and essential attribute(s) (*ṣifāt dhātiyya*), which is to occupy space; existence is a precondition for the realization of the latter, but given existence, they are entailed by the atom's attribute of the essence. (And further to the point made in the main text that the level of concern in this doctrine is with atomic entities, note that essential attributes are explicitly said to characterize "individual elements, and not aggregates" [*ṣifāt al-dhāt tarji'u ila'l-āḥād dūna al-jumal*]: Nīsābūrī, *Masā'il,* 238.) But as will be painfully evident from this formulation, this idiom is too involved to be adduced here without lengthy explanatory remarks, and therefore the reader is referred to Frank's more nuanced representation of the Baṣran focus in his above-cited article. As for direct Mu'tazilite texts, one of the most succulent treatments to be found is in Nīsābūrī's *Masā'il,* 37–47, where he discusses and defends the Baṣran thesis that an atom is an atom during its nonexistence.
32. This is stated plainly in Nīsābūrī, *Masā'il,* 46: "Nothing can inhere in an atom while it is nonexistent." It is also evident in 'Abd al-Jabbār's inclusion in the properties characterizing existent things "the possibility of . . . [their] inhering or constituting a substrate of inherence" in *al-Firaq ghayr al-Islāmiyya,* 232; cf. Frank, "Al-Ma'dum wal-Mawjud," 191. This is picked up by Rāzī in *Muḥaṣṣal,* 57, where he uses the claim that composition cannot be realized during nonexistence to argue against the Mu'tazilite view of nonexistents.
33. This is especially clear in a statement of Nīsābūrī's in *Masā'il,* 43, that seems to come close to our concerns: "It may be known that [something] existed before, and this knowledge would serve to distinguish it from other things. So this knowledge must necessarily attach to it [*muta'alliq bihi*]" (And cf. Frank, "Al-Ma'dum wal-Mawjud," 204.) Here of course, I have been training the focus on things under their aspect as objects of knowledge, and leaving out of focus the aspect of these objects as objects of power. This aspect, and the degree to which

the two are entwined, is stressed in ʿAbd al-Jabbār, *al-Mughnī, IV: Ruʾyat al-Bārī,* ed. Muḥammad Muṣṭafā Ḥilmī and Abuʾl-Wafāʾ al-Ghunaymī al-Taftāzānī (Cairo, 1965), 247.

34. Cf. Ibn Mattawayh's lexicographical remark on the meaning of *ʿaraḍa* in *Tadhkira,* 218–19.

35. Ibn Mattawayh, *Tadhkira,* 246. For Abū Hāshim's views, see also ibid., 245, and *Majmūʿ*, 2:312–13; Nīsābūrī, *Masāʾil,* 240–41. The role of appearance (*ṣūra*) in distinguishing *individual* human beings from another is paralleled by the role of the bodily structure usually referred to as *binya* (like *ṣūra,* also phenomenal) in distinguishing human beings from other animals. This is the topic of a much longer story, but succinctly, see ʿAbd al-Jabbār, *Taklīf,* 358–67; for discussion, see also Bernand, *Le problème de la connaissance,* 109–21.

36. Ibn Mattawayh, *Majmūʿ*, 2:313; ʿAbd al-Jabbār, *Taklīf,* 476, 467–68. The third quote appears in the context of the claim that the primary object of knowledge is the *dhāt* and not the *ṣifa*—an epistemological position that then yields an ontological claim about the criteria of identity.

37. Ibn Mattawayh, *Majmūʿ*, 2:305. Cf. *Tadhkira,* 238; see also ʿAbd al-Jabbār's discussion in *Taklīf,* 459–64. And for a discussion of the term *mubtadaʾ*, see Peters, *God's Created Speech,* 205–6.

38. See Ibn Mattawayh's catalog of generated accidents in *Tadhkira,* 37. Cf. ʿAbd al-Jabbār's passing reference to knowledge generated by inquiry in the context of his discussion of re-creation in *Taklīf,* 463.

39. Ibn Mattawayh, *Majmūʿ*, 2:306. Cf. ʿAbd al-Jabbār's remark in *Taklīf,* 454, concerning nonenduring accidents that "they cannot exist except at a single time [*fī waqt wāḥid*]," and that "it is impossible for them to exist *except in that time* [*fī ghayr dhālika al-waqt*]."

40. Indeed the remark extends to atoms, for the discussion is understood to provide conditions for the re-creation of all elements in reality; but as the re-creation of atoms was not a matter of dispute, the conditions are mainly of relevance for sifting the range of accidents.

41. Ibn Mattawayh, *Tadhkira,* 241. Cf. *Majmūʿ*, 2:306; cf. ʿAbd al-Jabbār's remarks about the particularity of *qudra* in *Taklīf,* 453–55. Cf. his remark about the time of a *maqdūr* as "elapsing": *taqaḍḍī waqti[hi]* (455).

42. Ibn Mattawayh, *Majmūʿ*, 2:306.

43. And while I have left out of the discussion the condition excluding generated accidents, it was a similarly austere conception of these accidents that was implicated in their exclusion from re-creation. See, for example, Ibn Mattawayh, *Majmūʿ*, 2:307.

44. ʿAbd al-Jabbār uses a suggestive expression here when he talks of "*taʿalluq al-qudra bi-jamīʿ mā waqaʿa bihā min qablu*" (*Taklīf,* 461).

45. Ibn Mattawayh, *Tadhkira,* 39.

46. Ibid., 41.

47. This seems to be the conclusion to be drawn from the rather convoluted passages in ʿAbd al-Jabbār's *Taklīf,* 372–73, where he comes nearest to broaching questions about the continuity of appearance. But ultimately his concern is with the structural continuity required for the inherence of life; phenomenal continuity is only part of this concern insofar as it is an indirect corollary.

48. Ibn Mattawayh, *Majmūʿ*, 2:314.

49. Ibid., 307.

50. Ibid., 313.
51. Note, however, an important difference between the two types of accident: there cannot be more than one phenomenal expression of life, whereas one can have different phenomenal appearances or forms. This means that in the case of composition, "the same *ta'līf*" (*'ayn al-ta'līf*) can be ambiguous between "the same phenomenal look," "the same accident (the same token)," *and* "the same *type* of accident." For the expression "the same life (*ḥayāt*)," only the second and third interpretative possibilities apply. With respect to composition, it is unfortunately not always obvious which interpretation the Baṣrans have in mind. It is not perfectly clear, for example, in ibid., where *ta'līf* is mentioned just before the quoted passage; but the context urges that the change in composition is understood at the metaphysical level of accidents (a change in token belonging to the same type). This is supported by *Tadhkira*, 246. Cf. 'Abd al-Jabbār, *Taklīf*, 475–76, where *'ayn al-ta'līf* must refer to the same tokens, and 473, where *ta'līf* is clearly used to refer to the metaphysical level ("*mā* ***fīhi*** *min al-ta'līf*"); the phenomenal form remains the same but the accident causing it changes.
52. 'Abd al-Jabbār, *al-Firaq ghayr al-Islāmiyya*, 167.
53. Of course, this picture is one that derives from a strict examination of the positions of the formal metaphysics developed by these Mu'tazilites and the pursuit of their consequences. At the same time, these theologians no doubt granted the vivid and concrete descriptions of the afterlife contained in the resources of the Qur'ān and the (endorsed) prophetic traditions. But as their rationalist approach to the interpretation of these resources should reveal, there were many different ways in which one might "grant" their sense, leaving plenty of leeway for interpretation.
54. Rāzī, *Arba'īn*, 286.
55. Jurjānī, *Sharḥ al-mawāqif*, 8:319 (as translated, the statement includes parts from both Ījī's text and Jurjānī's commentary); Avicenna, *al-Risāla al-aḍḥawiyya*, 51–52.
56. Jurjānī, *Sharḥ al-mawāqif*, 8:318–19 (again a patchwork of Ījī and Jurjānī).
57. Ibid., 319.
58. Ibid., 321.

APPENDIX
Translation of Mānkdīm Shashdīw, "The Promise and the Threat"

1. Mānkdīm is here referring to his introductory remarks on "the promise and the threat" in *Sharḥ*, 134–37.
2. The term here is *aḥkām*, but in many cases it is unwieldy to render the term *aḥkām* by any of the range of standard translations (such as "status," "ruling," "principle," "characteristic," "value," or the "consequence") by which I have sometimes referred to the deserts in question in the previous chapter. Thus, here I translate *aḥkām* directly as "deserts."
3. Reading *yuthību*, not *yathbutu*.
4. Therefore reading *shāqqa* as predicate instead of *al-shāqqa*.
5. In translating the term *ḥasan* ("good"), it is necessary to rehearse a point already made in the previous chapters concerning its normative force. Though unavoidable, this translation is not altogether satisfying because *ḥusn* has a

weaker normative value than the one carried by the term good in English usage. To say "it is *ḥasan* for/of someone to do *x*" will not have the force of a statement such as "it is good for someone to help those in need" (which suggests that one *should* help those in need). Its meaning is closer to that of a basic moral legitimacy, closer to the moral defense of an act than to an exhortation to perform it.

6. *Dhālika* omitted as otiose.
7. Here we jump from page 623 to 642, omitting the detailed discussion of the mutual interactions between deserts (*iḥbāṭ* and *takfīr*), and resuming with Mānkdīm's discussion of the means by which reward and punishment may be annulled.
8. The text has *isā'a kabīra*; but this must be a mistake, for the very opposite is intended: one cannot deserve blame for such a *small* offense given the magnitude of the good done.
9. In this and the next instance of the term *istibqā'* in this paragraph I read *istīfā'*. Note that "waive" and "annul" alternate as translations of the same term: *isqāṭ*.
10. Reading *mimman* instead of *man*.
11. Here we jump from page 647 to 666, passing over Mānkdīm's discussion of the scriptural evidence establishing the punishment of grave sinners.
12. Reading *lā yakhlū min* instead of *lā yakhlū immā*.
13. Omitting *dhālika*; the text is rather ungrammatical in the sentence that follows, but the meaning is clear.
14. Reading *la-istaḥaqqa* for *lā yastaḥiqqu*.

BIBLIOGRAPHY

Works in Arabic

Al-Qāḍī ʿAbd al-Jabbār Abu'l-Ḥasan al-Asadābādī. *Al-Mughnī fī abwāb al-tawḥīd wa'l-ʿadl:*

——. *IV: Ru'yat al-Bārī.* Edited by Muḥammad Muṣṭafā Ḥilmī and Abu'l-Wafā' al-Ghunaymī al-Taftāzānī. Cairo, 1965.

——. *V: Al-Firaq ghayr al-Islāmiyya.* Edited by Maḥmūd Muḥammad al-Khuḍ ayrī. Cairo, 1965.

——. *VI/1: Al-Taʿdīl wa'l-tajwīr.* Edited by Aḥmad Fu'ād al-Ahwānī. Cairo, 1962.

——. *VII: Khalq al-Qur'ān.* Edited by Ibrāhīm al-Ibyārī. Cairo, 1961.

——. *VIII: Al-Makhlūq.* Edited by Tawfīq al-Ṭawīl and Saʿīd Zāyed. Cairo, n.d.

——. *XI: Al-Taklīf.* Edited by Muḥammad ʿAlī al-Najjār and ʿAbd al-Ḥalīm al-Najjār. Cairo, 1965.

——. *XII: Al-Naẓar wa'l-maʿārif.* Edited by Ibrāhīm Madkūr. Cairo, n.d.

——. *XIII: Al-Luṭf.* Edited by Abu'l-ʿAlā' al-ʿAfīfī. Cairo, 1962.

——. *XIV: Al-Aṣlaḥ/Istiḥqāq al-dhamm/al-Tawba.* Edited by Muṣṭafā al-Saqā. Cairo, 1965.

——. *XV: al-Tanabbu'āt wa'l-muʿjizāt.* Edited by Maḥmūd al-Khuḍayrī and Maḥ mūd Muḥammad Qāsim. Cairo, 1965.

——. *XVII: al-Sharʿiyyāt.* Edited by Amīn al-Khūlī. Cairo, 1963.

——. *XX: Fi'l-imāma.* Edited by ʿAbd al-Ḥalīm Maḥmūd and Sulaymān Dunyā. 2 vols. [Cairo, n.d.].

Abū Sinna, Aḥmad Fahmī. "Naẓariyyat al-ḥaqq." In *al-Fiqh al-Islāmī, asās al-tashrīʿ*, edited by Muḥammad Tawfīq ʿUwayḍa. Cairo, 1971.

Al-Āmidī, Sayf al-Dīn. *Al-Iḥkām fī uṣūl al-aḥkām.* Edited by Sayyid al-Jumaylī. 2 vols. Beirut, 1984.

Al-Ashʿarī, Abu'l-Ḥasan. *Kitāb al-Lumaʿ fi'l-radd ʿalā ahl al-zaygh wa'l-bidaʿ.* Edited by Ḥammūda Ghurāba. [Cairo], 1955.

——. *Al-Ibāna ʿan uṣūl al-diyāna.* Beirut, 1990.

———. *Maqālāt al-Islāmiyyīn wa-ikhtilāf al-muṣallīn*. Edited by Muḥammad Muḥyī al-Dīn ʿAbd al-Ḥamīd. 2 vols. Beirut, 1999.

Al-Baghdādī, ʿAbd al-Qāhir. *Al-Farq bayna al-firaq*. Edited by Muḥammad Muḥyī al-Dīn ʿAbd al-Ḥamīd. Beirut, n.d.

Al-Balkhī, Abu'l-Qāsim, ʿAbd al-Jabbār, and Abū Saʿd al-Ḥākim al-Jushamī. *Faḍl al-Iʿtizāl wa-ṭabaqāt al-Muʿtazila*. Edited by Ayman Fu'ād Sayyid. Tunis, 1974.

Al-Bāqillānī, Abū Bakr ibn al-Ṭayyib. *Kitāb al-Inṣāf fīmā yajibu iʿtiqāduhu wa-lā yajūzu al-jahl bihi*. Edited by ʿIzzat al-ʿAṭṭār al-Ḥusaynī. Cairo, 1950.

———. *Kitāb al-Tamhīd*. Edited by R. J. McCarthy. Beirut, 1957.

Al-Baṣrī, Abu'l-Ḥusayn. *Kitāb al-Muʿtamad fī uṣūl al-fiqh*. Edited by Muḥammad Ḥamīd Allāh. 2 vols. Damascus, 1964–65.

———. *Sharḥ al-ʿumad*. Edited by ʿAbd al-Ḥamīd bin ʿAlī Abū Zunayd. 2 vols. Medina, AH 1410.

"*Dhimma*." In *al-Mawsūʿa al-fiqhiyya*. Vol. 21. Kuwait, 1992.

Al-Ghazālī, Abū Ḥāmid. *Al-Iqtiṣād fi'l-iʿtiqād*. Edited by I. A. Çubukçu and H. Atay. Ankara, 1962.

———. *Tahāfut al-falāsifa*. Edited by M. Bouyges. Beirut, 1962.

———. *Al-Mustaṣfā min ʿilm al-uṣūl*. Edited by Ibrāhīm Muḥammad Ramaḍān. 2 vols. Beirut, [1994].

Ibn Fūrak, Abū Bakr. *Mujarrad maqālāt al-shaykh Abi'l-Ḥasan al-Ashʿarī*. Edited by D. Gimaret. Beirut, 1987.

Ibn Ḥajar al-Haytamī, Abu'l-ʿAbbās. *Al-Zawājir ʿan iqtirāf al-kabā'ir*. Beirut, 1988.

"*Ḥaqq*." In *al-Mawsūʿa al-fiqhiyya*. Vol. 18. Kuwait, 1990.

Ibn Ḥazm, ʿAlī ibn Aḥmad. *Al-Faṣl fi'l-milal wa'l-ahwā' wa'l-niḥal*. Edited by ʿAbd al-Raḥmān Khalīfa. Cairo, AH 1347–48.

Ibn Manẓūr, Abu'l-Faḍl Muḥammad ibn Mukarram. *Lisān al-ʿArab*. 20 vols. Cairo, AH 1300–1307/1883–91.

Ibn Mattawayh, al-Ḥasan ibn Aḥmad. *Al-Muḥīṭ bi'l-taklīf*. Edited by ʿUmar al-Sayyid ʿAzmī. Cairo, [1965].

———. *Kitāb al-Majmūʿ fī l-Muḥīṭ bi-l-Taklīf (Paraphrase du* Muḥīṭ *du Qāḍī ʿAbd al-Jabbār)*. Edited by J. J. Houben, D. Gimaret, and J. Peters. 3 vols. Beirut, 1965–99.

———. *Al-Tadhkira fī aḥkām al-jawāhir wa'l-aʿrāḍ*. Edited by Sāmī Naṣr Luṭf and Fayṣal Budayr ʿAwn. Cairo, 1975.

Ibn Mufliḥ. *Al-Ādāb al-sharʿiyya wa'l-minaḥ al-marʿiyya*. Edited by Muḥammad Rashīd Riḍā. 3 vols. Cairo, AH 1348–49.

Ibn al-Murtaḍā, Aḥmad ibn Yaḥyā. *Ṭabaqāt al-Muʿtazila*. Edited by S. Diwald-Wilzer. Wiesbaden, 1961.

Ibn Nujaym, Zayn al-ʿĀbidīn. *Al-Baḥr al-rā'iq sharḥ kanz al-daqā'iq*. 8 vols. Cairo, n.d.–AH 1311.

Ibn Qayyim al-Jawziyya, Shams al-Dīn. *Iʿlām al-muwaqqiʿīn ʿan rabb al-ʿālamīn*. Edited by Ṭaha ʿAbd al-Ra'ūf Saʿd. 4 vols. Beirut, 1973.

———. *ʿUddat al-ṣābirīn wa-dhakhīrat al-shākirīn*. Edited by Zakariyā ʿAlī Yūsuf. Cairo, n.d.

Ibn Sīnā, Abū ʿAlī. *Kitāb al-Mubāḥathāt*. In *Arisṭū ʿinda al-ʿArab*, edited by ʿAbd al-Raḥmān Badawī. Vol. 1. Cairo, 1947.

———. *Al-Risāla al-aḍḥawiyya fī amr al-maʿād*. Edited by Sulaymān Dunyā. Cairo, 1949.

———. *Al-Shifā': al-Ilāhiyyāt*. Edited by G. C. Anawati, Sulaymān Dunyā, Muḥammad Yūsuf Mūsā, and Sa'īd Zāyed. 2 vols. Cairo, 1960.

Al-Iṣfahānī, Abū 'Abd Allāh Muḥammad ibn Maḥmūd. *Al-Kāshif 'an al-maḥṣūl fī 'ilm al-uṣūl*. Edited by 'Ādil Aḥmad 'Abd al-Mawjūd and 'Alī Muḥammad Mu'awwaḍ. 6 vols. Beirut, 1998.

Al-Jurjānī, 'Alī ibn Muḥammad. *Sharḥ al-mawāqif li'l-Qāḍī 'Aḍud al-Dīn 'Abd al-Raḥmān al-Ījī*. Edited by Maḥmūd 'Amr al-Dimyāṭī. 8 vols. Beirut, 1998.

Al-Juwaynī, Imām al-Ḥaramayn 'Abd al-Malik Abu'l-Ma'ālī. *Kitāb al-Irshād ilā qawāṭi' al-adilla fī uṣūl al-i'tiqād*. Edited by As'ad Tamīm. 3rd ed. Beirut, 1996.

Al-Kāsānī, 'Alā' al-Dīn Abū Bakr ibn Mas'ūd. *Kitāb Badā'i' al-ṣanā'i' fī tartīb al-sharā'i'*. 7 vols. Cairo, 1909–10.

Al-Khayyāṭ, Abu'l-Ḥusayn. *Kitāb al-Intiṣār*. Edited by H. S. Nyberg. 2nd ed. Beirut, 1993.

Mānkdīm Shashdīw, Aḥmad ibn al-Ḥusayn. *Sharḥ al-uṣūl al-khamsa*. Edited by 'Abd al-Karīm 'Uthmān. Cairo, 1965.

Murtaḍā al-Zabīdī, Muḥammad ibn Muḥammad. *Tāj al-'arūs min jawāhir al-Qāmūs*. Edited by 'Alī Shīrī. 20 vols. Beirut, 1994.

[Al-Nīsābūrī, Abū Rashīd]. *Fi'l-Tawḥīd*. Edited by Muḥammad Abū Rīda. Cairo 1969.

Al-Nīsābūrī, Abū Rashīd. *Al-Masā'il fi'l-khilāf bayna al-Baṣriyyīn wa'l-Baghdādiyyīn*. Edited by Ma'n Ziyāda and Riḍwān al-Sayyid. Tripoli, 1979.

Al-Qarāfī, Shihāb al-Dīn. *Kitāb al-Furūq*. 4 vols. Cairo, AH 1344–46.

Al-Rāzī, Fakhr al-Dīn. *Al-Arba'īn fī uṣūl al-dīn*. Hyderabad, AH 1353.

———. *Munāẓarāt jarat fī bilād mā warā' al-nahr fi'l-ḥikma wa'l-khilāf wa-ghayrihimā bayna al-Imām Fakhr al-Dīn al-Rāzī wa-ghayrihi*. Hyderabad, AH 1355.

———. *Al-Tafsīr al-kabīr*. 32 vols. Cairo, 1938.

———. *Muḥaṣṣal afkār al-mutaqaddimīn wa'l-muta'akhkhirīn min al-'ulamā' wa'l-ḥukamā' wa'l-mutakallimīn*. Edited by Ṭaha 'Abd al-Ra'ūf Sa'd. Cairo, n.d.

Al-Ṣafadī, Ṣalāḥ al-Dīn. *Al-Wāfī bi'l-wafayāt*. Edited by H. Ritter, S. Dedering, et al. 29 vols. Weisbaden, 1962–1997.

Al-Sanhūrī, 'Abd al-Razzāq. *Maṣādir al-ḥaqq fi'l-fiqh al-Islāmī*. 2 vols. [Cairo], 1954.

Al-Shahrastānī, 'Abd al-Karīm. *Nihāyat al-iqdām fī 'ilm al-kalām*. Edited by al-Fard Jayūm. Cairo, n.d.

Al-Sharīf al-Murtaḍā, 'Alam al-Hudā 'Alī ibn Ḥusayn. *Rasā'il al-Sharīf al-Murtaḍā*. Edited by Aḥmad al-Ḥusaynī. 3 vols. Qom, AH 1405.

Al-Suyūṭī, Jalāl al-Dīn. *Al-Ḥāwī li'l-fatāwī*. 2 vols. [Cairo], 1933.

———. *Kitāb al-Ashbāh wa'l-naẓā'ir fī qawā'id wa-furū' al-Shāfi'iyya*. Edited by 'Abd al-Karīm al-Fuḍaylī Beirut, 2001.

"Al-Tawba." In *al-Mawsū'a al-fiqhiyya*. Vol. 14. Kuwait, 1988.

'Uthmān, 'Abd al-Karīm. *Naẓariyyat al-taklīf*. Beirut, 1971.

Al-Zamakhsharī, Jār Allāh Maḥmūd ibn 'Umar. *A Mu'tazilite Creed of az-Zamahšarî (d. 538/1144) (al-Minhâğ fî uṣûl ad-dîn)*. Edited by S. Schmidtke. Stuttgart, 1997.

Al-Zarkashī, Badr al-Dīn. *Al-Manthūr fi'l-qawā'id*. Edited by Taysīr Fā'iq Aḥmad Maḥmūd. 3 vols. Kuwait, 1982.

Works in Western Languages

Adamson, Peter. "Al-Kindî and the Mu'tazila." *Arabic Sciences and Philosophy* 13 (2003).

Alami, Ahmed. *L'ontologie modale: Étude de la théorie des modes d'Abū Hāšim al-Ǧubbā'i.* Paris, 2001.

Allard, Michel. *Le problème des attributs divins dans la doctrine d'al-Aš'arī et de ses premiers grands disciples.* Beirut, 1965.

Arendonk, Cornelis van- [Joseph Schacht]. "Ibn Ḥadjar al-Haytamī." In *Encyclopaedia of Islam.* 2nd ed. Vol. 3. Leiden, 1954–.

Aristotle. *Nicomachean Ethics.* Translated by T. Irwin. Indianapolis, IN, 1985.

Arnaldez, Roger. "Ma'ād." In *Encyclopaedia of Islam.* 2nd ed. vol. 5. Leiden, 1954–.

Berkey, Jonathan. *The Transmission of Knowledge in Medieval Cairo.* Princeton, 1992.

Bernand, Marie. *Le problème de la connaissance d'après le Muġnī du cadi 'Abd al-Ǧabbār.* Algiers, 1982.

Black, Deborah L. "Psychology: Soul and Intellect." In *Cambridge Companion to Arabic Philosophy,* edited by P. Adamson and R. C. Taylor. Cambridge, 2004.

Brandt, R. B. "The Structure of Virtue." In *Midwest Studies in Philosophy, Volume XIII. Ethical Theory: Character and Virtue,* edited by P. French et al. Notre Dame, 1988.

Brecher, Bob. *Getting What You Want? A Critique of Liberal Morality.* London, 1998.

Brown, Daniel. "Islamic Ethics in Comparative Perspective." *Muslim World* 89 (1999).

Bulliet, Richard W. "Orientalism and Medieval Islamic Studies." In *The Past and Future of Medieval Studies,* edited by J. Van Engen. Notre Dame, 1994.

Calder, Norman. "Sharī'a." In *Encyclopaedia of Islam.* 2nd ed. Vol. 9. Leiden, 1954–.

Chamberlain, Michael. *Knowledge and Social Practice in Medieval Damascus, 1190–1350.* Cambridge, 1994.

Chehata, Chafik. "Dhimma." In *Encyclopaedia of Islam.* 2nd ed. vol. 2. Leiden, 1954–.

Cook, Michael. *Commanding Right and Forbidding Wrong in Islamic Thought.* Cambridge, 2000.

Corcoran, Kevin, ed. *Soul, Body, and Survival.* Ithaca, NY, 2001.

Dhanani, Alnoor. *The Physical Theory of Kalām: Atoms, Space, and Void in Basrian Mu'tazilī Cosmology.* Leiden, 1994.

Ess, Josef van. "The Logical Structure of Islamic Theology." In *Logic in Classical Islamic Culture,* edited by G. E. von Grunebaum. Wiesbaden, 1970.

———. "Mu'tazilah." In *Encyclopedia of Religion,* edited by M. Eliade. Vol. 10. New York, 1987.

Fakhry, Majid. "The Mu'tazilite View of Man." In *Recherches d'Islamologie: Recueil d'articles offert à Georges C. Anawati et Louis Gardet par leurs collègues et amis.* Leuven, 1977.

———. *Ethical Theories in Islam.* Leiden, 1991.

Farès, Bishr. "'Irḍ." In *Encyclopaedia of Islam.* 2nd ed. Vol. 4. Leiden, 1954–.

Feinberg, Joel. "Justice and Personal Desert." In *Doing and Deserving.* Princeton, 1970.

Frank, Richard M. *The Metaphysics of Created Being according to Abû l-Hudhayl al-'Allâf*. Istanbul, 1966.
———. "*Al-Ma'nà:* Some Reflections on the Technical Meanings of the Term in the Kalâm and Its Use in the Physics of Muʿammar." *Journal of the American Oriental Society* 87 (1967).
———. "Abū Hāshim's Theory of 'States': Its Structure and Function." In *Actas do IV Congresso de Estudos Árabes e Islâmicos, Coimbra-Lisboa 1 a 8 de setembro de 1968*. Leiden, 1971.
———. "Reason and Revealed Law: A Sample of Parallels and Divergences in Kalâm and Falsafa." In *Recherches d'Islamologie: Recueil d'articles offert à Georges C. Anawati et Louis Gardet par leurs collègues et amis*. Leuven, 1977.
———. *Beings and Their Attributes*. Albany, NY, 1978.
———. "*Kalām* and Philosophy: A Perspective from One Problem." In *Islamic Philosophical Theology*, edited by P. Morewedge. Albany, NY, 1979.
———. "Al-Maʿdum wal-Mawjud: The Non-existent, the Existent, and the Possible in the Teaching of Abū Hāshim and His Followers." *Mélanges—Institut dominicain d'études orientales du Caire (MIDEO)* 14 (1980).
———. "The Autonomy of the Human Agent in the Teaching of ʿAbd al-Ǧabbār." *Le Muséon* 95 (1982).
———. "Moral Obligation in Classical Muslim Theology." *Journal of Religious Ethics* 11 (1983).
———. "Bodies and Atoms: The Ashʿarite analysis." In *Islamic Theology and Philosophy: Studies in Honor of George F. Hourani*, edited by M. Marmura. Albany, NY, 1984.
———. "The Science of *Kalām*." *Arabic Sciences and Philosophy* 2 (1992).
———. *Al-Ghazālī and the Ashʿarite School*. Durham, NC, 1994.
———. "Currents and Counter-currents." In *Islam: Essays on Scripture, Thought, and Society: A Festschrift in Honour of Anthony H. Johns*, edited by P. G. Riddell and T. Street. Leiden, 1997.
———. "The Ašʿarite Ontology: I Primary Entities." *Arabic Sciences and Philosophy* 9 (1999).
Gardet, Louis. "Ḳiyāma." In *Encyclopaedia of Islam*. 2nd ed. Vol. 5. Leiden, 1954–.
———. *Dieu et la destinée de l'homme*. Paris, 1967.
Gianotti, Timothy J. *Al-Ghazālī's Unspeakable Doctrine of the Soul: Unveiling the Esoteric Psychology and Eschatology of the* Iḥyāʾ. Leiden, 2001.
Gimaret, Daniel. "Muʿtazila." In *Encyclopaedia of Islam*. 2nd ed. Vol. 7. Leiden, 1954–.
———. "La notion d' 'impulsion irrésistible' (*ilǧâ'*) dans l'éthique Muʿtazilite." *Journal Asiatique* 259 (1971).
———. "Matériaux pour une bibliographie des Ǧubbāʾī." *Journal Asiatique* 264 (1976).
———. "Les *uṣūl al-hamsa* du Qāḍī ʿAbd al-Ǧabbār et leurs commentaires." *Annales Islamologiques* 15 (1979).
———. *Théories de l'acte humain en théologie musulmane*. Paris, 1980.
———. *Les noms divins en Islam*. Paris, 1988.
———. *La doctrine d'al-Ashʿarī*. Paris, 1990.
Goldman, Alan H. "The Paradox of Punishment." In *Punishment*, edited by A. J. Simmons et al. Princeton, 1995.
Hallaq, Wael B. *A History of Islamic Legal Theories*. Cambridge, 1999.

Heemskerk, Margaretha J. *Suffering in the Muʿtazilite Theology: ʿAbd al-Jabbār's Teaching on Pain and Divine Justice*. Leiden, 2000.

Hershenov, David B. "Van Inwagen, Zimmerman, and the Materialist Conception of Resurrection." *Religious Studies: An International Journal for the Philosophy of Religion* 38 (2002).

———. "The Metaphysical Problem of Intermittent Existence and the Possibility of Resurrection." *Faith and Philosophy* 20 (2003).

Honderich, Ted. *Punishment: The Supposed Justifications*. Cambridge, 1989.

Hourani, George F. *Islamic Rationalism*. Oxford, 1971.

———. "Divine Justice and Human Reason in Muʿtazilite Ethical Theology." In *Ethics in Islam*, edited by R. G. Hovannisian. Malibu, CA, 1985.

———. *Reason and Tradition in Islamic Ethics*. Cambridge, 1985.

Hume, David. *Enquiries concerning Human Understanding and concerning the Principles of Morals*. Edited by L. A. Selby-Bigge. 3rd ed. Oxford, 2000.

Izutsu, Toshihiko. *The Concept of Belief in Islamic Theology*. Tokyo, 1965.

Jackson, Sherman A. "The Alchemy of Domination? Some Ashʿarite Responses to Muʿtazilite Ethics." *International Journal of Middle East Studies* 31 (1999).

Jaffer, Tariq. "Bodies, Souls, and Resurrection in Avicenna's *ar-Risāla al-Aḍḥawīya fī amr al-maʿād*." In *Before and after Avicenna*, edited by D. C. Reisman. Leiden, 2003.

Kamali, Mohammad H. "Fundamental Rights of the Individual: An Analysis of *ḥaqq* (Right) in Islamic Law." *American Journal of Islamic Social Sciences* 10 (1993).

Kleinig, John. "The Concept of Desert." *American Philosophical Quarterly* 8 (1971).

Lane, Edward W. *An Arabic-English Lexicon*. 8 vols. Beirut, 1968.

Leaman, Oliver. "ʿAbd al-Jabbār and the Concept of Uselessness." *Journal of the History of Ideas* 41 (1980).

———. Review of Margaretha Heemskerk's *Suffering in the Muʿtazilite Theology*. *Journal of Islamic Studies* 13 (2002).

Locke, John. *An Essay concerning Human Understanding*. Edited by P. H. Nidditch. Oxford, 1975.

MacIntyre, Alasdair. *After Virtue*. London, 1981.

———. "How Moral Agents Became Ghosts *or* Why the History of Ethics Diverged from That of the Philosophy of Mind." *Synthese* 53 (1982).

Madelung, Wilfred. "Imâmism and Muʿtazilite Theology." In *Le Shîʿisme imâmite. Colloque de Strasbourg (6–9 mai 1968)*, edited by T. Fahd. Paris, 1970.

Makdisi, George. "Ashʿarī and the Ashʿarites in Islamic Religious History." *Studia Islamica* 17 (1962) and 18 (1963).

———. "The Scholastic Method in Medieval Education: An Inquiry into Its Origins in Law and Theology." *Speculum* 49 (1974).

———. *The Rise of Colleges*. Edinburgh, 1981.

———. "Ethics in Islamic Traditionalist Doctrine." In *Ethics in Islam*, edited by R. G. Hovannisian. Malibu, CA, 1985.

———. *The Rise of Humanism in Classical Islam and the Christian West*. Edinburgh, 1990.

Marmura, Michael. "Avicenna on Primary Concepts in the *Metaphysics* of His *al-Shifāʾ*." In *Logos Islamikos: Studia Islamica in honorem Georgii Michaelis Wickens*, edited by R. M. Savory and D. A. Agius. Toronto, 1984.

———. "Soul: Islamic Concepts." *Encyclopedia of Religion*, edited by M. Eliade. Vol. 13. New York, 1987.

———. "Ghazali and the Avicennan Proof from Personal Identity for an Immaterial Self." In *A Straight Path: Studies in Medieval Philosophy and Culture*, edited by J. Hackett et al. Washington, DC, ca. 1988.

———. "Al-Ghazālī on Bodily Resurrection and Causality in *Tahāfut* and the *Iqtiṣād*." *Aligarh Journal of Islamic Thought* 2 (1989).

———. "A Medieval Islamic Argument for the Intrinsic Value of the Moral Act." *Corolla Torontonensis: Studies in Honour of R. M. Smith*, edited by E. Robbins and S. Sandahl. Toronto, 1994.

Martin, Richard C., Mark R. Woodward, and Dwi S. Atmaja. *Defenders of Reason in Islam: Mu'tazilism from Medieval School to Modern Symbol*. Oxford, 1997.

Mill, John Stuart. "Speech in Favour of Capital Punishment (1868)." In *Applied Ethics*, edited by P. Singer. Oxford, 1986.

Nader, Albert. *Le Système philosophique des Mu'tazila (premiers penseurs de l'Islam)*. Beirut, 1956.

Parfit, Derek. *Reasons and Persons*. Oxford, 1986.

Peters, Jan R.T.M. *God's Created Speech*. Leiden, 1976.

Reinhart, Kevin A. "Islamic Law as Islamic Ethics." *Journal of Religious Ethics* 11 (1983).

———. *Before Revelation: The Boundaries of Muslim Moral Thought*. Albany, NY, 1995.

Rorty, Richard. "The Historiography of Philosophy: Four Genres." In *Philosophy in History*, edited by R. Rorty, B. Schneewind, and Q. Skinner. Cambridge, 1984.

Schacht, Joseph. *An Introduction to Islamic Law*. Oxford, 1991.

Schopenhauer, Arthur. *On the Basis of Morality*. Translated by E.F.J. Payne. Indianapolis, IN, 1995.

Seigel, Jerrold. *The Idea of the Self*. Cambridge, 2005.

Smart, J.J.C. "Free-will, Praise, and Blame." *Mind* 70 (1961).

Smith, Jane I., and Yvonne Y. Haddad. *The Islamic Understanding of Death and Resurrection*. Oxford, 2002.

Sterba, James P. "Justice and the Concept of Desert." *Personalist* 57 (1976).

Stroumsa, Sarah. "The Beginnings of the Mu'tazila Reconsidered." *Jerusalem Studies in Arabic and Islam* 13 (1990).

Sverdlik, Steven. "The Nature of Desert." *Southern Journal of Philosophy* 21 (1983).

Taylor, Charles. *Sources of the Self: The Making of Modern Identity*. Cambridge, 1992.

van Inwagen, Peter. "The Possibility of Resurrection." *International Journal for Philosophy of Religion* 9 (1978).

Vasalou, Sophia. "Equal before the Law: The Evilness of Human and Divine Lies." *Arabic Sciences and Philosophy* 13 (2003).

———. "Subject and Body in Baṣran Muʿtazilism, or: Muʿtazilite *Kalām* and the Fear of Triviality." *Arabic Sciences and Philosophy* 17 (2007).

———. "'Their Intention Was Shown by Their Bodily Movements': The Baṣran Muʿtazilites on the Institution of Language," in *In the Age of al-Fārābī: Arabic Thought in the 4th–10th Century*, edited by P. Adamson. Forthcoming.

Wagner, E. "Munāẓara." In *Encyclopaedia of Islam*. 2nd ed. Vol. 7. Leiden, 1954–.

Watt, William M. *The Formative Period of Islamic Thought*. Oxford, 1998.

Weiss, Bernard G. *The Spirit of Islamic Law*. Athens, GA, 1998.

Williams, Bernard. "The Makropulos Case: Reflections on the Tedium of Immortality." In *The Metaphysics of Death*, edited by J. M. Fischer. Stanford, CA, 1993.

Wisnovsky, Robert. *Avicenna's Metaphysics in Context*. Ithaca, NY, 2003.

———. "Avicenna and the Avicennian Tradition." In *Cambridge Companion to Arabic Philosophy*, edited by P. Adamson and R. C. Taylor. Cambridge, 2004.
———. "The Nature and Scope of Arabic Philosophical Commentary in Post-classical (ca. 1200–1900 AD) Islamic Intellectual History: Some Preliminary Observations." In *Philosophy, Science, and Exegesis in Greek, Arabic, and Latin Commentaries*, edited by P. Adamson, H. Baltussen, and M.W.F. Stone. London, 2004.

INDEX

'Abd al-Jabbār, Abu'l-Ḥasan, 8; on causal nature of grounds of value, 97; on compensation for grief, 136–37; on consequentialist grounds for blame, 131–32; and definition of justice, 94; and goodness of blame, 102–6; and grounds of goodness, 89; Hourani's work on, 26–35; on *khiṣāl al-faḍl*, 135–36; on moral disagreement, 74; on moral motivation, 72; and qualification of God's act of punishing, 90; and use of legal resources in *al-Mughnī*, 39–57, 112–14
Abū Bakr, 135
Abu'l-Hudhayl, 146
Abū Sinna, Aḥmad Fahmī, 223n104
accidents. *See* entitative accidents
act of worship (*'ibāda*), 40, 52
'ādat Allāh (God's custom), 35
adultery (*zinā*), 43, 47, 112, 126
ahl al-'adl wa'l-tawḥīd, 94
akhdh (commission), 10
'Alī, 135, 227n35
allegorical interpretation (*ta'wīl*), 3, 15
al-Āmidī, Sayf al-Dīn, 70, 161
analogy (*qiyās*), 44, 56
apology (*i'tidhār*), 108–10, 124–25, 131
'āqil (rational or intellectually mature person), 104, 110, 111, 122, 131, 218n46
Aristotle, 22, 134, 201n23
al-Ash'arī, Abu'l-Ḥasan, 2, 4, 6, 198n10, 204n48, 206n4, 211n58
Ash'arites, 2, 4, 41, 161, 176; criticism of Baṣran proof of evilness of lies, 17–18; criticism of Mu'tazilite view of punishment, 128; definitions of legal values of acts, 70; view of belief, 7, 151; view of desert, 70, 85; view of grave sinners, 7, 149; view of moral values, 5, 7
al-aṣlaḥ (the optimal or most beneficial), 19, 28–29, 39
attributes, act-derived (*asmā'/ṣifāt mushtaqqa min al-af'āl*), 123–26, 141–44, 150–52, 225n16, 228n49, 229n51
attributes, modes of entitlement to (*wujūh al-istiḥqāq*), 123; essence, 138; entitative accident, 138–40; action, 141–44. *See also* attributes, act-derived; entitative accidents
Avicenna, 158, 164, 166–67, 177
'ayn (specific object), 151
'azīma (original binding force of legal ruling), 210n44

al-Baghdādī, 'Abd al-Qāhir, 10, 198n10
al-Bājūrī, Ibrāhīm ibn Muḥammad, 232n3
al-Balkhī, Abu'l-Qāsim, 2, 8, 9, 186
baqā' (endurance). *See* entitative accidents, enduring
al-Bāqillānī, Abū Bakr ibn al-Ṭayyib, 2, 57, 70
al-Baṣrī, Abū 'Abd Allāh, 44, 76, 88, 207n15
al-Baṣrī, Abu'l-Ḥusayn, 44, 51, 198n15

belief (*i'tiqād*), 127–28, 147, 174
belief (*īmān*). *See* believer
believer (*mu'min*), 6, 7, 148–52
beneficence (*tafaḍḍul*), 79, 81
blame (*dhamm*), 77–78; consequentialist grounds for, 131–32; eternal duration of, 121–22; goodness of, 104–6
British intuitionists, 27
Bulliet, Richard W., 14

Calder, Norman, 113
capacity for autonomous action (*qudra*), 10, 24, 134–35, 140, 141, 142, 143, 145, 147, 165, 202n26, 228n48
cause (*'illa*): legal (*'illa shar'iyya*), 50, 51, 56; necessitating (*'illa mūjiba*), 88, 96–102, 200n10; rational (*'illa 'aqliyya*), 51, 57
compensation (*'iwaḍ*), 19, 33, 58, 78, 80–82, 136–37, 212n63
composition (*ta'līf*), 167, 170, 175, 232n6
compulsion (*iljā'*), 75, 215n15
condition (*sharṭ*, pl. *shurūṭ*), 54, 98
courage (*shajā'a*), 135–36

daqīq al-kalām, 18
ḍarūra (necessity), 52
dawām (eternal duration), 119, 121, 129
Day of Judgment, 100, 117, 158, 159, 160, 161, 172
dayn (debt), 153, 209n39
death (*mawt*), 159–60
desert (*istiḥqāq*): causal nature of, 35, 95–102; conditions for, 75–76, 182–83; English translation of term, 64–66, 213n73; relation of to *ḥuqūq*, 59–62, 107
deserts (*aḥkām al-af'āl*): definitions of moral terms and, 72–74; eternal duration of, 119; as *ḥuquq*, 82–86; normative force of, 79–86; as reasons for action, 71–72; relation between grounds of value and, 96–102. *See also* punishment; reward
Dhanani, Alnoor, 18, 147
dhāt (essence, self, thing-itself), 138, 163, 165, 166, 167, 235n31, 236n36
dhātiyya. *See* God, essential attributes of
dhimma (legal responsibility), 47, 152–56, 231n68, 231n73
disobedience (*ma'ṣiyya*), 35, 125, 128, 130, 226n27
divine assistance (*luṭf*, pl. *alṭāf*), 19, 33, 48–49, 50, 51, 71, 132, 209n31

entitative accidents (*ma'nā*, pl. *ma'ānī*), 3, 21, 123, 127–28, 138–40, 141, 146, 147, 173, 201n21; enduring (*bāqiya*), 147, 172–74; personal identity and, 170–77
Ess, Josef van, 146, 229–30n56
evil (*qabīḥ*): acts and offences that are, 83–84, 107, 110–11; definition of, 72–73

fanā' (annihilation), 119, 161–62, 164, 165, 171
al-Fārābī, Abū Naṣr, 133
fasting, 51
fatwā (legal opinion, pl. *fatāwā*), 55
filial piety: Baṣran use of in justification of eternal punishment, 125; Baṣran use of as moral paradigm, 130–32
Frank, Richard M., 65, 138, 143, 146, 167, 201n16, 202n26, 205n60, 213n76

Gardet, Louis, 197n7, 229n52
al-ghā'ib (the otherworldly or unseen domain), 23, 24, 77, 128, 130
gharaḍ (end, purpose), 32, 52, 70, 88
al-Ghazālī, Abū Ḥāmid, 2, 12, 70, 158, 159, 166, 201n16, 232n4
Gimaret, Daniel, 15, 202n26, 211n53
God: ability to deserve, 23–25; essential attributes of, 3, 138; justice of, 19; unity of, 3–4
Goldman, Alan H., 217
good (*ḥasan*), 72–73
goodness (*ḥusn*), grounds of, 87–94, 106, 218n54, 218–19n57, 219n58
grave sinner (*fāsiq*), 6, 7, 22, 23, 112–13, 79, 148–52, 192–93
grief (*ghamm*), 35, 137
ground of value/act-description (*wajh*, pl. *wujūh*), 16, 20–23, 28, 46, 51, 52, 60, 88, 200n10, 218–19n57, 219n58; causal nature of, 96–102; consequentialist and deontological grounds, 51–52, 57, 209n43. *See also* goodness, grounds of

ḥadd penalties (pl. *ḥudūd*), 43, 47, 78, 85, 113, 224n123
ḥaqq (right/claim, pl. *ḥuqūq*), 42, 45–47, 52, 54, 88, 92, 107, 108, 121, 124, 208n23; and desert, 59–62; deserts as *ḥuqūq*, 82–86; *dhimma* and, 152–56; *ḥaqq ādamī/li'l-'ibād* (human right/claim), 42, 43, 46–47, 82, 107; *ḥaqq Allāh* (God's right/claim), 43, 46–47, 82, 85, 107; *ḥuqūq 'aqliyya*, 46; relation of to injustice, 59–61; relation of to justice, 94; relation of to welfare, 62. *See also* punishment; reward
hardship (*mashaqqa, kulfa*), 79–80
harm (*ḍarar*), 35, 217n34
al-Haytamī, Ibn Ḥajar, 43
Heemskerk, Margaretha J., 34–35, 81
ḥikma (reason, wisdom), 32, 135
Honderich, Ted, 214
honor, 42, 43, 61, 78, 111, 216n28, 228n49, 231n72. See also *'irḍ*
Hourani, George F., 26–35, 104–5, 200n10, 202n29, 203n38, 203n39, 204n45, 205n53, 218n54, 221n90
ḥukm (characteristic, quality, status, effect, judgment, pl. *aḥkām*, deserts), 16, 38, 74–75, 96–97, 99, 104, 131. *See also* deserts
Hume, David, 118

Ibn 'Ayyāsh, Abū Isḥāq, 34, 76, 147
Ibn Fūrak, Abū Bakr, 151
Ibn Ḥanbal, Aḥmad, 1, 2, 3, 206n4
Ibn Khallād, 'Alī, 211n53
Ibn Mattawayh, al-Ḥasan ibn Aḥmad, 8, 9, 97; on conditions for recreation of accidents, 172–74; on consequentialist grounds for blame, 131–32; and distinction between *aḥkām al-dunyā* and *aḥkām al-ākhira*, 114; on grounds of goodness, 88–89; on punishment as God's claim, 83–84; on qualification of punishment, 90; and time of deserving, 100–101
Ibn Nujaym, Zayn al-'Ābidīn, 59
Ibn Qayyim al-Jawziyya, Shams al-Dīn, 227n35
Ibn Sina. *See* Avicenna
al-iḥbāṭ wa'l-takfīr (frustration of reward and expiation of punishment), 76, 99, 129, 203n38, 221n87, 226n25
ijmā' (consensus), 44, 199n3
ijtihād (independent reasoning), 44, 58, 207n16
ikhtiṣāṣ (exclusive possession or assignment), 83, 120, 162
'illa. *See* cause
injustice (*ẓulm*), 5, 16, 59–61, 92–93
inṣāf (just treatment), 220n70
'irḍ (honor), 42, 78, 111, 231n69, 231n72, 231n73
Islamic law (*fiqh*), 4, 39, 43, 44, 45, 54; *dhimma* in, 153. *See also* legal theory

Jackson, Sherman, 17
al-jarḥ wa'l-ta'dīl (wounding and declaring just), 112
al-Jubbā'ī, Abū 'Alī, 2, 8, 205n51, 207n16, 217n41; and debate about *istiḥqāq al-dhamm*, 9–10; and view of function of revelation, 49, 209n31; and view of grounds of goodness, 87–88; and view of repentance, 39–40
al-Jubbā'ī, Abū Hāshim, 8, 31, 198n15, 207n15, 207n16, 220n79; and debate about *istiḥqāq al-dhamm*, 9–10; on recreation of accidents in resurrection, 170, 175; and theory of states, 3–4, 8, 139–40, 146–47; and view of function of revelation, 49, 209n31; and view of grounds of goodness, 87–88; and view of repentance, 40–41, 42;
jumla (material totality of atoms), 163, 167, 170
al-Jurjānī, 'Alī ibn Muḥammad, 82, 161, 165; on identity of resurrected persons, 178–80
al-Juwaynī, Imām al-Ḥaramayn, 2, 128, 211n58
justice (*'adl*), 94, 213n68

al-Ka'bī. *See* al-Balkhī, Abu'l-Qāsim
kaffārāt (acts of expiation), 210n44
kalām, 1, 4, 7, 12, 13, 16, 30, 44, 45, 54, 55, 56, 159, 167
Kamali, Mohammad H., 208n22
Kant, Immanuel, 134
al-Karkhī, Abu'l-Ḥasan, 44, 207n15
al-Kāsānī, 'Alā' al-Dīn, 210n44
khabar (predicative statement), 77, 120

al-Khālidī, ibn Shihāb, 196
Khārijites, 149, 182
khiṣāl al-faḍl (features of excellence, excellences), 135–36, 227n35
knowledge (*ʿilm*), 139, 140, 141, 142, 143, 145, 171, 228–29n49, 230n58; acquired knowledge (*ʿilm muktasab*), 16; necessary or self-evident knowledge (*ʿilm ḍarūrī*), 15–18, 46, 128–32, 163, 200n8

law (*sharīʿa*), 49
Leaman, Oliver, 31–33, 35
legal theory (*uṣūl al-fiqh*), 4, 38, 44, 48; Ashʿarite definitions of legal values of acts in, 70; *dhimma* in, 153; Muʿtazilite rationalism in, 57
life (*ḥayāt*), 139, 145, 146, 147, 159, 167, 170, 171, 233n14
Locke, John, 117, 118
luṭf. *See* divine assistance
lying: evilness of, 28, 31; proof of evilness of, 17–18

MacIntyre, Alasdair, 134, 201n23
major/grave sin (*kabīra*, pl. *kabāʾir*), 129–30, 229n66
Makdisi, George, 29, 54, 65, 199, 204n40
maʿlūl (causal effect), 97–98
al-Maʾmūn, 1
maʿnā. *See* entitative accidents
Mānkdīm Shashdīw, Aḥmad ibn al-Ḥusayn, 5, 8, 181, 198n15; and definition of necessary knowledge, 16; and justification of eternal punishment, 122, 124, 125, 129, 130, 151, 181
maqṣid (aim, purpose, pl. *maqāṣid*), 86, 226n27; *maqāṣid al-sharīʿa*, 210n44
Marmura, Michael, 166, 205n60
milk (property, ownership), 41, 65
Mill, John Stuart, 117
minor sin (*ṣaghīra*, pl. *ṣaghāʾir*), 129–30, 203n38, 220n80, 230n66
Miskawayh, 133
Moore, G. E., 22, 27, 201n23
moral knowledge. *See* knowledge, acquired knowledge; knowledge, necessary or self-evident knowledge
moral terms, definitions of, 72–74
moral values, objectivity of, 5–6, 19–20
motive (*dāʿī*), 75
muʿāmalāt (human transactions), 52
muḥsin (good-doer, benefactor), 122–23, 142, 225n16
mukallaf (subject of the law/of obligations), 50, 80, 161
mubāḥ. *See* permissible
Murjiʾites, 100, 101, 149, 151
musabbab (effect), 98, 101, 176
mutaʿallaq (relatum, object), 40, 139–40, 168, 199n17, 228n48; Baṣran debate over *mutaʿallaq al-dhamm*, 9–11, 39–40
al-Mutawakkil, 2
Muʿtazilite ethics: rationalism in, 15–20; theological aims of, 18–26
Muʿtazilites, Baghdadis, 24; and view of divine obligations, 28–29, and view of reward and punishment, 79, 190–92
Muʿtazilites, Baṣran and Baghdadi schools, 7–8
Muʿtazilites, five principles: commanding right and forbidding wrong, 197n6; the intermediate position, 6, 148, 150; justice, 4–6; the promise and the threat, 6, 148, 150; unity, 3–4
Muʿtazilites, future generations of, 102, 152
muwallad (generated), 172

Nader, Albert, 105n60, 229n53
nafs (essence, self), 138
al-Naẓẓām, Abū Isḥāq, 159
al-Nīsābūrī, Abū Rashīd, 8, 9, 55, 211n53
niyya (intention), 41, 226n27
non-existent (*maʿdūm*), 164–69, 234n24, 235n31, 235n32

obligatory (*wājib*), 72–73
offence (*isāʾa*), 83–84, 107–11, 124–25
offender (*musīʾ*), 110, 122–23, 142, 225n16

pain, justification of, 32–33, 34
permissible (*mubāḥ*), 72–73; relation of to *ḥasan*, 89–90, 219n59, 219n61
persistence (*iṣrār*), 40, 102, 112, 125–6, 128
personal identity: criterion of, 159–64; desert and, 157–58, 169–70; entitative accidents and, 170–77; Muʿtazilite doctrine of nonexistents and, 164–69; psychological continuity and, 169–77

Peters, Jan R.T.M., 145, 200n10, 202n26, 205n53, 221n90
power. *See* capacity for autonomous action
praise (*madḥ*), 77–78
prayer, 50, 52
prophethood (*nubuwwa*), 48, 207n17
punishment (*ʿiqāb*), 77–79, 187–89; eternal duration of, 119; *ḥuqūq* and, 60–62; justification of, 79–86; justification of eternal duration of, 121–32, 193–96; qualification as "good," 87, 89–93

qadhf (false accusation of adultery), 47, 78, 216n25
al-Qarāfī, Shihāb al-Dīn, 62
qudra. *See* capacity for autonomous action
Qurʾān: Baṣran view of *luṭf* in, 49; cosmic annihilation in, 161; createdness of, 1, 3; exhortation to forgiveness in, 85; punishment of grave sinners in, 149–50

ratio legis. *See* cause, legal
al-Rāzī, Fakhr al-Dīn, 2, 160–61, 166, 167, 177, 179, 180, 234n24, 235n31–32
reason (*ʿaql*), 45, 56, 135; rationally known moral values (*ʿaqliyyāt*), 49, 56; rationally known obligations (*takālīf ʿaqliyya*), 45, 48, 207n17; rationally known obligatory and evil acts (*wājibāt wa-qabāʾiḥ ʿaqliyya*), 59; rationally known prohibitions (*muḥarramāt ʿaqliyya*), 51
recommended/supererogatory (*nadb*, *tafaḍḍul*), 72–73
regret (*nadm*), 40, 43, 96, 98, 101–2
Reid, Thomas, 134
Reinhart, Kevin A., 29, 64–65, 204n40, 213n74, 219n66
repentance (*tawba*), 39, 42, 43, 96, 108, 110–11, 112, 113, 131, 206–7n11; and act-derived attributes, 124–27
resolution (*ʿazm*, *ʿazīma*), 40–43, 128
resurrection (*iʿāda*), 158–79; doctrine of nonexistents and, 164–69
retaliation (*qiṣāṣ*, *qawad*), 41
revelation (*samʿ*), 45; as divine assistance, 48–49; as particularisation of general moral knowledge, 50–53; relativity of revealed norms, 49–50, 51
reward (*thawāb*), 77–79, 184–86; eternal duration of, 119; justification of, 79–86
Ross, W. D., 27
rukhṣa (mitigation of legal ruling in case of hardship), 210n44

sabab (ground, cause, pl. *asbāb*), 46, 50, 54, 98–102, 172, 176
Said, Edward, 14
al-Sanhūrī, ʿAbd al-Razzāq, 154–55
Schopenhauer, Arthur, 223
shahāda (legal testimony), 112
al-shāhid (the worldly or perceptible domain), 23, 24, 77, 128, 130
al-Shahrastānī, ʿAbd al-Karīm, 2, 57, 128
sharʿ (revealed law), 45, 56
al-Sharīf al-Murtaḍā, 42, 62
Shīʿites, 198n15
al-Shīrāzī [Abū Isḥāq], 206n4
spirit (*rūḥ*), 159, 161
state (*ḥāl*, pl. *aḥwāl*), 120, 139, 140, 143, 147, 229n51. *See also* al-Jubbāʾī, Abū Hāshim, and theory of states
al-Sulamī, Muʿammar ibn ʿAbbād, 159
al-Suyūṭī, Jalāl al-Dīn, 155, 226n27

taklīf (God's imposition of obligations; divine Law), 32, 48, 80, 119, 205n50, 205n51; concept of person and, 145–46
tarjīḥ (preponderance), 70
tark (omission), 10
taʾwīl. *See* allegorical interpretation
temptation (*ighrāʾ*), 82
theft (*sariqa*), 43, 47, 85, 113, 124, 126
transitive acts (*afʿāl mutaʿaddiya*), 42, 84, 110
tuhma (accusation), 112–13
al-Ṭūsī, Naṣīr al-Dīn, 133

ʿUmar, 135
unbelief (*kufr*), 84, 114, 129, 151
unbeliever (*kāfir*), 6, 79, 148–52
usurpation (*ghaṣb*), 41, 42, 52, 53, 84, 109, 110, 126
ʿUthmān, 135
ʿUthmān, ʿAbd al-Karīm, 181

vain action (*ʿabath*), 31–33, 205n50
van Inwagen, Peter, 160

walī (legal guardian), 112
Weiss, Bernard G., 56
welfare (*maṣlaḥa,* pl. *maṣāliḥ*), 49, 50, 51, 62, 86, 132
Williams, Bernard, 214
willing (*irāda*), 139, 140, 141, 142, 143, 145, 163, 171, 174, 228–29n49
Wisnovksy, Robert, 166
wujūb al-naẓar (obligation to inquire), 20

al-Zamakhsharī, Jār Allāh Maḥmūd ibn ʿUmar, 122, 124, 125, 129, 151, 198n15
Zaydites, 198n15